**S/NVQ** Level **2**

**& Technical Certificate**

# Business & Administration

Carol Carysforth

**www.heinemann.co.uk**
✓ Free online support
✓ Useful weblinks
✓ 24 hour online ordering

**01865 888058**

**Heinemann**

*Inspiring generations*

Heinemann Educational Publishers
Halley Court, Jordan Hill, Oxford OX2 8EJ
Part of Harcourt Education Ltd

Heinemann is the registered trademark of Harcourt Education Limited

First published 2006

10 09 08 07 06
10 9 8 7 6 5 4 3 2 1

British Library Cataloguing in Publication Data is available
from the British Library on request.

10-digit ISBN: 0 435 46333 0
13-digit ISBN: 978 0 435 463 33 5

Typeset and illustrated by ↗\ Tek-Art, Croydon, Surrey
Original illustrations © Harcourt Education Limited, 2006
Cover design by Wooden Ark Studio, Leeds
Printed in the UK at Bath Press

**Websites**
Please note that the examples of websites suggested in this book were up to date at the time of
writing. It is essential for tutors to preview each site before using it to ensure that the URL is still
accurate and the content is appropriate. We suggest that tutors bookmark useful sites and consider
enabling students to access them through the school or college intranet.

# Contents

## Optional units on the CD

# Acknowledgements

## Author's acknowledgements

The advice and assistance of several people has been invaluable in helping to ensure that this book accurately reflects the way many tasks are undertaken by today's administrators. Their willingness to talk about their jobs and how various aspects of work are undertaken in their organisations has enabled the snapshots and case studies to reflect current business practice.

I am therefore indebted to the following people and organisations for their help: Phillip Green and staff at the Malt House, Manchester; Deborah Gorton and Carla Weall of Althams Travel Agency; Rob Simi of Moonfish, Manchester and Paul Carysforth, formerly also of Moonfish; Margaret Baines and Jane Barratt of St George's Surgery, Blackburn; David Knights of KC Mobility, Batley and Matt Neild, formerly also of KC Mobility; Harry and Kath Bretherton, Maureen Rawlinson, Claire Barnes and Catherine Carysforth.

Grateful thanks are also due to Christine Blackham, for her expert and efficient help in finalising all the IT units.

I am also extremely grateful for the advice and guidance provided by Margaret Reid, a Consultant in Administration, Technical Certificates and Key Skills to a leading awarding body. She is also a Lead EV in a number of business-related awards for the same awarding body. Her input helped to ensure that all the evidence guidance provided in this book is accurate, up-to-date and meets all the latest scheme requirements and her positive and efficient contributions throughout the project were very much appreciated.

Finally, I must express my sincere appreciation to the combined efforts of the Heinemann team – particularly to Jilly Attwood, my publisher on this project, for her friendly, positive approach and extremely competent manner – which combined to keep me calm and focused at critical moments! To Mary James, publishing manager, for her support and encouragement; to Roger Parker, for his expert editing as always; to Melissa Greaves, desk editor, for her scrupulous attention to detail and her patience and help with unpredictable file formats! Last, but by no means least, my thanks are also due to the ebullient Jenni Johns, Heinemann's visiting publisher from Oz, who worked with me so creatively on the planning of this book but who is now, sadly, only a shadow of her former self since England regained the Ashes.

Carol Carysforth
January 2006

This book is dedicated to Holly, the newest member of the Carysforth clan. May you be blessed with an open and enquiring mind, a warm heart and the confidence to believe that you can achieve your dreams.

The author and publisher would like to thank the following for permission to reproduce copyright material:

Samaritans, page 7
NHS, page 80
Virgin Retail Ltd, page 80
Save the Children, page 80

Crown copyright material is reproduced under Class License No. C01W0000141 with the permission of the Controller of HMSO and the Queen's Printer in Scotland, page 91.

The author and publisher would like to thank the following for permission to reproduce photographs:

Getty Images/Photodisc, page 1, 82, 156, 223, 248, 265, 343, 371
istockPhoto.com/Timothy Goodwin, page 3
Corbis, page 5
istockPhoto.com/Dragon Trifunovic, page 11
Richard Smith, page 27
Alamy, pages 70, 76, 146, 160, 177, 194, 240, 258, 270, 275, 306, 321, 323, 349
Corbis, pages 103, 143, 177, 179, 219, 251, 291, 296, 339
Getty, pages 133, 185, 238, 273, 331, 362
Royal Mail, page 203
Apple, page 215
Carphone Warehouse, page 216
Althams Travel Service Ltd, page 226
Press-images.co.uk, page 230
Railex, page 299
Kardex Systems UK, page 309
Suzi Paz, page 369

Getty, Unit 213 page 1, Unit 214 page 1, Unit 215 page 1, Unit 216 page 1, Unit 217 page 1

Every effort has been made to contact the copyright holders of material reproduced in this book. We would be glad to hear from any unacknowledged sources at the first opportunity. Any omissions will be rectified in subsequent printings if notice is given to the publishers.

# Introduction

Welcome to NVQ Business and Administration level 2. This book has been written to help you to achieve your award as easily as possible. It covers all the information for the two core units and the most popular option units. If you are on a Modern Apprenticeship scheme and are studying for a Technical Certificate at the same time, you will find special features included to help you. This means that you can develop your knowledge of key topics as you go – and saves you covering the same areas over and over again. You can find out more about the links to the Technical Certificate on page xi of this Introduction.

If you are new to NVQ awards then you need to take time to understand the scheme and what you have to do. This is because there is quite a difference between the way you achieve an NVQ and other awards, such as GCSEs.

# Key facts about your NVQ award

- NVQs are qualifications designed for people who are at work. They are not normally taken by full-time students unless special arrangements have been made for them to be assessed in a realistic working environment (RWE). Your tutor or trainer will give you more details about this if any of your assessments will take place in an RWE.
- NVQ awards are offered at different levels. The level you take usually depends upon how much responsibility you have. Level 1 is the first level for junior staff; level 5 is the top level and taken by senior managers.
- Business and Administration NVQs cover the tasks that are carried out by administrators working in different types of businesses and the skills that they need.
- All NVQs consist of a number of units, each covering a specific area of work. To obtain your level 2 award you have to do **five** units.
- **Two** units are compulsory because they cover skills required by all administrators.
- You then choose a further **three** units. These should be the ones that most closely link to your job role and the tasks you do at work so that the evidence you provide occurs naturally as you do your job.
- You are assessed on whether or not you can do tasks competently. This means that you must demonstrate or provide **evidence** to show that you can consistently carry out those tasks to a high standard.
- You also have to prove that you understand what you are doing and how it relates to your job. You will also be asked how you would adapt your skills if you changed your job or worked in a different type of office.
- Most NVQ candidates provide evidence in a **portfolio**. This is normally an A4 file which contains documentary evidence relating to your work. Electronic portfolio packages are now becoming more popular and if you are expected to store and record your evidence electronically you will be shown how to do this. You can find out more about types of evidence on page ix of this introduction.

### For Apprentices only

If you are on an Apprenticeship scheme then you will also be taking Key Skills qualifications in Communications level 2 and Application of Number level 1 as well as a Technical Certificate at level 2. The Technical Certificate will also test your knowledge of many areas of business and administration (see page xi). The Council for Administration (CfA) also recommend that you complete at least one IT unit from the optional units available.

# Who's who in the world of NVQ

You will be guided through the scheme by your **tutor**, **trainer** or **workplace supervisor**, depending upon where you work and where you are studying for your award. This person will be responsible for helping you to learn new skills and understand about the administrative tasks you will be carrying out. You will also learn about your organisation and other important aspects of work, such as your employment rights and responsibilities.

When you are competent at certain tasks you have to prove this to your **assessor**. This is the person who checks your evidence to make sure it meets the requirements of the scheme. Your assessor will visit you at work, for example to watch you perform some tasks and carry out **professional discussions**. This simply means your assessor will want to discuss certain aspects of your job role with you. It is called a professional discussion to differentiate it from a casual chat, because it is much more important. You can prepare for this by following the advice given throughout this book and, of course, by carrying out any preparation your assessor has requested on your assessment/action plan for a particular professional discussion. At the end of the professional discussion, your assessor may decide that more information is needed about your knowledge and understanding, and either verbal or written questions will follow the discussion. When your assessor is satisfied, you will be judged competent.

At certain intervals an **internal verifier** will also sample and check your evidence. This is normally done as you progress and when you complete the award. A final quality check is made by the **external verifier** who is sent by your awarding body. This is the organisation that will issue your final NVQ certificate, such as EDI, City and Guilds, OCR, Edexcel, IMI or SQA. You will not know which units are checked by a verifier but if your assessor has judged you to be competent in those units, then normally there are no problems.

# What is 'evidence'?

You might think you should just be able to tell your assessor that you can do a task but unfortunately that isn't enough! You have to provide proof of your abilities. There are two main ways in which you can do this.

- **Performance evidence** is direct proof of how you work. There are two types of performance evidence.
  - **Work products**, such as documents you have created. This could be a diary page or telephone message, email or typed document – depending upon the unit you are doing. It is even better if it has your own notes on it or if you have your draft notes together with a final version. Alternatively you can keep a work diary or work log of tasks you do and then use this as a basis for a professional discussion with your assessor (see below).
  - **Observation** by your assessor when you are at work, such as when you are dealing with a customer or sending a fax or email. In this case it is better if your assessor visits you at a time when you are busy doing various jobs – and you just act naturally and get on with your work.

- **Supplementary evidence** is used in situations when there is no direct performance evidence, such as when you are trying to prove that you behave in a certain way or understand something. Again there are two types of supplementary evidence.
  - **A professional discussion** between you and your assessor will give you the opportunity to demonstrate how you would behave in certain situations or circumstances. Your assessor will identify which situations or circumstances you need to be prepared to discuss.
  - **Witness testimony** is a signed and dated statement from your line manager, supervisor or colleagues to confirm something you have done. It is often easier to write a full description yourself and then ask your boss or supervisor to sign and date this statement to confirm it is true.

# Key facts about evidence

For your award you do not collect evidence separately for the core units. Instead you use the evidence you collect for your option units to count twice, wherever possible. This means, for example, that you prove that you can communicate information (Core Unit 201) through the tasks which involve communication in your option units. You then cross-reference this evidence from the option unit to cover the appropriate sections of core unit 201. Two features of this book will help you to do this more easily, as you will see on page xi of this introduction.

Many administrators think that they must always provide a piece of paper to prove what they have done. This isn't true! As you will see with the suggestions for evidence in this book, there are several other ways. For example, you can note the location of documents that are used by everyone – such as the procedures to follow if there is an emergency evacuation or your organisation's grievance procedures. You don't need to make a copy for your portfolio. Similarly, if you produce lots of documents on a computer, don't print out all of them. It is sufficient to print out one or two and to refer to where the others are saved on your system. You can then show these to your assessor if requested.

## IMPORTANT!

Make sure that you read all the information and guidance notes issued by your awarding body so that you understand:

- the performance indicators for the units you are doing
- the knowledge that is required
- the recommended evidence suggested by your awarding body
- the way in which you must record your evidence.

Ask your tutor or trainer to explain anything that you are unsure about.

# Key features in this book to help you achieve your award

In addition to the knowledge and information you need to be able to carry out various tasks, the following features have been included to help you achieve your award more easily.

- **How to ...** features summarise the steps required to do a task properly. These features link to many of the performance indicators. These are the tasks you have to prove you can do competently.
- **Evidence planning** sections in the core units help to prepare you for collecting suitable evidence for the option units so that it can be used as evidence for the core units.
- **Evidence collection** sections in the option units suggest appropriate evidence that you can collect that is not always paper-based!
- **CU Link** features show you how the evidence you collect in the option units may link to the core units so that you can cross-reference the evidence to both units.
- **What if?** features tell you what to do if you are unable to provide a particular type of evidence during the time you are being assessed.
- **Snapshots** and **Case studies** in the option units enable you to see how specific tasks are carried out in different types of organisation.
- **Changing places** features give you examples of other ways in which certain tasks may be undertaken. This is important because your assessor will ask you to demonstrate that you would be able to transfer your skills if you changed your job in the future.
- **Over to you** sections enable you to check your own knowledge of the information given so far and investigate some aspects further on your own.

**Suggested answers** to all the Over to you sections are given on the CD-ROM to enable you to check your answers and ideas, as well as an invaluable **Use of English** section to help you to improve your communication skills.

You should note that the Snapshot, Case study and Changing places features have not been included in the IT units on the CD. This is because the evidence requirements for these units are slightly different. Full details are given at the start of each IT unit.

# Links to Technical Certificate

If you are also studying for a Technical Certificate then you should note that Technical Certificate topics are mainly covered in the sections listed below. The topics on which you need to focus will vary, depending upon the scheme issued by your particular awarding body. More details about individual topics can be found in the index at the end of this book.

| Topic | Units and pages |
|---|---|
| Business objectives and policies | Unit 202, pages 77 – 100 |
| Communicating verbally and in writing | Unit 210, pages 2 – 34 (CD) |
| Communicating by telephone | Unit 219, page 332 – 361 |
| Communicating by email | Unit 213, pages 2 – 24 (CD) |
| Computer created documents | Units 214, 215, 216 and 217 (CD) |
| Continuous improvement and personal development | Unit 201, pages 55 – 64 |
| Contract of employment | Unit 202, pages 112 – 118 |
| Data Protection and copyright legislation | Unit 202, pages 151 – 153 |
| Dealing with other people | Unit 201, pages 65 – 75; Unit 203, page 119, 200, 217; Unit 206 page 278 – 282 |
| Diversity and discrimination legislation | Unit 202, pages 132 – 142 |
| Employment rights and responsibilities (including employment legislation | Unit 202, pages 101 – 131 |
| Information management/filing systems (paper based and electronic) | Unit 209 pages 300 – 330 |
| Internet software | Unit 213, pages 24 – 32 (CD) |
| Health and safety legislation and risk assessments | Unit 110, pages 161 – 193 |
| House style | Unit 201, page 13; Unit 217, page 24 (CD) |
| Planning, targets and meeting deadlines | Unit 201, pages 35 – 54 |
| Security and confidentiality | Unit 202, pages 144 – 159 |
| Time management and working effectively | Unit 201, pages 40 – 45; Unit 204, page 225 |
| Using office equipment | Unit 220, pages 363 – 388 |
| Waste – minimising/environment | Unit 201, page 24; Unit 220, page 376, 377 |
| Working with other people | Unit 201, pages 65 – 75; Unit 202, pages 132 – 138 |

# Links to Key Skills

At the end of each unit you will find a reminder to check if any of that unit's evidence can be cross-referenced to a Key Skills award. It is useful to note that if there is a specific reference in the CU link sections to Communications in Core Unit 201, it is quite likely that some of your evidence will also count towards your Key Skills Communications award. It is sensible to check the matrix issued by your awarding body which shows where possible key skills opportunities occur in the Business and Administration core units and your chosen option units. However, you should check carefully with your assessor before assuming that the evidence you are offering will definitely meet the requirements of both.

# Unit 201

# Carry out your responsibilities at work

**Unit summary and overview**

This core unit has four sections:

- Communicate information
- Plan and be accountable for your work
- Improve your own performance
- Behave in a way that supports effective working

Good communication skills are essential for all administrators, and that includes you! This is because you will regularly be involved with receiving and passing on information to your colleagues at work, as well as to your external contacts such as customers or clients. You must also be able to read and understand the written information you receive so that you can identify the key points to pass on to other people. In addition, you will be expected to contribute usefully to discussions and provide written information that is accurate, clear and easy to read.

## Link to option units

Your evidence for this unit will be generated and assessed through the option units that you select. This is because your option units should reflect the main areas of your job role, so your evidence will occur naturally as you carry out your day-to-day work. For each option unit in this book, therefore, you will find guidance notes to show how evidence can be cross-referenced to this unit.

Within this unit you will also find suggestions to help you plan your evidence. These will help you to make the most of opportunities for obtaining evidence as you progress through the scheme.

All administrators must also be able to take responsibility for themselves and their own performance without being constantly monitored. This means producing high-quality work to agreed deadlines. It also means taking the correct action if anything upsets these plans so that, wherever possible, remedial action can be taken in good time. This doesn't mean turning a drama into a crisis, or keeping quiet in the hope that no-one will ever notice that something has gone wrong!

If you prove that you can carry out the tasks you are given correctly and to the right standard *and* demonstrate that you are eager to learn more, you are likely to be given additional responsibilities. This is all part of a continual development process that starts when you learn how to analyse your own performance, objectively consider the feedback you receive from other people, and constantly review your own performance.

Wherever you work you will be expected to cooperate with your colleagues and your employer and to behave professionally. This includes setting high standards for yourself and working productively and courteously with all your colleagues, no matter what your personal views are. Finally, it means responding positively if you are asked to change or accept a new challenge, even if this worries you at first. How to cope with this type of situation is one of the many skills you will learn in this unit, as you discover how to effectively carry out your own responsibilities at work.

# Communicate information

You communicate with other people every day – when you talk to them face-to-face, send a text message, make a telephone call or write an email. You also regularly receive communications from other people – by post, telephone, face-to-face and online. Until you start work for an employer, your communications are mostly between you and your friends and family, and are always informal and usually friendly! There may be odd misunderstandings or minor difficulties but, by and large, the consequences of errors are unlikely to result in serious problems or financial loss. When you start work the situation changes. You are now involved in sending and receiving a wide range of business communications, such as:

- taking and writing messages for your supervisor or your colleagues
- being given instructions about how to use equipment or what to say to a customer
- reading and replying to emails
- telling your supervisor or your colleagues about a situation
- contributing to a team discussion to help to solve a problem
- finding and summarising information your supervisor wants
- creating a variety of business documents – such as fax messages, letters to customers, reports etc.

At first, this can be a bit nerve-wracking. As you will know, it is one thing to answer your mobile and quite another to make a business telephone call to an important customer. Similarly, until now most of the written material you will have dealt with has probably been fairly straightforward. Now some documents you handle will be more complex or contain terms you do not understand. Even more crucial, the potential for misunderstandings and serious consequences is far greater. If you get something badly wrong the business could lose an order or you could seriously inconvenience an important customer or your boss. It is therefore very important that all your communications are sent in good time and are accurate in every respect.

This section contains hints and tips to help you to do this. It also suggests ways in which you can plan to collect evidence through your option units to prove that you are an effective communicator.

# The importance of effective communication

In business, people always communicate for a purpose. They may want to give or receive information. They may want to make or cancel an arrangement or to provide an explanation. They may want to make an enquiry. Therefore, when you communicate with your colleagues and customers on a business matter there will always be a reason – and so, too, when they communicate with you.

A communication is only effective if you successfully achieve your purpose. This means that:

- you make contact with the correct person, or leave a message that he or she later receives and understands
- your recipient understands every part of the communication, in every respect, and is left with no doubts or unanswered questions
- you have made contact in time for the information to be useful and for a response to be made, if required.

You can obtain this result only if:

- you have all the information you need before you start
- you speak, or write, clearly and in words and phrases your recipient will understand
- you don't miss anything out
- you use the correct 'tone' so that you don't annoy or upset anyone
- your information is accurate
- you send the communication at an appropriate time (for example, if a meeting is cancelled or rearranged those due to attend must be told as quickly as possible, so that they can make appropriate other arrangements).

Some people are far better communicators than others. They speak clearly and keep to the point! They include all the required information but don't distract or bore their listeners with irrelevant details. They are courteous yet friendly. When they are writing they keep their sentences short, use correct spelling and punctuation and don't use words their recipient wouldn't understand. As a first step to developing these skills yourself, check the table below to see how many you have already!

**Find out**

Your tone of voice speaks volumes about your attitude! Try it out. Say 'All right' four ways. The first time you are delighted, the second time you are furious, the third time you are resentful, the final time you are reassuring someone.

## Effective communicators ...

| ALWAYS | NEVER |
|--------|-------|
| Speak and write clearly, concisely and accurately | Communicate until they are clear about what they are writing or saying |
| Listen carefully when other people are communicating | Answer the telephone and try to do something else at the same time |
| Make careful notes if a verbal message is long or complex | Try to remember detailed information they are told |
| Check information is accurate before passing it on | Guess an answer, because it's quicker than looking it up |
| Ask for an explanation if they do not understand something | Worry about looking foolish if they ask someone to repeat or explain something |
| Check that information is complete and nothing is missing | Miss out important information the recipient will need |
| Think carefully about the needs of the recipient | Use informal terms, slang or expressions the recipient wouldn't understand |
| Are polite and courteous | Upset people by being tactless |
| Communicate promptly | Delay making contact |
| Select the best method of communicating, based on the situation | Give long, complex or critical information verbally without also confirming it in writing |
| Check that messages they have left have been picked up by the recipient | Leave important messages without checking later that they have been received |
| Work hard to continually improve their communication skills | Assume that communication skills aren't important |

# Focusing actively when others are communicating

A good starting point for developing your communication skills is to improve your ability to focus on what other people are saying so that you really listen. Most people are pretty pathetic listeners. This includes you if you find your mind wandering almost as soon as someone starts to talk to you, or if you regularly interrupt people to have your say. You are a good listener only if you can normally repeat back accurately what you have just heard. If you can do this then you may find many of your friends confide in you when they have worries or are upset. This is because good listeners help us to feel better by allowing us to talk about a problem, even if they can't offer much practical help at the time.

In a social situation, none of us is expected to be a good listener all the time. Finding yourself trapped at a party with someone who could 'bore for England' often means desperate measures are called for! At work, though, you have fewer options. You cannot afford to cause offence and it is likely that some of the information is important. You must therefore listen carefully to make sure that you understand what you are being told. You also need to make sure that you have all the information you need. If you have any gaps, then you will need to ask questions to obtain the missing details – but if you haven't been listening then you probably won't realise this until it's too late!

### The art of active and reflective listening

**Active listening** means that you concentrate on the other person, not yourself. Not only do you hear the words, but you also consciously note other details, such as whether the speaker was nervous, impatient, stressed or worried. This means that you are more likely to respond both appropriately and tactfully to the situation.

**Reflective listening** means that you restate what you have heard at regular points in the conversation to check your understanding as you go. It is sensible to use different words or you will begin to sound like a parrot! For example, if the speaker tells you that he rang your office last Monday, Wednesday and Friday, then you could say 'Have I heard you correctly? You telephoned to speak to someone *three* times last week?'

## How to ... Actively focus on information other people are communicating

- Focus on the person speaking. Look at the speaker if he or she is in front of you. If you are on the telephone in a busy office you can even close your eyes to shut out other distractions.

- Don't interrupt – you can't listen and talk at the same time! If the information is important, start making notes. If you don't understand something, put a question mark for checking back later.

- If the person is in front of you try to assess his or her attitude from body language and tone of voice. Also, give positive feedback yourself, such as a smile or nod to show that you understand what is being said. On the telephone, listen carefully for non-verbal signals such as a sigh or hesitation. Whilst it is no use nodding your head to show you understand, you can still give positive signals by laughing or smiling during the conversation. (Smiling affects the sound of your voice.)

- If your mind starts to wander, then deliberately switch yourself back on again. If you've missed some important information, politely ask for it to be repeated.

- You will be distracted if you are in a hurry, upset, annoyed, uncomfortable or trying to do two jobs at once, or have just thought of something important you need to say. If you are in a terrible rush or if the speaker is upsetting you in some way, then get assistance promptly. Otherwise make yourself focus on the task in hand. If you struggle to remember what you must say next unless you speak immediately, write down a 'prompt' word so that you won't forget.

- Don't react emotionally to what you hear. For example, if someone is complaining it may be tempting to take the statements personally, take offence and start to defend yourself. If you feel that you are being deliberately insulted then get help to deal with the situation.

- If the speaker is taking a long time to get to the point, or keeps adding unnecessary details, politely interrupt to review the notes you have made so far. This will help to keep the conversation on track.

- At the end of a conversation always check that you have noted down all the key points correctly and have agreed with the speaker what action you will now take.

**Did you know?**

Samaritans – which provides telephone, email and face-to-face support to anyone who is depressed or has a personal problem – has started offering coaching to organisations to teach staff communication skills. Their volunteers are particularly skilled at active listening because this is crucial to helping people who contact them – so Samaritans can put this skill to good use by teaching other people too. You can find out more at www.samaritans.org.

**Find out**

Check how good a listener you are by seeing how much of a conversation you can remember afterwards. Then compare what you can recall with someone else who was also listening and see how far you agree!

# The importance of questioning things you are not sure about

It is in everyone's interests that you understand what someone is saying to you. This may mean asking questions to check your understanding. This is nothing to be ashamed of. Many people preface a question with the phrase 'I'm sorry, but could you just explain ...'. In this case they apologise for interrupting – they don't apologise for asking! It is far better to check at the time than to guess an answer or to omit important information.

Whereas your listening skills are tested if you talk to someone who takes ages to get to the point, your questioning skills are tested to the extreme when the speaker is abrupt, curt, very shy or very nervous. In this case the conversation may be very short indeed because many details are missing. Unless you spot this quickly, and ask the right questions, you may well find yourself trying to solve a problem or taking action with only half the information you need.

### Reasons for questioning things you are not sure about

- You must check that your understanding of a situation is correct and that your information is accurate.
- You must make sure you know the name of the person you have been speaking to and how to contact him or her again if necessary.
- You must make sure you have all the information you need to take action.
- You save yourself the embarrassing job of having to go back to ask a number of questions later.
- You can save yourself looking silly if a specialist term or jargon is used that you don't understand.

Knowing that you need to ask questions is one thing. Actually asking them is quite another, particularly if someone is talking very quickly or if you are worried that you will look foolish. To help, read the guidelines in the 'How to ...' box below.

**How to ...** Question any points you are unsure about

- Never accept a word, term or statement you don't understand without asking what it means. Simply say 'I've never heard that word before. Could you please spell it for me and explain what it means?'
- Names, addresses and phone numbers are vital information. Check spellings and other personal details as you go – and repeat them back to be doubly sure.
- If someone is speaking too quickly, politely ask him or her to slow down so that you can take notes. Then ask the person to start again.

- If it is obvious you are going to have to ask several questions to fill in some gaps, simply explain that this is necessary so that you can do your best for the person you are talking to.

- Ask your questions one at a time and note down the answers.

- Ask your questions in a logical order.

- Don't ask unnecessary personal questions, and phrase your questions tactfully. For example 'Could you give me your date of birth, please?' is always better than 'How old are you?'

- Try to use appropriate pauses in the conversation to ask questions as you go, rather than storing them all up for later. You can often use body language to do this (see page 19), such as a quizzical look or a slightly raised hand.

- Ask an appropriate 'follow-up' question if you don't get a full answer the first time or if you are uncertain whether you understood the information correctly.

- Write down the answers, then you won't have to ask people to repeat themselves.

- As a fail-safe, at the end of the conversation, always check that you have a contact number or email address so that you can get in touch again if necessary.

- Always end by thanking the person who has given you help or assistance.

## Over to you

1 Practise active and reflective listening with a friend or colleague. Ask the person to tell you about something interesting he or she has done recently. The description should last about three or four minutes. Listen carefully, then try to summarise it back accurately *without* making notes. Don't forget to restate information back at appropriate points to check your understanding as you go. Then reverse roles.

2 Practice your questioning skills too by working with a friend or colleague. Ask the person to describe a place he or she likes to visit or has visited recently without saying where it is. It should be somewhere you would recognise or know about. Your task is to find out where it is by asking appropriate questions. The better you are as a questioner, the fewer questions you should need to ask! Then reverse roles.

3 A recent survey by Royal Mail identified that addressing individuals by the wrong sex or spelling people's names wrongly was a major 'turn-off' for customers.

**Over to you** Continued

**a** You are on the telephone to a caller who says her name is Mrs Keane. She tells you that one of her children, Sam, has been ill recently. Identify two questions you should ask immediately, bearing in mind the Royal Mail's survey.

**b** Suggest the main reasons why people have problems with the way other people spell their family names. Then suggest four examples of difficult names. These could include some that you have found hard to spell in the past.

**c** How many first names can you identify that could denote either a male or a female? Compare your ideas with other members of your group.

## Evidence planning

You will obtain your evidence for this unit through the option units you select. However, you should find this easier if you start to plan opportunities for evidence collection now, whilst this section is fresh in your mind. That is because it will be easier to obtain evidence relating to your verbal communications (such as your listening and questioning skills) in option units where you regularly deal with other people face-to-face, rather than those where you don't.

If you haven't yet chosen your option units, now is the time to discuss your ideas with your tutor or trainer. Remember that you need to choose three from a total of 24. There may be only three that fit your job role, but it is likely that you will have a wider choice. In that case you may find it better to look at option units that cover the different types of skills you need to demonstrate in the core units. Remember that the earlier you choose your option units, the sooner you can start to plan how to obtain your evidence, as you will see on page 26.

### Did you know?

Business communications are either **internal** or **external**. Internal communications are kept within the organisation, whereas external communications are sent to customers and contacts who work elsewhere. At the start of your career it is normally sensible to ask someone else to check any written communications that you intend to send outside the organisation.

## Snapshot – The changing world of business communications

Traditionally there were only a few methods used to communicate information. Written information was sent to external contacts in a business letter and to internal contacts in a memo. Urgent written information was sent by fax and the office telephone system was used for urgent verbal communications. Until mobile phones became commonplace, administrators often struggled to contact someone who was away from the office.

Electronic communications have changed all this. Mobile phones mean most people can be contacted at any time. Emails enable written information to be sent instantly both internally and externally together with attachments, such as spreadsheets, word-processed documents or presentations. Most businesses have a website and many sell goods over the Internet. Staff information is available on the firm's intranet. Instant messaging enables staff to contact each other and receive immediate written replies. Laptops, smartphones and devices like the Blackberry enable people to answer emails even when they are travelling.

All these developments have dramatically affected the work of many administrators. They will have to deal with their own emails and, in many cases, those of their boss or team leader too. They may be interrupted by instant messages from their boss or team members, be involved in 'virtual' meetings, and be expected to keep in regular contact with colleagues travelling on company business. It may be their responsibility to provide updated information to the web or intranet team – some will even post updates on the sites themselves. Administrators therefore have even greater responsibilities as communicators but more varied and interesting jobs as a result!

# Structuring and presenting information clearly and accurately

Information is structured when it is grouped or ordered in a logical or methodical way. An obvious example is a calendar. Dates are in numerical order and listed under each month. You can therefore find any date you want quickly and easily.

Information is well presented when it is clear and easy to read. If you had a calendar with one page per month hanging on your wall, and the dates underneath were in large type and clearly displayed in rows and columns, then it would be easy to see and understand at a glance. It would not be much help

to have a calendar on the wall that showed the whole year at once because the information would be too small to be useful.

Sometimes the order in which information is structured and presented is crucial. If you were told how to log on to your computer in the wrong order it wouldn't work. Similarly, you wouldn't expect instructions for heating a pizza to tell you to put it into the oven before telling you to open the box! Neither would it be very wise to put important instructions about completing a form at the end, rather than at the beginning. The way to avoid these problems when you are preparing communications is to check that you know what you have to do before you start, and then to proceed methodically.

## How to ... Prepare to present information

- Make sure that you know exactly what information you are meant to provide.

- Obtain the information and put it into a logical order.

- Check whether it should be presented in writing or verbally.

- Find out who will be receiving it and what they already know. This will affect what you should say or write (see page 15).

- If you have to prepare a written document, find out which form of communication you must use (email, written message, report etc.), and whether there is a specific layout or house style you must use (see page 13).

- If you have to give the information verbally, find out whether this will be face-to-face or over the telephone.

Bear in mind that there is normally a standard structure to presenting information, whether verbally or in writing:

- Start with an introduction (e.g. what has happened so far).

- Develop the topic (e.g. what could be done next).

- End with a conclusion and/or action plan (e.g. what now needs to be done and by whom).

# Structuring and presenting written information

Some business documents have specific layouts, or formats, which determine the way in which information is structured; this is referred to as the **house style**. This means that certain documents are always set out in the same way, so external people always see the same 'corporate image' no matter who they are dealing with. In this case, not only will all business letters be prepared on letter-headed paper, but even the margins, spacing and layout of the date and address may be identical. Some large organisations also specify the typeface and font size to be used and include an example of the specific layout in a reference manual. Alternatively, you may have a template on your computer system which is set up in the required style and format. In smaller firms, or those that are less rigid about layout, you would simply be expected to copy what other people do.

## How to ... Structure and present written business information

- Follow the house style for a document if this is specified. Or check the files and copy the layout of a similar document that a more experienced colleague has prepared.

- Remember that headings help people to see what is coming next. A main heading goes at the start. You can then use section headings if you are dealing with several topics, as you can see in the example below.

### An example of a document with headings and a consistent layout

**THE MAIN HEADING**
The main heading is always the most important. It is often typed in capitals and bold. It is better not to underline it as this can look too clumsy or fussy.

**First section heading**
Section headings enable you to group information into different sections. This makes it easier for the reader to find specific parts of the document quickly.

**Second section heading**
Section headings are less important than a main heading. One way of showing this is to use bold but not to use capital letters.

**Third section heading**
Be consistent. Headings of the same importance should be the same style and all the spaces before and after them should be the same.

**Fourth section heading**
Finally, put your name (or the author's name) and the date at the bottom of the document for reference.

Name
Date

### Find out

The documents that usually have specific formats in business include: business letters, emails, printed message forms, memos, fax messages and meetings documents. If you prepare any of these documents as part of your job, check that you know the format you must use in your workplace.

Documents where you may be able to choose your own layout include: a message for someone which is not on a pre-printed form, a short report for your boss, and your own notes on something you have found out. Check if this is the case where you work.

### Find out

Another word used to describe the importance of headings is **weighting**. The most important you could call 'A', then 'B', 'C' and so on. In a long document you would then decide what style to use with each 'weight' of heading to show how they decline in importance. You can see how this works in this book. Find three examples of different types of heading in the text and see how the style changes.

**How to ... Continued**

- Use paragraphs to separate continuous text. Your first paragraph should introduce the topic or give the reason for the communication. Subsequent paragraphs should develop the topic and give further details. The final paragraph should state what action you will take (or expect to be taken) next.

- Numbered paragraphs denote a specific order; bullet points indicate that the order is not important. Both are useful for splitting up text so it is easy to read.

- If you include graphics, charts or tables, make sure these have headings so the reader can see how these relate to the text.

- Remember that all business documents are dated and the sender's or creator's name is normally included.

- Never forget that accurate spelling, punctuation and grammar are important in all written documents.

### Structuring verbal communications

You may think that a good structure and clear presentation applies only to written communications, but that isn't true. We all know people who take ages to get to the point of a conversation or someone who describes minor incidents in great detail but fails to mention something that is important. In both cases it is much harder to understand what they are saying. You will know about this if you have very elderly relatives who find it difficult to communicate precisely what they mean. This may be excusable at 87 years of age, but it isn't usually acceptable at age 17 or 27!

To structure your verbal communications properly you need to think before you speak, so that you put your information in a logical order. This is why, with formal presentations, people prepare by making notes beforehand.

To present your verbal communications properly you need to speak at the right speed for your audience, at the right volume, and use words they will understand. You would therefore speak more quickly and softly in a group of three than you would to a room of 20 people. You should also use a different approach if you are going to be speaking to someone over the telephone than if you are talking to the person face-to-face. This is because the listener cannot see your facial expressions or any gestures you make, so has only your voice as a guide.

*Unfortunately gestures of frustration or despair are wasted on the caller!*

## How to ... Structure and present information verbally

- Allow enough time to prepare properly for formal situations, such as an interview, a review meeting with your boss or an occasion when you have been asked to give a short explanation or presentation.

- Write clear notes that summarise the key points you must include.

- Check that your key points are in a logical order.

- Reduce these to 'key words' that will prompt you if you just glance down at your notes.

- Look pleasant, smile and look at the people you are talking to. If you are nervous, take a deep breath.

- If necessary introduce yourself, so that people know who you are.

- Speak to people clearly and use the right volume. Don't shout or mutter!

- Don't gabble. It's very tempting to talk quickly if you are nervous but this will mean it is difficult for people to understand you.

- Make sure your body language matches the words you say (see page 19).

- Give people 'thinking time' if you are giving complicated information or asking for a decision.

- If you are shy, try to forget about yourself and think instead about the information you are providing.

- Be prepared to answer questions. Ask for these to be at the end if you are worried they will distract you part-way through.

- If you are asked a question, think before you reply. If you don't know the answer then say so. Don't be tempted to waffle! Remember that you can always offer to find the information later.

### Remember

You can find out more about communicating over the telephone on pages 334–351 in option unit 219: Use a telephone system.

### Find out

Do you change the words you use and the way you speak when you are at work? If not, then perhaps you should! Everyone speaks in a lazier way at home or with their friends – and you are also far more likely to use slang or current expressions such as cool, wicked, awesome or ace. Normally this isn't very wise if you want to give a professional impression at work, particularly to your older colleagues and customers. Remember, it's perfectly possible to speak a little more formally and still be pleasant and friendly!

# Adapting your communications to meet the needs of others

Marie has a responsible job for a national children's charity. As part of her work she gives short talks to groups who want to know more about the work done by the charity. She also visits people who have raised money and who want to present a cheque, to thank them for their efforts. In the last few weeks these groups have included year 6 pupils at a primary school, students of a university, the directors of a large company, the staff of a supermarket (visited in their lunch break) and a group of pensioners at a community centre.

Although the overall message that Marie is giving is always the same, she obviously adapts it each time depending upon her audience. This is because it

would hardly be appropriate to speak to a group of directors using the same language as she used with the year 6 pupils! She also tells stories to illustrate the work that is done when she has more time or is speaking to an audience that would appreciate this. Equally, the literature that Marie chooses to take with her also differs. For a presentation to the directors she took illustrated booklets on the work that was done, together with the charity's accounts to show how the money was used. For the youngsters, she took colourful leaflets with lots of illustrations.

Although this is quite an extreme example, you also have different 'audiences' with different needs.

- Your internal contacts will know most of the technical jargon and phrases used in your type of business, whereas your external contacts won't.
- You may be able to send informal chatty notes or emails to your colleagues in your own office but you should be more careful if you are sending messages to your boss or other senior staff, to other departments or to any staff you do not know.
- Your business contacts will expect efficient, professional and prompt responses that quickly get to the point, whereas some private customers may need more careful handling and more detailed explanations.
- Some of your external contacts may be very young, quite elderly or have particular needs. For example, English may not be their first language or they may need literature provided in large print format because they have a visual impairment.

In all these cases you can solve the problem for yourself and your recipients if you think about their needs rather than your own! Simply put yourself in the shoes of the other person and think about what you would want or need in that situation. Then do it!

## Did you know?

It is useful to check your draft written communication, or your ideas for what to communicate verbally, with someone else – preferably someone who will understand the needs of the person you will be communicating with. If there is no-one who can help you, put your draft notes away for a day if you can afford the time, and then read them again when they have gone 'cold'. It is then much easier to spot mistakes or identify information that is hard to understand.

## The importance of confidence

Confidence is important because we are far more apt to believe what someone is saying if they appear to know what they are talking about! As a simple example, imagine you put the TV on tonight to hear the presenter say: 'Er, well, this is the news. Today, um, three people – or was it four? – were arrested as they, er, um, broke in – no, sorry – as they were just leaving a bank in Southall – sorry Southport.'

You would be amazed. We are used to hearing television presenters, actors, politicians and others in the public eye speaking smoothly and confidently, no matter what the situation or how large their audience. We never think that perhaps they might be nervous or feel panicky in case they make a mistake.

In business you may sometimes be asked to communicate in situations that perhaps seem unnerving. It isn't easy to talk to strangers or speak out at a meeting, particularly if you are shy. The problem, however, is that if you don't make an effort your lack of confidence can be misinterpreted. People may think you are ignoring them deliberately, not interested in contributing, not interested in your job, being stuck up, being lazy ... the list is almost endless! Even worse, it can be very embarrassing to watch someone who is obviously in agony through nerves. In this case the whole thing becomes a dreadful ordeal for everyone.

So what can you do? The first step is to find out whether lack of confidence is hampering you or not. In some cases people can actually be a bit over-confident and not think about others as much as they should. Find out how you rate by doing the quiz below. Then take steps to improve your confidence if this is necessary.

## Over to you

Check how confident you are by answering the following questions. Then see how you score. If your result shows that you struggle in this area, don't worry. Talk to your tutor, trainer or supervisor about ways in which you can work to improve your self-confidence.

### How confident are you?

Answer each of the questions below and then award yourself 1 point for each A, 2 points for each B and 3 points for each C. Then check what your score means on page 389.

1 Your boss asks you to greet a group of visitors in reception and bring them to his office. Do you:
   a Greet them nervously and walk in front of them in silence?
   b Introduce yourself, say why you are there and explain where you are going? 2
   c Introduce yourself and start a conversation with them about their journey as you walk along?

2 How often do you feel you have an 'invisibility' problem in shops or restaurants because assistants or waiters seem to ignore you?
   a Frequently.
   b Sometimes – in which case I try to get their attention.
   c Rarely. I check that they know I'm waiting when I arrive. 3

3 Your friend is planning a huge party for her twenty-first birthday. Are you
   a Dreading it and looking for an excuse not to go?
   b Quite looking forward to it – it really depends on who else she invites?
   c Counting the days (you are the ultimate party animal)? 3

4 Your firm is organising a summer social event with a meal in a local restaurant. You end up sitting between two people you've never met before. Do you:

a Sit quietly, waiting for one of them to talk to you?

b Listen to them both and try to contribute to the conversation?

c Introduce yourself and try to find a topic of mutual interest?

5 At a team meeting you think of a good idea to suggest. Do you:

a Raise your hand a little, but put it down again if your team leader doesn't acknowledge you immediately?

b Wait for a suitable pause then raise your hand and get attention by addressing your team leader by name?

c Interrupt immediately before you forget your idea?

6 You overhear your supervisor going mad because a bad mistake has been made. Do you:

a Go cold with fear, because you think it must be your fault?

b Suspend judgement until you are told what is wrong?

c Listen carefully for clues to find out whose fault it is?

7 Your boss has asked you to give a short presentation to a small group of people about a topic you know well. Are you:

a Tired out because of lack of sleep and so nervous you can't speak properly?

b Suffering from butterflies but know that you've prepared as much as possible?

c Looking forward to the challenge?

8 When you phone a business customer to pass on some important information you are redirected to voicemail. Do you:

a Panic and put the phone down?

b Put the phone down whilst you prepare what to say, then ring back and leave a message?

c Leave a short message and include your name and number?

9 Your supervisor has asked you to send an email to everyone in the organisation asking for volunteers to be first aiders. Do you:

a Spend all morning drafting it and then email it to her to check before you send it to everyone?

b Draft it out and ask a colleague to check it quickly on your screen before you click 'send'?

c Just write it and send it (it takes you about 2 minutes)?

10 Your firm is supporting a local charity collection and your boss suggests you dress up and help to collect money. Do you:

a Say you'll help but only behind the scenes?

b Agree but only if you can collect with someone else?

c Have a bet with your colleagues that you'll collect more than they will?

## How to ... Communicate more confidently

- Prepare what you are going to say in advance for formal events. (See How to structure and present information verbally, on page 15.)

- Don't use 'fillers' or annoying mannerisms, such as 'hmmmm' or 'you know'. If you are apt to do this, reduce the length of your sentences.

- Take a deep breath to calm your nerves and speak a little more slowly than you normally do.

- Use positive words ('Yes, certainly', 'I will' or 'I'll find out' not 'I can't', 'Who me?' and 'I doubt it!').

- Use positive body language: stand up straight, hold your head high, look at people – and smile!

- Believe in yourself. Focus on things you are good at and tell yourself that you can do this, too!

- If you have to start a conversation with strangers, concentrate on making them feel at their ease to take your mind off yourself. A general topic, such as whether they had a good journey, or even the weather, will usually break the ice.

- If you are seriously struggling then opt for honesty! Rather than hide in a corner in a room full of people, attempt a wobbly smile and say: 'Sorry but I find it really hard to talk to someone I don't know.' Unless you are very unlucky this should help to start a conversation!

**Remember**

You will sound more confident on the phone if you just stand up when you are talking. Try it!

# Non-verbal communication and its impact on other people

Non-verbal communication (NVC) is often referred to as **body language**. This is because it comprises all the gestures and facial expressions you use when you are communicating with someone as well as the way you stand and even *where* you stand. Body language sends messages to people. Realising how these messages are interpreted means that you are more aware how your body language affects other people – and you can also read the messages other people are sending to you. This may or may not be the same as the words they are saying – as you will see.

## Facial expressions

Your face is the most expressive part of your body. Without thinking about it you will smile, frown, scowl, nod, blink, stare and grimace many times a day. You may pull a face to send a silent message to a friend. You will register

many emotions on your face – surprise, disappointment, joy, boredom, annoyance – even sexual attraction.

Children are particularly interesting to watch because they haven't learned to conceal any of their emotions. If a child is upset or disappointed or bored it is absolutely obvious. As adults we are expected to 'mask' these feelings when they are inappropriate. So if your friends buy you a birthday present that you think is dreadful, you are not supposed to stare at it with a horrified look on your face. Similarly, if a customer – or your boss – appears when you are busy it is generally unwise to glare or frown because you are annoyed at being interrupted. Neither is it advisable to rest your head on your hand and stare dreamily out of the window when your supervisor is talking about the new key targets that must be achieved!

## Gestures

Gestures can be useful because they can add emphasis to what you are saying. You can also use them to communicate to someone who is some distance away – which is much better than shouting. There are only two things to be aware of. Gestures can also be a distraction – for example, if someone waves his or her arms around like a windmill when speaking. There are also some gestures, as you are aware, that aren't socially acceptable and which should be completely avoided at work!

Common gestures in Britain include:
- giving the 'thumbs up' to express approval
- rubbing your hands together with glee – or simply because you're cold!
- rubbing your thumb against your fingertips to signal money
- tapping your feet or drumming your fingers if you are impatient
- clenching your fists or showing the whites of your knuckles if you are anxious or in pain
- crossing your legs and folding your arms if you feel you need to defend yourself – even clutching a folder or bag across your body for added protection

- lowering your head if you feel negative or under attack
- leaning forwards if you are interested and leaning back if you feel very relaxed or confident
- putting your hands on your hips if you feel aggressive
- touching your hair or tossing it back if you are female/smoothing your hair and straightening your tie if you are a male – in either case to get attention.

## Posture – and all the rest!

Everyone looks more confident if they sit or stand up straight. You can immediately tell if someone is miserable or depressed because they hunch themselves up, trying to make themselves look smaller (or lower) than they really are. We also look down if we are upset or disappointed, as you will see if you watch any football player's reaction after missing a penalty. We do the opposite when we are thrilled and are even known to leap in the air (or punch the air) if we are really delighted!

In western cultures we prefer to leave a gap between ourselves and other people we don't know very well. If you travel to the Middle East you might find yourself constantly moving backwards to maintain the distance you prefer! You will also turn your body towards someone you like and want to talk to. If you only want to stop for a few moments you will turn your body and head towards them – but not your feet.

You will use 'mirror' gestures with someone you agree with. Watch for this with other people. One person will fold his arms, and then the other. Then one person will change to resting her head on her hand, and the other will follow.

Finally, expect people to touch things they own and are proud of. This can range from 'stroking' a new car to demonstrating a new laptop or even holding on to the arm of the new person in their life! This type of possessiveness is why people get annoyed when someone sits in 'their' chair or uses another personal object without permission.

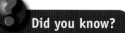

**Did you know?**

Research has shown that not only do pessimistic people look down more, they think better when they do this! Conversely, if you are an optimist you will have your best ideas when you look up.

**Did you know?**

Bowing and curtseying to royalty came about because people tried to make themselves look smaller in stature to show that they weren't as important in terms of class or status. If we feel less confident we try to 'shrink' by hunching our shoulders, if we feel confident we stand tall. We also use phrases that reflect how size makes us feel: 'I wanted to crawl into a corner' or 'He made me feel ten feet tall.'

Try this out with a partner. Talk about a topic that interests you. Your partner can do anything except look at you. He/she can read a paper, look out of the window, examine his/her fingernails, watch other people. Then see how long you can keep on talking when it is obvious no-one is listening. Unless you are very unusual you will slowly find yourself becoming more and more distracted (or irritated) until you give up altogether.

## The impact on others

Watching someone's body language can help you to understand how they feel. Start by discounting obvious physical reactions. If it's 28 degrees in your office today the reason why people are waving their hands in front of their face is to keep cool, not to attract your attention!

Then see if you can analyse their facial expressions, gestures and movements correctly. Then be aware how *your* facial expressions, gestures and movements affect other people. As a start, imagine how people who entered your reception area would react if you scowled at them all as they arrived!

# Discussions in business

There are many different types of discussion in business. There are very informal 'chats', such as occasions when you and your colleagues are talking together in your office. Then there may be times when your supervisor or boss is in your office and talking to you all, either informally or in a team briefing or a team discussion about a particular topic. Then there may be more formal occasions when a special meeting is held to obtain ideas, to solve a problem or to decide on something jointly.

You may be included in all these events, but to what extent do you participate? Do you think that just being there is enough? Or do you perhaps think that no-one is interested in your views? Or do you feel you could often help to improve the final outcome if you made some sort of contribution?

Basically, when it comes to discussions, some people are a joy and others are a complete pain! So what separates the two?

- **Positive contributions** are made by people who prepare in advance, arrive promptly, participate purposefully, listen to other contributions, don't upset anyone and keep their promises afterwards.
- **Negative contributions** (or worse) are made by people who are unprepared, arrive late, either don't participate or never shut up, jump to conclusions, never listen, annoy or insult other people and don't do the jobs they agreed to do.

Some responsibility obviously falls upon the leader of the discussion to ensure, whenever possible, that people know the topic in advance so they have time to think about it. It is also sensible if people are aware that they should arrive on time. If there are likely to be arrivals over five or ten minutes it can be useful to offer soft drinks or coffee at the start. This helps to relax people and encourages them to talk to each other informally. When everyone has arrived the session can then get under way.

Everyone should also know that they are expected to be courteous. This means listening when other people are speaking and helping to move the discussion forward. It also means responding politely to other people's suggestions – no matter what their private views are. There is nothing worse than someone who makes no effort to contribute but pours cold water over everyone else's ideas. If the whole group is focused on working together productively then a discussion can have a very positive outcome, particularly as many heads are usually better than one when it comes to thinking of new ideas.

## How to ... Contribute positively to discussions

- Unless the topic is a complete surprise, think carefully about what you can contribute before the discussion starts or read any information that you have been given in advance.

- Arrive on time and listen carefully whilst the leader outlines the topic and the aim of the discussion.

- Make brief notes if you think you may want to refer back to something that has been said.

- Be positive and constructive. Try to make suggestions that build on other people's good ideas.

- Ask questions if you don't understand something or want to clarify a suggestion.

- Don't talk for the sake of it, just to hear the sound of your own voice!

- Never 'rubbish' an idea because you didn't think of it, or make personal remarks about the person who suggested it.

- If you are nervous or shy, team up with someone else who feels the same and help each other to contribute. Being shy doesn't mean you never have a good idea!

- Be prepared to accept an outcome that is rather different from your ideal. This is because many discussions result in a compromise. Alternatively there may be good reasons why an idea has had to be adapted or changed to be acceptable.

- If you volunteer to follow something up afterwards or agree to help with a follow-up task, do so.

## Over to you

1   Do this activity in a group. Obtain a copy of a job application form. This can be the form used by your employer, your training organisation, your college or one you have downloaded from the Internet.

Although job application forms are rarely identical, they are all structured documents which present their information in a logical order.

Working in small groups, compare at least four different forms and allocate each a score out of five for each of the following categories:

●  first impressions

●  clear and easy to read

●  questions asked in a logical order

●  questions easy to understand

●  plenty of space to answer questions.

Then compare your scores to identify the best form of all, as agreed by everyone.

2   With your supervisor's agreement, obtain examples of two or three non-confidential business documents you have prepared. If you work for a large organisation with a specific house style then select different types of documents that show this. If you work for a small business where you aren't given any specific guidance, select different types of documents you have prepared yourself.

If you can, compare these with examples brought by other members of your group to see how they vary. For documents where you have been able to choose the layout and presentation, in each case explain the factors that influenced your decision.

3   Nabila has been asked to give a talk to everyone on how they can reduce waste in the office. She has made some notes, but they are a bit jumbled.

a   Look at Nabila's notes and put them into a more logical structure for her talk. Decide four or five sub-headings under which Nabila could group the information.

### NABILA'S NOTES

**Reducing waste**

Easiest to focus on jobs we all do.

Filing is one. Can reuse old folders by turning inside out.

Photocopying. Should do two-sided copies whenever possible.

Producing documents. Proof-read everything on screen. Take test copy and check that before printing more.

Also reuse old box files, lever arch files, ring binders etc where possible.

NB – should also take test copy of photocopies to check, too.

Can reuse envelopes for internal mail.

Put tops back on all pens after use (tightly).

Filing – remove any plastic wallets or polypockets from old papers so they can be reused.

Check emails carefully before sending or printing.

Don't print out emails unnecessarily.

Also store and use all photocopying and printer paper properly according to instructions.

Filing: when clearing files, recycle old papers if non-confidential, shred rest for packaging.

Make old forms/letter heads etc into scrap pads.

Screw tops on liquid paper tightly after use.

Don't take more photocopies or print more copies than really needed – wastes toner/ink/paper.

Reuse paperclips/bulldog clips.

Emails – Send an email attachment rather than a print-out.

Convert old unwanted stationery into scrap pads

Use solar cell calculators.

    **b**  Nabila is very nervous. What would you suggest to help her to give her talk clearly and more confidently?

**4**  Prove you can interpret body language! Match the actions in the table below with the messages that they are most likely to convey. Bear in mind this isn't an exact science, because much depends upon the person and the situation, so you may find that some examples overlap.

| Interpreting body language | |
|---|---|
| **The action** | **The message** |
| A Nodding the head | 1 Surprise |
| B Scratching the head | 2 Relaxed |
| C Shaking the head | 3 Displeasure, disagreement |
| D Winking | 4 Interested |
| E Frowning | 5 A shared joke or secret |
| F Wrinkling nose | 6 Defensiveness |
| G Raising eyebrows | 7 Impatience, annoyance |
| H Tapping the foot | 8 Dislike, distaste |
| I Folding arms against chest, crossing legs | 9 Confident, determined |
| J Leaning back, legs outstretched | 10 Agreement, understanding |
| K Leaning forwards | 11 Disagreement, disbelief |
| L Standing upright | 12 Puzzlement |

**5**  Your friend Bridget often makes you laugh with tales from her workplace, but today she is annoyed. Two weeks ago she went to a talk on making offices more environmentally friendly – a topic she feels strongly about. As a result she decided to hold a discussion with her colleagues to see how they could apply the ideas in their own workplace. According to her, most people arrived late, and two of them, Sarah and Nathan, started chatting between themselves. Rupel went on endlessly about how environmentally friendly her last company was. Ian, from accounts, who expressed no interest at the start, seemed to fall asleep. Janet, who according to Bridget never has any good ideas herself, poured cold water on everyone else's. Then a row broke out between Rupel and Janet, who traded insults before the meeting broke up in disarray. Bridget's boss still thinks the idea is worth pursuing and has asked her to lead a follow-up discussion and to be more focused on getting the best out of the team. Bridget says her blood is running cold at the thought.

    **a**  Suggest the actions that Bridget should take *before* the discussion to ensure it is better organised than the last one.

    **b**  Bridget decides to lay down a few ground rules to encourage positive contributions from everyone. Help her to decide what these are.

c At the last meeting, the following remarks were made. In each case suggest a more tactful way of making the same point.

i You're off your head if you think that'll work.

ii If you'd just shut up for one moment, someone else might be able to get a word in.

iii How long is this thing going to go on for anyway?

iv Can you never think of anything sensible to say?

## Evidence planning

Think about the times at work when you do each of the following activities:

- receive verbal information and instructions, and have to ask questions if you are not sure of something

- have to provide clear information, confidently, to other people

- have to adapt the way you communicate to meet the needs of other people

- are expected to contribute to a discussion.

For each of these, think about the type of information involved and the option unit to which this relates.

Now start a communications log sheet on which you can record these occasions. Each time put the date, what you did, the subject matter and the option unit to which this relates. Attach to your log sheet any relevant written communications you have received or written – such as a message you have written to someone or notes on a discussion you attended.

You can then use this information in various ways:

- You can use it as a basis for a professional discussion with your assessor about the ways in which you communicate at work.

- You can use it as a basis for asking for witness testimony from your supervisor or colleagues to prove what you did.

- You can use it to help identify future occasions on which your assessor can observe you or during which you could produce a tape or video to prove what you did.

# Written information you need at work

Written and printed information is referred to constantly in every office. More arrives each day both by post and electronically and new documents are created by staff throughout the day. Most of this information is stored for future reference in computer directories, in filing cabinets, in box files or lever arch files, on bookshelves and in folders.

The type of written information you see at work will depend upon your job role. Generally, however, most administrators use written information that falls into the following categories:

- documents relating to external contacts, such as customer and supplier records
- documents relating to internal matters, such as meeting notes, expense claims and holiday leave records
- directories, telephone lists and address books containing contact names and numbers
- other reference sources, such as dictionaries, timetables, equipment handbooks and stationery catalogues
- company information – from staff newsletters to advertising leaflets and company brochures
- newspaper and magazine articles on relevant topics
- information that has been downloaded and printed from the Internet.

As a first step you should make sure you know exactly where to find information you need. Ideally you will keep information that relates specifically to your own job in your desk or nearby, in appropriate files or folders. Shared information should be stored centrally, where it can be accessed easily by everyone. You should put away new information you obtain promptly, in the correct place, so that your working area stays neat and tidy and you can quickly find whatever you need.

### Did you know?

You will work far more quickly and efficiently if information you frequently need is close by. Save time by making your own copy of lists or papers you often need to borrow, and by storing information you regularly use in folders in your desk drawers.

# Confirming and reading written material to find information

If you are asked to find information that is contained in written documents, then there are several things you need to do.

- *Check you know what you are looking for.* Make sure you clearly understand the information you need to find. It always helps to write this down and to keep referring to it, then you don't get distracted by anything you are reading.
- *Find out how you should present the information.* You may have to provide it verbally, write it in a message, send an email or provide a photocopy. Or you may be expected to extract the key points and summarise these (see page 29).
- *Find the correct document or source.* You may be told to refer to a specific document to find information, or you might simply be asked to find certain information and it is up to you to decide where to look. If you are struggling, ask for help, rather than disappear for ages on a massive search. When you think you have found it, confirm with the person who made the request that you are correct before you go any further.
- *Check that the information is still up to date.* Many documents and reference books are regularly revised, such as telephone lists, timetables, stationery catalogues and price lists. Always check that the version you are referring to is the most recent, so the information is still relevant.
- *Check you understand the format of the document.* The information may be contained in a document that is short or long. It may comprise continuous text, it may be sub-divided under headings and into bullet points, have tables or graphics or include illustrations. Start by doing the 'flick test' to see how it is structured. How long is it? Is there a summary or contents page at the start? Is there an index and is it in alphabetical order? What sections or headings have been used? This will give you a quick appreciation of how the document is set out and what it contains.
- *Read it more carefully.* Focus on the specific parts of the document that contain the information you need. Read this more slowly and check you understand it. Ask someone if there are words or phrases you do not understand.
- *If possible, highlight the information you need.* If you are allowed to mark the document, then it often helps to use a highlighter pen. This means you will find the information more quickly if you are interrupted and have to continue with the task later.

At this point, if the request was straightforward, then you should be able to supply the information that was needed.

Rather more skills are required if you are asked to pick out the main points from a longer document and make written notes in which these are summarised in a logical order.

**Remember**

If you are asked to find information from books or online, then limit your search to three or four appropriate sources. Otherwise you are likely to end up with far more information than you can cope with.

## How to ... Extract the main points from written material

- Start by reading the material to get the overall meaning.

- Read it again more slowly. If you are allowed to mark the document then highlight each key point. If not, then see if you can take a photocopy and highlight this document. Otherwise list them on a separate piece of paper. Ignore examples or descriptions used just to illustrate something.

- Re-read the document and check that you haven't missed out anything important.

- Write out the points you have identified in proper sentences.

- Check if there is a sensible sequence or order that should be followed.

- Group together any connected information. You might want to put this under appropriate sub-headings.

- Decide a suitable heading for your document.

- Draft out your information and check it carefully to ensure that your punctuation, spelling and use of English is correct.

- Add your name and the date at the bottom. It is also useful to state the source of your information, such as the name of the handbook or magazine and the date of publication, in case you need to refer to it again.

### Did you know?

The key facts when you are taking a message normally include: the date and time of the call, the person's name, organisation or address, telephone number and dialling code, reason for calling. You can find out more on pages 351–361 in option unit 219: Use a telephone system.

### Did you know?

One advantage of email is that you can communicate easily and quickly with many people. One major disadvantage is that everyone can also see all your spelling and punctuation errors! You will find out more about creating emails if you choose option unit 213: Use IT to exchange information, on the CD-ROM.

# Providing written information that meets other people's needs

All communications created in business are for a purpose, as you saw on page 3. This purpose affects many things, including the type of document that is created, its format, the tone and style as well as its length and design.

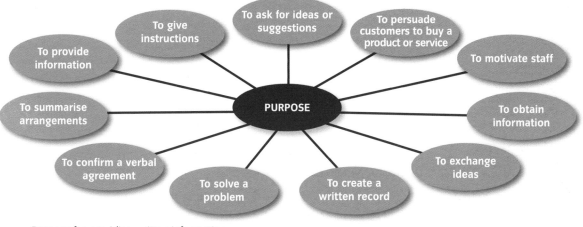

*Reasons for providing written information*

Before you can start to provide written information you need to know:

- what type of information is required
- why it is needed
- who wants it, and what they already know
- how quickly it must be supplied.

Only then can you decide the best document to prepare – as you can see from the table below.

| Types of written documents and their features | | |
|---|---|---|
| **Type of document** | **Sent to** | **Features** |
| Business letter | External contacts | Formal, slower than electronic methods, impersonal, provides permanent written record |
| Email | Internal and external contacts | Informal, rapid, other documents can be attached, can be sent worldwide very easily |
| Fax | External contacts, other branch offices or departments some distance away | Fast, useful for order confirmations on official paper, originally also for graphics and photographics before these could be sent electronically |
| Form (for completion) | Internal and external contacts | Used to collect information in a systematic manner. All sections must be completed accurately |
| Instant Messaging | Internal and external contacts | Immediate exchange of information online, can attach/send other documents |
| Memo | Internal contacts | More formal than email, provides permanent record if filed |
| Message or note | Internal contacts | Short and informal. Usually left on recipient's desk unless absent or on holiday |
| Report (informal) | Internal contacts | Gives clear account of an event or investigation under specific headings |
| Report (formal) | External contacts | Gives clear account of an event or investigation under specific headings |

## Deciding what to write

It is one thing to identify which type of document would be most appropriate, it is quite another deciding what to say! If you are writing a short message or email to a friend this is usually easier than writing to your boss or a customer, simply because you are less worried about making a mistake and looking foolish. Here is some advice:

- Decide how to display the document (see pages 11–14). Remember that you may have to follow a specific structure or house style.
- Choose the right words for your audience.
- Decide on your introduction, what you will say next and how you will end your document.
- Write fluently and grammatically.
- Check your spelling and punctuation.

The notes in the next How to ... box should help you.

**Remember**

Few people are good at writing at the start, but practice often makes perfect! Don't be afraid to show your drafts to other people, and don't take offence when they make positive suggestions to improve them.

## How to ... Provide written information accurately and clearly

- Think before you start.
- Jot down notes summarising the key points you need to include. Your task now is to extend these into a proper written document.
- Keep it simple! Don't use long sentences or words you don't fully understand.
- If you are writing by hand, make sure you use a pen that doesn't smudge, and write neatly so that every word and figure is readable.
- Avoid slang and colloquial expressions and the use of abbreviations, such as 'thanks', 'OK' or 'haven't', unless you are writing an informal note to a close colleague.
- Be polite. Say 'please' or 'I would be grateful' if you want someone to do something.
- Use proper sentences and paragraphs, even in an email.
- Don't use jargon or technical terms your recipient wouldn't understand.
- Try to avoid ending a document with 'thank you' on its own, unless it's an internal email.
- Try to vary the length of sentences to add some variety – but remember that commas should be used to separate items in a list or to denote a pause.
- Try to avoid repeating a word in a sentence. Think of an alternative instead.
- Check the spelling of any unfamiliar word in a dictionary. Run the spellchecker after you have completed the document, but remember that this cannot spot alternative words (e.g. from/form or wed/weed), so you need to do a final check yourself.
- If you are preparing the document on a computer, run the grammar checker when you have finished but remember that this has limitations too! If a suggestion seems weird, check with a colleague or ignore it.
- If you have had to key-in columns of figures, ask a colleague to check them with you so that you are absolutely certain they are correct.

**Did you know?**

The correct way to quote the title of something such as a newspaper, magazine, report or television programme is to put it into italics, like this: 'He reads *The Times* but I prefer *OK!*'

**Did you know?**

You can customise your spellchecker to correct any words that you regularly misspell or mistype if it doesn't do this already. Start by typing the word in your usual wrong way (e.g. grammer). Now highlight the word. Then press your *right* mouse button and *left* click on AutoCorrect. Then select the option you want (grammar). (In Office 2003 you just click on the correct option at the top.) From now on this word will auto-correct whenever you make the same mistake.

### Over to you

1 You should have already found out the format used in your organisation for each of the documents listed in the table on page 30. Now identify examples of reasons why they are sent. Do this by finding an example of a letter, a memo, an email, a report and a fax.

For each example, identify the main reason or purpose why it was sent, the type of recipient (e.g. internal or external; business contact or private individual), and then decide how this affected the way the information was written and presented.

2 Test your current ability to write grammatical sentences, spell words correctly and punctuate sentences properly by doing the quiz below. Then refer to the answers and notes on the CD-ROM to help you to improve your weak points.

### Communication quiz

This quiz is in four sections. Complete every section before you check your answers with those on the CD-ROM.

**Section 1**

Ten of the following words are spelt incorrectly. Identify them and write the word correctly.

| | | | |
|---|---|---|---|
| receipt | cemetery | reference | desperate |
| competent | prestigious | awfull | accidental |
| budget | foreign | colleage | honour |
| disappear | parallel | innoculate | permenant |
| irrelevent | fourty | embarrass | accommodate |
| appropriate | payed | alchohol | hygiene |
| definately | recommend | honorary | sincerly |

**Section 2**

Choose the right word from each of the pairs in italics.

1 She was worried that she might *loose/lose* her bracelet because the safety chain was *loose/lose*.
2 He told her to *accept/except* the *check/cheque*.
3 She said she would *waive/wave* her *right/rite* to the money.
4 He said he was *confident/confidant* that his *personal/personnel* documents were in order.
5 She was *complimented/complemented* on the *stationery/stationary* that she had designed.
6 *Their/They're* keen on going *their/there* for *their/they're* holidays.

### Section 3

Punctuate each of the following sentences correctly and add any capital letters that are required.

1  on his trip he will be visiting paris brussels rome and amsterdam
2  jacks sister will be arriving on saturday on the ten oclock flight from new york
3  did you buy a copy of the daily mail yesterday when you were in durham
4  the office desk as we know it will soon cease to exist according to a study called working in the twenty first century
5  Its doubtful she will want a key to the members new locker room as she thinks its size makes it impractical.

### Section 4

Rewrite each of the following sentences correcting the errors.

1  Me and Clive is going to the meeting.
2  She never gives him nothing but trouble.
3  BA are a very large airline.
4  Each of the documents have to be checked.
5  Was it Kelly that spoke to you?
6  Lend us your pen, will you.
7  Does you come here alot?
8  I'm alright thankyou.
9  This is the page what Jane wrote.
10 Less people work here now.

3  You have three short notes to write. Make sure that in each case you include the relevant information and your 'tone' is appropriate for the person you are contacting. Check your finished work with your tutor or trainer.

**a** The first note is to your supervisor, Ken, to ask if you can leave half an hour early on Thursday because your brother has qualified for an athletics final and you would like to watch him. It is up to you if you wish to include an offer to work later on another occasion to make up your hours!

**b** The next note is to your best friend at work, Jenny, who is off today, to let her know that you have borrowed her calculator because yours has gone faulty.

**c** The third note is to a customer, Russell Barnes, who called in yesterday. He had lost the instructions to the timer for the automatic watering system he bought last year. You have found a copy and photocopied them for him. Write a brief note you could include on a compliments slip when you send the copied instructions to him.

**4** Your supervisor is interested in recycling used paper and cartridges in the office and buying recycled paper. She has heard that some charities welcome used ink and toner cartridges, too. She also wonders if all the used drinks cans are recyclable, and has asked you to find out more.

Search online for information on recycling paper and cartridges by using a good search engine such as www.google.co.uk. Investigate two or three websites which you find easy to understand. Some may specifically relate to recycling schemes that operate in your own region. Try to find at least one website relating to a charity scheme. Print out the relevant information you find.

Identify the main points from your printouts, and summarise these in a short document. Use appropriate headings to ensure that the information is clearly set out. Check your finished work with your tutor or trainer.

## Evidence planning

Identify occasions when you carry out the following activities at work:

- reading written material that contains information and extracting the main points – either for yourself or for other people

- preparing and providing accurate, clear written information to other people.

Now look at the type of information you prepared in each case and decide to which option units these documents relate. This is likely to depend upon the topic of the material and/or the reason you were asked to provide it.

Include copies of these documents in the evidence you collect for each option unit, and make sure that you do this for any future written material you prepare and provide. These are valuable work products that are important as evidence of your written communications.

## What if?

What should you do if either:

- you are not involved in any discussions during the time you are taking your award

- the written material you have created does not directly link to any of your chosen option units?

In either case, talk to your assessor who can arrange to observe you at work, talk to you about your job and ask you questions during a professional discussion and show you how to link the written material you have as evidence to the scheme as a whole.

# Plan and be accountable for your work

People vary in their ability to make plans. You can see this when people prepare to go on holiday. At one extreme is the person who costs out a holiday carefully, works out a savings plan, makes all the arrangements six months ahead, lists everything to take and packs a few days ahead, sets off with a map, guidebook, itinerary and a contact checklist as well, and will go only to restaurants thoroughly researched in advance. At the other extreme is someone who suddenly decides to go away, throws a few things in a bag the night before and leaves. This might sound wonderful but there can be a few problems with this approach – not least running out of money, not being able to find anywhere to stay or forgetting to take some essential items. If one of these happens to be a passport then the whole trip may be off!

Interestingly, in business, neither of these approaches to planning is ideal. In the first case there is no flexibility, whereas the second approach would lead to chaos. Obviously businesses cannot just decide to do things on a whim, regardless of whether they can afford them or not. Similarly, they cannot just put things off, or cancel arrangements because they never got around to sorting out the details. So businesses have to plan – but they also have to be flexible enough to incorporate changes when these are needed. To be successful, as you will see in unit 202: Work within your business environment, they need to make plans, set targets and work steadily towards achieving these.

This idea of planning doesn't just relate to the organisation as a whole or its managers. It also involves you! It is your responsibility to meet any targets and fulfil any commitments that are part of your job role. This section looks at the best way to do this, even on very busy days, and is essential reading if your normal approach in your private life is to hope that you remember everything and just keep your fingers crossed!

> **Remember**
>
> A **deadline** signifies the very last date by which a task must be completed. Never assume this is some vague, flexible date you can ignore if you want! The 'countdown' to an important deadline should be flagged up in a diary or planner rather like an early warning system.

## The importance of planning your work and your accountability to others

The plans and promises we make vary in their ability to affect other people. If you plan to go shopping and then can't be bothered, you are the only person likely to be affected. If you make a promise to go with a friend and then change your mind, this will affect someone else as well. If you make a commitment which involves several people and then don't deliver, you will probably be extremely unpopular. This will be the case at work if you cannot manage your own workload effectively, store up problems and then expect other people to drop everything to help you out.

During the average day at work you will have several routine tasks to do on a regular basis. You will also be given specific jobs to do by your supervisor or manager. You may also have other commitments. You may have made arrangements to meet someone at lunchtime, to telephone a customer with some information and attend a team meeting. You will be expected to organise your day so that you fulfil *all* your responsibilities. If there is a crisis then it is likely that you will have to rethink your priorities as you will be expected to select the key tasks to do. You will then either leave the rest until another day or ask your supervisor if someone can help you.

In your private life you may rarely write down what you need to do and plan the best way to go about doing everything. At work, this is very dangerous. You could easily spend too long doing unimportant work or even forget to do an important job altogether. In this case you will be letting down the person who gave you the task. If other people have to be drafted in to help to rescue the situation then they are unlikely to be very pleased, especially if they too are busy. If this happens on several occasions you will rapidly start to become 'public enemy number one'.

Both your boss and your colleagues must be able to rely on you to do your job effectively – as you should be able to rely on them. This means that they expect you to:

- plan and manage your own daily workload effectively
- prioritise your work effectively, so that you do the most urgent and important tasks first
- be flexible and prepared to change your plans when necessary
- listen and contribute responsibly when new or important tasks are being discussed so that you make sensible suggestions about deadlines that will affect you
- make sure you know the deadline for all tasks that are your responsibility

- plan how to do the work so that it is done correctly and on time
- let people know if there is a problem that could affect the overall outcome, in plenty of time for action to be taken.

If you act as a professional and responsible member of your team and can be trusted to fulfil your commitments on a regular basis, you will not only be a more valued colleague but will also be more efficient and be able to take on more interesting and challenging jobs. It is also highly likely that you will enjoy your work more.

### Did you know?

You will work more efficiently if you record tasks to do and things to remember in a proper planning system. Use the one that works best for you. This may be a diary, a notepad, a personal digital assistant (PDA), a wall planner or a simple 'to do' list. Some people like Post-it notes, but these have limitations. You can't put much on one note, they can look untidy, and there can be dangers if you fasten them to your computer screen. According to a court martial in 2005, when the ship HMS Trafalgar ran aground off the coast of Skye on a training exercise, part of the problem was caused by all the Post-it notes stuck on the screens of the navigational instruments!

# The importance of agreeing realistic targets for your work

The targets you agree to may relate to several small tasks or one large one. If this job is particularly long or complex you may be expected to agree to interim targets that help to contribute towards the achievement of the main task.

You may be expected to agree targets relating to:

- deadlines
- quality and type of work
- the resources you can use.

There is obviously a link between these items. Many jobs can be done very quickly and to a very high standard if money is no object. If you were asked to organise the production of 1000 leaflets and told you could use a professional agency, regardless of cost, this is a lot different from being told to do the same job using the office photocopier. And if your office has only a small, old-fashioned copier you will find the job harder than if you have a modern all-singing and all-dancing version with lots of automated features.

No matter which resources you use, however, it would never be acceptable to produce a leaflet which is crumpled, full of errors and ten days late!

There is, however, a trade-off between speed and type of work. A task that is complex, detailed or high quality will take longer to do than one that is not. If you are asked to find a suitable hotel for your boss in the middle of Birmingham you will (or should) do a much better job if you are given ten or fifteen minutes rather than expected to have the answer in three minutes flat. Similarly, in five minutes you can photocopy 20 pages but not 2000 and could prepare a simple table but not a complicated spreadsheet.

You need to be aware of what you can personally achieve in a certain time and what you cannot. It is no use having unrealistic ideas about what is possible and then getting in a panic or just making a mess of the job. If a deadline is not negotiable then you must ask for help if you know that, on your own, the task would be unachievable.

**Did you know?**

You need resources to do any job. These include materials, equipment, skills and time. You can also class other people as resources if you can rely on them for help.

**Remember**

An achievable timescale is the time period in which you can complete a job to the standard required with the resources you have available. If the task will take you a long time, setting interim deadlines will help you to check your progress regularly and keep on schedule.

## How to ... Agree realistic targets and an achievable timescale

- Know your own capabilities and skills. This includes which tasks you can do easily, which give you problems, and how long it takes you to do routine jobs.

- Find out all about a task before you make any promises. This includes knowing how complex it is, how much work is involved, and the quality required.

- Find out what resources are available. Bear in mind the better your resources the faster or more easily you are likely to be able to do a job.

- Find out the proposed deadline. This may be flexible or immovable.

- If the deadline is flexible, calculate how long it will take you to do the work based on the type of task and the resources. Then suggest an achievable completion date and be prepared to give reasons to support your suggestion.

- If the deadline is immovable, explain that you will need help. This could mean the assistance of other people, or it might mean taking other work off you so that you can do the urgent task first. In this case be prepared to suggest the tasks other people could do for you, to 'free you up' to concentrate on the one you are discussing.

### Did you know?

If you want to impress people, argue for more time than you need and then challenge yourself to try to beat the personal deadline you have set for yourself. Most people are thrilled to find work arriving on their desk earlier than they expected, rather than later. Of course, if you do this every time, do be aware that someone will eventually call your bluff!

# Planning your work

Planning means deciding the best way to do something, taking into account the key factors involved. The aim is make the best use of your time and the other resources you need. Normally you will get better results more quickly if you plan rather than act on impulse, because you will have thought about what is involved in advance.

There are several other benefits:

- You will normally save time in the long run, because you won't have to back-track.
- You will get more jobs done each day than someone who doesn't plan.
- You will do the most important and urgent tasks and only leave tasks that don't matter as much.
- You will make far fewer mistakes – or preferably none at all!
- You will be well organised.
- You will be able to check your own progress.
- You are far more likely to meet your targets.
- You will be far less stressed and have more confidence in your own abilities to do difficult tasks.

### Did you know?

Good planning pays dividends in your private life. Good task and time management means you get more done each day – which helps you to live life to the full. Good project management is invaluable if you ever have to arrange a major event, like a wedding or house move.

## Planning your day-to-day work

This is sometimes called **task management**. This involves thinking about how to cope with all the different tasks you have to do every day, especially when you are very busy and have more than you can do in one day. How do you decide which ones to do now and which you can leave until tomorrow?

Quite simply you divide up all your jobs and assign them different priorities. These tell you which jobs must be done first, and which you can leave until later.

### How to ... Prioritise the jobs you do each day

Assign one of the following four categories to every job that crosses your desk:

- *Class A* tasks are both urgent and important – do these FIRST.
- *Class B* tasks are urgent but not important – do these NEXT.
- *Class C* tasks are important but not urgent. If you leave these, they will soon become urgent.
- *Class D* tasks are routine jobs which are not urgent or important. Do these last.

The following day, look at the jobs you left and reassign them, according to how they should now be categorised.

## Planning how to do a longer or more difficult job

This is sometimes called **project management**. In this case you really need some blank paper, a pen or pencil and some quiet time whilst you think and concentrate. Your aim is to end up with a comprehensive list that includes everything you need to do, in the right order and which takes into account your final deadline and the resources you need. You also need to know how to 'factor in' possible contingencies. These are the things that might go wrong and how you will cope with them.

There are several steps in this process and these are outlined in the diagram opposite.

## Project management and prioritising

If you are planning how to work on a complex task, you will have a slightly different way of deciding which tasks to do first.

### Planning and project management

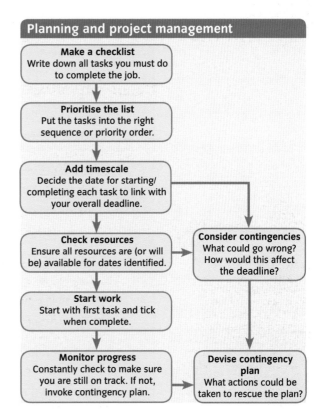

**Make a checklist**
Write down all tasks you must do to complete the job.

↓

**Prioritise the list**
Put the tasks into the right sequence or priority order.

↓

**Add timescale**
Decide the date for starting/completing each task to link with your overall deadline.

↓

**Check resources**
Ensure all resources are (or will be) available for dates identified.

→ **Consider contingencies**
What could go wrong? How would this affect the deadline?

↓

**Start work**
Start with first task and tick when complete.

↓

**Monitor progress**
Constantly check to make sure you are still on track. If not, invoke contingency plan.

→ **Devise contingency plan**
What actions could be taken to rescue the plan?

- Tasks that are urgent and important still come first. These now include
  - tasks that are crucial to the overall job
  - tasks that involve other people
  - tasks where there could be delays
  - tasks that you have been asked to complete quickly.
- Tasks that will take a long time to do must be scheduled to start before those that will take only a short time.
- Tasks that you must finish before something else can be done must be done at an early stage.

Remember that your priority list can easily change if the overall task is long or complex. A new request, a minor delay or an unexpected problem can change your list from one day to another.

## Time management

**Time management** means being self-disciplined about the use of your time so that you don't waste time doing unnecessary things. Good time managers are normally able to achieve far more in the course of the average working day. This is because they do jobs when they are scheduled to be done, rather than when they feel like it. They are also firm about interruptions. They discourage people from distracting them when they are busy, and are equally sensitive enough not to disturb anyone else at the wrong time, either.

**Over to you**

1 Test your own time management skills by doing the quiz below. Do they need improvement? Decide how frequently you do each of the following by answering 'often', 'rarely' or 'never' for each question.

**Can you manage your time?**

How often do you ...

1 Get distracted reading irrelevant items when you are looking for information online?

2 Put off doing jobs you don't want to do?

3 Stop doing a job because you're bored, not because you've finished it?

4 Have to spend ages looking for what you need because your desk is such a tip?

5 Chat to people who pass by your desk?

6 Make a mess of a job and then have to start it again?

7 Have to retrace your steps because you forgot something the first time?

8 Find yourself running late for some reason?

9  Spend more time trying to decide what to do than actually doing it? 2

10  Find yourself half way through an urgent job when it's time to leave for the day? 2

**Score yourself**     14

Give yourself 0 points each time you said 'often', 1 point each time you chose 'sometimes' and 2 points each time you said 'never'. Then turn to page 389 to see how you fared!

2  Suggest how you could solve each of the following time-wasting problems. Compare your ideas with other members of your group or with the suggested answers on the CD-ROM.

   a  A new colleague doesn't seem to be able to start work until she has discussed the last episode of *EastEnders* with you.

   b  It takes you about ten minutes to find anything in the filing basket.

   c  There is normally a queue whenever you want to use the photocopier.

   d  You can never remember the addresses of websites you use regularly so have to hunt for them all over again.

   e  Although you keep important notes clipped together, you always have to plough through them all before you can find the one you want.

   f  It takes you absolutely ages to find any document you have saved on your computer.

3  Mia has made out a 'to do' list for tomorrow but hasn't decided in which order she should do her jobs. Start by grouping each job into A, B, C or D depending upon its priority. Then rewrite the 'to do' list showing the order you would tackle the jobs within each group.

Check your answers with those on the CD-Rom.

> **TO–DO**
> Water the plants
> Book hotel for Ken's trip to Dublin in two days' time
> Send a refund cheque to a customer
> Book a room for a sudden safety meeting tomorrow afternoon
> Photocopy documents for the safety meeting
> Find out the flight times to Dublin, check with Ken and book the flight
> Get filing up to date
> Report photocopier breakdown to the leasing firm
> Order photocopying paper – nearly out!
> Unpack and check a stationery order that arrived today

## Evidence planning

You can now practise your planning skills by thinking about the evidence you will need to prove that you can plan and are accountable for your work. As a first step, think about evidence that proves that you can make the best use of your time and resources on a day-to-day basis.

The easiest way is to keep a record of the tasks that you have to do and the way in which you prioritise these. Quite simply, just keep your 'to do' lists, diary or notebook safely. Instead of throwing away notes or emails you receive that make you change your plans, keep them.

Ideally you should present this information as part of your evidence for one of your option units, but you can also use it as the basis of a professional discussion with your assessor about the way you plan and are accountable for your work.

## Snapshot – How efficient is your office?

According to research by BACS Payments Schemes Ltd, the average office worker loses nearly three hours of time a day through time-wasting activities, much of it caused by inefficient working practices.

The worst offenders are PC problems, computer errors or crashes and printer jams – all of which lose their users up to 48 minutes a day. Dealing with colleagues – especially those who can't make their minds up or are noisy – loses another 34 minutes a day. Unnecessary phone calls and meetings, too many emails and searching for information that has been filed wrongly are other culprits.

The result is that whereas most people agree that the phone and their computer are both essential they also feel that the barrage of unwanted communication and complicated technology have both created more problems than they have solved.

According to the research, the worst region in the country for time wasting is the East Midlands with 88.5 working days a year lost, and the best is the North East which only loses 74.5 days.

To help to save time, BACS has published a light-hearted book which includes tips to stop time-wasting. You can download *The Little Book of Time Wasting* at www.paymedirect.co.uk.

## Using resources wisely

Time is just one resource you can waste or use wisely. Others include physical resources (equipment, materials etc.), information and people.

- **Equipment** includes large items such as computers, photocopiers, printers and shredders, and small items such as calculators, punches, staplers and scissors. Large items should be used according to instructions, small items you use regularly should be kept close at hand and in good working order. The last thing you want when you reach out to punch or staple twenty pages urgently is a shower of bits all over your desk or an empty stapler or – even worse – one that jammed last time you used it and is still stuck.
- **Materials** includes paper, pens, folders, envelopes, CDs, paper-clips and dozens of other small items. You need to identify the right items for the job you are doing and make sure enough are available for when you need them. This may mean placing a special order. It may also mean learning the difference between the various types and weights of paper or sizes of envelopes.
- **Information** includes all the reference sources and details you need to do the task(s) you have been allocated. It can include the office files, company brochures, catalogues, reference books, your organisation's intranet and, of course, the Internet. Bear in mind that too much information is almost as bad as too little, because you don't know where to start and then get swamped and confused. Start by identifying the type of information you need to find, then deciding the most appropriate place to find it. Finally, check it is up to date before you use it.
- **People** may not like to be considered a resource but that's what they are! A helping pair of hands or wise advice should be treasured, not squandered. This means thanking people who assist you and returning the favour as soon as you can.

## Effective working methods to help you to achieve your plan

Working methods relate to the way you go about a task. Sometimes you will be told exactly what to do, at other times you may be able to make many decisions yourself. There are several factors that influence working methods, as you can see in the diagram below.

Features that influence working methods

You need to check any specific requirements before you start. You should also understand the implications of ignoring these or adopting sloppy working methods yourself. These are illustrated in the example below.

Louise and Bushra are friends and work together. Individually, though, they are very different and work in different ways. Louise is well organised. Her desk is neat and tidy. She plans carefully and thinks before she acts. She is careful, methodical and takes pride in doing a good job first time.

Bushra is great fun but far more slap-dash. She doesn't have Louise's experience, but instead of taking her time and thinking about things – or asking for advice – she is far more apt to guess what to do, sometimes with dire results.

Now look at the difference when they are each given an urgent photocopying job to do by Sam, their boss, who needs 20 copies of a 15-page report for an important meeting.

Louise starts by checking that the original is good quality and that the pages are in the right order. She carefully removes the staple from the pages using a staple remover. She knows that company guidelines state that all documents should be photocopied double-sided where possible to save paper, so she sets this on the machine. She also sets the automatic staple option. She then places her original in the document holder and takes a test copy to check the print is correctly positioned and is straight on every page. The paper tray is low, so Louise refills this and throws away the empty packaging in the rubbish bin. During the print run there is a paper jam and three pages are spoiled. Louise puts these in the paper recycling box and then sets about remedying the problem. She has been trained how to do this but sometimes forgets, so she double checks the instructions to make sure that she does this safely. If she couldn't remedy the problem she would put a notice on the machine to stop other people using it until it could be repaired. When she has cured the paper jam she completes the job, carefully collects the copies and looks around to make sure she hasn't forgotten anything. She then leaves the photocopying room and hands over the copies, plus the original just before the meeting starts.

Bushra doesn't bother checking the original but simply assumes it must be fine. She tugs at the staple to remove it and some pages tear at the top. She puts the pages into the document holder and keys in the copies required. She refills the paper, when this is needed, but leaves the used packaging on the floor. Part way through, when the paper jams, she hazards a guess at what to do and is lucky not to burn her hand. Eventually she has to go and ask Louise for help. Louise points out that some of Bushra's copies look crooked and suggests she redoes them. She also reminds her she could have set the staple option and will now have to do this manually. By now Bushra is struggling for time. She hurriedly starts to staple the copies that have been done and, in her haste, knocks several sets on the floor. In even more of a rush she

**Remember**

It's *always* quicker to think through a task before you start, then to concentrate and work carefully – simply because you do a much better job with fewer mistakes. As you become more experienced, you'll learn to do this at speed, too!

abandons the idea of redoing any pages, frantically staples the rest and rushes out of the room.

You wouldn't be surprised to know that although Sam was relieved to get the copies 10 minutes after the meeting started, he was less amused to discover there were only 12 sets, and eight of these were unusable with missing pages, crooked text or staples placed so that part of a page was unreadable. In fact, no two sets seemed to be the same. To make matters worse one of the participants was Sam's own boss, who acidly observed that the 'double-sided' rule was obviously not being followed any more in Sam's department. To cap it all, he then received complaints from other staff about the state of the photocopying room that afternoon.

Plan to be tidy and organised:
- Tidy your desk regularly and always before you leave each night.
- Use desk aids and tidies to store pens, paper-clips and other small items.
- Keep your diary, notebook and Post-it notes together at one side or in your top drawer.
- Aim for a file-free desk top with only the work you are doing on the top.
- Bin unwanted stuff regularly.
- Keep vital reference information or deadline lists safe by pinning them up or taping them to your desk.
- Check out the electronic aids that can help you. You'll find several ideas on pages 228–233 in option unit 204: Manage diary systems.

### Did you know?

Do you have deskitis? According to the office products firm Avery, this stands for Dump Everything Seldom Keep it Tidy! You qualify if the top of your desk is strewn with personal items (teddy-bears, nail files, magazines and personalised mugs are favourites) and covered in files, papers and other documents. Only 30 per cent of those surveyed cleared their desks daily, 20 per cent doing so very occasionally, and 16 per cent only when everything threatens to fall on the floor! To help, Avery have launched a 'refresh your desk' campaign at www.averyrefresh.co.uk.

## How to ... Confirm effective working methods

- For any task that you are planning to do, check the specific rules that you must follow when you do the work. These may include organisational procedure, guidelines, safety rules or codes of practice (see page 52).

- Identify any preferences your boss (or the person giving you the job) may have. These might include the order in which you have to do the work, the resources that must be used or how the work is presented.

- Ask for guidance if there is anything about the task, or how it should be done, that you do not understand.

- Adopt effective working methods yourself. These include
  – setting out the equipment and materials you need at the start
  – working in a clear space
  – working methodically
  – having a place for everything and everything in its place
  – finishing one job before you start the next
  – tidying up when you have finished.

# Problems that can occur and how to report them

Plans may have to change for several reasons. Some of these may be good news – such as finding out you have more time to do a difficult job, or something which sounded complicated is now being simplified. Unfortunately at other times the change is needed because a problem has occurred. You need to know how to react in this situation, and the best response will normally depend upon the type of problem and its possible effect.

You can roughly divide problems up into two types:

- *Minor problems*. These cause a minor inconvenience more than anything else. With a little thought you can usually adjust what you are doing and keep going. Normally, as part of your responsibilities you will be expected to solve most of these yourself, although you may check out a proposed solution with your supervisor before you go ahead.
- *Major problems*. These are issues that could have serious consequences and therefore need very careful thought. These shouldn't be kept to yourself! Sometimes you may find a 'crisis meeting' is called to discuss the problem. This is useful because a group of people think about all the aspects before deciding on the best solution. The support of other people who may be affected by a problem or who can contribute to the discussion is invaluable.

## Did you know?

It is always better if you can suggest a solution to a problem. This shows you want to help to solve it. But never be tempted to take matters into your own hands and implement any solution that is outside your area of responsibility without obtaining permission first.

## Types of problems

Problems normally relate to issues of resources, quality, type of task or deadlines. If any of these change unexpectedly then this causes a problem. If several occur simultaneously then your first instinct may be mild hysteria. Here are some examples:

- A vital piece of equipment breaks down.
- Pre-ordered materials don't arrive on time.
- A colleague who is helping you goes off sick.
- The task is extended for some reason.
- The first draft is unacceptable and has to be redone.
- The deadline moves closer.
- You hit a technical difficulty that you don't have the skills to solve.
- You are still waiting for other people's contributions and are stuck until you get them.
- You have dozens of other jobs on your desk and simply cannot do the work by the target date.

## The action to take

The most appropriate action to take obviously depends upon the type of problem that has occurred, how serious it is, whether you can put it right yourself, whether you have a good idea but need permission first, or whether you urgently need help!

The following checklist should give you useful guidance on the type of action to take and when to take it.

| Solving problems | | |
| --- | --- | --- |
| **Solve it yourself if** | **Ask for permission if** | **Ask for help if** |
| The problem is only minor<br><br>It directly relates to your own area of responsibility<br><br>No-one else is involved<br><br>You are not breaking any company rules<br><br>You can easily solve the problem | Not solving the problem could create serious problems<br><br>Your idea for a solution would cost money<br><br>Your solution exceeds your area of responsibility<br><br>Your solution involves other people | The problem will have serious consequences if it isn't solved quickly<br><br>Many people will be affected<br><br>You haven't a clue how to solve it<br><br>You have an idea but are worried it won't work<br><br>You desperately need advice or assistance |
| **Example** | **Example** | **Example** |
| It is taking longer to do a task than you thought, so you take a short lunch break to complete it. | Your supplier has let you down. You can use a different one but the prices are higher. | You are told by a senior member of staff that the room you booked for a customer presentation has been double-booked and you can no longer use it. There are no other rooms available. |

### Over to you

1 Does planning and being well organised come naturally to you, or do you treat both as an optional extra? Do the quiz below to find out.

#### Are you a natural planner?

Answer each of the following questions True or False. Give yourself 1 point for every True and no points for every False. Then check your score on page 389.

1 You've already planned what you will be wearing tomorrow – and know it is clean.
2 You normally check the weather forecast before planning a day out.
3 The floor area in your bedroom is clear of clutter.
4 Before you go shopping, you make a list so you won't forget anything.

5 You never forget a birthday because they are all noted in your diary.
6 You always carry a notebook and pen with you at work, in case you need to write anything down.
7 You enjoy thinking about the future and planning what you will do.
8 Your friends often ask you to help plan events and days out.
9 You rarely forget or lose anything.
10 You can always find what you put away.

2 Re-read the working methods used by Louise and Bushra when they were photocopying. Assuming part of the problem is the fact Bushra hasn't been trained how to do this properly, make a list of the key areas you would want her to improve if she worked in your office.

3 For one task you do regularly, identify the working methods you use (or should use!) at work. Then explain how these help you to do a good job first time.

4 You have been asked to assemble 500 customer information packs to be taken to an exhibition to be held in three weeks' time. They will be given to visitors who call at the stand. Each pack will contain:

- a letter from the managing director, which his PA is providing

- a map showing the best route to the company, which you need to download and print out in colour from the website

- a brochure about the company, to be provided by Tim in marketing

- a brochure about your products, to be provided by Ali in sales

- an enquiry form, which you have to create and photocopy.

The folder is being designed and printed by an outside firm and is due to be delivered in ten days' time. You also have to arrange with Samina in marketing for the completed packs to be collected and taken to the exhibition.

a How many people are you depending upon to do this task well? List them.

b Which tasks do you have to do yourself? List these in the right sequence for doing the work.

c What resources will you need to do the task? List them.

d What interim deadlines or reminders would you put in your diary to make sure nothing is forgotten or delayed?

e Suggest four things that could go wrong. In each case say what action you would take.

Compare your ideas with other members of your group, or check with the answers on the CD-ROM.

## Snapshot – Bad luck or bad management?

Administrators who work in the media know all about working to tight deadlines. You can hardly publish a newspaper a day late or hand over information for a radio programme an hour after it was broadcast! When things go wrong, it is also likely that the news will become common knowledge, as staff of the BBC found when its problems filming a series about the wonders of ancient Egypt were reported in the *Sunday Times*.

Some members of the crew argued that bad management had caused costs to spiral way over budget. This included more people travelling to Egypt and more money spent on reconstructions and props than planned. They claimed these could have been foreseen at the start.

The BBC argued differently. It said that all overspends were authorised and the problems were simply due to bad luck. These included security problems, terrible weather and many of the staff catching infectious diseases that prolonged filming.

Although it is not usually good tactics to rely on superstition to explain away problems, perhaps on this occasion the newspaper was right in suggesting that it could just be the Curse of the Pharaohs that had struck again!

# Keeping other people informed about progress

At the start of your career you may have the happy notion that you should be left alone to get on with your work and that you will do better if no-one keeps pestering you for information or progress reports. This may sound reasonable but is unrealistic if you think about it from the point of view of your boss and your colleagues.

Your boss – and more experienced colleagues – will know that problems can occur at any time. They also know that whilst some people will quickly make a fuss, others will keep quiet and try to cope. In fact, if anyone has been silly enough to criticise you when you have raised a problem in the past, you will probably be tempted to do just that. The risk is that if you *don't* manage to put things right on your own, the problem will get worse.

There are therefore several reasons why you need to keep people informed about your progress:

- You won't have to go to bed worrying how to solve a problem on your own.
- You can get help and advice if a problem occurs, and support from other people.
- People can factor in any possible delays in time to change their plans (see below).
- You don't give everyone a scare when you announce a serious problem when it's too late to do much about it (see below).
- Your boss can plan how to allocate the rest of the work coming into the office effectively, because your workload is known.

# Giving sufficient notice if plans need to be revised

If you keep quiet and say nothing, everyone will expect you to meet the deadline you have agreed. If there is the slightest hint that you will not, then you are better to give people as much notice as possible. This gives them far more scope for taking action than a last-minute panic.

Notify the person concerned and give the reason for the problem. Hopefully this is because of something outside your control, rather than the fact that you made a total mess of the job first time round! Apologise for the delay and suggest a new deadline time or date. Be prepared to be as flexible as you can. You may have to be prepared to reshuffle your work to fit this in. If you have a serious problem managing your workload then talk this through with your supervisor.

**Remember**

If you fail to meet a deadline, the task now becomes even more urgent and should therefore move up on your priority list for completion. There may therefore be a 'knock-on' effect with your other work.

# Acknowledging and learning from your mistakes

When you are given a task, and agree to do it, it is up to you to keep your promise even if the job is a bit harder than you thought it would be. This is what responsibility is all about. You can't suddenly decide it's all too much for you and dump it on someone else!

What you can do, as you have seen, is discuss problems that occur with other people in good time for a solution to be found. This is relatively easy for problems that are outside your control. You cannot help a deadline date moving forwards, the photocopier breaking down or the stationery supplier losing the order. These types of problem are always easier to deal with because you can focus on solving the difficulty – and ask other people to help you.

The situation is rather different if you are the *cause* of the problem in the first place. Here are examples:

- You lost (or forgot) important information so couldn't finish the job – or did it incorrectly.
- The task is a mess and needs to be redone.
- You took on too much work and couldn't do it in time.
- You promised something you weren't capable of doing.
- It has taken you five times longer than you thought it would.
- You forgot you'd booked three days off next week.
- You forgot all about it!

You then not only have to take responsibility for the work you haven't done, but also for the reason it hasn't been done! This is never pleasant for anyone, at any stage of his or her career. But your actions in this situation will be remembered for a long time. One strategy is to go for immediate pain but long-term respect. Or you can try to dodge the issue or push the blame on someone else. The risk is that you will be caught and no-one will ever trust you again.

# Guidelines, procedures and codes of practice relevant to your work

Several of the tasks you do as part of your job may have to be done in a certain way. This is because you have to follow guidelines, procedures or codes of practice. You will learn more about these in unit 202: Work within your business environment, but you will find a useful summary in the table below.

| Types of instructions you must follow | What they are | Examples for administrators |
|---|---|---|
| Guidelines | Instructions on the best way to do a task based on 'best practice' | Using email<br><br>Researching on the Internet<br><br>Using the photocopier<br><br>Remedying a printer problem |
| Procedures | Step-by-step instructions issued by the organisation to link with the systems in operation | Booking in visitors and issuing visitor badges<br><br>Logging in to the computer system<br><br>Processing expense claims |
| Codes of practice | Advice on how to comply with laws or regulations; e.g. on health and safety, data protection or discrimination | The use of display screen equipment (i.e. computers)<br><br>Disclosing personal data on staff and customers<br><br>Access for disabled visitors |

**Did you know?**

If you don't like rules and regulations, don't apply for a job at the Department of Trade and Industry. It drew up a policy document on 'foliage strategy' which told staff where any plants they brought into the office must be positioned and how they should be cared for and disposed of. The problem? It took six pages and 2000 words to describe this in detail!

Some of these will be well known to you because they relate to tasks you do every day, such as logging on to your computer or using the photocopier. Others may be less familiar because a task is new. It is always wise to check with your supervisor or a more experienced colleague if there are any specific instructions or procedures you must follow before you attempt any new task so that you always work safely, comply with organisational instructions and never unwittingly break the law.

1  Kate is always encountering problems. In the last two days she has had a catalogue of disasters. For each of these, decide whether they were preventable or not preventable. For each preventable problem, say what Kate could have done, but obviously didn't. For each problem that was not preventable, suggest what Kate could do next.

   a  There is a thunderstorm as she is about to send an urgent fax, so she is told she can't use the machine.

   b  She loses the printed copy of the spreadsheet she has been asked to update, on which her boss had written the new figures.

   c  She has to send an urgent package to Dublin and has just found out that Royal Mail workers are on strike.

   d  Her printer jams, for the fourth time this week, when she is printing out an urgent report. Arif, who has mended it for her each time, is on leave today.

   e  Because she stood in for an absent colleague on reception for an hour, Kate doesn't have time to finish the report she is preparing until tomorrow, rather than today as she promised.

   f  She cannot read the writing on some rep's reports she has to enter into the database before the sales meeting tomorrow.

2  A trade delegation of Chinese visitors is coming to your organisation next month and you have been asked to help with the arrangements. You will be helping to create folders containing samples of your products, photographs of the production process used and information sheets that must be translated into Chinese.

   a  You have five tasks listed to do first: order the special stationery and folders; ask production for the product samples; start producing the information sheets; book the photographer; and find out how long the translation agency will need to do the work. If you could complete only four of these, which would you choose, and why?

   b  Your boss asks you to prepare a contingency plan which lists the possible things that could go wrong. What would you include?

   c  Identify four reminder dates that you would enter into your diary to ensure that you kept to the agreed timescale.

   d  If you encountered a problem, do you think the deadline is negotiable or not? Give a reason for your answer.

   e  Your boss asks you to keep her informed each week of your progress. Suggest three reasons why this is necessary.

   f  The following problems occur. In each case state what you would do. In your answer you should identify those difficulties you could resolve yourself (and state what you would do) and those you must report to your boss immediately.

i   The printer tells you the special folders will be delivered a day later than planned.

ii  Your departmental photocopier is out of action the day you were going to copy the information sheets for posting to the translation agency.

iii When the translation agency receives the sheets they say there is more work than you originally specified and it will take longer to do.

iv  The photographer rings to say his camera must have been faulty. None of the photographs have come out and he will have to take them all again.

v   You suddenly spot two typing errors in one of the information sheets you prepared and sent to the agency.

vi  The managing director's PA phones and asks for a sample pack a week before the Chinese visitors arrive. You are not expecting these for another two days.

## Evidence planning

Create your own plan which identifies how you are most likely to obtain your evidence for this section of the unit. For two or three specific tasks that you identified on page 49, check that you have the following information:

1 What type of targets relate to that task – such as the deadline(s), quality or quantity of work to be completed and the resources that you can use?

2 Are there any guidelines, procedures or codes of practice that you must consider when you do each task?

3 What working methods you will use (or have used) to achieve the agreed result – such as how you will do the work, use equipment, obtain information or communicate with other people. How could you prove these are effective? One way is to consider whether they could be improved – and if so, how?

4 What problems might occur? You may have identified these in advance in a contingency plan. If problems actually occur when you are doing your work, make a note of these together with the action that you took at the time.

5 Keep records of any progress meetings you attend, even if these are just informal discussions with your boss or colleagues.

6 Keep a note of any mistakes you made and the action you took to put matters right.

**7** Keep any documentary evidence that relates to this task and witness testimony to support your claim that you worked effectively and achieved your targets.

You will be expected to link this evidence to the option units you have chosen. Do this by identifying the option unit to which each task best relates.

## What if?

What should you do if either:

- no problems occur during the time you are being assessed
- there are no guidelines, procedures or codes of practice that you have to follow
- you don't make any mistakes when you are doing your work, nor miss any deadlines
- you struggle to link the tasks you have done to one of your option units?

In the first three cases, be prepared to answer 'what if?' questions. Quite simply, your assessor will ask you what you *would* do if any of these situations occurred – such as 'What would you do if you suddenly discovered you had made a mistake?'

If you are struggling to decide to which option unit your plans relate, ask your tutor or trainer for advice. If this poses a serious problem then you could instead plan to have a professional discussion with your assessor about this area of your work.

# Improve your own performance

Who do you think is responsible for your future job prospects? Your employer? Or someone else? The true answer to this question is you. It obviously helps if you work for an organisation that is supportive and encourages its staff to constantly improve. It also helps if you have a boss or supervisor who gives you new challenges to broaden your skills and experience. But unless you respond positively to these opportunities they will be wasted. And if they don't exist, but you are keen enough, you will find other ways of moving forwards.

Why would you want to do that? There are three main reasons:

- It is good to see how far you can get if you put your mind to it.
- Your working life will be far more enjoyable and interesting as a wider range of jobs will be open to you.
- You will earn more – which means you can spend and save more!

However, you will move 'onwards and upwards' only if you can look at yourself objectively, analyse what you do now and what you need to be able to do in the future. That is what this section is all about.

**Did you know?**

Most people underestimate their own potential. Have you ever wondered how far you could *really* go if you gave yourself a chance?

# The importance of continuously improving your work

If you work hard and generally do a good job, you may think that there is very little that you have to improve. This is fine, if you are happy doing what you do now for the rest of your life. If you want to move forwards, you need to look at this from a different viewpoint.

- No-one is perfect. So, whereas you will have some skills that are strengths, you will also have some weaknesses. What are they?
- You will feel confident about doing some jobs, because they are familiar and you understand what you are doing. But there may be others you are less happy to take on. What are they?
- You will see or know other administrators who do other types of work. What do they do that you would like to try? What would you need to know to be able to do these tasks?
- What type of job would you like to be doing in four or five years' time? What would you need to learn or do in the meantime to achieve this goal?

If you think about these questions carefully you will have a broader view of yourself, your current job and your future career. You can then decide the best way to take advantage of opportunities that occur to broaden your skills and experience both now and in the future. At the same time you will work towards increasing the number of areas you can count as strengths and decreasing any weaknesses.

A useful first step is to set yourself one simple goal. Anything that you handle or which has your name on it has to be 'right first time'. If anything is returned for re-doing because someone has changed his or her mind, that's fine. But if anything is returned because you have made a mess of it then you have failed to meet that goal on that day. Then see on how many consecutive days you can achieve it!

> ### Did you know?
>
> In 2005, the average salary for an administrator was £22500, according to the annual OfficeTeam Workplace Survey. London was the highest paying region (£27800) and the North the lowest (£19500). This difference reflects the different cost of living in each region so, in real terms, you would earn about the same. You can find out more at www.officeteamuk.com – and check out the most recent survey.

# Encouraging and accepting feedback from others

**Feedback** is the response you receive from other people in relation to your work and performance. If you start to consistently achieve the 'right first time' goal, then you should find people start to make complimentary remarks about your work. In fact, if they don't, you will probably be disappointed! This is quite reasonable. Most people do better if they are encouraged and praised, and this is one of the benefits of receiving positive feedback.

There are, however, a few other aspects relating to feedback that you need to think about.

- What do you do if no-one says anything? How do you encourage people to give you feedback?

- How do you react if you receive negative feedback? Obviously this will depend upon whether the speaker is tactful or hurtful – but some people have a natural inclination to either hit back or burst into tears whenever they are criticised, however mildly!
- Most feedback is informal, like 'Thanks, that's a great job' or 'Oh, dear, what are you like?'. This gives us all the information we need! But on other occasions feedback is formal, as you will know if you are on an apprenticeship. This is also the case if you have performance reviews or appraisal interviews at work when a note is made on your employment record. This is important if you later apply for promotion or want a good reference. How should you prepare for one of these occasions so that you give a good impression?

## Encouraging feedback

Most people would prefer to have some type of feedback rather than none, simply because it is very disheartening to do your best and have it taken for granted. In this case you may be tempted to work harder and harder and, if still nothing is said, give up. Rather than do this, encourage feedback and look for other signs, in the following ways:

- Ask your colleagues for feedback when you are working with them. You can do this quite informally, as with 'I left those on your desk last night. Are they OK?' Remember that if you are not sure whether to believe the verbal answer you can always check body language for confirmation! (See page 19.)
- You can take the same approach with your boss, but you may gain more if you explain that you actively want to improve your work and you would therefore appreciate regular feedback. A simple statement like 'I'd find it really helpful if you could tell me if you are happy with the work I do for you' should make the point quite easily.
- Assess your own work by what happens to it afterwards.

  – If it is used without any amendments or corrections and you met the deadline, you have obviously done a good job.
  – If it comes back for amendment or – even worse – someone else is asked to sort it out, then find out what was wrong and why you weren't given the chance to put it right yourself. It may be because you were busy. Or it may be because the originator thought you'd make a mess of it again!
  – If it is shown round the office as an example of the work everyone should produce then you will obviously be very popular with your boss, if not with all your colleagues!

### Find out

Does your organisation have a system for encouraging and recording compliments as well as complaints? If not, why not suggest it? This will motivate everyone – provided, of course, that the staff do a good enough job to earn a few!

## Accepting feedback

If informal feedback is complimentary, don't blush or say 'Don't be stupid' – otherwise it's likely to be a long time before anyone tries to repeat the experience. Accept any compliment graciously, by saying thank you and smiling.

If you are given feedback formally, and told you are doing a great job, you have every reason to be proud. Just don't brag about the session to the rest of the office, for fairly obvious reasons. And don't let it distract you from continuing to work hard – otherwise the next session may be less positive.

Of course, if the feedback is negative you may be gritting your teeth, rather than smiling. The remarks may whirl around in your head for ages, so that you feel resentful or bitter. Or you may just want to run into a corner and hide. Even people who appear to just shrug off criticism may be very hurt inside.

If it helps, this may not be your fault. It may be because the person who was giving you feedback wasn't constructive, tactful or thoughtful. This may have been deliberate but often isn't. It can be difficult to criticise someone without them taking offence! On the basis that you are not perfect, you will occasionally have to cope in this situation, so look at the box below for some tips.

### How to ... Cope with negative feedback from other people

- Listen carefully to what is being said. *Honestly* assess whether the criticism is justified or not.

- If you are not clear what is meant, ask for a specific example.

- If you think the accusation is unfair, say so, with reasons, and ask the speaker to suggest what you should have done.

- If the accusation is fair, try to analyse the situation by concentrating on where the 'task' went wrong. Did you forget the instructions? Were you in a rush? Did you fail to check it properly?

- Don't be over-defensive and give a detailed explanation about what went wrong – and never put the blame on anyone else.

- Decide whether you can remedy the problem yourself or whether you need help. This would be the case, for example, if you needed more experience or greater skills to do a task properly.

- If you get angry, or feel your sensible suggestions are being rejected, then ask if you can think about the matter and continue the discussion at another time. In the meantime, try to see the situation from the other person's point of view.

- If your boss is very critical but rarely praises you, try to explain how this makes you feel – quite simply and unemotionally. Just say that you would find it easier to focus on improving your weak areas if feedback sessions also included your strengths, too.

- Finally, remember that no-one ever likes being criticised. Ironically, though, negative feedback goads people into action far more often than compliments. So if you only ever received good feedback you probably wouldn't improve as much!

# Formal feedback – and putting improvements into practice

The best feedback sessions are those that end in the creation or updating of a personal development plan after both you and your supervisor have identified areas where you are doing well, areas where you could improve and how this could be done. This is the usual format of performance review or appraisal interviews.

If you work for an organisation that has formal feedback sessions you will normally be given the opportunity to plan for these in advance. There may be a form that you complete and give to your supervisor ahead of the session, which identifies the areas you wish to discuss.

- Think carefully about your work and the aspects that you are good at. Try to think of examples to support your opinion.
- Which work areas worry or concern you? Why? Is this because you have never been shown properly or because you have always been weak at this type of work? What help do you need to improve at these tasks? How long do you think it would take before you would be satisfied with your performance?
- Which areas would you like to develop in the future? What additional skills would you need? How would this fit in with the work done in your organisation and its future plans?

At the session your supervisor will comment on your strengths and weaknesses and suggest areas you should concentrate on improving and developing. There may also be suggestions and ideas you had never thought of, such as taking on new responsibilities or learning new skills, or talk of future opportunities provided that you put some agreed improvements into practice first. These improvements should therefore be summarised in terms of the specific targets you need to achieve before the next review session.

# Targets for improvement

Setting targets helps you to achieve a goal. Ideally your targets should be SMART. This means they are:
- **Specific** – precise and clearly state what you intend to do
- **Measurable** – you can easily check if you have achieved it
- **Achievable** – sensible so that you can attain it
- **Realistic** – it must achievable with the resources you have
- **Time-related** – it should have a set date for achievement or review.

Therefore a target to learn how to update the customer database within the next two months is a SMART target whereas a vague idea that you might learn Japanese someday is definitely not!

The next stage is to write down your targets on a personal development plan or a learning plan (see page 63) for discussion at your next review session and to decide the best way of achieving them.

# The value of learning and development to improving your work and your future career

Some improvements you can make on your own. These relate to your personal attributes and characteristics and areas where you know you are slack! If you are told you should be tidier or more punctual or improve your attention to detail, then it is very much up to you to get on with this. The remedies may be painful but are fairly obvious! Put things away when you have used them, get up earlier and take more time to proof-read or check your work.

In other cases you may need to undertake further learning and development to improve your performance. If you struggle to understand spreadsheets, have been asked to help prepare presentations but have never used PowerPoint and are worried about the idea of dealing with important customers over the telephone, then it is not realistic to think that you can improve these areas without any help. The added benefit, of course, is that you not only improve your performance in your current job, but you also gain additional skills that will help you to further your career. This is because you can apply for better paid, more responsible jobs, as you increase your skills and experience.

If you want to take a more proactive role in deciding your future, a useful strategy is to look at the type of advertised jobs you would like to do in the future and measure the skills required against those you have now. This is often called a **skills analysis** because you identify your personal skill gap. You now need to look for opportunities to close this gap, as you will see below.

## Find out

Check out your sources of information for training opportunities and career development at work. These may include your human resources department and your trade union learning rep, who will be able to tell you about internal training and e-learning opportunities.

You can also check your local newspaper, at your library, local college and online – for example at professional organisations such as Reed Training – where you can look through personal development, IT and Admin courses. Go to www.reed.co.uk/training to find out more.

## Snapshot – The growth of ULRs

If you work in an organisation with a recognised trade union, a key source of help and advice may be your union learning rep. They were introduced in 2002 to work with employers and employees to give advice on training and personal development and to suggest training opportunities. They often help to mentor young workers on Apprenticeships – so you might have already met your ULR.

In 2002, when the scheme started, there were over 4500 ULRs, all of whom are given special training themselves before they are allowed to assist their colleagues. The government now estimates there will be at least 23 000 by 2010, helping over half a million union members to access courses.

# Main career progression routes available to you

The world is your oyster! One reason is that business administration is a superb way of starting a career that can go in many different directions. You could stay in administration and progress to being a manager or supervisor. You could move into a related, but specialist area, such as marketing, sales or human resources, or work in a specialist industry, such as education, health or law. You could aim to become a personal assistant (PA) to a leading business person. You could choose to travel and work abroad. You could decide to teach or train administrators yourself one day – or even write books on the subject!

The first step, as you will be aware, is to achieve your NVQ 2 award. Then it is quite likely – and logical – that you will progress to NVQ 3. It is at that stage that you can think about the next step you would like to take. This is likely to involve taking more qualifications as well as developing new skills. However, if you are keen to achieve your goal – and are working in an area you enjoy – then continuing to improve should be enjoyable. If it isn't, then you should rethink the route you have chosen.

You can start by studying the chart below, to see the route you might be tempted to follow. Remember that you can choose to specialise at any point – in either different types of admin work (legal, medical, school, agricultural etc.) or in different functions in business (sales, marketing, human resources etc.). You will find out more about these on pages 88–90 in unit 202: Work within your business environment.

## Main career progression routes for administrators

| Types of jobs and example job titles | Qualification level |
|---|---|
| Company secretary<br>Senior officer<br>Senior manager<br>Executive officer | Level 5/post-graduate/professional qualifications |
| Senior Administrator<br>Office Co-ordinator<br>Office Manager<br>Administration Manager<br>Practice Manager (medical)<br>Group Administrator<br>Personal Assistant | Level 4/degree/professional qualifications |
| Administration Officer<br>Secretary/PA<br>Medical/legal/school secretary<br>Human Resources Administrator<br>Sales/Marketing Administrator<br>Medical Administrator<br>Office Administrator/Supervisor<br>Admin Coordinator<br>Clerical Officer | Level 3 vocational and skill qualifications |
| Trainee Administrator<br>Admin Assistant<br>Admin Support Assistant<br>Clerical Assistant | Level 2 vocational and skill qualifications/GCSEs |
| Trainee Admin Assistant<br>Junior Administrator<br>Office Assistant | Level 1 vocational and skill qualifications/GCSEs |

### Find out

Most people have a preferred learning style. One famous study, by Honey and Mumford, identified four main styles.

- **Activists** prefer to learn by doing; they don't like a lot of theory.

- **Reflectors** like to listen and watch someone else before they try something new.

- **Theorists** like to research and read lots of information on a topic.

- **Pragmatists** like putting ideas and information into practice and applying new things to their own job.

Which is yours and how do you think this relates to the type of learning activities you enjoy the most?

# Learning and development opportunities available to you

Even the longest journey starts with a single step! The first stage for you is to work out what to do next. You can then chart your progress, review it systematically and move on to the next stage. This is far more effective – and less overwhelming – than having some vague plan in your head over the next four or five years.

## The role of a learning plan that meets your own needs

If you are on an Apprenticeship programme then you will already know about **individual learning plans** (ILPs) because you will already have one! This outlines all the aspects of learning you have agreed with your employer and/or training provider. Your plan will have been completed after your initial assessment and updated after your induction, and will then be regularly reviewed. The benefit is that you can record and update all your achievements whilst you are on your current scheme. The drawback is that you may not feel there is enough room to record individual learning opportunities that relate to your personal and work skills development or include the outcomes of performance review discussions or feedback you receive at work. In this case, there is nothing to stop you creating a much simpler and shorter version which notes down the items *you* want to record.

If you are not on an Apprenticeship then you may never have heard of an ILP! In this case you already have the flexibility to design one that suits your own needs.

On page 63 is an example of a design that has some items already entered. You don't need to copy this design. You can simply use it as a guide.

## Reviewing your progress and updating your learning plan

It is important to keep your learning plan up to date by reviewing the targets you have achieved, and those you have not. There may be a valid reason why one or two have 'slipped'. You must then decide whether to move these forward or whether to drop them altogether. This is quite acceptable if you have changed your mind about the areas you want to develop or if your job has changed.

Talk to your supervisor to identify new opportunities for targets that you still want to achieve. This is easier if you limit your targets to three or four at once, rather than writing down everything you can think of!

Remember to keep your old learning plans safe until you have updated your curriculum vitae (CV) to include your new skills. Then your CV will reflect your additional abilities if you apply for a new job in the future.

## Learning Plan

| Name | Chloe Slater | Organisation **Glazier Products** |
|---|---|---|
| Job title | Admin Assistant | Department (if applicable) **Sales** |
| Date created | 7 March 2006 | Review date 14 June 2006 |

### JOB SKILLS AND KNOWLEDGE

| Skills/knowledge to be developed | Activity/opportunity | Target achievement date | Result on review date |
|---|---|---|---|
| Telephone skills | Work shadow Joanne or Faizal | 30 April 2006 | |
| Team work | Team training day | 4 May 2006 | |

### PERSONAL DEVELOPMENT

| Area for growth/ development | Activity/opportunity | Target achievement date | Result on review date |
|---|---|---|---|
| Assertiveness | In-house course | 16 March 2006 | |

ADDITIONAL COMMENTS In this section record additional/unexpected opportunities since the last review date and their results and the reasons for good or poor progress in particular areas and notes on additional goals you want to include in your next plan.

Attended one day course on using new database system on 2 May.

Have put name down for first aid training when next held.

### Over to you

1  Identify all the ways in which you currently receive feedback at work. Summarise the outcomes and explain the type of information they give you. Then say whether you think the feedback you receive matches your own perception of yourself.

2  If you wanted to encourage feedback from someone, suggest how you could do this.

3  Juanita, Carla, Faisal and Jim work together. They are all having performance reviews with their supervisor, Kate. Juanita comes out of the office in floods of tears because Kate mentioned that her proof-reading skills needed improvement. Carla comes out boasting about how Kate said she had a rosy future. Faisal comes out and just says it went OK. Jim comes out chuckling, saying that he and Kate had a good laugh.

   a  As Juanita's friend, what would you say to her?

   b  What do you think the others think of Carla and Jim – and why?

    **c**  Do you think Faisal was right to keep quiet? Give a reason for your answer.

    **d**  You are due to talk to Kate tomorrow. What will you do to prepare for your review?

**4**  Carry out a training needs analysis on yourself. Do this as follows:

    **a**  List the skills you have now.

    **b**  Find out those you will need for a job you want in the future by looking at job advertisements for this type of job.

    **c**  Identify the skills you will need to acquire to bridge this gap.

    **d**  Suggest how you might achieve each of these, bearing in mind the opportunities available to you and your own learning style.

## Evidence planning

For this section you can use evidence from any performance reviews or appraisals you attend. You will need to provide evidence that you:

- receive feedback from other people
- have improved your own work as a result
- have noted how further learning and development could improve your performance
- can follow through a learning plan that meets your own needs, then review your progress and update this plan.

The easiest and best approach is to keep all of the evidence related to your personal development and future ambitions in a special folder that you can refer to in discussions with your assessor.

## What if?

What should you do if either:

- your organisation doesn't have performance reviews or appraisal interview
- you don't receive much feedback on your performance?

Your assessor will expect you to encourage feedback from other people, and to act on it to improve your work. This doesn't have to be formal feedback – you can obtain informal verbal feedback and keep a note of this. You can also supplement this with witness testimony.

If you have performance reviews with your tutor or trainer, then you can include these records as part of your evidence. Supplement it with a learning plan which you have devised yourself and which lists your personal goals and how you intend to achieve these.

# Behave in a way that supports effective working

It may seem strange to be reading a section on behaviour at work. After all, you are old enough to work and earn your own living. You may therefore think it is a bit insulting to suddenly be told how you should be behaving!

This may be true if you have already been working for some years when you read this book. If you have only recently started working full-time then the situation is a little different, simply because the way you need to behave as a professional administrator in a working environment is rather different from anything you have met before. You can't even compare it with part-time jobs you may have had in the summer or at weekends because you are doing a different job and – presumably – looking at building a career. Your 'image' is therefore important. This is how other people see you – your colleagues, customers and other contacts you have at work.

Many people are unaware of the image they create. They are also not aware of times when they irritate their colleagues. If you work with someone like that, perhaps a good idea is to leave this book open on your desk at this section, next time they are nearby!

## Over to you

If you still think you've nothing to worry about, do the quiz below to see if you are nice to work with! Unless you get a very good score, continue reading where you left off.

### What kind of colleague are you?

Decide your answers to each of the following questions. Then score yourself according to the key on page 66. Check your score on page 389.

1  In a team meeting you suddenly realise you forgot to tell your friend where to meet you at lunchtime. Do you:
   a  ring immediately and try to speak in a hushed voice?
   b  hide your phone under the desk and send a text?
   c  ask to be excused a minute, then ring from the nearest loo?

2  When you get really angry and fall out with someone, do you:
   a  stop, count to ten and then walk around for a bit?
   b  burst into tears?
   c  use a few choice swear words and have a major row?

3  You go to the water-cooler for a drink and empty the bottle. Do you:
   a  replace it?
   b  clear off quickly, before anyone spots you?
   c  ask someone else to do it because you've never worked out how?

**Over to you** Continued

4 You have been asked to relieve a colleague on reception whilst she has her lunch – a job you find boring. Do you:
  a arrive 10 minutes late because you nipped out to buy a magazine?
  b arrive on time but in a bad mood?
  c arrive 5 minutes early and ask if there's anything you need to know?

5 How often do you chew gum at work:
  a most of the time?
  b rarely?
  c never?

6 It is your turn to make the coffee. Do you:
  a do it?
  b look busy, and hope someone else will offer to do it?
  c disappear to the photocopier room for a while?

7 It's a very hot day in summer. What are you wearing on your feet:
  a flipflops?
  b trainers?
  c sandals or loafers?

8 How often do you 'borrow' things from other people's desks when they're not around:
  a often?
  b rarely?
  c never?

9 A friend sends you a joke by email. Do you:
  a laugh, then delete it?
  b forward it to a few select people in the office?
  c forward it to everyone you know?

10 You take a message for Jo who sits two desks away. Do you:
  a tell her?
  b ring her?
  c email her?

**Score yourself:**

For questions 1, 4, 5, 7 and 8, give yourself 2 points for (a), 1 point for (b) and no points for (c).

For questions 2, 3, 6, 9 and 10, give yourself 0 points for (a), 1 point for (b) and 2 points for (c).

# Why the way you behave in the workplace is important

There are several reasons why your behaviour at work is important.

- You are paid to work cooperatively with a group of people you don't know very well. Some of them you will like, others you may not. Regardless of this you have to get on with all of them, and this often means making adjustments to your behaviour.
- People will visit your organisation – from customers or clients to other business contacts, even delivery or maintenance workers. They will judge the organisation on how the staff behave, and that includes you.
- You are sending out signals all the time to your boss about your professionalism (or lack of it). This creates an image which you will find very difficult to change, no matter how long you work for an organisation, and can affect your long-term promotion chances and may even influence the reference you are given if you want to change your job.
- You are less likely to work productively or effectively if you are not focused on what you are doing and can relate well with your colleagues.
- If you start to fall out with people then you are unlikely to enjoy going to work very much.

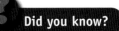

**Did you know?**

First impressions matter! Research has found that bosses are very slow to change their mind about their staff. Employees who were a bit silly, thoughtless or immature when they started working for an organisation are often horrified to discover that ten years later their boss still thinks they are the same and is still hesitant to give them very much responsibility!

# Setting high standards for your work

On page 56, you read that a good first, simple goal is 'right first time'. Even though you might not always achieve it, this means you are setting a high standard in the sense that all your work is usable. If anything has to be amended, it is because the instructions have changed and not because you made a mess of the job.

This is a useful goal to start with, but isn't enough on its own. The reason is two-fold:

- Some people will accept your work as 'usable' because they are in a hurry, not very fussy or are being kind! They may still think there is room for improvement.
- 'Right first time' does not necessarily mean that it is the best that can be achieved. You may be able to suggest improvements that can be made that will make it even better.

Of course there is a balance. You can't disappear for days tidying the stationery cupboard because you want everything to be absolutely perfect. The time and attention you give to any job should be in direct relation to its importance. So a printed report for an external customer must be absolutely perfect, whereas a short note to your colleague needs to be legible and understandable but does not need to be to the same standard.

**Find out**

What are the pet hates of the people in your office? One top-ten list of irritating habits and worse is shown below:

- sniffing
- eating smelly food in the office (e.g. egg sandwiches)
- tuneless humming or whistling
- shouting on the phone
- being unable to move around quietly
- using a computer with the volume on loud
- slurping coffee
- chewing gum
- not smelling clean and fresh
- constantly moaning.

Now double-check that none of these applies to you!

The first important skill to develop is attention to detail. Quite simply this means being fussy about anything that goes out from your desk. You need to develop a critical eye so that errors seem to leap off the page (or screen!) and you hate to see lop-sided printouts or photocopies, staples that obscure any print, or higgledy-piggledy punched papers in a file. In other words, you become a bit of a perfectionist.

It also helps if you are persistent and don't like being beaten! This gives you extra motivation and energy if you have a difficult job to do, if you are under pressure, or if something is taking longer than you thought it would at first. If you throw up your hands and give in, whine and moan, or ask someone else to do it, then you are being defeatist. You are also becoming one of the irritating colleagues in the list on page 67!

If you show that you are committed to achieving high standards in all your work you will soon find that you will be trusted to do more difficult and responsible jobs which call for accuracy and care. You will also work more quickly if you get in the habit of making a good job of everything first time, simply because you won't have to re-do it. You will also be highly valued by everyone you work with.

## Understanding your own needs and rights

Your colleagues have the right to expect you to behave responsibly towards them, and your employer has the right to expect you to be competent at the work that you do. You have legal rights too, of course, which you will read more about on page 101–129 in unit 202: Work within your business environment.

However, it isn't practical or appropriate to refer to your legal rights just because you find someone is hard to deal with because they are hyper-critical or because their bad habits drive you mad or because they foist work on you at the last minute. These things can be fairly common occurrences at work and you have to learn how to stand up for yourself – nicely! Another word often used for this is **assertiveness**. The trick is to learn to assert your own rights without upsetting anyone. This includes:

- standing up for yourself
- learning to say 'no' nicely because it isn't your job or you are genuinely too busy to help
- asking for more information without feeling inadequate
- giving an explanation without feeling guilty.

Assertiveness isn't easy and sometimes you will get it wrong. But if you keep trying then you will gradually get better at stating your own case without upsetting anyone.

## How to ... Understand (and assert) your needs and rights

**Your legal rights**

- You have the right to be treated fairly and reasonably by your boss and your colleagues and never to be asked to do anything illegal.

- Your employer must observe all your statutory legal rights, including providing a safe working environment.

- You have a legal right not to be bullied, victimised or harassed at work.

Your organisation has rights, too.

**Your needs**

- To produce high-quality work you need the right equipment and resources. You also need time to do the work properly.

- You should be given appropriate training to learn how to do new tasks or acquire new skills.

- Tasks should be explained clearly so that you know what you have to do, and any deadline should be specified.

**If you need to assert your rights**

- Listen carefully whilst the statement or request is being made.

- Use the word 'I' when you respond, not 'you', to explain how you feel; e.g. 'I don't think that's possible' *not* 'You expect the impossible.'

- Bear in mind that the other person has the right to a view, too! So be prepared to acknowledge this.

Then state, clearly and pleasantly, why you disagree or can't comply with the request being made.

**Remember**

You have a legal right not to be bullied, victimised or harassed at work (see also page 122). Check out online sources of help at www.bullyonline.org/workbully and www.kickbully.com.

# Taking on new challenges and adapting to change

When you learn about your legal rights and responsibilities in unit 202 you will also find out that your employer has the legal right to expect you to be prepared to change as the job changes. An obvious example is if new technology is introduced so that some work that was done manually – such as filing or keeping a diary – is now done on computer. It would be quite impossible for an organisation to function efficiently and productively if staff could simply refuse to do anything different or anything new.

However, it is one thing knowing that you must adapt, it is quite another doing this willingly or actually looking forward to it. Much will depend upon your temperament and the type of change that is envisaged.

## Showing a willingness to take on new challenges

Some people are more adventurous than others in all areas of their life. In fact, they quickly get bored if things remain the same. They enjoy challenges and will actively seek them out if necessary.

You may not be quite so bold, but it is sensible not to shrink away from new opportunities. Often the idea may seem more scary than the reality! For this reason, if your supervisor asks if you are willing to do something different, it is wise to ask to think about it if you are nervous, rather than just refuse. Or say that you would be very willing but would like to know more about what is involved and the training or support you will receive.

## Adapting readily to change

Change is inevitable wherever you work. It could be a minor change, such as a colleague leaving and jobs being reassigned or the office furniture being changed around. Or it could be a major change, such as a move to new premises or a complete reorganisation of the company.

Many people shy away from change. This is understandable if they are settled in a job with colleagues they know well and suddenly find that they are expected to move location or work in a different team of people. They are worried that they will not be able to cope or readjust to the new situation. If this happens to you it helps to put it into perspective by remembering that, in a year's time, the changes will all be history!

The main concerns about change usually fall into the following categories:

- job security (e.g. reduced income or redundancy)
- status (e.g. lower graded job than before)
- prestige (e.g. learned skills no longer needed)
- social ties (e.g. team disbanded, working with new group of people)
- personal anxieties (e.g. may dislike new work, may not be able to cope).

You can work through this if you have the opportunity to find out more about the changes involved and can discuss your anxieties. You may even be able to agree to a trial period where you try out the new arrangements on a temporary basis.

Of course, you may have the opposite response to change and welcome it with open arms – either because you enjoy something different, welcome new experiences or consider that working with new colleagues would probably be an improvement! Whatever your natural instincts, it is still sensible to find out as much as you can about the changes that will affect you personally and then focus on all the positive benefits that are likely to come your way as a result.

**Find out**

All organisations must keep changing to survive. If change worries you, try to work out why. Do you feel threatened or insecure or worry that you cannot cope? In this case, who can give you the information and support that you need to feel better?

# Treating others with honesty, respect and consideration

Imagine, for a moment, a workplace where people treated each other with disdain; lied and cheated and took great pleasure in seeing other people humiliated or hurt. Would you like to work there? Obviously not! At a very basic level, for people to work together harmoniously and productively each of the following is important.

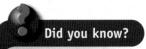

**Did you know?**

A major benefit of being truthful is that you don't have the worry of trying to remember the lies that you've told!

## Honesty

You need to be able to trust people and they need to be able to trust you. Whilst you may never think of stealing someone's money or looking in their bag, what about telling their secrets or saying one thing to their face and another behind their back? And will you be honest if you do something wrong that affects them? If you are wise – yes. Because you will then retain their trust and that means a lot.

## Respect

This means realising that everyone has strengths as well as weaknesses. It also means recognising that people may be different from you but still have a right to different opinions, ways of working and ways of living. No-one likes to feel that someone looks down on them or belittles them behind their back, and this type of behaviour makes people feel miserable and insecure. Ironically it is often the person who is causing the problem who is the one who doesn't deserve any respect!

**Remember**

There is a big difference between tolerating someone and respecting them!

**Did you know?**

**Office politics** is the term often used to describe bitchiness at work – by both men and women. You know you are a victim if someone takes the credit for work you have done, if colleagues who 'crawl' to the boss or tittle-tattle are rewarded, if a colleague puts you down in public to make himself look good, or if a 'friend' who promised to support you suddenly has amnesia about your conversation when you need her!

If you ever work in an organisation where this type of behaviour is encouraged, then the best answer is to look around for alternative employment in a far happier environment.

## Consideration

We all want our feelings to be taken into consideration so that we are treated like individuals. We don't want people to talk to us as if we are stupid, ignorant or don't exist. We simply want people to remember that we have opinions too. If you feel like that, remember that other people deserve your consideration just as much as you deserve theirs.

# Types of behaviour that show that you treat others properly – and those that don't

Even if you exclude overt office politics, there are other types of behaviour that can demonstrate whether you are naturally honest, respectful and considerate of your colleagues. There are also behaviours that indicate exactly the opposite – as you can see in the table below.

| Do | Don't |
|---|---|
| Look people in the eye when you are talking to them | Look at the floor, smirk or blush when you are giving an explanation |
| Give examples to prove what you are claiming is true | Try to change the subject if things get tough! |
| Keep your eye on other people's property if they leave the room | Help yourself to other people's personal belongings (or sit on their desk!) |
| Learn how to keep a secret. This literally means not telling *anyone*! | Think that sharing someone's secret with your best friend doesn't count |
| Observe basic courtesies, such as saying 'please' if you want something and thanking people who help you | Take people's assistance and support for granted |
| Listen when people are talking | Interrupt people when they are speaking |
| Ask people for their opinions and ideas | Force your own ideas on people |
| Respect people's need for privacy | Tell tales, gossip or speculate about people's private lives. |
| Admit you're in the wrong when you make a mistake, and apologise | Put the blame on someone else for your mistakes |
| Compliment people who have done well | Make cruel jokes or comments about people or try to leave them out |
| Think about the effect on other people of what you say and how you behave | Assume that you are no better or worse than anyone else |

Today many organisations aren't willing to leave it to chance that their employees will behave properly towards one another. They issue formal policies that state the behaviour they expect and the consequences of this not being followed.

These policies are necessary because employers have a legal responsibility to ensure that their employees aren't harassed, bullied or victimised at work but are treated courteously, fairly and with respect. Their employees, too, are responsible for thinking about their own behaviour and how it might affect other people.

Many organisations have coupled their **behaviour at work policies** with those on **equality and diversity**. This also links to their responsibilities under discrimination laws. You will find out more about these in unit 202: Work within your business environment.

Of course, there is also negative behaviour that isn't illegal but just a nuisance – such as the person who you find really difficult to deal with. In this case you may be dealing with a simple personality clash where both of you unwittingly irritate the other. One method of dealing with this is to decide exactly what it is about this person that gets to you and then deciding the best way of dealing with this. Alternative ideas include: talking about the matter using your new-found assertiveness skills; behaving in an unexpected (but pleasant!) way yourself – such as paying compliments; walking away rather than getting involved; or doing nothing for at least a week rather than acting in haste.

**Find out**

If you are having a problem with a visitor or customer you will learn what to do in option units 203: Manage customer relations and 206: Deal with visitors.

**Find out**

Check if your organisation has any policies related to the behaviour of staff at work or rules in the staff handbook that you must obey.

# How to help and support others and why this is important

Sometimes the best way you can help or support someone else is simply by listening. People often feel better for just talking about a problem – it is almost immaterial whether you can offer practical assistance. Even your boss may want to let off steam to a sympathetic ear on occasion – when a contract has been lost, a difficult meeting has just ended or an unreasonable customer has just left.

At other times you need to be aware of occasions when you should offer practical help. Imagine, for one moment, trying to rush around to complete several jobs before you go home whilst your colleagues are sitting around surfing the net for cheap holidays, doing a crossword or reading the paper! Surely nothing could be more irritating. Now reverse roles. Could that possibly be you who is taking it easy whilst one of *your* colleagues is struggling to cope? If so, you should hang your head in shame – or be prepared to admit that you are a person who will never give help but never ask for it either.

This is the main point. If you want help and support yourself then you must be prepared to offer it in return – not just when it's convenient (that's the easy bit) but sometimes when it isn't and you really have to put yourself out to do it. This type of gesture is worth a lot and helps to unite staff and bind them together so that they are stronger as a group. They know that they can rely upon each other for help and support whenever it is needed. This makes them all more productive – and far happier at work as a result.

## Over to you

1   It is said that disrespect is the first step towards bullying. Do you think this statement is true or false? Give a reason for your opinion.

2   You work with four colleagues. In each of the following situations below state what you would say to your friend and what you would advise them to do. Check your ideas with those on the CD-ROM.

   a   Joanne, your receptionist, is furious because she has been told that she has to go home and change. She is wearing a miniskirt and crop-top. She comes to you to ask for your opinion.

   b   Jacqui completely lost it with her supervisor when she was told off for being late for the third time this week. She is now upset and tearful.

   c   Meraj is worried because she has been told she must transfer to the IT section and work on the help desk. She is scared that she won't be able to cope with the work.

   d   Zilpha has been asked if she would be interested in taking on the job of team leader. She is scared that she will lose her friends and not be able to cope.

   e   Jack is forever falling out with Miranda over the silliest of things. He claims she is bossy, critical and interfering and this gets on his nerves. Miranda is older than Jack and more experienced but isn't in charge of him.

3   You have been asked to give a short talk to new staff on an induction course next month. This should focus on the way staff should treat each other to promote effective working.

   Prepare for this by summarising the way in which you think staff should behave towards one another, with reasons. Include one or two examples from your own experience to explain what you mean. Check your ideas with your tutor or trainer.

## Evidence planning

Identify the times when you have been involved in any of the following:

- specifically set yourself high standards and worked to achieve these
- were asked to take on new responsibilities or challenges
- were involved in a change at work that affected you (e.g. a change of location, colleagues or a change involving the work that you do)
- gave other people help and support.

Now check the evidence that you have. Do you have memos, emails or personal development plans to support your claims? Will your supervisor or colleagues give you witness testimony?

Finally, identify the option units(s) under which you can appropriately place this evidence.

## What if?

What should you do if either:

- you aren't expected to take on any new challenges or changes during the period when you are being assessed
- there are no opportunities to demonstrate your help and support for your colleagues over this period?

Always remember that you can have a professional discussion with your assessor which includes what you *would* do if any of these situations occurred. It is also worth noting that changes and challenges don't have to be major ones, and you may often give help or support in many minor ways. These will count just as much as doing this on formal occasions!

## Key skills reminder

If you are taking Key Skills awards, remember to discuss with your tutor or trainer how your evidence for this unit may also be able to count towards those awards.

# Work within your business environment

**Unit summary and overview**

This core unit has four sections:

- Work to achieve your organisation's purpose and values
- Apply your employment responsibilities and rights
- Support diversity
- Maintain security and confidentiality

Administrators work in a wide range of organisations, large and small. Some businesses may produce or manufacture goods whereas others provide a service. Some may be small family-owned businesses while others are very large with hundreds of employees. Despite these differences the tasks administrators carry out are often very similar – such as handling information, producing documents, working with other people and using IT as part of their day-to-day work. However, the type of information they handle will differ depending on the organisation, and so will the issues that concern the people they contact. There are other differences. They may work to tight deadlines in a high-pressure industry such as newspaper publishing, or be more focused on following the correct procedures, such as in a bank or local authority.

Wherever you work, your employer will expect you to work effectively and support the business aims and objectives. Even more importantly, this is a legal right of all employers, as you will see on page 78. If you fail to work towards the objectives of the organisation then this could be grounds for you to be disciplined or even dismissed. It is therefore sensible to know what these objectives are, in addition to knowing about your other employment responsibilities and rights.

Your employer will also expect you to work harmoniously with your colleagues and relate positively to your customers. In today's working environment this means appreciating the needs and beliefs of people from a wide range of backgrounds and circumstances.

Finally, you will be expected to maintain the security and confidentiality of your employer's property and any sensitive information you handle. This, too, is a legal responsibility of all employees.

As you progress through this unit you will be involved in finding out more about your current organisation, as well as the terms and conditions of your employment. You will learn more about the laws that apply wherever you work in relation to issues like discrimination, security and confidentiality. Your wider knowledge of your working environment will help you to understand your current organisation better and settle more quickly into any new job in the future.

**Link to option units**

Your evidence for this unit will be generated and assessed through the option units that you select. This is because your option units should reflect the main areas of your job role, so your evidence will occur naturally as you carry out your day-to-day work. For each option unit in this book, therefore, you will find guidance notes to show how evidence can be cross-referenced to this unit.

Within this unit you will also find suggestions to help you plan your evidence. These will help you to make the most of opportunities for obtaining evidence as you progress through the scheme.

# Work to achieve your organisation's purpose and values

All organisations have a reason, or purpose, for their existence. They decide what they want to achieve – their **aims** – and how to achieve them. Staff then work towards achieving specific **objectives**, or **targets**, which all contribute towards these aims.

In a large business the purpose of the organisation and its aims and objectives are often common knowledge. They are often issued in formal documents such as the mission statement and the operational plan. They may even be listed on the organisation's website. If you work for a small firm you may find that nothing about aims is written down. This does not mean that there is no purpose, aims or objectives. The owner(s) will undoubtedly know what they want to achieve, even if this has not been put in writing!

**Find out**

What is your organisation's main purpose, how does it hope to achieve this, and how you can help? Discuss your ideas with your supervisor.

All employees are paid to work towards achieving the aims and objectives of the business. So every task you do should help your employer to achieve the main purpose, provided of course that you carry it out properly. Despite this, you will no doubt often do tasks without realising how they contribute towards the organisation. You may also not be aware how some of the little things you do can support or undermine your employer's purpose and values.

In this section you will learn how to find out more about how your organisation works and how you can help or hinder it. You may then look at your job in a new light! You should certainly appreciate what you need to do to help your organisation to achieve its objectives.

# The sector in which your organisation operates

**Did you know?**

**Industrial sectors** include all the businesses that produce or make something, so there is a product of some type at the end.

**Service sectors** include retailers and all the businesses that provide a service, such as banks, schools, hairdressers and hospitals.

You will often hear people talk about their job by saying which type of business they work in. Examples are 'I'm in construction – but I understand you are in retailing?', 'No, I used to be in banking, but now I work in telecommunications.'

Administrators are quite unusual because they can work in almost any type of business. Construction companies like Barretts and McAlpines employ administrators. So, too, do retail stores, banks and telecom companies such as Vodaphone and British Telecom.

A list of all the different types of businesses in the UK would be huge so, to make life easy, they are put into groups known as **sectors**.

## How to ... Find out which sector you work in

You can do this in two stages.

1   Identify whether you work in an industrial sector or in a service sector by answering the following question: *Does your firm produce or make something, or does your employer provide a service?*

2   Now look at the chart opposite and find your sector.

  - Look down the blue column if you work in the industrial sector (i.e. your employer produces or makes something).

  - Look down the red column if you work in the service sector.

  To help you, examples of businesses in each sector are given alongside.

3   If you have a problem identifying your sector then don't be afraid to ask your supervisor, tutor or trainer for help. You may work in an unusual industry or for a business that covers more than one sector.

## Identify your sector from these examples

### INDUSTRIAL SECTORS

*In this case your employer produces or makes something*

| | |
|---|---|
| **Agriculture and fishing** | farmers, forestry businesses, landscape gardeners, fish farms, animal breeders |
| **Biotechnology, medical and chemical** | makers of chemical products and pharmaceuticals |
| **Construction and building services** | road and house builders, electricians, joiners |
| **Energy and water** | electricity, gas, oil and water companies (including bottled water producers) |
| **Mining** | quarries, gravel pits, coal mines |
| **Manufacturing and engineering** | makers of food, metal, plastic, glass, wood, leather and other products; textiles and all types of equipment and machinery |
| **Publishing, printing and packaging** | book and newspaper publishers and printers |

### SERVICE SECTORS

*In this case your employer offers a service to other businesses, private individuals or both*

| | |
|---|---|
| **Business services** | advertising, marketing and recruitment companies, cleaners, security services |
| **Creative services and media** | film, video, radio and television companies, graphic designers and photographers |
| **Education** | schools, colleges, training organisations, driving schools |
| **Financial services** | banks, building societies, insurance companies |
| **Health and social work** | hospitals, nursing homes, dentists, opticians |
| **Hospitality and catering** | hotels, restaurants |
| **Information technology (IT) and telecoms** | software developers, computer consultants, mobile phone network providers |
| **Personal services** | hairdressers, beauty therapists, children's nurseries |
| **Professional services** | solicitors, accountants, architects, vets |
| **Public admin and defence** | government offices, local councils, police, fire service |
| **Real estate** | estate agents, auctioneers, surveyors |
| **Retail and wholesale** | shops and superstores, chemists, garages |
| **Transport, storage and distribution** | cargo and passenger transport by road, rail, sea and air |
| **Travel, tourism and leisure** | travel agents, tour operators, airlines, sports centres, cinemas |
| **Voluntary organisations** | charities and community organisations |

# Your organisation's mission and purpose

A recruitment agency wanted to employ a trainee administrator and the owner of the business was carrying out the interviews. The owner asked each applicant why he or she thought he was in business. Only the final interviewee gave the answer 'to make a profit'. She got the job because the owner said she was the only one who understood the main purpose of his business and would therefore appreciate how and why he ran the business as he did.

Would you have answered like this? And how should you answer if your interview is in your local NHS hospital or for a charity like Save the Children?

Another way of grouping organisations into sectors is by **ownership**. Most businesses are privately owned but some, like NHS hospitals, are owned by the government on behalf of everyone. Then there are voluntary or charitable organisations that raise money to do good work. In each case, the purpose of these organisations is different as you can see from the table below.

|  | Private sector | Public sector | Voluntary sector |
|---|---|---|---|
| **Examples** | Shops, stores, builders, manufacturers, banks, vets, hairdressers | Government departments, local councils, NHS hospitals, state schools | Oxfam, Amnesty International, Samaritans, Friends of the Earth, Cancer Research UK |
| **Purpose** | To make a profit | To provide a quality service to the community | To provide a free service for the needy. To promote a particular cause |
| **Achieved by** | Increasing sales. Lowering costs | Meeting targets. Must operate within a budget | Raising money by appeals, charity shops etc. Keeping running costs as low as possible |

**Find out**

Do you know how your organisation is owned? Find out and then think about how this affects its main purpose.

## How the main purpose affects the objectives

The main purpose of the business will affect the way the business is run and the decisions that are made at every level.

**Privately owned businesses** must make a **profit**, so the emphasis is always on increasing sales or the number of customers and keeping costs low. This is because the higher the sales and the lower the costs, the greater the profit that is made each year.

**State owned businesses** want to keep costs low and get **value for money**. Most of them are expected to break even. This means they must not spend more than the money they receive to operate. They normally have a strict budget and targets to meet. Examples include: hospital targets relating to patient waiting times for treatment; school targets relating to achievements in examinations; and police targets relating to solving crimes.

**Charities and other organisations** in the voluntary sector aim to raise as much money as possible from donations and other sources and keep costs low, so they have a large **surplus**. This is spent on supporting the main aims of the organisation. So, for example, Shelter uses the surplus to assist the homeless; the RSPCA uses it to help animals – and so on.

## The mission statement

Many large organisations have a mission statement, especially those in the public and voluntary sectors. Some organisations call this their **vision statement** instead. Others have both a mission statement and a vision statement.

Because mission statements reflect the main purpose of the business you will see a difference between them.
- **A privately owned business** will mention customers, employees, the cost of its products, value for money or profits. An example of a privately owned business is easyJet, the cut-price airline.
- **A state-owned organisation** will mention the service it provides as well as the work it does. It will often include statements on quality, efficiency and customer service. An example of a state-owned business is the United Kingdom passport service.
- **A charitable or voluntary organisation** will focus on the service it provides or its aims in helping the needy. An example is Amnesty International, which is concerned with upholding human rights.

**Did you know?**

All private business must make a **profit** to survive. Profit equals income from sales minus the cost of running the business.

**Did you know?**

State owned businesses are known as the **public sector**. They receive public money raised through taxation and so are held accountable to the government and the general public for their performance and spending.

**Did you know?**

A **mission statement** may state
- the main purpose of the business and what it aims to achieve
- the activities it is doing to achieve its purpose
- the values and beliefs of the organisation.

**Find out**

Does your organisation have a mission statement? If not, talk to your supervisor about the type of information it would include if there were one.

### Over to you

1 Check how mission statements vary by looking at the mission statements for the three organisations on page 82. Even if the names were missing you should be able to identify the main purpose of each organisation and its ownership.

---

#### Mission statements

**EasyJet**

To provide our customers with safe, good-value, point-to-point air services. To effect and to offer a consistent and reliable product and fares appealing to leisure and business markets on a range of European routes. To achieve this we will develop our people and establish lasting relationships with our suppliers.

**United Kingdom Passport Service**

The UKPS mission is

'Confirming nationality and identity, enabling travel'

By focusing on:
- quality, integrity and security
- excellence in customer service
- developing and motivating staff
- efficiency and value for money
- innovation and improvement.

**Amnesty International**

Amnesty's mission is to undertake research and action focused on preventing and ending grave abuses of the rights to physical and mental integrity, freedom of conscience and expression, and freedom from discrimination – in the context of our work to promote all human rights, as articulated in the Universal Declaration of Human Rights.

---

2 Obtain a copy of the mission statement for your college or training organisation and suggest two ways in which its administrators help to achieve the main purpose of the organisation. Compare your ideas with other members of your group or with the suggestions on the CD-ROM.

# How your organisation compares to others in the sector

Businesses will always aim to do as well as others in their sector, if not better. In the private sector it means that their sales and profits are increasing. In the public sector it means they are providing a better service and giving better value for money. In the voluntary sector it means they are raising more money.

- **In the private sector**, businesses compare themselves against their competitors.
  - A large firm looks at its **market share**. This shows how much of the total consumer market the firm holds in relation to its competitors. Normally it will want to increase its share each year by attracting customers away from competitors.
  - A small firm will be interested in *retaining or increasing sales and profits*. Its accountant will be able to provide useful comparisons with other organisations in the sector and locality, based on financial data such as average sales and profit.
- **In the public sector**, organisations such as police forces, schools, colleges, universities and hospitals, publish **performance tables** so that everyone can compare their performances. Council Tax charges are also compared, together with services, so that taxpayers can see which local authorities offer the best value for money.
- **In the voluntary sector**, charities compare performance in terms of the *amount of money they raise*. They are aware that there is a limit to the amount the public will donate to charities each year and they must therefore be inventive to try to retain or increase their share.

**Did you know?**

For comparisons to be any use, you must compare like with like. Alton Towers doesn't compare itself with BBC Television and your local hospital isn't interested in Tesco because they are doing different things. Tesco will, however, compare itself with Asda and Sainsbury (and vice versa), the BBC will respond to programme schedules issued by ITV and Sky, and the performance of hospitals across the country is compared in national league tables.

**Find out**

Which businesses does your organisation compare itself with? How does it find the information it needs to make a comparison?

## Snapshot – Checking out the competition

Your organisation will be well aware of its main competitors. These may be direct competitors who offer exactly the same type of products or services to the same people. Alternatively they may produce similar goods or services that people may choose instead. So Next keeps an eye on the prices and stock offered by Top Shop and River Island but also monitors George at Asda and knows that you could easily decide to buy a pair of shoes instead of a new outfit.

Large organisations have several ways of checking each other out. They read press reports, employ 'mystery shoppers' to visit their competitors, and pay a market research company to provide the information they want.

Small firms are just as keen to know about their competitors but sometimes have to be more inventive to find out. One boss of a recruitment agency sent each new member of staff to register with one of his rivals to check out their

**Snapshot** Continued

service and report back on what they were offering. Estate agents regularly check the property adverts placed by their competitors, and travel agents monitor the offers made by their rivals on the high street and online. Others get to know their competitors in person so that they can exchange information about the trade, cooperate with each other where possible and keep a joint eye out for any new threats.

As a result of this, one mother of a learner driver was surprised to be given the cold shoulder by everyone in the waiting room when she accompanied her daughter to the test centre. As the learners departed with their examiners she was aware that those left had gone in a huddle. Eventually one man approached her and asked, quite sharply, when she had set up her driving school business – given that she had arrived in a driving school car. She was astounded and explained that, at the last minute, her daughter's instructor had been taken into hospital but had lent them the car for the test because it was the one her daughter was used to. The man immediately apologised. It transpired that the group all ran local driving schools and had thought they had a new, unknown competitor in their midst!

# Supporting your organisation's mission and objectives

**Did you know?**

Long-term aims are easier to achieve if they are broken down into small steps. Whether you are trying to lose weight, get fit or complete an NVQ award it is always easier if you set short-term goals and targets for yourself. In business, short-term goals are called **objectives** or **targets**.

You have already seen that many organisations identify their main purpose in a mission statement. This helps the business to decide its aims. These are the long-term goals it hopes to achieve – such as increasing sales and profits, expanding into new areas or offering new services or products.

All businesses have long-term aims for the organisation as a whole. They then divide these into short-term objectives and targets for staff and departments to achieve. These are often quite specific. For example, an objective related to increasing sales might be to reduce the prices on selected products by 5 per cent or to increase Christmas season sales by 10 per cent. Senior managers will then decide how to achieve these objectives and set targets for each department or team. So the sales department or sales team may have a target of increasing sales each month by 5 per cent whereas the marketing team may be set a target to produce a new, exciting Christmas catalogue by late September. All departments will be set targets for spending to keep these to budget levels.

Some objectives and targets will directly relate to your own job as an administrator, others may not. For example, you will be able to help your team to offer a better service by answering the telephone promptly or by taking accurate messages and passing them on quickly to the right person.

You may be less able to affect the results of other objectives, such as obtaining more customers or developing new advertising campaigns.

**Find out**

Do you, your team or your department have specific targets to achieve? How many of these relate to your own job role and in what ways?

## Over to you

1 The pie chart below shows the market share of each of the major supermarkets in March 2005. Use it to answer the following questions. Some suggested answers are given on the CD-ROM.

  **a** Which supermarket has the largest market share?

  **b** Suggest two main purposes of a large supermarket that may be included in its mission statement.

  **c** ASDA lost 2 per cent of its market share between December 2004 and March 2005. What type of actions do you think it may have taken to try to recover this?

  **d** Suggest two ways in which Asda staff may help the business to achieve its aim of increasing its market share.

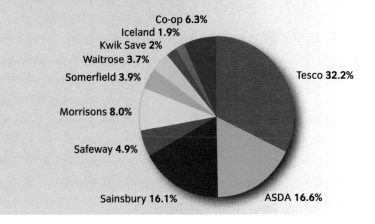

**Over to you** Continued

2 For each of the following businesses, identify two organisations in the same sector that it will probably compare itself to. Try to suggest one that is in direct competition (i.e. offers the same type of product of service to the same people) and one that offers a similar but alternative product or service. If you are stuck, look for ideas in the answer section on the CD-ROM.

   **a** Perrier

   **b** Oxfam

   **c** Pret a Manger

   **d** Pizza Hut

   **e** *The Sun* newspaper.

3 Imagine you have friends who run each of the following businesses. Now suggest ways in which they could find out information about their competitors. Be imaginative but remember to keep all their activities legal!

   **a** a local newsagent

   **b** a sandwich shop

   **c** a garden centre

   **d** a bookshop.

*There are many ways to find out what your competitors are doing!*

Although you will obtain your evidence for this unit through your option units, you may find this easier if you start planning now, while this section is fresh in your mind. Basically you will need to prove to your assessor that you understand this section and that you regularly work towards achieving your organisation's objectives.

You may find it helpful to prepare a short set of notes on which you summarise the information you find out about your own organisation as you work through this section. This will help you to decide how best to relate your evidence to your option units (see page 97). Keep these available as a 'prompt sheet' if you are asked questions relating to this section of the unit in a professional discussion with your assessor.

You can use any title you want. One suggestion is 'Notes on my business environment' but do choose a different one if you prefer.

1   Start with the name of your employer, the main activity of the organisation (i.e. what it does) and the sector it is in. This should be the main sector related to its activities but you might also want to add whether it is in the private, public or voluntary sector, too, as this will affect its main purpose.

2   If your organisation has a mission statement then you should have obtained a copy or talked to your supervisor or boss about the main purpose(s) of the business. Either attach the mission statement or summarise the main purpose yourself in a short statement.

3   You should have found out how your organisation compares itself to others in the sector. Ask your supervisor or boss if you are still not sure and include this information.

4   Finally, add the objectives or targets that apply to your department, to your team or to your own work as an administrator, and say how these support the overall purpose of the organisation.

Save your work as you will add to this information sheet as you progress through this section.

# Your main responsibilities at work

The duties and responsibilities of administrators are often included in job advertisements. They are also summarised in a job description. This document is often sent to job applicants so that they can check exactly what type of work they will be expected to carry out. This prevents anyone applying for a job if they wouldn't want to do the work or be qualified to apply. An example of an administrator's job description is shown on page 88.

## A job description

**CAPITAL SERVICES LTD**

**Job Description**

| | |
|---|---|
| Department: | Sales |
| Job title: | Sales Administrator |
| Hours of work: | 37.5 per week, normally 9 am – 5.30 pm Monday to Friday |
| Salary scale | £12,000 – £14,000 |
| Responsible to: | Sales Supervisor |
| Responsible for: | Not applicable |
| Job purpose: | To provide administrative support for the sales team<br>To handle customer enquiries by phone, post and online<br>To help to prepare sales documents and sales literature |

**Duties and responsibilities**

1 Receive telephone calls, deal with general enquiries and take messages for team members as necessary.
2 Send out sales literature to customers, as requested.
3 Monitor online customer requests and responses and forward these to members of the sales team.
4 Keep the customer database up to date.
5 Keep the departmental files up to date.
6 Assist in the preparation and distribution of mailshots to customers.
7 Assist in the preparation and updating of sales literature.
8 Type documents, letters, reports and memos using Word.
9 Attend any training course or team events as requested by the Sales Supervisor.
10 Maintain staff confidentiality at all times and be aware that breach of this could lead to instant dismissal.
11 Undertake any other relevant duties that may be identified.

This job description will be the subject of regular review and possible amendment in line with company priorities. The post holder may also be required to undertake related tasks that are not specifically mentioned above.

### Did you know?

Most administrators do the following tasks at work:

- They communicate with other people.
- They produce, store and retrieve documents.
- They use IT systems and software.
- They answer the telephone.
- They operate standard office equipment.

Does this describe your job? What else do you do?

If you compare advertisements or job descriptions for a number of administrative jobs you will find certain similarities. These relate to the core skills and abilities required by almost all administrators. You may also undertake specific tasks that are related to your particular job, department or organisation.

# Your role and contribution in the organisation's structure

All organisations need some type of structure to operate productively. Even a small firm will have specific job roles for the staff, so there may be a general manager, along with technical experts and/or others responsible for sales and administration. A local travel firm may have a branch manager, several travel advisers and a branch administrator. A vet's surgery may be run by three partners with four veterinary assistants and a receptionist/administrator. A car dealership may have a manager who oversees four sales staff, three mechanics and an office administrator.

Larger organisations employ more staff and normally group them into departments.

- Many large manufacturing companies are structured into departments related to the different **functions** carried out by staff, such as Purchasing, Sales and Marketing, Finance (or Accounts), Production, Human Resources (or Personnel), IT and Distribution. A large organisation in the service sector wouldn't need a production department, and unless the organisation is in the retail or wholesale trade it will be unlikely to have purchasing and distribution departments.
- Many organisations have specialist terms for their departments, relating to the type of work carried out there.
  - Hospitals have departments such as Radiography, Physiotherapy and Maternity to reflect specialist services for patients.
  - Colleges and universities often have departments linked to the courses they offer, such as Art & Design, Health & Social Care, IT & Business Administration, as well as functional areas such as Student Services and Finance.
  - Large legal firms divide their operations into different areas of law such as employment, property, probate etc.
  - Your local council will name its departments after the services it offers, such as Housing, Education and Social Services.

## Your role and the structure of the business

In a small firm, administrators provide a wide range of support services to all, or most, of the staff. Your exact duties will depend on the type of organisation you work for and whether you are the only administrator. If there is a small team of administrators some tasks will probably be shared and other more specialist jobs will be the responsibility of certain individuals.

In a large organisation, administrators are normally employed in various departments and their specific duties will depend on which department they work in.

- In a **sales department**, administrators may liaise with representatives, keep customer records up-to-date and arrange hospitality for visitors.
- In a **finance department**, administrators may keep financial records, prepare spreadsheets and process expense claims and payments.
- In a **personnel** or **human resources department**, administrators may keep staff records up-to-date, schedule interviews and arrange training events

- In a **specialist department** – such as the education or housing departments of a local authority – administrators support the specialist staff employed to deliver that particular service.

# Policies, procedures, systems and values of your organisation that are relevant to your role

You have already seen that a business needs to decide what it wants to do or achieve, and then sets objectives to achieve these goals. The business also needs to decide something else – how to achieve the goals.

## Deciding how to achieve the aims and objectives

There is often more than one way to achieve a goal, and some methods are more ethical than others. Your personal goal might be to get rich. You could do this by working hard, marrying into royalty or robbing a bank. The first is admirable, the second is pretty unrealistic and the third is illegal! Basically, if you decide to take shortcuts, you have to accept the risk that things may not go very smoothly. The same applies in business. For example, a business could probably increase sales by passing off cheap substandard products as high-quality goods; it could lower costs by paying very low wages and retain staff by giving such poor references that no one else will employ them. Needless to say, none of these are ethical or even legal practices.

Reputable businesses, of course, would not behave like this. They often have stated values and then draw up policies that explain what the business believes in and what it will and will not do. For example, there may be a policy relating to customers that states they will never be misled, and a policy relating to staff that forbids bullying or harassment. Ethical organisations often go beyond their legal responsibilities – such as allowing staff longer holidays than the legal minimum, or having a generous returns policy for customers who change their mind after making a purchase.

### Snapshot – Moral matters

One way of deciding the main values of a business is to ask the customers. The Co-operative Bank did this in 1992 when it asked its account holders for their views. In 2005, the Co-operative Insurance Society (CIS) – its sister company – polled 44 000 of its policyholders for the same reason. As a result it has drawn up its Ethical Engagement Policy which states its main concern when choosing its suppliers as well as how it will invest the £20 billion it holds in insurance funds for its customers. The new policy covers issues such as human rights, the arms trade, environmental impact, labour standards, animal welfare and corporate governance (i.e. how businesses are run). This reflects the main issue identified by 97 per cent of customers that the Co-op should not invest in companies unless they have strong safeguards against fraud, bribery and corruption. Ninety-five per cent were also against firms that pay excessive salaries to directors.

The Co-operative Bank, too, has long been famous for its high values and claims that 34 per cent of its customers have become members specifically because of its beliefs. It will not provide its services or deal with any groups that go against its main principles. In 2005 it was involved in a dispute when it asked the organisation Christian Voice to close its bank account because it had allegedly made several comments against homosexuals that did not accord to the values of respect and tolerance for others held by the bank.

You can find out more about the Co-operative Bank's ethical policy on issues such as human rights, global trade, the environment and animal welfare – and how it puts its beliefs into practice – at www.co-operativebank.co.uk.

### Find out

Are your organisation's values written down? These may include ethical policies (see the snapshot on the Co-operative Bank), or they may be related to issues like health and safety, equal opportunities, data protection, dealing with customers, paying suppliers' bills and dealing with discrimination, bullying or harassment. If there are no written policies, talk to your supervisor about the values of the business. When you reach page 95 you will be able to check out your own values, too!

Of course, simply writing down a policy does not ensure its success! In a large firm, with several written policies, staff could still behave unethically, whereas in a small firm without a formal policy the staff may still have very high standards.

## The role of systems and procedures

Once a business has decided its objectives (and its values and policies) it then needs to have a practical way of making sure these are achieved. This is where systems and procedures are invaluable.

A **system** is a formalised method of doing something. It is devised so that a large number of people will do the same thing in the same way. It is normally required when specific objectives or results must be achieved. The best example of a complex system with which you are already familiar is the UK traffic system. This has been designed to enable a large number of people and vehicles to use the same roads, at the same time, with a high degree of safety and the minimum of delays and inconvenience. Generally it is only when people do not follow the system (e.g. drive through red traffic lights) that these objectives are not achieved.

**Procedures** support a system because they tell users what to do. As a road user you follow a specific procedure when you cross a busy road. If you are a driver then you must follow the procedures as set out in the *Highway Code*.

If you are still unsure, in any way, about how all these aspects relate to one another, check out the figure below.

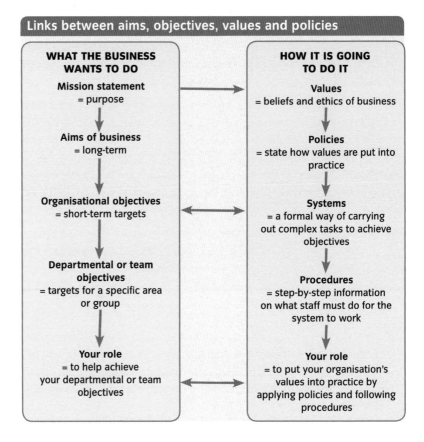

**Links between aims, objectives, values and policies**

| WHAT THE BUSINESS WANTS TO DO | HOW IT IS GOING TO DO IT |
| --- | --- |
| **Mission statement** = purpose | **Values** = beliefs and ethics of business |
| **Aims of business** = long-term | **Policies** = state how values are put into practice |
| **Organisational objectives** = short-term targets | **Systems** = a formal way of carrying out complex tasks to achieve objectives |
| **Departmental or team objectives** = targets for a specific area or group | **Procedures** = step-by-step information on what staff must do for the system to work |
| **Your role** = to help achieve your departmental or team objectives | **Your role** = to put your organisation's values into practice by applying policies and following procedures |

**How to ... Follow the systems and procedures relevant to your role**

- Identify the systems and procedures that relate to your role. The easiest way to start is to think about the main procedures that relate to the tasks you do – and which system they support. As an example, every office has a filing system. When you add or remove documents from a file you should follow the same procedure as everyone else.

- Check the office handbooks and manuals you refer to. These will contain procedures that you probably carry out every day without thinking. For example, there will be a particular procedure to follow if you send a fax, clear a paper jam in the printer or take multiple photocopies. There will also be procedures you must follow in an emergency, such as when the fire alarm sounds or if an accident occurs.

- If there are very few written procedures that seem to apply to you, think about why you do particular tasks the way that you do, such as filing documents, taking a telephone message or dealing with visitors. This is probably because you are following a procedure that someone has shown you, even though it isn't written down.

## Over to you

1 Study the job description on page 88 and answer the following questions *as if it were your job*. You can check your ideas with the answers on the CD-ROM.

   **a** Identify four duties that directly relate to the function of the sales department.

   **b** Identify three duties an administrator could be asked to do in any department.

   **c** Identify three responsibilities that are likely to be included in every job description at Capital Services.

   **d** Explain why you think item number 11 and the statement at the end have been included.

   **e** If you were asked to clean the floor one day do you think you could reasonably refuse? Give a reason for your answer.

   **f** If you were asked to collect the post one day do you think you could reasonable refuse? Again give a reason for your answer.

2 Most sporting teams have aims and objectives. An amateur ice hockey team has three main aims as its overall mission or purpose: it wants to attract more sponsorship, win more matches and be respected in the league for its professionalism and responsible attitude. Its objectives include: winning the league this season; raising enough money from sponsors and other sources to play at in at least one European competition; and improving the overall performance of individual players.

   **a** Suggest three ways in which team members can help the team to achieve its main aims.

   **b** Suggest three ways in which team members can help to achieve the team objectives.

   **c** Suggest two actions that could be taken by the players that would demonstrate the team did not have very high values!

Compare your ideas with other members of your group or your supervisor, tutor or trainer. Some suggested answers are also given on the CD-ROM.

**3** The following are objectives for a business organisation.

- Open three more branches next year.
- Reduce the number of customer complaints.
- Provide a more rapid response service to customers.
- Devise a new advertising campaign.
- Reduce wastage.
- Attract 5 per cent more customers over the next 12 months.
- Retain 5 per cent more customers over the next 12 months.
- Reduce staff turnover.
- Improve and update the company website.
- Become more environmentally friendly by recycling waste paper and used toner and printer cartridges.

  **a** Identify those that are likely to be the most relevant to the work of departmental or team administrators.

  **b** For each objective you identify as relevant, suggest one way in which administrative staff could help to contribute towards its achievement.

Check your ideas with the answers given on the CD-ROM.

**4** What are *your* values? Are you a very ethical person, or do you think nothing really matters except not getting caught? Do the quiz below and find out!

### Quiz – What are your values?

**1** You think it is OK to be late for work:
  **a** never
  **b** only in a crisis or an emergency
  **c** whenever you can get away with it.

**2** At your workplace you can earn a bonus based on target achievements. Do you:
  **a** work extra hard?
  **b** accept that some months you might not do as well?
  **c** fiddle the figures if you can?

**3** You think it is OK to help yourself from the stationery cupboard:
  **a** never
  **b** not as such, but you've often taken a work pen or pencil home without thinking about it
  **c** any time, especially from a large firm – you know they'll never miss it.

4  You are in a rush to meet a friend and are delayed by a customer with a complex query. Do you:
   **a** accept you will be late and will have to apologise to your friend?
   **b** find someone else to help them?
   **c** tell the customer anything to get rid of them?

5  You are hoping your friend will get a job in your firm. Do you:
   **a** help by rehearsing her for the interview?
   **b** put in a good word for her with your boss?
   **c** encourage her to lie about her qualifications?

6  You help with a team task but your supervisor thinks you did all the work. Do you:
   **a** put your supervisor straight?
   **b** tell the others you were all praised?
   **c** happily enjoy all the credit?

7  In an average day, the time you spend personally surfing on the Internet and sending personal emails is:
   **a** five or ten minutes at most
   **b** about half an hour
   **c** as long as you can get away with.

8  You desperately need a day off to attend a friend's wedding but have used up your personal leave allowance. Do you:
   **a** offer to work extra hours in exchange or take the day off without pay?
   **b** fiddle the holiday rota and claim you still have a day due?
   **c** call in sick?

9  In the office kitchen is an honesty box for the biscuit fund. You put money in:
   **a** every time you take a biscuit
   **b** once a week
   **c** only when someone sees you take one.

10 Your student brother asks if you can do lots of personal photocopying for him. Do you:
   **a** say he should use a college photocopier or ask his tutor for help?
   **b** agree to do a few pages if your supervisor agrees?
   **c** wait until everyone is out at lunch and do the lot?

11 One of your jobs is to enter approved appointments in the office diary for the Purchasing Manager. A rep from an unknown company offers you a huge box of chocolates to slip his name in a gap next Tuesday. Do you:
   **a** refuse and tell him to write in for an appointment like everyone else?
   **b** laugh and tell him you don't like chocolates?
   **c** accept happily?

12 You overhear two staff from another office laughing about the way they have fiddled their expenses. Do you:
   **a** Quietly mention it to your supervisor?
   **b** Keep it to yourself (no-one likes a sneak)?
   **c** Ask them what it's worth for you to keep quiet?

**Your score**
Give yourself 2 points for every (a), 1 point for every (b) and 0 points for every (c) you answered. Check your score on page 390.

## Evidence planning

1 Obtain a copy of your job description and highlight all your main responsibilities at work. If you don't have a job description, ignore this task and move to task 2.

2 Start a work diary that summarises the tasks you do each day. Because this is a summary you need to spend only five or ten minutes at the end of every day just jotting down the jobs you have done. Keep this for three or four weeks – or until it gives a good picture of the work you do. It is also valuable to include information on how and where you worked with other people and occasions when you improved your own learning because of something that happened. Ask your supervisor to countersign and date your diary to confirm that it reflects your job role – then you can use it as witness testimony.

3 From the information in your work diary, and your job description if you have one, note down the main aspects of your job and your responsibilities and add this to the information sheet you started on page 87.

4 Write a brief note about how your organisation is structured and how your role fits into this. Add this to the sheet.

5 Find out whether there is an official document that lists your team's objectives. Otherwise find out what your supervisor considers are the current objectives for your own team or department. For each one, think about the tasks you do that contribute towards its achievement. Then decide which option unit these tasks relate to. This will then help you to identify the option units where you can best obtain your evidence for this section.

6 For each of the policies, systems and procedures that you have identified relate to your role, decide the option unit(s) to which each one relates. Bear in mind that some may relate to more than one unit. You can then supply evidence that you follow the policies, systems and procedures that are relevant to your role in those units.

## How to ... Apply your organisation's values and put them into practice

- Make sure you know what your organisation's values are by obtaining a copy of the written policies and/or talking to your supervisor or boss about the company values.

- Identify which policies directly relate to your own job role and make sure that you put them into practice as part of your work.

- Watch an experienced member of staff whose behaviour you admire and take note of how he or she handles difficult situations.

- Treat everyone you deal with – customers, colleagues, callers – with respect and courtesy.

- Obey instructions you are given and policies and procedures that relate to your job, no matter what you think of them. If you genuinely think they can be improved, talk to your supervisor.

- Don't cheat your employer by misusing business supplies, equipment or time when you are paid to work.

- Don't talk about people derogatively behind their backs.

- Don't tell lies – even little white ones. There is a difference between misleading someone and being tactful!

- Thank people who help you and return the favour when you can.

# Work with outside organisations and individuals in a way that protects and improves the image of the organisation

As long as your employer is paying your wages, it is reasonable to expect you to be supportive of the organisation – and you are hardly doing this if you are disloyal when outsiders are present. This doesn't have to be outright criticism of your boss or giving away business secrets. A huge sigh, raising your eyes to heaven or telling people that the place is always like a madhouse says volumes, especially to a prospective customer or one of your competitors!

## **How to ...** Protect and improve the image of the organisation

- Never send out any documents unless they are error-free.

- If you make a promise, keep it – or explain in advance exactly why you have a good reason for not doing so.

- Don't write emails or send text messages you wouldn't be happy for anyone at work to read.

**Remember**

One of your legal responsibilities is to work towards your employer's objectives. You don't do that if you undermine the reputation of the business by making snide or sarcastic comments to people, sending out documents full of errors or being curt with customers.

It isn't just what you say that affects the image of your organisation. When you are dealing with people outside your organisation then you are an advert for your employer in everything you do. So being dismissive with a caller, sending out a letter with three spelling mistakes or posting a parcel with insufficient stamps to cover the cost are all sending a message to the recipient. And the message is not one that you would really like them to hear!

**How to ...** Continued

- Always act professionally. This means keeping your temper and not becoming over-emotional. If you have a personal worry or problem that is affecting you then talk to your supervisor in private.

- Always refer to your organisation positively when you hear it being discussed by outsiders.

- Be loyal to your colleagues and members of your team.

- If you are visiting an outside organisation or regularly deal with visitors, make sure your appearance reflects the image of your organisation

- Set yourself high standards and aim to achieve them.

# Seek guidance from others when you are unsure about policies, objectives, systems and values

Even the most experienced employees sometimes need to double-check what to do in a new or difficult situation. This is far better than guessing what to do and getting it wrong. In that case you may then need to apologise and ask for help to solve a problem that you have caused. All sensible bosses would far rather you asked for advice in the first place.

If you work for a small firm then your supervisor will probably be the person to ask if you are unsure about any of these areas. If you work for a larger firm and have a mentor to guide you, then you can ask this person.

**Find out**

A **mentor** is a more experienced colleague who will give you informal advice at any time. Many large organisations allocate mentors to new employees. Even if there is not an official mentor, is there a more experienced colleague who you can ask for on-the-spot advice and guidance when you need it?

If none of these options apply, then you would need to contact a responsible person who works in the relevant area. So if you need guidance about dealing with a customer, contact Customer Service or Sales. If there is a problem relating to a colleague, then Human Resources (sometimes called Personnel) would be best. If the query relates to money, contact Finance or Accounts.

The golden rule is not to take any action on your own initiative if an issue is outside your job role or area of responsibility.

## Over to you

1   Check that you know the policies, procedures, systems and values of your organisation that relate to your own job role. Some of these may have been given to you at induction, others may be in a staff handbook. If you are unsure about these, ask your supervisor if you can discuss the matter. In addition, find out who else in the organisation could help you if you had a query when your supervisor was not available.

2   During a bad week you are faced with each of the following problems or queries. In each case state what you would do if this happened. Where possible use the policies, procedures, systems and values that you would apply at work. Discuss your suggestions with your tutor or trainer and/or check your ideas with the answers on the CD-ROM.

   a   A customer is furious that one of your colleagues, Don, promised to call her back twice but hasn't. You don't like Don – you think he's a show-off and basically useless. What will you say to the customer?

   b   A colleague suddenly finds that her purse has gone missing and starts to accuse everyone in the office. What would you tell her to do?

   c   You regularly collect items from one of your suppliers. Joe, who works there, starts to joke about how you should change your job as he thinks your firm will be out of business within a year. How would you respond?

   d   Four students call in to your firm collecting for a charity. Although you know there is a petty cash fund for small items you are not sure whether it covers charity collections. What would you do?

   e   You see one of your colleagues helping herself to a stack of blank CDs from the stationery cupboard. When she spots you she shrugs and says: 'Everyone else does it – why not me?'

   f   You have been helping to collect money for a staff night out. You know everyone has given £5 and there are ten people in your office, including you, but somehow you have £55 in the kitty. What would you do?

## Evidence planning

Start a work log on which you note occasions when you actively:

- follow policies, systems and procedures as part of your day-to-day tasks
- put your organisation's values into practice
- protect or improve the image of your organisation when you are dealing with outside organisations or individuals
- ask for guidance because you are unsure about your objectives, policies, systems, procedures and values.

Ask your supervisor to countersign your log and date it to confirm its accuracy. You can refer to this log when you are gathering evidence for the option units you have chosen.

## What if?

What should you do if:

- your organisation doesn't have a written mission statement
- your organisation has no stated values
- you think you may struggle to obtain some of the evidence bearing in mind your organisation and job role?

Your assessor will be aware that not all candidates work in businesses with written mission statements and stated values. You should ask your employer for guidance, as you saw on pages 96–97.

If there are any other parts of this section that don't seem to apply to your organisation or your job role, then talk to your tutor or trainer who may be able to help you to identify evidence opportunities linked to your option units.

# Apply your employment responsibilities and rights

From the moment you are officially offered a job with an organisation you have certain legal rights – and so does your employer. Your employer is responsible for ensuring that the organisation complies with all the laws and regulations that relate to its employees, customers and everyone else with whom it has dealings. In many cases these will include specific laws and regulations that relate to a particular industry and how it operates.

All employees are responsible for ensuring that they comply with the employment laws that relate to them. If either an employee or the employer fails to comply with one or more of their responsibilities then there may be repercussions because the other party has the right to take legal action.

It is important that you know about your own rights, as an employee. However, you also need to know what your responsibilities are and the possible consequences of ignoring or disregarding these.

**Did you know?**

All employees and employers have legal rights and responsibilities. Your rights are your employers' responsibilities, and vice versa.

# Aspects of employment that are covered by law

In the UK, there are laws that cover most, if not all, of the main aspects of employment. These apply to every business in the UK, no matter how small or large and no matter what they do. They can be divided into the following main areas:

- health and safety at work (including fire safety and first aid)
- data protection
- employment rights and responsibilities
- pay and pensions.

## Health and safety at work

A safe environment at work is a legal requirement throughout Europe. Both employers and employees have to abide by the Health and Safety at Work etc. Act and the various Regulations that have followed it.

Large organisations often have a health and safety officer who has overall responsibility for health and safety policies and training. In others, there may also be a safety committee, made up of representatives from management and

**Find out**

All employees must have access to the Health and Safety at Work etc. Act, either by a notice in the workplace or by receiving a leaflet. If there are more than five employees the business must also have a safety policy and have procedures that all employees must follow in an emergency. Check that you know what these are now, and that you are aware of your own legal responsibilities under the Act.

**Find out**

The Health and Safety (Display Screen Equipment) Regulations apply to almost all administrators because they cover computers in the workplace – including how the workstation should be set up, how computers should be used, rest periods and free eye tests for regular users. Check the details on page 166–167 in unit 110 and find out whether these Regulations apply to you.

employees. This group is responsible for checking that legal requirements are being met. Many businesses have safety representatives who attend meetings of the safety committee. These representatives are appointed by recognised trade unions and elected by union members, not by the employer. If none of these exists, the employer must still consult with employees over health and safety matters, either direct with employees or through a nominated employee representative.

The main Act relating to health and safety is the **Health and Safety at Work etc. Act 1974**. This is an 'umbrella' Act under which other Regulations can be passed to ensure that health and safety laws are always up to date. The Act applies to all work premises regardless of size and relates to anyone there, such as employees, visitors and any maintenance workers or contractors working on the premises.

The Act puts an equal responsibility on employees to be responsible for their own health and safety as well as that of other people who may be affected by their activities and actions and to cooperate with their employer on health and safety issues. Regulations are different from the Act. As you will see on page 165–166 in unit 110, some apply to all workplaces and to all employees. Others apply to most administrators – but not all of them. Then there are many other Regulations that focus on other types of jobs – such as the Work at Height Regulations 2005 which were designed to help to protect construction workers and others who work on high buildings. You can find out more on pages 163–164 in unit 110 and decide how many are relevant to your role. If you are involved in reducing health and safety risks at work as part of your job role, then you may want to choose option unit 110 which covers all these areas.

## Data protection requirements

The Data Protection Act 1998 restricts the use of personal information stored on computer and in structured paper files. All employers must ensure that all personal data is processed fairly and lawfully, kept up to date and not retained longer than necessary. Normally this relates to information held on customers and staff. Your employer will probably have a policy to ensure that the business complies with the Act and will expect you to abide by it when you are handling personal information. Under the Act you can also ask to see any information held about you, though your employer can make a small administrative charge for supplying this.

Further information on this Act is given on page 151.

## Employment rights and responsibilities

You have two types of employment rights and responsibilities.
- **Statutory employment rights**. These are the legal rights of every employee in Britain as set down in the laws and regulations that have been passed

by the government. All employers must abide by these. For example, employees have the right to be paid at or above the national minimum wage rate for their age and to receive statutory sick pay (SSP) if they are ill for at least four consecutive days.

- **Contractual employment rights**. These are additional rights that are contained in a contract of employment. As an example, many people are paid above the minimum wage rate and their starting salaries will be shown in their contracts. Similarly, many employees benefit from a company sick pay scheme if they are ill which pays more than SSP. Contracts of employment vary from one organisation to another and from one job to another – as you will see on page 115.

## More about your statutory rights and responsibilities

Broadly, you can divide employment laws into two main groups:

- **Laws relating to equality of opportunity, fairness and discrimination**. Some laws aim to ensure that everyone is given the same opportunity and treated fairly at work regardless of superficial differences that have nothing to do with their ability to do a job – such as sex, race, disability, religion, belief or sexual orientation. From 2006 it will also be unlawful to discriminate on grounds of age. You will find out more about discrimination laws on page 139–141.

There are also laws to ensure that part-time and fixed-term workers are not treated less favourably than full-time or permanent workers and to ensure that women and men are paid the same for doing the same job (see below). 'Fixed-term' refers to temporary workers who are given a specific

**Remember**

Several laws give you legal rights at work. Understanding the main ones and the aspects of employment they cover helps you to understand your own rights better and to see the reasons for many company policies on equal opportunities, discrimination and other related areas, such as health and safety and data protection.

end date when they start work, such as staff taken on by a resort hotel or theme park just for the summer months.

- **Laws relating to working conditions.** These have constantly tried to improve the rights of workers in areas such as: the number of hours they can be required to work; their minimum holiday entitlement; maternity, paternity and parental leave; flexible working; and how disputes are handled.

## Pay and pensions

Pay is obviously very important to all employees and for that reason there are several laws giving employees rights relating to this.

Under the Equal Pay Act 1970, a man and a woman doing exactly the same work or work of 'equal value' must be paid at the same rate unless the employer can prove there is an important difference between them that has nothing to do with their gender, such as different qualifications or experience in the job.

All workers must be paid at least at the national minimum wage rate for their age. Unfortunately this doesn't apply to 16 and 17-year-old Apprentices.

Full-time employees have the right to four weeks' paid holiday each year (i.e. 20 days' leave). Part-time employees have the same right in proportion to their working hours – so someone working two days each week would have eight days' paid holiday a year. There is no legal entitlement to have bank holidays with pay unless this is stated in the contract of employment. If you left your job and hadn't taken your holiday leave then your employer must pay you for this.

You are entitled to an itemised pay statement which shows gross pay, all deductions and take-home pay. You should know the reason for all deductions that are made. Your employer cannot make any deductions without your written permission apart from income tax and national insurance (which are required by law) unless these are specified in your contract of employment. The only exception is if you have earlier been overpaid by mistake. Retail workers responsible for cash or stock cannot have more than 10 per cent of their gross wages deducted to make up for any shortfall.

Pregnant women automatically qualify for maternity leave for a minimum of 26 weeks. Many have the right to receive a minimum level of pay during this time and those who have worked for longer with an employer can take additional unpaid leave. Similarly most working fathers can now take up to two weeks' paid leave following the birth of their partner's baby – known as paternity leave. Most employees who adopt a child have similar rights and are entitled to statutory adoption pay.

**Did you know?**

Unison, the largest trades union in the UK with over 1.3 million members, launched a campaign in 2005 to improve pay for all young people, including Apprentices. It argues that almost a half of 16 and 17-year-olds today work for a pittance. It has also launched a website, Trouble at Work, in conjunction with the National Union of Students. You can find out more at www.unison.org. uk and www.troubleatwork. org.uk.

Employees who are dismissed because there is no work for them to do (known as redundancy) are entitled to a lump-sum payment based on their age, length of service and weekly pay, up to a specified amount.

A summary of the main aspects of your employment that are covered by different statutory laws is given below.

| Main aspects of your employment covered by law | |
| --- | --- |
| **Aspect of employment** | **The law says . . .** |
| Data protection | The Data Protection Act 1998 states that you have the right to see computer records about you or paper files containing your personal details. Your employer can make a small charge for providing this information. |
| Disputes at work | The Employment Act 2002/2004 (Dispute Resolution) Regulations state that all businesses must have grievance and disciplinary procedures. These must be followed before any ongoing disputes are referred to an Employment Tribunal. |
| Employee consultation | Under the Employment Relations Act 1999, employers must consult employees about key decisions and changes that will affect them, such as redundancies (i.e. there is no work for you to do). |
| Equal opportunities and discrimination | You must be treated fairly and not discriminated against on grounds of race, gender, disability, religion, belief or sexual orientation. From 2006, discrimination on grounds of age will also be unlawful. You must also not be subject to harassment or victimisation for any reason. (See page 140 for discrimination laws.) |
| Equal pay | The Equal Pay Act 1970 states that men and women doing the same work or work of 'equal value' to the business must be paid at the same rate. The only exceptions are when there is an important difference unrelated to gender (e.g. the man is better qualified) or between the two jobs (e.g. the man does more dangerous work). |
| Flexible working | Under the Employment Act 2002, you can apply to work flexibly if you have a child aged under 6 (or a disabled child under 18) provided you have been working for at least 26 weeks. Your employer can refuse but only for certain specific reasons. |

### Did you know?

The Work and Families Bill introduced in 2005, includes plans to extend maternity leave to 9 months by 2007 and 12 months by 2009. Unpaid maternity leave for new fathers may also be increased to 6 months by 2007. In addition, leave will be introduced for workers who need to care for sick or elderly relatives.

**Main aspects of your employment covered by law** Continued

| Aspect of employment | The law says ... |
| --- | --- |
| Health and safety | All employees have the right to work in a safe environment. Full details are given in option unit 101. |
| Maternity, paternity and parental leave | Under the Employment Relations Act 1999, pregnant women, expectant fathers and adoptive parents have legal rights to take special leave. All parents must be allowed limited (unpaid) time off in a family emergency. |
| Part-time and temporary workers | Under the Part-time Workers (Prevention of Less Favourable Treatment) Regulations 2000 and the Fixed Term Employees (Prevention of Less Favourable Treatment) Regulations 2002, part-time and temporary workers must be treated in the same way as their full-time colleagues and have the same opportunities in relation to areas such as training and promotion. |
| Pay and pensions | Under the National Minimum Wage Act 1998, employees aged over 18 who are not in an Apprenticeship must be paid a salary that is at or above the national minimum wage for their age. The Employment Rights Act 1996 states that you must receive an itemised payslip showing your pay and deductions. If there are more than five employees and your employer does not have an occupational pension scheme, you must be given access to a stakeholder pension scheme. |
| Redundancy | Under the Employment Rights Act 1996, employees have the right to receive redundancy pay if they are dismissed after having been continuously employed for at least two years. |
| Study time | Under The Right to Time Off for Study or Training Act 1998, if you are 16 or 17 you have the right to be given reasonable time off to study or train for a qualification up to NVQ2. If you are 18 you have the right to complete training you had already begun when you first started work. |
| Trade union membership | Under the Human Rights Act 1998, all employees must be allowed to join a trade union or staff association if |

| Main aspects of your employment covered by law Continued | |
|---|---|
| **Aspect of employment** | **The law says . . .** |
| | they want to and cannot be disciplined or dismissed for doing so. If their workplace doesn't recognise a union they can still join one independently, if they wish. |
| Working hours | Under the Working Time Regulations 1998, you can only be asked to work a maximum of 48 working hours per week, averaged over a 17-week period unless you are in an exempt occupation; 16–18-year-olds are limited to 40 hours a week and night work is not allowed. Under the Employment Rights Act, noone can be forced to work on a Sunday. |

# Industry-specific legislation and regulations relevant to your role

Businesses have a legal obligation to find out all the laws and regulations that apply to their particular operations and comply with these. They must also make sure that their employees are equally aware of their own legal responsibilities based on their job roles. It is never acceptable for anyone to say that he or she broke a law out of ignorance of its existence! This would apply to you if you thought that it wouldn't matter if you played loud music in the street at 4 a.m. It would equally apply to a shopkeeper who thought it was acceptable to sell alcohol, cigarettes or fireworks to children, and to a car salesman who lied about the mileage of a used car he was desperate to sell. Ignorance of the law is never an excuse!

Employees are often told about the laws and regulations that apply to their job role during induction – when they are told about the company and introduced to their colleagues. They will be told about company policies that they must follow. If they refuse, they could be disciplined or even dismissed.

Examples of these types of laws and regulations include the following.

- All establishments that deal with food have to abide by food safety laws and those that apply to food labelling, weights and measures and food handling. Employees who handle food must wear special uniforms and protective gloves, tie their hair back and/or wear a hairnet or hat, and follow specific procedures if they cut themselves or are ill.

**Did you know?**

Anyone working in sales should know the main consumer laws. All products must be safe to use, do what they are intended to do, be of satisfactory quality and match their description. If consumers buy the goods on credit, then the agreement must comply with the Consumer Credit Act. The laws apply whether goods are sold in a shop, by mail order or online.

As a customer you should know your rights when you are making a purchase. Option unit 203, Manage customer relations, gives more information, and you can also find out more online at www.consumerdirect.gov.uk.

### Find out

Talk to your supervisor and find out what industry-specific laws and regulations apply to your organisation. If your supervisor isn't sure, then go to www.businesslink.gov.uk and click on 'sectors'. Identify your own sector (this will be the same one you identified on page 87). Then click on the section that lists the laws that apply to your sector. Print this out and use this as a base for discussion with your supervisor. Then think about how they relate to your own job role.

- All road haulage and distribution companies will be aware of laws and regulations relating to transport and driving. This includes all relevant health and safety legislation as well as specific issues such as drivers' hours and laws relating to safe and secure loads.
- All organisations that deal with large amounts of money, such as banks and building societies, must know about regulations relating to money laundering and profits from criminal activities. These have meant that specific forms of identification must be given by new customers.
- All organisations that operate a website to sell or market their products must comply with several regulations, such as the E-commerce (EC Directive) Regulations and the Distance Selling Regulations 2005.
- Organisations need to be aware of their responsibilities in relation to environmental legislation. This covers issues such as air, water and noise pollution, the disposal of waste materials and the use of packaging.

As an administrator, you may not be as directly involved with the laws and regulations that affect your employer as some other members of staff, but this does not mean that you can ignore them. You are as responsible as everyone else in the business for making sure your organisation fulfils its legal responsibilities.

### Over to you

1 Test your own knowledge of your statutory rights from what you have read so far by answering true or false to each of the following questions. Then check your answers on the CD-ROM to see how many you scored.

a You can insist on taking New Year's Day as a holiday.

b As a 16-year-old apprentice you can insist on being paid the national minimum wage rate.

c Last month your employer overpaid you by mistake and this month has deducted the money from your pay. This is illegal.

d A lorry driver who loses his licence for drink driving can legally be sacked.

e If you work full-time your employer must give you 20 days' holidays a year.

f You have a serious family crisis. Your employer must give you special leave with pay.

g You have a serious family crisis. Your employer must give you special leave but does not have to pay you.

**h** A worker involved in food preparation can be sacked for failing to wear the uniform and hat provided.

**i** All employees have a responsibility to cooperate with their employer on health and safety issues.

**j** Your employer can refuse to tell you what is in your staff record.

**2** In Table A below are several examples of laws and regulations that apply to specific industries. Imagine that, as an administrator, you are applying for a job in each business listed in Table B. By reading the name carefully and thinking about the type of issues covered by each law, try to match each one to the business to which you think it is most likely to apply.

| Table A | |
|---|---|
| 1 | Controlled Waste Regulations 1992 and Hazardous Waste Regulations 2005 |
| 2 | Protection of Children Act 1999 |
| 3 | Private Security Industry Act 2001 |
| 4 | Copyright, Designs and Patents Act 1988 as amended by the Copyright and Related Rights Regulations 2003 |
| 5 | Goods Vehicle (Licensing of Operators) Act 1995 |
| 6 | Licensing Act 1964 |
| 7 | Sunday Trading Act 1994 |
| 8 | Employment Agencies Act 1973 |
| 9 | The Proceeds of Crime Act 2002/ Money Laundering Regulations 2003 |
| 10 | Package Travel, Package Holidays and Package Tours Regulations 1992 |
| 11 | Control of Misleading Advertisements Regulations 1988 |
| 12 | Building Act 1984 and Building Regulations 2000 and Town and Country Planning Act 1990 |

| Table B | |
|---|---|
| A | A restaurant that sells alcohol |
| B | An architect or surveyor |
| C | A large supermarket |
| D | An agency that offers young workers temporary jobs |
| E | A casino |
| F | A primary school |
| G | A travel agent |
| H | A book publishing company |
| I | A football club that regularly hosts major events |
| J | A road haulage company |
| K | An advertising agency |
| L | A hospital disposing of hypodermic needles |

> ### Evidence planning
>
> For your evidence for this unit you will need to prove to your assessor that you act within your responsibilities and rights. You will do this through the option units you have chosen.
>
> You may find it useful to start to collect the information you obtain that relates to your responsibilities and rights as you progress through this section. The easiest way is to label a file folder 'My employment responsibilities and rights'. Start by adding the information you have found on industry-specific legislation that relates to your job. Then add any information on health and safety, data protection and other employment rights that you have. If you are on an Apprenticeship then these should have been given to you at induction.

**Remember**

Both employers and employees have to obey all statutory laws and any contract that they have jointly signed. If they do not, then they are in breach of the law and there may be legal repercussions. If an employee is in breach then he or she can be disciplined and may be dismissed. If an employer is in the wrong, then an employee can take legal action and may be awarded damages or compensation.

# Why legislation is important for both employers and employees

Laws uphold and protect the rights of employers and employees because there is a system in place to protect both parties if the law is disregarded.

This is why legislation is so important. No matter where you work or what you do, you have certain basic rights in law. So, too, does your employer. If there is a disagreement then experts will refer to the law to make a decision. There is even a specific process that both employees and employers have to follow if there is a dispute related to employment rights. Most disputes are resolved quickly and informally, but in some cases they go much further – as you will see from the snapshot relating to an employee of the Woolwich Building Society on page 112.

### Steps in resolving a dispute

- **An informal discussion** should be the first step. Often a problem may be due to a simple misunderstanding that can be remedied quickly and easily without going through a formal process.
- **Formal procedures** are the next stage. The Employment Act 2002 (Dispute Resolution) Regulations requires all firms to have specific procedures for dealing with dismissal, disciplinary action and grievances in the workplace. All employees must be told what these are. You will normally find that this information is given to you as part of your contract of employment (see pages 113 and 120).
- **Arbitration** may be needed if negotiations within the workplace are unsuccessful. Acas, the Arbitration, Conciliation and Arbitration Service, operates an arbitration scheme that can be used by both parties. The arbitrator will listen to both sides, ask questions and assess the situation,

bearing in mind general principles of fairness and good practice, and then decide how the dispute could be solved. If the parties agree then the matter is settled. If not, the complaint will go to a tribunal.

- **Employment tribunals** are like an informal court set up to deal with employment disputes. Although no one wears a wig or gown, it is still a court. A legally qualified chairperson is in charge and usually sits with two non-legal (lay) people. One of these will be chosen to identify with the employer's view (such as a business person) and the other to identify with the employee's situation (such as a trade union representative). Normally a claim must be made to a tribunal within three months of the original problem or complaint.

  The panel listens to both sides of the argument and may ask witnesses questions. It considers the employee's previous behaviour and work history and the actions taken to solve the problem by the employer. This will include checking the disciplinary or grievance procedures that operate in the organisation and whether or not they have been followed. The panel then comes to a decision. If the employee wins the case the tribunal can order that he or she be **reinstated** (i.e. given his/her old job back), given a similar job or financially compensated. Because most employees would not want to return to work for an employer in this situation, the most usual outcome is a **compensation award**. However, this will be reduced if the tribunal thinks the employee contributed to the problem or could have obtained another job sooner.

- **An appeal** is the final stage if there is an argument about a point of law. Either the employer or employee can appeal against a tribunal's decision. The first step is to take the case to the Employment Appeal Tribunal. Beyond that, the case can be taken to the European Court of Justice. In rare cases this can mean that British law has to change because of the European decision.

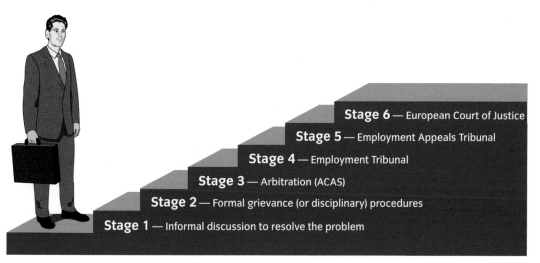

*The steps in resolving a dispute. Remember that most disputes are resolved at an early stage!*

## Snapshot – An administrator changes the law!

When Michelle Alabaster became pregnant in 1996, she never thought that one day she would be responsible for changing the maternity pay of thousands of British women. Michelle worked as an administrator with the Woolwich Building Society, now owned by Barclays Bank. Although she had received a 12 per cent pay rise shortly before taking maternity leave, her maternity pay didn't take this into account. Her employer had followed government regulations and calculated maternity pay based on her wages earlier in her pregnancy – before her pay rise. Michelle thought this was unfair. The Maternity Alliance, which supported her case, helped her to argue that this broke European sex discrimination law as she was underpaid throughout her maternity leave.

The case was first heard at an employment tribunal in Ashford, Kent. It then went to the Employment Appeal Tribunal and the Court of Appeal in London. By 2005 it had reached the European Court of Justice in Luxembourg which found in her favour. As a result, all British firms must now calculate maternity pay to include any pay rises during pregnancy. In addition, other women who were treated like Michelle may now be able to claim against their employers.

Michelle herself received £204.53 – plus £65.86 interest. Although it took her nine years to get this small amount of compensation she wasn't interested in the money. Instead she was delighted that the ruling will help to prevent other new mothers losing out financially at work because they are pregnant.

## Main terms and conditions of your contract of employment

### Did you know?

Your contract of employment defines the legal relationship between you and your employer. When you have both signed it, then it is binding. Because it is so significant, it is important that you understand the items it contains and how these will affect you at work. This is because the document defines the actions that you and your employer can take, and those you cannot.

After you have been working for your employer for more than one month you have the legal right to receive details of your terms and conditions of employment in writing. This must be sent to you within two months of the date when your employment started. You may receive this information in a letter or in a more formal document, called a **contract of employment**. Or your document may just summarise the **main terms of employment** and state where you can find other essential information.

### Key items in a contract of employment

Your letter, contract or statement of main terms must contain certain specific items. Other items of information must also be provided but can be in a separate document, or you must be told where you can find them.

*Within the contract* must be the following information:

- your job title
- your hours of work
- your place of work
- the main terms and conditions of your employment
- your pay and other benefits, such as sick pay and holiday pay
- the date on which your employment started
- the name of your employer
- your own name.

*Additional information* that can be given in a separate document, but must be provided somewhere, is as follows:

- in some cases, if the job is temporary, the date on which the job will end
- details of any trade union agreements that relate to you
- details of your employer's grievance and appeals procedures (see page 120).

*Further information* to which you must have access includes:

- details about sickness benefits and sickness entitlement if you are ill
- pension scheme details
- how much notice you must give if you want to leave the job
- details of your employer's disciplinary rules and procedures (see page 120).

An example of a statement of the main terms of employment is shown below. It is called this because a full contract would contain all the information. Like many organisations, Capital Services Ltd prefers to summarise the main terms and refer its employees to other documents for further details.

**Find out**

Your contract of employment should be kept in a very safe place so that you can quickly refer to it. This would be vital, for example, if you wanted to check whether your employer could take a certain action or ask you to do something. Before you finish this section, find out what your contract says. Then ask your tutor, trainer or supervisor about any terms in it you don't understand.

## Statement of main terms of employment

This statement, together with the Employee Handbook, forms part of your Contract of Employment and sets out the main terms of your employment with Capital Services Ltd.

**Name**: Holly Watson

**Job Title**: Sales Administrator

**Place of work**: Capital Services Ltd, Melling Street, Brankston, BR3 2RE

**Date of commencement of employment**: 2 October 2006

**Salary**: £12,000 per annum plus employee bonus scheme

**Date paid**: 28th day of each month by BACS credit transfer

**Hours of work**: 37.5 hours each week over 5 days, Monday to Friday

**Holidays**: Annual holiday entitlement and holiday pay is calculated on the basis of 20 days for each full calendar year of employment plus 8 statutory public/Bank Holidays. The annual entitlement increases with length of service, details of which are provided separately. The holiday year runs from 1 April to 31 March and unused holiday entitlement may not be carried forward from one year to the next.

## Statement of main terms of employment Continued

**Holiday pay**: Normal rate for all holidays including statutory public/bank holidays.

**Sick pay entitlement**: You will be entitled to paid absence due to sickness or injury under the company's sick pay scheme on the following basis:

Up to 8 weeks' service: Nil; After 8 weeks' service: Up to 2 weeks at full pay and 3 weeks at 50% pay in any 12-month period. You may also qualify for statutory sick pay.

**Absence from work**: Your supervisor's permission must always be obtained in advance for planned absence. In the case of an unexpected absence you must notify your supervisor by 10 am on the first day whenever possible. To qualify for statutory sick pay and payment from the company's sick pay scheme, you must complete a self-certificate when your absence lasts from 0.5 to 7 days, including Saturday or Sunday. A doctor's or hospital certificate must be produced for all absences exceeding 7 days.

**Health and safety at work**: All employees must comply with the company's health and safety policy and with all the rules laid down by the Health and Safety at Work Act and all other relevant regulations. A copy of the health and safety policy and the relevant requirements will be issued during your induction period.

**Notice**: This contract can be terminated by notice by either party as follows:

Notice by employer: Under 1 month's service – Nil; Over 1 month's but less than 5 years' service – 1 month; 5 years' service or more – 1 week for each completed year of service up to a maximum of 12 weeks

Notice by employee: Under 1 month's service – Nil; Over 1 month – 1 month

**Disciplinary rules and disciplinary procedures**: The disciplinary rules and procedures are fully explained in the employee handbook.

**Grievances and grievance procedure**: If you have a grievance relating to your employment, you have the right to express this in accordance with the company's grievance procedure. This procedure is described fully in the employee handbook.

**Date of issue of this document**: 2 October 2006

I acknowledge receipt of my Statement of Main Terms and the Employee Handbook and confirm that I have read and understand these documents. I understand that any amendments to this statement will be agreed with me and confirmed in writing within one month.

**Signed** ………………………………………………………………… (Employee)

**Signed** ………………………………………………………………… (Employer)

This contract is subject to the information submitted on your application form being correct. The company reserves the right to withdraw any offer of employment or to terminate your employment without notice if any information provided by you is found to be false or misleading.

# Understanding your contract of employment

There are two important aspects to your contract that you need to understand:
- the terms and conditions of your employment
- your contractual rights and responsibilities (some of these will be listed in your contract but others will not, as you will see on page 116).

## 1 Your terms and conditions of employment

If you compare your own contract with a friend, with a more senior colleague at work or even with the example on page 113–114 you are likely to find certain differences. This is because the exact terms and conditions of your jobs are unlikely to be the same. As long as your employer includes all the essential items you read about on page 113, and doesn't include anything that is against the law, this is quite permissible. Here are some things to look out for:

- **Payment terms.** Your contract will state your salary or wages, how often you will be paid and the method of payment. Details of any bonus or commission schemes will also be included.
- **Working hours.** The working hours for different groups of employees may vary. Some may work specific hours, others may be expected to work flexible hours in which case the specific starting and finishing hours may be omitted from the contract.
- **Holiday leave.** All employees who work full-time have the legal right to a minimum of 20 days' paid holidays – often referred to as annual leave. Some employers may be more generous and this would be stated in the contract as well as any restrictions. For example, if your employer is very busy at a certain time of the year, holidays may not be allowed then except with special permission. You will have a legal right to time off on a Bank Holiday only if this is stated in your contract.
- **Sick pay.** Many employers operate a company sick pay scheme and will pay their employees for a maximum number of days at their normal rate of pay. The number of days will vary between organisations. Your contract will also state what you must do to notify the organisation if you are unfit for work to qualify for sick pay.
- **Other leave arrangements.** Your contract will give you information on allowable absences from work and state which are paid and which are not. (See also page 126–127.)
- **Disciplinary and grievance procedures.** Basic information must be included in the written statement of employment and this must also state where the employee can find full details of the procedures (see page 119–122).
- **Notice and termination of contract.** There is a minimum amount of notice that you, or your employer, must provide if the contract is terminated. This is to allow you to find another job or your employer to replace you. Some employers extend this, particularly for senior staff who may be more difficult to replace.

**Did you know?**

One national retailer has a rule that staff must not drink alcohol or eat garlic or curry the night before they work in the store because of the effect on customers. Several manufacturing businesses include in their workers' contracts the right to stop and search employees (and their cars) as they leave the premises if they suspect a theft.

Guidelines on dress will tell you what you can and cannot wear.

- **Specific responsibilities and codes of behaviour**. These may be stated in the contract and more details will be provided in separate documents, such as an employee handbook. There may be specific rules for employees relating to confidentiality, use of company equipment and guidelines on dress. There may be policies on health and safety, the use of IT equipment, equal opportunities, maternity, paternity and parental leave, breaks from work, emergency leave and welfare for staff (such as help if someone is ill for a long time).
- **Additional information**. This will vary from one organisation to another. There may be details of the company's occupational pension scheme, links with trade unions, staff development opportunities and your responsibility to attend certain training courses.

### 2 Your contractual rights and responsibilities

A contract of employment gives you and your employer two types of rights and responsibilities.

- The first are **express rights and responsibilities**. These are the ones that are specifically listed in a contract – such as the fact that an employee has to work 37.5 hours a week and will get 25 days' holiday.
- The second are **implied rights and responsibilities**. These may or may not be put down in writing because they are supposed to be so obvious that they don't need to be listed. This is fine if you know what they are! If you don't then you could perhaps risk doing something wrong. To help, a summary of your rights and responsibilities, and those of your employer, are given opposite. These include your implied rights and responsibilities.

## Summary of employee and employer responsibilities, including implied terms

| YOUR RESPONSIBILITIES/ YOUR EMPLOYER'S RIGHTS | YOUR EMPLOYER'S RESPONSIBILITIES/YOUR RIGHTS |
|---|---|
| **You must:** <br> • Meet all the terms of your contract <br> • Follow health and safety regulations <br> • Comply with other laws related to your work <br><br> **In addition your employer can expect that you:** <br> • Are reasonably competent and possess the skills you claimed at the interview <br> • Are 'ready and willing ' to do the work and will do what any 'reasonable' employee would do in a situation <br> • Will take reasonable care of your employer's property (e.g. equipment and furniture) <br> • Will work towards the objectives of the organisation <br> • Are prepared to carry out reasonable instructions and requests <br> • Will be honest <br> • Will not disclose confidential information <br> • Will behave responsibly towards other people at work <br> • Will be prepared to change when the job changes (e.g. when new technology is introduced into the workplace) | **Your employer must:** <br> • Meet all the terms of your contract and notify you of any changes within one month of these being made <br> • Comply with all statutory employment law and regulations <br> • Provide a safe working environment <br> • Provide appropriate training <br> • Allow you to join a trade union or staff association <br> • Allow you access to confidential records kept on you <br><br> **In addition, you have the right to expect that your employer will:** <br> • Treat you reasonably <br> • Give you the opportunity to participate in and be consulted on company matters that would directly affect you <br> • Never ask you to do anything that is illegal |

## Over to you

1 Your friend Holly has received from Capital Services the 'statement of main terms' document shown on page 113–114. Read this carefully and help her to understand it by answering the following questions. You can compare your answers with those on the CD-ROM.

   **a** Holly can't remember whether she will work fixed hours every day (e.g. 9 a.m. to 5 p.m.) or more flexible hours. According to the contract, which is more likely to be correct?

   **b** Holly wants to visit her relatives in Australia next year and would like to take extra paid holidays. She thinks one way to do this would be to 'save up' holiday from this year. Can she do this?

**Over to you** Continued

c  Holly finds out that her supervisor, who has worked there for several years, has more holidays than she has. She wonders whether she can complain. What do you think?

d  What must Holly do if she wakes up one morning with 'flu?

e  Why do you think Holly won't qualify for sick pay from her first day at work?

f  Why is it important that both the employer and the employee must give notice if the contract is being terminated?

2  Now refer to your own contract of employment to answer the following questions.

a  Identify three express or explicit terms that it contains.

b  State three implied terms that are not included because they are considered obvious.

c  Identify three legal responsibilities of your employer after you have both signed the contract.

d  If you deliberately ignored the terms of your contract of employment what do you think would happen – and why?

## Evidence planning

As part of your evidence for this unit, you will need to prove to your assessor that you carry out your responsibilities to your employer in a way that is consistent with your contract of employment.

1  Prepare for this by looking at your option units to see whether you can identify examples of related responsibilities linked to your contract of employment. Check these against both the express terms in your contract and the implied terms listed on page 117. You should find it relatively easy to identify occasions, for example, when you must be honest, carry out reasonable instructions and act responsibly towards other people in the organisation!

2  Now put a copy of your contract of employment into the folder 'My employment responsibilities and rights' you started on page 110.

# Work grievances and guidance on employment issues

An issue may occur at work because you have a query or problem. You may think something is unfair or unjust and want to find out whether you have a justifiable complaint to make. Alternatively, your employer may have a complaint about you – which you may, or may not, agree with! In either case you need to know what to do next.

The action to take will depend on the type of problem you have, the structure of your organisation and whether there is a recognised trade union at your workplace.

## You have a query or think something is unfair

Although there are a number of reasons why you may think something is unfair; problems and disputes often arise in the following areas:

- **Pay**. Have you not been paid in accordance with your contract, has your pay been calculated wrongly, or do you think you are being paid unfairly because someone else is getting paid more to do the same job?
- **Working conditions**. Are your working hours not as agreed, or do you have a problem relating to time off or holidays? Have your terms and conditions been changed so that they are worse than before?
- **Job content**. Have you been asked to do a different job or work in a completely different way from what you have done in the past?
- **Discriminatory or unfair treatment**. Do you feel you are being treated less fairly than your colleagues or are being harassed, victimised or bullied at work?
- **Contested disciplinary action**. If you have been disciplined, do you think this was unfair or unjustified, or do you think the correct procedures were not followed?

## Step one: Check your disciplinary and grievance procedures

Although most problems and queries are resolved informally, you really should know the formal procedures that exist in case you are less fortunate. Your contract of employment will tell you where to find your organisation's grievance and disciplinary procedures. If you have a problem it is sensible to read these, as well as your contract, as a first step. The type of information to check is likely to include the following (see also the chart on page 120).

*If you have a grievance:*
- the terms and conditions of your contract of employment
- the procedure to follow if you have a grievance
- who is eligible to accompany you to a grievance interview
- how to appeal against a decision that is made.

### Find out

Find out whether your employer has written grievance and disciplinary procedures and obtain a copy of each. Then read the information that will tell you what to do if you have a grievance and what your employer would do if you were being disciplined.

*If your employer is taking disciplinary action and you need guidance and support:*

- your contractual terms and the organisational rules that you have to abide by
- the procedure your employer must follow to discipline you
- who is eligible to accompany you to a disciplinary interview
- the stated penalties for different types of offences, including those that could result in instant dismissal
- how to appeal against a decision that is made
- the length of time any type of warning would stay on your record.

## Typical grievance and disciplinary procedures

| Grievance procedures | Disciplinary procedures |
|---|---|
| These tell the employees what action to take if a dispute or problem cannot be resolved informally and if the employee feels there is a legitimate complaint.<br><br>There are several stages:<br>• The employee should be asked to put the grievance in writing. There may be a specific form to complete.<br>• The next stage may be to investigate the complaint within the department<br>• The employee and manager meet to discuss the issue and talk about how the problem could be resolved. It is at this meeting that the employee may wish to have a trade union rep or colleague present.<br>• If the employee does not agree with the decision, he or she can appeal – normally to a more senior manager.<br>• If there is still a problem the complaint may be pursued outside the organisation, such as with Acas. | These state what action the employer will take if an employee breaches his/her contract, fails to follow an instruction, does not fulfil his/her responsibilities or disregards organisational rules.<br><br>Again there are several stages and normally only senior managers can issue written or final warnings.<br>• The employee should be informed, in writing, that there is a problem and told the reason for any action being considered.<br>• A disciplinary interview should be arranged to discuss the problem and to decide the action to be taken. If the matter needs investigating then the employee may be suspended on full pay until this is completed.<br>• The action taken will vary depending on the seriousness of the offence. This may be:<br>  – a verbal warning for a first or minor offence<br>  – a written warning for subsequent minor offences or a more serious offence<br>  – final warning for repeated offences or a very serious offence.<br>• Dismissal can follow a final warning or be the first step if an employee commits gross misconduct.<br>• The employee has the right of appeal against the decision, normally to a more senior manager or outside the organisation (e.g. to Acas) if he/she is arguing that a dismissal was unfair. |

## Step two: Ask for advice

It is often easier for employees if there is a recognised trade union in the workplace. This is because union reps will give advice on individual rights and support employees involved in grievance or disciplinary hearings. Most encourage their members to ask for help and advice if they have a problem. They can then:

- discuss the problem with the employee and employer to try to resolve it quickly and informally
- advise the employee about his or her legal rights and whether there is a valid complaint (by either side)
- refer any complex legal queries to the union's branch or head office for clarification
- attend grievance or disciplinary meetings with the employee, as a witness
- support and advise the employee if a problem goes before an employment tribunal (this may be the case if the employee has been dismissed and wants to claim it was unfair).

Even if you work for a very small business there is still a lot you can do to find out about your rights – as you will see below.

## Step three: check whether you can solve the problem informally before you take action

If you have a grievance then it is worth exploring all other alternatives before you take formal action, particularly if the matter is relatively minor. Most businesses pride themselves on having good relations with their staff and good communications. Asking to see your supervisor in private and then quietly, rationally and reasonably discussing the problem may be all that is needed, especially if you are willing to listen to suggestions and work positively towards finding a solution.

If you are being formally disciplined then you need to obtain help and advice quickly – but unless you have committed a serious offence it is likely that you will receive an unofficial verbal warning first. This is your opportunity to solve the problem informally by taking note of what you have been told.

**How to ...** Access information and seek guidance about your employment rights and responsibilities

You can do this in several ways.

- **Check your documents**. These include your contract of employment, any staff handbooks containing rules or guidelines, other manuals relating to your job or your workplace.

**How to ... Continued**

- **Ask for advice**. If you still haven't resolved your query, and your organisation recognises a trade union, then see your union rep. Alternatively you could obtain advice from a staff association rep or works committee rep, if there is one. Alternatively, you could ask for advice from a member of the human resources or personnel department, or the person responsible for staff issues in your firm. Or you could ask your supervisor or an experienced colleague. However, you should remember that this person may not be an expert on employment law.

- **Go online**. Several websites give easy-to-follow information online. A good one is www.worksmart.org.uk, run by the TUC. An alternative is www.acas .org.uk. You may remember that this is the organisation which mediates in disputes, too. Tiger is an interactive website linked to Acas at www.tiger.gov.uk and covers the national minimum wage, maternity/paternity rights, adoption rights, flexible working rights and employment relations. Or you could go to www.troubleatwork.org.uk which was highlighted on page 104. The BBC also has information online linked to its Watchdog programme at www.bbc.co.uk/watchdog/guides_to/employmentlaw. Or you may prefer BBC Radio 1's One Life website at www.bbc.co.uk/radio1/onelife/work/rights. This also gives advice on coping with a range of problems at work including bullying and harassment – as well as how to cope with an office romance!

- **Consult an expert** (free). You can talk to a specialist employment law adviser at your local Citizens Advice Bureau or see what CAB has to say online at www.adviceguide.org.uk. Some solicitors (known as CLS solicitors) offer a first half hour at no cost to discuss the basics of the problem. If you visit anyone in person remember to take your contract of employment, your organisation's grievance and/or disciplinary procedures and any other documents or handbooks that relate to your query.

# Witnessing or experiencing discrimination or bullying at work

By law, your organisation should have a written policy which outlaws discrimination in your workplace and tells you what you should do if you have a complaint. All employers must also take prompt action if any employee complains about discrimination, harassment, bullying or victimisation and investigate these thoroughly and fairly. If the complaint is upheld, then action must be taken to minimise any chance of a recurrence.

Any organisation that fails to take the issue seriously is in breach of the Health and Safety at Work etc. Act 1974 and is also breaching the individual's contract of employment. In addition, it may also be liable under the Sex Discrimination Act and/or the Race Relations Act (see page 140). The penalty – for both the employer and/or the person breaking the law – can include a fine, a compensation payment and even a jail sentence.

## What are discrimination, bullying, victimisation and harassment?

Discrimination means treating someone differently and unfairly because of a reason totally unrelated to his or her job. In Britain it is illegal to discriminate against employees just because they are a certain sex, a particular race, have a disability, have certain beliefs or belong to a particular religion, or because they are gay or bisexual. You will find out more about these laws on page 139–141.

Discrimination matters because employers should be concerned only with people's abilities to do the job. It also matters because discrimination can make anyone's life a misery, as well as denying very capable people the opportunities they deserve. Wise businesses recognise this and have policies in place to prevent it. They also take action against any individuals in the organisation who disregard them.

Discrimination can occur at any stage of the employment process – such as during an interview, when selecting people for promotion or offering training opportunities. It also occurs if someone is treated differently on a day-to-day basis, for example if they are bullied, victimised or harassed. Such behaviour normally results in acute stress for the person concerned, who can suffer a range of symptoms from sickness, headaches and sleeplessness to a serious loss of confidence in his or her own abilities.

The problem is that many people hesitate to say anything for a variety of reasons:
- They are not sure whether they are really being bullied or harassed.
- They don't think they have enough proof.
- They are worried that things will get worse if they report it.

There are two points to note if you feel like this. The first is that most organisations would not like to find themselves in an Employment Tribunal, defending a discrimination case, because the penalties can be so severe. So check the How to . . . box on page 124 to find out what to do if you have a case yourself or witness someone else in this situation. The second point is that if you feel that you have no choice but to resign, then you can still take legal action because you can claim what is called **constructive dismissal**. This means you felt you had no choice but to leave your job because the situation became so unbearable.

### Did you know?

- **Bullying** is when one person is singled out for unfair treatment by someone else or a group of other people.
- **Victimisation** is when one person is singled out for unfair treatment, particularly after complaining about a discrimination issue
- **Harassment** is unwelcome behaviour that offends, frightens or upsets someone.

All these are illegal and employers must take action to stop them.

### Did you know?

Bullying behaviour includes:
- constantly criticising someone
- deliberately leaving someone out of things
- giving someone impossible targets
- shouting at or picking on someone
- making fun of someone
- humiliating someone or making them feel useless
- giving someone all the horrible jobs to do
- being cruel or hurtful
- making threats.

## How to ... Take action if you experience discrimination or bullying

- If possible, confront the person concerned. Calmly state that his or her behaviour is not acceptable and for it to be stopped.

- Start a diary. Tell the person concerned you are doing this and that you will write down any future incidents that occur. This is very important because it will provide a written record.

- Tell someone! Start with a work colleague or friend that you trust. You may find that you are not alone in being bullied.

- Tell your union rep, safety rep or staff rep concerned with safety matters. This person should help you to make a formal complaint and give you support throughout the grievance procedure.

- Tell your manager or supervisor; or, if one of these people is the problem, go to see that person's manager. Take your diary with you but don't part with it!

- If you are on an Apprentice programme, tell your trainer, tutor or assessor and ask for guidance.

- If nothing is done, lodge a formal grievance. Make sure you take your union rep or a colleague to every meeting you have to attend.

- If life is utterly miserable then resign. State in your resignation letter that you have had no choice but to do this because of their failure to investigate your concerns about discrimination or bullying. Then hotfoot it to your local Citizen's Advice Bureau with your diary, your letter and all your evidence for advice on whether to pursue a legal case. And find another job in a decent firm!

### Find out

Find out whether your employer has a written policy on discrimination and/or a policy that tells you what to do if you feel you are harassed, victimised or bullied. If not, check with your supervisor the correct procedure you should follow.

## How to ... Take action if you witness discrimination or bullying

Take the person concerned for a coffee and talk through the checklist above. Then support them every step of the way!

### Evidence planning

1   Write a note to add to your folder 'My employment responsibilities and rights', stating your where your organisation's disciplinary and grievance procedures and any policies or procedures relating to discrimination, harassment, victimisation or bullying are routinely kept.

2  If you ever have to find out information yourself or seek guidance, make a note of what you did, or keep copies of any emails you sent and printouts you made. Add these to your folder.

# Procedures to follow if you are ill or need time off work

Your contract of employment should give you clear guidance on what to do if you are ill or need time off work for any reason – or it should tell you where to obtain this information.

## Sick leave

The actions you must take to comply with your organisation's sick leave requirements will vary, depending on where you work. This is why it is important to check your own contract of employment and not rely on what a friend of yours might say!

The procedures you must follow may include one or more of the following.

- **Notification**. You must tell someone you are sick as soon as possible – normally as early as possible on the first day you are ill. You may have to do this in person unless you are seriously ill or in hospital. You then need to check the rules to see how often you have to keep in touch after that, if you are off for a long time. Bear in mind that you must comply with these rules to be able to claim sick pay, either from your employer's scheme or statutory sick pay (SSP).
- **Certification**. Most businesses want self-certification forms for the first week and then medical certificates after that, but some may not want any certificate for a very short absence of one or two days. You can certainly expect to have to provide regular medical certificates signed by your doctor throughout a long-term absence, wherever you work.
- **Return to work discussions**. These are becoming more and more common, especially if someone has been absent for a long time or is frequently absent. You may also be asked to see a company doctor or occupational health services person for a separate report on your illness. It is sensible to do this because a refusal could go against you and enable your employer to dismiss you – ill or not.

**Remember**

Even with the most generous company sick pay scheme there will be a limit to the number of days per year that you can be absent with pay, no matter how ill you are. It is sensible to know what your contract says so that you don't get a nasty shock if you are ill two or three times and suddenly find your pay has stopped and you have to rely on SSP instead.

## Time off work

There are various reasons why you will want time off work. In each case the procedure to follow might be rather different.

**Find out**

Check your contract of employment, staff handbook or other information you have been given to find out exactly what you need to do if you want time off – either for a holiday or in an emergency or special circumstances.

- **For holiday leave**. The number of days allowed will be stated in your contract. Most organisations insist that staff book their holidays in advance, so that they can always ensure that key jobs are covered. This means that you may not be able to take your holidays at the same time as your colleagues. It is always important, therefore, to get permission before you make any firm arrangements.

- **With pay, usually to link with your statutory rights**. As well as maternity, paternity, adoptive and parental leave – and attendance at antenatal classes for pregnant women – employees can also take 'reasonable' time off with pay for other specified reasons. These include:
  - duties as a safety rep, employee representative or trade union official
  - looking for another job if they are to be made redundant
  - young people studying for a relevant qualification.

Your staff handbook or contract should tell you what to do in this situation, otherwise ask your supervisor.

*In most organisations you need to book time off in advance.*

- **Without pay, in certain circumstances.** These include:
  - emergencies concerning a dependant (although good employers will allow time off with pay for the funeral of a close relative)
  - taking part in certain trade union activities
  - carrying out a public duty, such as being a member of a jury (the jury members are recompensed by the court).

  Some employers are more generous and, for example, give paid leave for emergencies involving a dependant. In this case, this will be stated in the contract. Again your staff handbook or contract should tell you what to do, otherwise talk to your supervisor.
- **At your employer's discretion, in other situations.** These are normally personal crises and commitments that occur at the last minute. They can be as varied as your friend getting married, moving house, terrible toothache or the washing machine blowing up and a repairer being available only between 9 a.m. and 12 a.m.! If you are lucky, your employer will have a policy to cover these situations, too, so that all staff are treated in the same way. Most employers try be fair in these situations to prevent people deliberately 'taking a sickie' because they think it's the only way to get time off.

Whether your employer has a policy or not, the guidelines in the How to . . . box below might help.

---

### How to ... Ask for time off work

- Check whether you have a legal right to the time off or are asking for a favour. Your employee handbook or any of the websites on employment rights on page 122 will tell you.

- Check whether your firm has a policy for booking holidays or asking for time off. If it does, follow it.

- If you are asking for a favour bear in mind the following.
  - Pick your time. Don't ask when your supervisor is trying to do three things at once.
  - Don't ask in public. It is easier to give an explanation (or plead!) if you are talking to your supervisor in private.
  - Remember to say 'please'!
  - Normally your previous history will be a factor. If you never or rarely ask for time off you will have a stronger case.
  - Don't expect time off with pay if you are desperate.
  - Offer a 'trade'. Can you make up the time by working through your lunch-hour, coming in early or staying late? With luck your offer will be turned down – but it will be appreciated.

**How to ...** Continued

- If your request is granted say 'thank you'! And don't take advantage of your boss by staying away longer than necessary. If the washer repairer comes at ten not eleven then go back to work, not on a shopping spree for the rest of the morning!

- If your request is turned down, try to accept it with good grace. Don't sulk. Instead ask for the reason and find out whether there was anything you could have done to get a different answer.

## Snapshot – Get back to where you once belonged!

According to the Confederation of British Industry (CBI), the total cost of sickness absence in 2003 was £11.6 billion with an average cost per employee of £588. It is therefore not surprising that many organisations have turned their minds to ways of encouraging employees back to work as soon as possible.

British Airways estimates that absence from work costs it £60 million a year. It is trying to reduce its current high average of 17 days absence per employee per year to 10 days maximum by introducing return-to-work discussions as well as offering a £1000 bonus to staff who take fewer than 16 days' sick leave over the next two years.

Royal Mail has gone one step further. In 2004 it started a scheme whereby employees with 100 per cent attendance over six months were entered into a draw. Thirty-seven won a new car, 70 won £200 holiday vouchers and 90 thousand won £150 vouchers. Unsurprisingly its attendance levels rose by 11 per cent. The scheme was so successful that Royal Mail announced it was repeating it in 2005.

Despite their apparent popularity with staff, many have criticised these schemes, arguing that they tempt people who are genuinely ill to go into work when they are not fit. They argue that good workplace relations are more valuable together with sensible time-off policies for staff.

Tesco wouldn't agree. It has taken a different approach to sickness. To cut unplanned absence it introduced a trial scheme whereby it no longer paid its workers for the first three days off sick. If workers are ill for more than three days, they can claim sick pay and also get compensation for the previous unpaid days. The aim is to stop people 'taking a sickie' for personal commitments or for a day off just because they don't feel like working.

# Information recorded in personnel records, why these are needed and how to report changes

All organisations keep records on their employees for two main reasons.

- **Legal requirements**. Employers record some information to prove they comply with the law, such as hours worked, holidays taken and pay rates. All employers must also have records of their workers, the date they started and how much they earned, for tax purposes. Health and safety law also requires them to keep records of accidents, injuries, diseases and dangerous occurrences.
- **For management decision-making**. Basic information, such as the number of people employed, helps managers to decide whether existing staffing levels are correct or more are needed, particularly if the business is thriving. Information on absences, sickness levels, lateness and staff turnover is also important. For example, high staff turnover could indicate that pay rates are uncompetitive (and should be raised) or some other factors are making staff unhappy.

## The information that is recorded

Information kept on individual workers is likely to include the following.

- **Personal information** – name, address, date of birth, sex, education and qualifications, work experience, and details of any disability. Next-of-kin details may also be recorded. Your NI number and tax code on starting work will also be noted.

**Did you know?**

Numerical data from personnel records can be analysed quickly and easily using computerised systems. Information on the number and type of workers also helps organisations to check whether they really are recruiting a diverse range of employees in accordance with their stated equal opportunities policies. You will read more about this on page 132.

- **Employment history** – the date you first started with the organisation, any training you have undertaken and qualifications you have obtained, promotions you have obtained and the date. Past and present job roles and titles will also be noted.
- **Current terms and conditions of employment** – your current job role, pay, contracted hours, holiday entitlement and a copy of your contract of employment (in case there is any query or dispute), together with any changes that have occurred.
- **Work record** – your lateness record, your sickness record, any other times you have been allowed time off from work, details of any warnings you have been given or grievances you have made, details of any accidents you have had, results of any performance appraisals you have had.

## Reporting changes

How to report changes may depend on whether the information is kept manually – on a simple card record – or on a computer system. It will also depend on whether staff information is kept by your manager or in your department or held centrally, in a personnel or human resources department.

Wherever the record is kept, your employer will want to ensure it is accurate and up to date. In a large organisation your staff handbook will state who you should tell if your personnel details change – for example if you move house, change your name or achieve a qualification. In a small business you will need to tell your supervisor or boss. Changes to your job role and work record should be recorded automatically. If you want to check that these are accurate, don't forget that – for a small charge – you can ask to see your own record at any time.

**Find out**

Find out whether your personnel record is kept on a manual or computer system, and what you should do if you are moving house and want to change your address.

### Over to you

1 Six members of staff at Capital Services were grumbling one day about several aspects of their employment. Some were considering lodging a formal grievance and have asked for your advice. For each of the complaints, state whether you think the person has a valid complaint in law and, if so, recommend the best action he or she should take. You can check your ideas with the answers on the CD-ROM.

   a Hannah is furious that she was refused permission to take a week's holiday in June because three other staff have already booked their holidays for that same week.

   b Joshua is annoyed that, when he asked to see a copy of his personnel record to check that all the information was accurate, his request was refused.

c Samira is upset because she says her new boss often criticises or makes fun of her in front of other people and is always finding 'emergency' jobs she must do at her normal leaving time of 5 p.m. even though everyone else is allowed to leave.

d Poppy is complaining she has never had a contract of employment or anything in writing despite the fact she has worked at the firm for four months.

e John is complaining on behalf of his friend, Sam, who has just left the company. Despite working there for two years Sam has been told he can't have a reference because Capital Services doesn't provide references.

f Mohamed says that, in his opinion, the worst feature of Capital Services is that it doesn't have a company sick pay scheme.

2 Your friend changed her job three weeks ago and has now discovered that she is pregnant.

a Suggest three ways in which she could find out what her rights are.

b Research one of these ways yourself and find the answer.

c She says her new firm boasts about its 'family-friendly policies'. Use one or more of the sources of information listed on page 121–122 to find out what this means.

Discuss your ideas with your tutor or trainer or with other members of your group.

## Evidence planning

1 Add to your folder 'My employment responsibilities and rights' any information relating to the procedures you must follow to give notification if you are sick and/or if you want time off – unless this is already included in your contract of employment. Make a note of any procedures you must follow to book your holidays or if you need time off in an emergency. Then add any information you have been given relating making changes to your staff record.

2 If you follow any of these procedures at any time, keep a record. Alternatively you could ask the colleague you dealt with for witness testimony to say that you followed the procedure correctly.

3 Keep your folder safely. You can use the information to help you answer questions from your assessor to prove that you can access information about many of your employment rights and responsibilities and understand your rights related to your job.

**What if?**

If you never need to ask for guidance on your rights and responsibilities while you are taking your award, your assessor can ask you 'what if?' questions. This might be 'What would you do to check your rights if you heard a rumour that your firm might be closing down?' In this case, you will find it useful to look back at the table on page 117 and the How to . . . box on page 121 for ideas!

**Find out**

Do the administrators or apprentices you know match the profile opposite? Do you match it too, or are you different? According to the *Free to Choose* report published by the Equal Opportunities Commission, Apprenticeships are perpetuating gender segregation or even making it worse because careers guidance focuses on 'traditional' careers (such as engineering for boys and admin for girls) and so, too, do work experience placements for students. To help, it has launched the website www.works4me. org.uk to help young people find out more about the full range of career options. You can find out more about gender barriers at www.eoc. org.uk.

# Support diversity

Who are you and how would you describe yourself? The fact that you are reading this book means that you are statistically most likely to be female, aged between 16 and 19 and able-bodied. There is also a 90 per cent chance that you are white and studying as an Apprentice on a work-related training programme. How do we know this? Because statistics tell us that in the UK most administrators are female, most people taking a level 2 administration award are on an apprentice programme, and 92 per cent of young people on Apprenticeships are white.

This last figure comes from the Learning and Skills Council's (LSC's) *Equality and Diversity Annual Report 2003*–4. The LSC is the national body responsible for vocational training in the UK and one of its key aims is to widen participation to more people in Britain. 'By 2010 we want young people and adults, whatever their background, to have knowledge and skills that match the best in the world.' The LSC would therefore prefer more ethnic minority students to take advantage of vocational training opportunities and less gender bias in some occupations. It wants to make learning easier for disabled students and has launched 'e2e' – a flexible programme to attract more young people to employment, education or training. These types of action are carried out by organisations that support diversity who look at the actions they can take to widen access for everyone.

## The meaning of diversity and why it should be valued

In 2005, Live8 gigs took place in the capitals of all the G8 countries in the world as well as in Johannesburg. The aim was to put pressure on the leaders at the G8 summit to 'make poverty history' in Africa. The G8 countries are the richest in the world and Bob Geldof and Bono led a campaign to get more aid, debt relief and better trade opportunities for Africa.

Were they successful? That depends on your viewpoint. Africa certainly benefited but there is still a long way to go. An early criticism of the G8 was: 'How can eight white men in suits know what is best for Africa'? The answer is by asking the people who know and listening to the response! The G8 leaders and their advisers were well aware of this and consulted with African leaders and representatives from major charities about the problems before any decisions were made. They did not assume they automatically knew what was best for people different from themselves.

This is at the heart of the diversity argument. We live in a diverse world. In other words people come in many varieties, not just one! They aren't even just white or black, male or female, young or old. They come from a huge variety of ethnic and cultural backgrounds and have different religions and beliefs. They may be heterosexual or gay. Some are able-bodied but others are not. In addition they have different personalities, backgrounds and experiences. So it is impossible to think that you can easily understand or empathise with the needs or wishes of people who are different from you.

What do you do when you meet someone who is very different from you? People react in different ways. Some actively protest against diversity – such as extreme right-wing parties like the BNP. Some try to ignore anyone who isn't like them, either through fear or prejudice. Others are more open-minded and realise that judgements aren't possible until you get to know people as individuals. They also realise it is good if we can understand other people better. This isn't just so that we can all live together peacefully. The other main benefit is that we broaden our own knowledge and increase our experiences – and become wiser in the process.

### Did you know?

Many people felt that a key factor in London winning the Olympic bid was the fact that it took 30 children of all nationalities to Singapore to take part in the final presentation. In the words of the Bishop of London: 'London is a whole world in a city. There is no more diverse community on earth and there could be no better place for the 2012 Olympic Games.' He was referring to the fact that London is the world's most culturally diverse city with more than 50 ethnic communities of 10 000 or more people, speaking more than 300 languages. The city's restaurants offer more than 70 national cuisines.

## The value of diversity

Imagine, for one moment, that you work in an office with ten other people. Now imagine that these are all white males aged between 40 and 50. What do you think they would talk about, apart from work? Football? Cricket? Their families? The news last night on TV? Whatever their interests might be, it is unlikely that they would have much in common with your own if you are much younger.

Now imagine that these ten people are all your own age, gender and ethnic group. Would this be better or could there be the odd problem? For example, if you needed advice who would you ask? And who could help if you couldn't understand an elderly customer or someone from a different ethnic group?

The great thing about diversity is that it can give us different perspectives on a topic. We might not want to be close friends with people who are much older than us or very different in other ways, but we can still find it fascinating to talk to them and learn more about the world.

From a business point of view there are several advantages diversity can bring to an organisation, such as staff understanding the needs of a wider range of customers. You will find out more about this if you continue your studies to level 3, but your common sense should tell you that a mobile phone shop staffed only by elderly pensioners would be as silly as a Help the Aged helpline manned only by teenagers.

This is why many businesses have written diversity policies. These state why and how the organisation supports diversity. Part of this process often involves educating employees and helping to develop their knowledge and awareness of other people and their sensitivities.

# Being sensitive to people's needs, abilities, background, values, customs and beliefs

There are two main reasons why people are insensitive or intolerant to the needs of others.

- They are prejudiced or judgemental, often using stereotypes to justify their views.
- They are worried because they don't know what to do when they have to relate to someone different from themselves – so take the easy route and ignore them!

## What is prejudice?

Prejudice is when you make a negative judgement based on an opinion that cannot be supported by facts. Your judgement may, however, be supported by a **stereotype**. Stereotypes are generalisations we are all apt to use when we don't know enough about a person or a group of people. This usually results in a false mental picture of a person or group based on the group they belong to. It doesn't help, of course, that the media frequently promotes stereotypes.

- In many soaps on TV, such as Coronation Street and EastEnders, regional differences are emphasised. Do all Northerners really live in terraced houses? Are all EastEnders 'on the make'? Are all Liverpudlians work-shy? Does everyone who comes from Glasgow enjoy a fight after a night in the pub?
- In TV adverts you will still often see the 'perfect' family of mother, father and two children – with mother in the kitchen preparing the meal – despite the fact that 'life isn't like that' for most people these days.
- In magazine adverts you will see page after page of skinny female models, mostly white and mostly under 25 – despite the fact that in Britain in 2005 the average clothes size is 16.
- Tabloid newspapers love labels: 'yobs', 'chavs', 'neets', 'hoodies'. This saves space for banner headlines!

If stereotypes and labels are recognised for what they are, that's fine, but that's not always the case. Young girls become anorexic trying to look like Kate Moss, while elderly people are scared when they see two young lads wearing hoods. And this is when judging people according to a stereotype causes problems – for everyone, including you.

The problem is that you may not realise you are doing this. You will have formed your own attitudes and beliefs from several sources – as the diagram below shows. You may not even realise you hold some views until someone challenges you or you are involved in a different situation. This doesn't matter, provided you are prepared to step back and reassess why you think the way that you do.

You can find out more about your hidden prejudices in the 'Over to you' section on page 142–143.

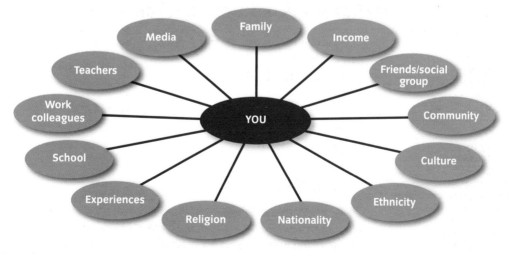

*Factors that influence your attitudes and beliefs.*

## Coping with new situations

Some people love new experiences and actively seek them out – such as backpackers who travel the globe for a year or more, happily finding out more about different countries, cultures and people. Others are more restrained and prefer a more fixed routine. They see their family and friends on a regular basis. They may work at the same place for several years. Then, especially if they are quite shy or reserved, they may struggle if they are forced into something that is completely unfamiliar. An obvious example is a life change that brings them into contact with new and different people. Consider these examples:

- A 50-year-old man enrols on an IT course where everyone else is under 25 and is worried about looking foolish.
- A female trainee administrator starts working for a construction company where everyone else is male. She comes from a family of three sisters and isn't sure how to cope.
- A blind girl gets a job as a sales administrator in an office where no one else has a disability and no one has a clue how to deal with her.
- A Muslim girl who has attended a girls-only school persuades her parents to let her attend a large mixed college to take a law course.
- An Indian family buy a house next to an elderly white couple.

What happens next depends on the behaviour of both sets of people. If the newcomer is outgoing and confident and the group is open-minded there will be no problem – but this doesn't always happen. In this case you should remember that it is always worse for the person who is 'different' from the rest. It is far easier to be one of several people already on an IT course or working in a sales office than it is to be the 'new' 50-year-old or blind person who suddenly has to get to know everyone.

> **Remember**
>
> The better you get to know someone who is different, the more you identify with them as an individual – and this is when stereotypes get blown away completely!

*It can be hard to be different unless you're made welcome.*

So, what would you do to make someone different feel welcome? In this situation you should find the guidelines ··below·· useful.

## How to ... Interact sensitively and respect other people's different backgrounds, abilities, values, customs and beliefs

- Adopt as your motto 'do as you would be done by'. In other words, always treat other people as you would like to be treated yourself.

- Challenge your own prejudices and stereotypes by working out what these are and identifying how they are likely to affect your behaviour.

- If you are nervous because someone is different, focus on the person and not the difference. For example, if a man is in a wheelchair don't let this stop you being friendly. Focus on his face, greet him with a smile and talk to him as you would talk to anyone else.

- Learn more about the cultures and beliefs of people you are likely to meet at work. If your visitors regularly include Muslims it is helpful to know that they only eat Halal meat, never eat pork, never drink alcohol and fast during Ramadan. Similarly, if you deal with Jewish people, you should know that they only eat Kosher meat, never eat pork or shellfish or take milk and meat at the same meal. At the very least this will stop you offering inappropriate refreshments.

- Learn how to deal sensibly and sensitively with someone who has a disability of some type so that you aren't nervous about approaching him or her (see page 141 and 281–2). Then find out more from the Disability Rights Commission at www.drc-gb.org.

- Think about the words you use. Don't use racist language, slang or derogative phrases that ridicule groups of people: e.g. 'Play the white man', 'She's barmy', 'He's a right girl', 'She's well past it', 'He's queer'.

- Don't be a snob! You should be just as polite and friendly to the office cleaner as you are to the boss.

- Be patient if you work with anyone who has learning difficulties or finds it harder to grasp certain tasks than you. Normally if the task or explanation is appropriate they do very well, so make it your job to try to find the best way to help them.

- Be curious but polite. Chat to someone who has a different background, culture or belief – or who has overcome a disability – to find out more. Most people like talking about themselves and will happily answer questions if they aren't too personal.

- If you feel that you would benefit from specific training to understand or communicate with different customers better, talk to your supervisor.

# Learning from other people

At work one day you are told that your office will be dealing with the needs of an elderly black man who is visiting the country. He will be seeing a woman in her eighties before leaving to meet a middle-aged blind man for a chat.

What would be your reaction? Would you think this would be one of your more boring jobs – one, really, that you could do without? How interesting do you think any of these people could be? Or would you reckon they are just wrinklies, really, with little to offer?

Would it make any difference if you then found out that the elderly black man was Nelson Mandela, the woman in her eighties was the Queen and the blind man was David Blunkett MP? Would that change your perception of the event, the people involved and the importance of the arrangements just a bit?

Regardless of any personal beliefs, most people would admit that Nelson Mandela would be fascinating to talk to and the Queen has had a wealth of experience as head of state. For years, successive prime ministers have found their weekly Tuesday meetings with the Queen invaluable, particularly when they encounter problems and difficulties. Given her vast experience, there is little she hasn't seen before and she can therefore give them useful advice based on her wider knowledge. David Blunkett MP is walking proof that anyone who is blind can forge a career in politics if they work hard enough.

This example should demonstrate that there are several reasons why you can find it invaluable to learn from others:
- They may have unique experiences or be able to explain more about cultural differences and beliefs
- They may have a wealth of experience which will help you to put problems and difficulties into perspective
- They may provide a role model for you to live up to.
- They can give you advice which may stop you making a mistake or help you to make a difficult decision.
- They can help you to interact with people you haven't met before or are unsure about.

If you are open-minded and welcome the opportunity to constantly develop your knowledge and skills, then one day you may find that people are asking for your opinions and views and trying to learn from you, too!

## Find out

Diversity Leaders UK is a charity dedicated to promoting inclusivity in the workplace and society by various means. One of these is through the annual British Diversity Awards in June to a range of different businesses including the media. Another is by developing a Diversity Practice Index against which businesses can be assessed to be awarded a diversity kitemark.

You can find out more at www.diversityleaders.org. uk – including whether your favourite TV programme has won an award for diversity excellence, like Soul Deep, Holby City and Only Human – Autism did in 2005.

# Your organisation's procedures and legal requirements in relation to discrimination legislation

**Find out**

What policies exist in your workplace relating to equal opportunities or diversity? What procedures do you have to follow to ensure that you never fall foul of discrimination legislation?

Originally many organisations developed **equal opportunities policies**. These stated that the business would ensure that everyone would be given the same opportunity regardless of their gender, race, culture, sexual orientation or disability. You would often see these statements included in job advertisements. Critics have argued that many of these policies are meaningless and have not helped to improve diversity in the workplace.

Today many organisations prefer to have a **diversity policy** which states why and how they support diversity. This helps everyone to identify the practical steps that are being taken, such as providing existing staff with more information and training. This can include setting up staff networks by which employees can discuss their concerns and suggest information they would find helpful – such as on cultural differences related to their customers; obtaining and posting information on the staff intranet or noticeboards and arranging disability awareness training or visits by speakers who can give greater insight into cultural or religious differences that would be helpful to staff.

In addition, of course, everyone should be aware that they must also comply with all discrimination legislation. This should be emphasised as part of any diversity training. All employees should know the main UK laws that deal with discrimination and the possible effects on the business if any of the staff or customers experience discrimination.

## Discrimination legislation

The first laws to be passed, in the 1970s, had the aim of preventing discrimination on grounds of sex and race. Disability discrimination followed in the 1990s and has been expanded since. In 2004, businesses had to improve access for disabled people where required, and by 2006 the public sector must promote equality for the disabled in all aspects of their work. In 2003, legislation was passed to outlaw discrimination on grounds of religion, belief and sexual orientation. From 2006, discrimination on grounds of age will no longer be lawful (see the snapshot on awards and diversity at the ETS).

Discrimination is often divided into two types.
- **Direct discrimination** is where one group is obviously excluded, such as 'Only men considered' or 'Only white applicants need apply'.
- **Indirect discrimination** is where a condition makes it more difficult for one group to comply, such as 'All applicants must be over 1.8 metres tall', 'Only those with English as a first language need apply'.

Details of the current Discrimination Acts are given below. The new age discrimination legislation will be based on the European Employment Directive. It is expected to include:

- the right for employees to ask if they can carry on working after the statutory retirement age (employers do not have to agree, however)
- a ban on firms using age as a basis for recruitment or promotion (employers will be able to set an upper age limit for recruitment only if this can be justified)
- the right for workers to claim unfair dismissal if they are sacked without going through the proper process.

However, critics have said that this will not help older workers who are forced out when they reach the age of 65. As things stand, provided the employer has given correct notice, this will still be legal.

| The law | What it says |
|---------|--------------|
| The Sex Discrimination Act 1975 (as amended) | It is unlawful for anyone to be directly or indirectly discriminated against or harassed on grounds of gender (or gender reassignment). <br><br> In employment, the Act applies to recruitment and selection for jobs and promotion, training, the way you are treated at work, dismissal and redundancy. There are some exceptions, such as acting and live-in jobs, if the employer can show that a Genuine Occupational Qualification (GOQ) applies to that job. |
| The Race Relations Act 1976 (as amended) | It is unlawful for anyone to be discriminated against or harassed on grounds of colour, race, nationality or ethnic origin. Again both direct and indirect discrimination apply, although the definition of the latter is broader. <br><br> The Act covers other areas in addition to employment, such as education, vocational training, access to goods and services and social protection. Again there are a few special circumstances under which discrimination may be justified (such as some restaurants, for authenticity) but these are relatively rare. |
| The Employment Equality (Sexual Orientation) Regulations 2003 | It is unlawful to harass, victimise or discriminate (either directly or indirectly) against workers because of their sexual orientation, whether they are bisexual, lesbian, |

| The law | What it says |
|---|---|
| | gay or heterosexual. This includes employees, agency workers, vocational trainees and any other workers at the organisation. |
| The Employment Equality (Religion or Belief) Regulations 2003 | It is unlawful to discriminate, harass or victimise anyone on the grounds of their religion of belief. This does not, however, include political beliefs. The regulations relate to issues such as the provision of a 'quiet room' for prayer, time off for special religious events, choice of menu in worker canteens, social events (at which non-alcoholic drinks must be available) and dress codes. |
| The Disability Discrimination Act 1995 (as amended) | This Act is concerned with discrimination against people with disabilities in employment, when obtaining goods and services, buy/renting land or property and in relation to access to business premises. The disability may be physical, sensory or mental, must be relatively long-term and includes long-term progressive conditions, such as MS and cancer. Public bodies must have clear policies and action plans to tackle discrimination and no employer must treat a disabled person less favourably than able-bodied persons unless this can be justified. Employers must also be prepared to make reasonable adjustments to the workplace to enable a disabled person to do the job. In this case, discrimination is not divided into 'direct' or 'indirect' but is based on the grounds that less favourable treatment cannot be justified. |
| The Gender Recognition Act 2004 | This Act gives transsexual people the right to live and work in their new gender for all legal purposes. |

**Did you know?**

According to the Equal Opportunities Commission (EOC) each year around 30 000 pregnant working women are sacked, made redundant or leave their jobs due to discrimination. Five per cent of the 441 000 women who are pregnant at work each year were put under pressure to hand in their notice when they announced their pregnancy. Others have been denied promotion, bonuses and training opportunities and even verbally abused. Most suffer in silence. As a result the EOC has launched its Pregnant and Productive campaign to inform more women of their rights and give greater support, especially for small businesses. Find out more at www.eoc.org.uk/pregnancy.

## Snapshot – Awards and diversity at the ETS

The Employment Tribunal Service (ETS) deals with claims for unfair dismissal and makes awards for compensation when these are successful. According to the 2004/5 ETS report the average award in that period was £14 158 for sex discrimination cases, £19 114 for race discrimination cases and £17 736 for disability discrimination cases. However, in other cases the awards have been far higher.

In one notable case in 2003, a 22-year-old former trainee car sales executive won nearly £180 000 for sexual harassment after working for just one week in a new job. Needless to say the harassment was serious and her ex-employees had done nothing to support her or prevent managers or supervisors harassing junior staff. In 2005 a homosexual office manager was awarded £35 000 when he successfully sued his ex-employers for breach of contract, unfair dismissal and victimisation because of sexual orientation. He was the first worker in the UK to win a case under this legislation.

The ETS deals with around 100 thousand claims a year from all sections of the community. Little wonder, then, that in 2003 it set up a Diversity Working Group and in 2004 it replaced its Equal Opportunity Statement with a Diversity Policy. This sets out its standards in relation to the employment of staff and meeting the needs of users at tribunals. It aims to ensure that:

● users receive fair and equal access to ETS's services

● staff are fairly and equitably treated in the workplace

● staff and users are treated with dignity and respect for their human rights.

It produces information booklets in eight languages and provides documentation in large print, braille, on disk and on audiotape for anyone with a visual impairment and a special number for anyone who is hard of hearing to call. You can find out more at www.ets.gov.uk and more about discrimination at the Equal Opportunities Commission (www.eoc.org.uk), the Commission for Racial Equality (www.cre.org.uk) and the Disability Rights Commission (www.drc.org.uk).

## Over to you

1 Colonel Collins commanded the space shuttle Discovery in July 2005. Before becoming an astronaut Collins was an Air Force flight instructor and previously piloted and commanded shuttle flights in 1997 and 1999. From this information, decide what you think Collins is like by suggesting: family background (parents' jobs/income/home family life); gender; date of birth; whether you think Collins is disabled; own family life. Then check your ideas against the reality in the answers on the CD-ROM.

**2** Complete each of these statements with the first phrase that comes to your mind. Then decide how much you believe them. Then decide how these thoughts and generalisations can affect your attitude and behaviour.

    **a** All old people are …

    **b** Muslim women are all …

    **c** White people are all …

    **d** Northerners are …

    **e** Southerners are …

    **f** All students are …

    **g** Deaf people are …

    **h** All teenagers are …

    **i** Women drivers are …

    **j** Men are good at …

**3** To what extent do you think a deaf person in your office can help you to understand other people with a disability? Give a reason for your answer.

**4** To what extent do you think the staff in your workplace reflects the diversity of your customers? What benefits or drawbacks do you think there are as a result? Discuss your ideas with your tutor or trainer.

## Evidence planning

When you are gathering evidence for your option units you have to prove to your assessor that you interact with other people sensitively, respecting their diversity. You can plan how to do this in the following ways.

1 Make a list of the people you deal with on a regular basis. This list can include both your colleagues and your customers. Make a note of those people who are different from yourself in terms of age, nationality, ethnic origin, religion, gender or in any other way.

2 Think about the reasons why you interact with them and what you have learned from them and about them since you first knew them.

3 Identify the option unit(s) which would be most appropriate for including your evidence. This could be a log you keep of occasions when you deal with your customers or colleagues or witness testimony from your colleagues. You should be aware that your assessor will probably at some stage want to watch you when you are dealing with other people.

## What if?

What should you do if either:

● your organisation doesn't have any procedures linked to diversity or discrimination that you have to follow

● you deal with very few people who are different from you

● you would struggle to prove what you have learned from other people?

In all these cases your assessor may ask you 'what if?' questions to cover these areas. For example: 'An older Polish woman starts work in your office. How would you make her feel welcome? Do you think there is anything you could learn from her?' or 'One of your colleagues keeps making fun of a young Chinese girl who works in the next office. Last week he upset her. What do you think you should do in this situation?'

# Maintain security and confidentiality

We are all aware of the importance of looking after our own possessions – and the distress that is caused if we lose something we treasure or, even worse, have it stolen. Today, security of possessions isn't just a case of keeping them under lock and key. Most people are aware of other threats – such as identity theft and 'phishing' – which occur when someone unwittingly gives away personal information relating to their credit card or bank account.

All organisations have similar concerns. The premises, equipment and any money and finances need to be secure. So, too, does important information and documents. A business is likely to be more concerned about the information stored on a computer than the value of one laptop or PC. The computer may be insured but the information stored may be irreplaceable. This is why back-up copies should be made and stored in a separate secure area. In addition, the organisation has legal responsibilities for the security of information under the requirements of the **Data Protection Act**.

Information can be secure, however, only if there are security systems in force and if people treat confidential matters with respect. It is obviously useless to store important and confidential information safely if someone in the office is telling everybody what they contain!

For that reason there is usually a range of systems in place to try, as far as possible, to minimise both security and confidentiality risks.

# The importance of maintaining security and confidentiality

Security systems are sometimes described as 'ways of keeping intruders out and valuables in'. They are not put in place to protect just buildings and equipment but also the people who work in the organisation, their personal possessions and the information they handle.

The security measures in place will differ, often depending on the type of information that is processed. Organisations that deal with highly secretive work will obviously be more security conscious than others. You would hardly expect to walk into MI5 with the ease in which you could stroll into your local college! And even the smallest firm would not like to think that someone could enter the building at will and take anything they wanted.

Maintaining security and confidentiality is therefore important for the following reasons:
- to prevent buildings from being entered or vandalised by unauthorised persons
- to protect employees from personal attack or assault
- to minimise burglaries and theft (this includes theft and misuse of information, as well as theft from employees)
- to keep the organisation's computer system safe from hackers and viruses
- to keep the organisation's future plans secret from its competitors

**Did you know?**

When you are online – at work or at home – you are broadcasting your presence to anyone who is interested. This is why a **firewall** is essential. This software acts as a protective barrier and regulates access to your computer. You also need antivirus software plus software that regularly checks for security breaches. Never open email attachments from unknown senders or reply to spam emails, and never ever tell someone your password.

**Did you know?**

A **security risk assessment** identifies risks based on several factors, such as:
- the type of business
- where it is situated
- the type of building and its design
- the number of staff employed
- the number of visitors it deals with each day
- the number and type of valuables kept on the premises
- the type of information it handles
- the times of day it is open.

The systems and procedures put into operation are then designed to eliminate or minimise these risks.

- to meet the organisation's legal responsibilities for information security and use under the Data Protection Act (see page 151), Copyright, Designs and Patents Act (as amended, see page 153) and other relevant laws.

For that reason, there may be several systems in your workplace to maintain the security of property and information.

## Maintaining the security of property

The systems that you have to follow will depend on the risks that have been identified in your workplace and the preventative measures that have been taken.

### Control over entrances and exits

Usually the number of entrances and exits is kept to a minimum and visitors can use one specified entrance. Some exits may be for emergencies only. These can normally be opened only from the inside, or they may open automatically when the alarm sounds. These must never be left or wedged open, for any reason.

Entrances to company car parks are usually protected by barriers that will open when a special ID card is inserted, or staff may be issued with vehicle passes that must be displayed on the windscreen. There may be a gatehouse with security staff to oversee the car park and monitor access by staff and visitors alike.

Entrance to highly secure buildings or areas may be by keycode, keypads that read fingerprints or voice recognition. Electronic badges that trigger doors to open automatically can also be worn by nominated holders. Often two or more of these methods are used in conjunction with each other for greater

security; so, for example, in addition to an electronic badge the holder also has to enter a PIN.

### Control over visitors

Visitors may be issued with passes that must be returned when they leave. Their name, organisation and date/time of arrival will be logged into the visitor's book. This provides an immediate check on the number of visitors in the building if there is an emergency evacuation. The procedure to follow is often printed on the back of visitor passes for reference.

Restricted areas should be clearly marked and staff should challenge or report visitors who appear to be unauthorised or who are in a restricted or unexpected area. The easiest way is to make a polite enquiry to ask whether the visitor is lost and to offer help. If the reaction is strange or suspicious, do not press the matter, just leave and tell security or your supervisor.

### Control over buildings

All buildings are usually illuminated during the hours of darkness so that anyone trying to enter can easily be seen. Burglar alarms and anti-scaling devices, such as spikes on roofs and walls, also help to deter intruders. CCTV cameras may be used to flash from one area to another at constant intervals or to provide continuous film that can be studied in the event of an incident.

Keys should be restricted to nominated holders and a list of these should be kept in a secure place. All windows and doors should be checked each night and rooms as well as toilets checked to ensure they are empty.

### Protection for staff

Walkways and car parks should be illuminated at night and security cameras installed. Anyone working in vulnerable (public) areas should have a panic button behind their desk and be protected by a toughened glass screen. All staff who may have to deal regularly with members of the public should be trained in how to reduce tension if a potentially violent situation threatens.

Special security arrangements should be in place for the handling or transportation of cash. This is not just for banking money but also for emptying vending machines or cash registers on the premises.

### Protection for equipment

All valuable items should be tagged or security marked for identification. Alarms should be fitted to computers. If a piece of equipment is very valuable it can be anchored by a special security chain. There should be specific procedures that state how old computers can be sold or disposed of.

Valuable items should be stored well away from public areas and goods received should be unpacked, checked and put away promptly. All stationery items and small items of equipment should be stored in a lockable storeroom or cupboard and access restricted to those responsible for storing and issuing the stock.

## How to ... Help to maintain the security of property

- Always lock away money – even the biscuit fund!
- Fasten windows at night and/or if the office will be empty.
- Lock the office door if everyone will be absent, even for only a short time.
- Keep keys in a safe place and keep a list of the holders of master keys.
- Never think that a stranger is a member of staff or has an automatic right to be in the building. Ask whether you can help and/or check with someone else.
- Don't leave handbags on desks or wallets in coats if you leave your office.
- Don't take unnecessary personal valuables to work, such as credit cards or your passport.
- Never allow anyone to remove any equipment or other items from your office in your supervisor's absence, even if they show you ID.
- Don't leave anyone alone in the office. Telephone for assistance in this case.

### Did you know?

A research team from Glamorgan University discovered that many second-hand, supposedly 'clean', computer hard drives still contained personal or sensitive information on individuals. The original owners, which included several large organisations, were breaking the Data Protection Act by failing to dispose of the information effectively.

Simply 'deleting' data on the hard drive still leaves it recoverable. Alternatives are to use a program like Infosec 5 to wipe the data or to pay a professional data destruction agency to clean the disk. The National High-Tech Crime Unit recommended a cheaper option: remove the hard drive before selling the computer and smash it up, then dispose of the bits in an environmentally sound manner!

## Maintaining the security of information

Information may be kept on computer or in a paper-based filing system. It may be stationary or in transit – either in a briefcase, folder or on a laptop. There are several reasons why it could be confidential.

- It may include personal details about staff that they would not wish other people to know.
- It could be about new product developments or include lists of customers, both of which would interest competitors.
- It could relate to financial information or employee negotiations that would result in unfavourable publicity for the organisation if it were given to the media.
- It could refer to possible internal plans that have not yet been agreed.
- It could include passwords or access codes that would be invaluable to a hacker or thief.

It could even be a combination of these. For example, if sensitive talks on a possible sale of the business were leaked to the press there might be banner headlines about possible redundancies, which would be awful for the staff and may even be totally untrue.

For these reasons a variety of security measures are used to protect important or confidential information. These will vary, depending on whether the information is held on computer or on paper (hard) copy.

### Information held on paper
- All confidential documents are put into an envelope before being despatched, even those for internal distribution.
- Only a limited number of named individuals receive confidential documents.
- Files containing sensitive information are locked in special filing cabinets and issued only to nominated people. Photocopying is also restricted.
- Sensitive documents are destroyed in a shredder and never placed in a wastepaper bin.
- Fax machines can be programmed so that confidential messages can be stored in memory and printed out only when the correct password has been entered.
- High-level confidential work should be done in a separate area, well away from public areas.

### Information held on computer

Computer security can be threatened in a variety of ways. Hackers may attempt to gain access to a computer system to steal or corrupt the data, virus attacks can destroy data or infect the whole system. Information may be stolen or passed to competitors. Small businesses are particularly vulnerable to staff misuse of company websites and lack of care in relation to security, such as forgetting or sharing user IDs and passwords and/or copying and forwarding emails unnecessarily.

**Did you know?**

Home shredders have become a 'must have' item for many people (with sales rising by over 25 per cent since 2004) since they became aware that criminals can rummage through their rubbish to find personal documents such as bank statements and till receipts and use these for identity theft or credit card fraud.

**Did you know?**

Microsoft Office 2003 includes Information Rights Management. This means managers can restrict the printing, copying and forwarding of sensitive email and documents. You can find out more at www.microsoft.com/uk/evolved.

The increase in cybercrime has resulted in a surge in the sale of security software and the use of external IT specialists who operate intrusion detection systems and regularly test their clients' network and keep them up to date on the latest threats.

**Find out**

Identify the security system that is in operation in your organisation to protect computer data. Find out whether this includes a monitoring system or automated protection systems, and whether critical data is backed-up every day so that it can be recovered quickly in an emergency.

## How to ... Maintain the security and confidentiality of information

- If you work in a public area, position your computer screen so that it can't be read by visitors.

- If you are creating a confidential document on computer and are worried someone might see it, start a second document and switch windows if someone approaches. Do this quickly by pressing Alt + Tab. If you leave your desk, save your document and exit the program.

- Never leave your computer logged into email when you leave your desk.

- Think twice before you copy or forward an email to someone, especially if it's going outside the organisation.

- Be careful about the information you disclose over the telephone, no matter how charming or persuasive the caller. It could be a competitor trying to find out more about your existing customers or your charges!

- Never 'gossip' with a customer or give away internal information unnecessarily. Keep your explanations brief and focused on the topic. Don't be led astray by flattery, shared confidences or sympathy for your heavy workload!

- If you are not sure whether you should disclose information, simply say you don't have it and will have to find out. This saves having to explain why you won't tell. Then refer the request to your supervisor.

- When you are photocopying sensitive documents, check you haven't left a copy on the glass before you leave.

- Keep a folder in your desk so that you can always put sensitive documents inside if you have an unexpected visitor. Lock away all work-in-progress papers relating to anything confidential in this folder every night.

- Pick a sensible password for your computer that you'll remember without writing down. A good tip is to pick something in your life no one would know about and add a number! So if you've just bought an outfit in Funky Fashion for £19.99 why not 'Funky1999'?

- Follow all the systems and procedures in your organisation that relate to security, whether you agree with them or not!

- If you identify any security lapses or flaws, report them promptly to your supervisor.

# Legal and organisational requirements in relation to security and confidentiality

## The security of business premises and staff

There are no laws that relate specifically to the security of staff or business premises, although your employer does have a duty to ensure your health and safety under the Health and Safety at Work etc. Act (see page 161). This includes, for example, taking the necessary steps to protect you from violence at work, and monitoring or eliminating any security risks that could endanger you – as you saw on page 145.

Unfortunately some small businesses do not give adequate consideration to security until something goes wrong – a strategy that has been criticised by many security professionals as this often puts staff at risk. An example is when the last person to leave is given the responsibility to lock up and set the alarm. This puts anyone who works late at risk, including women and junior staff, and means they can also be blamed if anything goes wrong with the alarm or someone later breaks in. The recommended procedure is that two people should be responsible for locking up together, that managers should have responsibility for security and no young person should be left to lock up or work alone in an office. All keyholders should be managers or senior staff who have received training on the procedure to follow if they are called to the premises because the alarm has sounded out-of-hours.

Businesses where staff often work late or at weekends are recommended to employ part-time security guards on an hourly basis so that staff are protected at vulnerable times.

### Find out

Find out the security procedures that are in force in your organisation – including who locks up, who sets the alarm, who the nominated keyholders are for responding if the alarm sounds out-of-hours, and what protection there is for anyone who works late or wants to work during a weekend. You can also see what the Home Office advises at www.homeoffice.gov.uk/crime/preventionadvice/index.html.

## The security of information

There are several laws relating to the security and/or use of information. Two of the most important are described below.

### The Data Protection Act 1998

This Act regulates how personal information can be collected, stored, processed and distributed by business organisations. The first Data Protection Act in 1995 regulated the use of information processed on computer. This was introduced because there was concern about the type of information held about people on computers – such as whether it was correct, whether information was held against people's wishes and what it was used for. The Act gave people rights about the information that could be held about them, who could hold it and how it could be used. The Data Protection Act 1998 extended the original Act to cover data held in paper filing systems, too.

All businesses that hold data on individuals are called **data controllers**. They must be included on a national register held by the Information Commissioner's Office. This office is responsible for enforcing the Act and ensuring freedom of information. If an organisation fails to comply or contravenes the Act, then the Information Commissioner has the power to issue an enforcement notice or an information notice against that data controller. An enforcement notice tells the data controller what action to take (or what activities it must stop). An information notice is a request for details. The Information Commissioner also has the power to search premises if there is evidence of contravention. Failure to comply with a notice or obstructing a search are criminal offences.

As you saw on page 105, under this Act an employee who wishes to obtain access to his or her personal files can do so, subject to a small charge.

The main principles of the Act and the rights of individuals are summarised below.

---

## Find out

The Freedom of Information Act 2000 has given the public new rights to obtain information held by many public sector organisations. As an example, parents can now ask their local authority why their child didn't get a place at the school of their choice. The organisation can charge a fee to cover searching, photocopying and postage but has to comply unless it can plead special exemption. One example of the latter is information relating to national security. If you work in the public sector, find out what your organisation has done to cope with requests for information it holds.

---

## The Data Protection Act 1998

This Act requires all organisations that process personal data on individuals to be listed in the register of data controllers, held by the **Information Commissioner**.

**Data** refers to
- information recorded or processed by computer
- information that is part of a relevant filing system or forms part of an accessible record (e.g. health records, social services records).

**The principles of the Act**

1 Data must be obtained and processed fairly and lawfully. Normally this means the individual (called a **data subject**) has given consent. Explicit consent is required for sensitive data relating to religious or political beliefs, racial origin, trade union membership, physical or mental health or sexual life, criminal convictions.

2 Personal data must be held only for one or more specified and lawful purposes and not processed for another reason.

3 The data should be adequate, relevant and not excessive.

4 Personal data must be accurate and kept up to date.

5 Personal data must be kept no longer than is necessary.

6 Data must be processed in accordance with the rights of data subjects (see below)

7 Data must be stored to prevent unauthorised or unlawful access, loss, destruction or damage.

8 It must not be transferred outside the EU unless the country to which it is being sent also protects the rights of data subjects.

**The rights of individuals (data subjects) include:**
- the right to access data held about them
- the right to prevent processing which would cause damage or distress
- the right to prevent processing for direct marketing purposes
- rights in relation to automated decision-taking (e.g. deciding creditworthiness on the basis of personal information)
- the right to take action to correct, block, erase or destroy inaccurate data
- the right for compensation if damage is suffered through contravention of the Act.

**Exemptions under the Act relate to data held for the following reasons:**
- purposes of national security
- crime detection and taxation purposes
- health, education and social work
- research, history and statistics
- domestic use only.

**Copyright, Designs and Patents Act 1988 (as amended)**

All businesses must comply with copyright legislation. This limits the action that can be taken with information which has originated elsewhere. If the business allows this to be copied or distributed freely then it will be breaking the law. This doesn't just mean photocopying information in a book or articles in a newspaper and handing it to someone. If you scan them into your computer and send them to someone as an email attachment then that too is against the law. Original documents created within the company or by an employee in the company's time are exempt, because the business will own the copyright.

The reason is to protect the rights of people who create original work. So if someone writes a book or a computer program, composes a song, makes a film or creates any other type of artistic work, the law treats that work as the person's property (or copyright). The law applies just as much to information on the Internet as it does to that in printed form. A related term you might hear is **intellectual property** (IP). Copyright is one type of IP. Other types include designs for products, trademarks for brands and patents for inventions. You can find out more at www.intellectual-property.gov.uk.

Anyone who wishes to make use of someone else's work must get permission to do so and, on occasions, must be prepared to pay a fee. The law of copyright does allow students (but not businesses) to take one copy for private study or for research purposes. Businesses, on the other hand, must obtain a licence from the appropriate agency, such as the Copyright Licensing Agency or the Newspaper Licensing Agency.

**Did you know?**

Copyright law also applies to music downloaded from the Internet. If this is done illegally it is classed as 'music piracy'. After sending warnings direct to computer desktops the British Phonographic Industry (BPI), which represents recording companies, is now taking court action. Fines have been issued to householders who continue to download music files illegally rather than use legal download services such as iTunes.com and napster.co.uk.

### Other organisational requirements

One method of checking the information that is created, downloaded and stored on business computers is to monitor staff activities. Programs exist that can record every keystroke made by staff from the second they log on until they log off for the day. Their emails are monitored as well as the websites they visit and the information they download. A key aim is obviously to prevent undesirable or pornographic material being accessed; but concern was expressed, by the TUC and others, that staff monitoring was a breach of their human rights. To help to solve the problem the Information Commissioner has drawn up codes of practice relating to staff surveillance by employers, such as the use of CCTV, the interception of email and the monitoring of Internet use and telephone calls. A key requirement is that employers should issue computer or IT policies that make staff responsibilities clear. They can also include these in their contracts of employment.

All organisations may include other requirements relating to confidentiality and security of information in staff contracts of employment. An example is a restriction on direct communications between staff and direct competitors and/or specific requirements relating to the disclosure of information. Flouting these rules is taken very seriously and can result in dismissal.

There may be rules and procedures you have to follow in relation to vetting customers, such as asking for proof of identity. On the telephone, automated systems can request the customer to enter an account or ID number and this can be followed by verbal security checks, such as asking for specific personal details such as date of birth, postcode or mother's maiden name. These types of check are routinely used by banks and credit card companies before any account details are disclosed to callers.

**Find out**

The British Security Industry Association represents UK security companies – not just those that provide security guards but organisations that produce alarms and CCTV systems or specialise in physical security, information destruction and consultancy. You can find out more about these organisations and how they are using technology to improve security systems at www.bsia.co.uk.

*Staff must beware of surveillance policies!*

Are you a cyberloafer? In other words do you surf the Internet or use your computer to send personal emails or instant messages to friends and relatives? According to a survey carried out by employment law firm Peninsula in 2004, some employees spend as much as three hours a day surfing the web!

A 2005 survey by Clearswift – a company that makes web blocking and monitoring software – found that in a typical 100-person company almost 1700 working days a year are lost to cyberloafing. According to other statistics, at its height the weekly cost to employers in the UK of employees accessing Channel 4's Big Brother website while at work was £1.4 million!

If these figures are to be believed, it is not surprising that employers have taken action. One in three has disciplined staff and 40 per cent of employers have sacked someone for email or Internet abuse.

How legal is this? The TUC has registered its concern about snooping by employers by eavesdropping telephone calls, monitoring emails and Internet use and using CCTV or other tracking devices to check activities during working hours. It supports Dutch research that people allowed to cyberloaf for short periods are more productive, suffer less stress and enjoy their work more.

So what are your rights? Under the Data Protection Act your employer cannot spy on you without your knowledge unless you are suspected of criminal activity. This is why many organisations issue staff with a copy of their IT policy that says what monitoring is in place. Or you might find the rules on computer use are included in your contract of employment. In this case, if you break the rules you have no option but to cope with the consequences.

## Procedures to follow if you have concerns about security and confidentiality

Your responsibilities don't just stop at cooperating with your employer by following security procedures. They also include taking the appropriate action if you spot a security risk or think that confidential information is being disclosed. This may mean:

- taking action yourself
- reporting the risk promptly to the appropriate person.

## Taking action yourself

Quite obviously you should never be expected to put yourself in danger, but this does not mean to say you cannot carry out common sense actions yourself. These would include:

- closing an open window before you go home
- logging out a colleague's computer that had been left on by mistake

**Remember**

Research has shown that *you* are probably the weakest link in your employer's IT security system! Many employees can't be bothered following even basic security procedures, can't resist opening dodgy emails, pick absolutely obvious passwords (like the words 'password' or 'letmein') and even write their password on a Post-it note and stick it on their desk!

- locking away valuables if you are leaving the office (or locking the office door)
- asking someone who appears lost whether you can be of assistance
- moving confidential papers away from a reception desk – or covering them up – when a visitor appears
- checking cabinets are locked before you leave for the night and putting keys in a desk if they have been left out
- having a quiet word with a colleague if you overhear sensitive information being discussed with a customer.

## Reporting the risk

If you work for a large organisation you will probably have to report different types of risks to different people. For example, a broken window may be reported to maintenance, an IT problem to your IT department and a suspicious person to security. If you work in a small business then your first contact would normally be your supervisor.

If you are concerned about a breach of confidentiality then always speak to your immediate supervisor first. This is because the information and/or problem may be specific to your own office or department.

The main point is that you report a worry to someone! Even if this is proved to be a false alarm it doesn't matter. It is far better that this is the case than you shrug, decide a possible problem is nothing to do with you, and later find there is a serious breach of security that you could have prevented.

### Did you know?

Louise Large's suspicions about a customer led to the discovery of a multi-million fraud ring! Louise, a Laura Ashley shop manager, became suspicious about a customer's behaviour when he tried to get a refund for an £80 dress previously bought in Dundee. She alerted security and used the radio link to warn other stores. The man was followed and watched by police who discovered he was part of a fraud ring obtaining refunds on millions of pounds worth of stolen property.

**1** Suggest two types of confidential information that will be dealt with by each of the following organisations:

   **a** a hospital

   **b** a solicitor

   **c** an accountant

   **d** a school

**2** A new employee starts work in a small firm with six members of staff. On the third day you can see she is very upset. You find out that she is distressed because all the staff seem to know everything about her – from her date of birth to why she left her last job. She is also annoyed that her salary also seems to be public knowledge.

   **a** Suggest four ways in which these lapses could have occurred.

   **b** Recommend steps the firm should take to prevent this happening again.

**3** Read the information on the Data Protection Act on page 151–152 and then answer the following questions.

   **a** Three of the following types of data are included in the Act. Which are they?

      • employee records held by the employer

      • customer records held by a supplier

      • a database of your friends on your home computer

      • police records

      • social services files.

   **b** Three of the following activities are an offence under the Act. Which are they?

      • a business sells its staff database to a finance company so it can write to them to promote its services

      • your employer gives the tax office information about your earnings without your consent

      • you ask your bank for details of the information they hold on you but they refuse, saying this is confidential

      • your local college asks students to voluntarily identify their ethnic origin when they enrol on a course

      • your brother, who runs his own business, refuses to register as a data controller as he says that the Act doesn't apply to small businesses.

**4** Decide what you would do if each of the following situations occurred in your own workplace. Then check your answers with your tutor, trainer or supervisor.

**a** Your office window won't close for some reason.

**b** You see someone you don't recognise loitering around the office on several occasions.

**c** A man walks in and delivers a really weird looking parcel. He isn't in uniform.

**d** Your computer is running slowly and then starts crashing, unexpectedly.

**e** A visitor gets very aggressive when she is talking to your receptionist.

**f** You are given a six-page confidential report to copy and in the process 'mislay' one page. No matter how hard you search you can't find it.

**g** You return from holiday and can't remember your computer password.

**h** A telephone caller is urgently trying to reach one of your colleagues who left the office an hour ago. He asks for her address and phone number.

**i** A colleague asks you to do 200 photocopies of a magazine article so that he can send them out to customers.

**5** In one organisation there was chaos when Samantha had her bag stolen when she attended a training day in a nearby hotel. The bag contained her purse, passport, three credit cards, a cash card, her house keys and her car keys. She had also been to the bank in the lunch break and drawn out £300 because she was going on holiday in a few days' time. The bag 'disappeared' when she left it in the room at the lunch break, thinking the door was going to be locked.

**a** If you were on the training day, what would you have advised Samantha to do next – and why?

**b** To what degree do you think she was responsible for her own misfortune? Give a reason for your answer.

**c** If you were asked by your supervisor to write short guidelines for all staff on bringing personal property to work, what would you include?

**d** What procedure would you follow in your own organisation if you lost something personal and valuable at work?

## Evidence planning

You will have to prove to your assessor that you preserve the security of property and the confidentiality of information in your own workplace. You will do this while you are gathering evidence for your optional units. However, you will find this easier if you start to plan now. You can do this in the following way.

1 Obtain a copy of any security guidance documents or security procedures that relate to your own workplace. These include computer or IT policies. Don't worry if you work for a small firm where there are none. Instead, make a note of the actions you have to take if there are security issues. Your answers to question 4 in the 'Over to you' section above may help you.

2 Carry out a security check of your own office area and workstation. Assess your own actions before you start looking at anyone else! Decide what security risks there may be related to your own job role and how you deal with these.

3 Keep safely any memos, emails or other instructions you receive that relate to either security or the confidentiality of information.

4 Decide which types of security issues, risks and actions apply to the option units you have chosen. As obvious examples, any IT units you have chosen will link to IT security risks/password procedures whereas units related to customers and visitors will link to controlling access, recording visitors, issuing badges etc.

5 Decide the confidentiality issues which apply to the option units you have chosen. Examples could be how you deal with requests for confidential information or how you store confidential information.

6 If you need to report any concerns about security or confidentiality, keep a record of the memo or email you sent and the result. If you make a verbal report, remember that you can always ask for witness testimony to prove this.

## What if?

What should you do if you don't have any security concerns or worries about confidentiality at work during the time you are taking your award? Your assessor will ask you what you would do if you *did* have a problem. For example: 'What would you do if you overheard a colleague giving confidential information to a customer?' or 'What would you do if a stranger called and said he had come to collect the office laptops because they needed upgrading?'

## Key skills reminder

If you are taking Key Skills awards, remember to discuss with your tutor or trainer how your evidence for this unit could also count towards those awards.

# Ensure your own actions reduce risks to health and safety

## Unit summary and overview

This option unit is divided into two sections:

- identifying hazards and evaluating risks

- reducing risks to health and safety.

Hazards and risks exist in all workplaces and can jeopardise the health and safety of those who work there. All employers have a legal responsibility to minimise or eliminate hazards and risks and need the cooperation of their employees to achieve this. If you are involved with identifying and dealing with hazards and risks in your area, then this unit would be suitable for you.

As you work through this unit you will learn about your legal responsibilities and find out how to evaluate and reduce the health and safety risks that are relevant to your own area of work.

You will obtain your evidence for this unit under the two sections on pages 176 and 181. First, however, it is important that you know about the relevant health and safety laws that cover your job and understand what is meant by hazards and risks in the workplace.

# Legal duties for health and safety as required by the Health and Safety at Work etc. Act 1974

All employees have certain legal duties relating to health and safety no matter where they work or what job they do. This is common sense because carelessness, ignorance or just plain stupidity can cause accidents that can affect many people – the person concerned, colleagues and even visitors to the business.

Employers also have legal duties. This means that health and safety is a joint responsibility for both employers and employees and these duties are defined in the Health and Safety at Work etc. Act 1974 (known as HASAW for short). This Act governs health and safety in the workplace in the UK and applies to all work premises and to anyone who is there. This includes employees, managers, visitors and external contracted workers, such as plumbers or builders.

The agency that enforces the Act is the Health and Safety Executive (HSE). An HSE inspector can visit any industrial premises without warning to investigate an accident or complaint or to carry out a random inspection. Offices and shops are inspected by an environmental health officer employed by the local authority.

Businesses with more than five employees must draw up a written safety policy and have safety procedures that everyone must follow in an emergency, if an accident occurs or if they are doing certain types of work. Businesses must monitor the risks in the workplace and take action to eliminate or reduce these as much as possible. They must also follow up employee concerns and investigate any accidents.

The main provisions of the Act are shown below.

## Link to core units

As you gather your evidence for this unit you should also obtain evidence for your core units. Watch for the CU link logo which suggests how the evidence you may collect may count towards both this unit and your core units.

Remember that you might be able to identify other links yourself, because of your own job role and the evidence you have obtained.

Talk to your assessor if you need further guidance on how your evidence should be cross-referenced.

## Did you know?

Under the Health and Safety at Work etc. Act, both employers and employees have legal responsibilities. Anyone who ignores the Act and is negligent can face criminal prosecution.

## Find out

To comply with HASAW, all businesses must display the main terms of the Act in a notice for their employees to read, or provide them with a leaflet summarising the law on health and safety. Can you locate yours?

---

### The Health and Safety at Work Act 1974

1 Applies to all work premises. Anyone on the premises is covered by and has responsibilities under the Act, whether employees, supervisors, directors or visitors.

2 Requires all employers to:
   - 'as far as is reasonably practicable' ensure the health, safety and welfare at work of their employees. This particularly relates to aspects such as
     - safe entry and exit routes
     - safe working environment
     - well-maintained, safe equipment
     - safe storage of articles and substances
     - provision of protective clothing

**The Health and Safety at Work Act 1974** Continued

    – information on health and safety
    – appropriate training and supervision
- prepare and continually update a written statement on the health and safety policy of the company and circulate this to all employees (where there are five or more of them)
- allow for the appointment of safety representatives selected by a recognised trade union. Safety representatives must be allowed to investigate accidents or potential hazards, follow up employee complaints and have paid time off to carry out their duties.

**3** Requires all employees to:
- take reasonable care of their own health and safety and that of others who may be affected by their activities
- cooperate with their employer and anyone acting on his/her behalf to meet health and safety requirements
- not interfere with or misuse anything provided for health, safety or welfare.

# Your duties for health and safety as defined by specific legislation

There are many regulations that cover specific aspects of health and safety. For example, a duty of all employees is to 'correctly use work items provided by their employer, including personal protective equipment (PPE), in accordance with training or instructions'. This is because HASAW states that employees must cooperate with their employer and not misuse anything provided for health and safety reasons. However, PPE isn't specifically included in that Act because it is covered separately – in the Personal Protective Equipment at Work Regulations.

**Did you know?**

HASAW is an 'umbrella' Act under which other Regulations are passed. These are introduced and/or revised regularly to ensure that health and safety laws are always up to date.

HEALTH and SAFETY at WORK etc. ACT

**Manual Handling Operations**
**Personal Protective Equipment**
**COSHH**
**PUWER**
**etc.**

Personal protective equipment may not apply to you if you work in an office because most office workers don't need to wear items such as hard hats, safety specs or safety boots, unless there are special circumstances. However, many regulations will apply to you as an administrator. A good example is the Health and Safety (Display Screen Equipment) Regulations which apply to anyone who uses a computer.

The table below summarises the main points of the regulations that apply to all office employees. It also identifies those that are most likely to apply to you as an administrator.

## Health and Safety Regulations that apply to all employees

**Workplace (Health, Safety and Welfare) Regulations.** These cover four specific areas: (a) the work environment (ventilation, temperature, lighting, space); (b) safety (in respect of traffic routes, floors, windows, escalators, stairs etc.); (c) facilities (toilets, water, seating, rest areas); (d) housekeeping (maintenance and cleanliness). (See also page 165.)

**Fire Precautions Act and Regulations.** All business premises must possess a fire certificate and have suitable fire precautions – such as fire-resistant doors, fire extinguishers, break-glass alarms, a fire alarm system and a protected means of escape.

**Employers' Liability (Compulsory Insurance) Regulations.** All limited companies must take out insurance so employees who are injured at work can claim compensation.

**Health and Safety (First Aid) Regulations.** All organisations must provide adequate and appropriate first-aid equipment and facilities and trained first-aiders. The number of first-aiders must be appropriate to the risks in the workplace.

**Health and Safety (Safety Sign and Signals) Regulations.** – Safety signs must be displayed to identify risks and hazards that cannot be eliminated and written instructions must be provided on how to use fire-fighting equipment.

**Reporting of Injuries, Diseases and Dangerous Occurrences Regulations (RIDDOR).** All organisations must notify the Health and Safety Executive (HSE) of any serious or fatal injuries and keep records of certain specific injuries, dangerous occurrences and diseases.

## Additional regulations that apply to all or most administrators

**The Display Screen Equipment Regulations.** All employers must assess the risks to staff using VDUs and workstations, pay for eye tests and spectacles/lenses if these are prescribed for VDU work, and plan work activities to incorporate rest breaks. (See also page 166).

**Additional regulations that apply to all or most administrators** Continued

**The Control of Substances Hazardous to Health Regulations (COSHH).** All hazardous substances (such as toxic cleaning fluids) must be clearly labelled and stored in a special environment and users provided with protective clothing.

**The Electricity at Work Regulations.** These govern the design, construction, use and maintenance of electrical systems.

**The Noise at Work Regulations.** These require employers to check noise hazards and reduce these where possible and provide ear protectors if necessary.

**The Provision and Use of Work Equipment Regulations (PUWER).** These relate to the maintenance and safety of all work equipment. Employers must make regular checks and inspections and provide appropriate training and instructions for users.

**The Manual Handling Operations Regulations.** These govern the way items should be lifted and handled. Preferably an automated process must be used, but if items are moved manually employees must be trained properly to minimise injury. This means not trying to lift weights that are too heavy and bending their knees to take the strain and keeping their back straight.

**Personal Protective Equipment at Work Regulations.** Protective clothing and equipment must be provided when risks cannot be eliminated. They must be free of charge, fit properly and be kept in good condition.

### Over to you

1 Find a copy of the health and safety poster in your workplace or at college and write down the names and job titles in the boxes. One box gives details of the trade union or other safety representatives in your workplace and one states the names of competent persons appointed to assist with health and safety and their responsibilities. If you have received only a leaflet and cannot find a poster, then ask your supervisor for the names of those people responsible for health and safety in your workplace. Keep these names safe as they will contribute towards your evidence for performance indicator 1 (see page 180).

2 If you haven't received a copy of the leaflet summarising health and safety law, you can obtain this free of charge from the HSE website. There are also several useful free leaflets available – a full list is given at www.hse.gov.uk/pubns/index.htm. Download or print any other leaflets that would help you to understand the law better in relation to your own job role, such as *An Introduction to Health and Safety, Working with VDUs, Health and Safety Regulations and Manual Handling*.

**3** On the HSE website you can access a special area relating to health and safety in offices or you can go direct to this area at www.hse.gov.uk/office/index.htm. These leaflets and information offered cover the main areas of health and safety that the HSE considers apply to office workers. Download or print any information that you think is particularly relevant to your own job role and keep it for reference.

## Important regulations for most administrators

The following regulations are likely to be particularly relevant to your job role.

### The Workplace (Health, Safety and Welfare) Regulations 1992

These complement the Health and Safety at Work etc. Act and provide more details related to the minimum conditions that employees can expect in relation to their working environment, safety, workplace facilities and general 'housekeeping' (i.e. maintenance and cleanliness). The main aspects are shown in the table below.

**Main aspects of the Workplace (Health, Safety and Welfare Regulations) 1992**

**Work environment**
- Ventilation must be effective.
- There must be a reasonable temperature during working hours (minimum 16°C but no maximum is stated).
- Lighting must be adequate and, where necessary, emergency lighting.
- There must be sufficient space for employees to work safely (a minimum of 11 cubic metres for each 'permanent' person).
- Workstations must be suitable for the people who use them.
- There must be protection from adverse weather conditions for any workstations that are outside the building.

**Safety**
- Traffic routes must enable pedestrians and vehicles to circulate safely.
- Floors must be properly constructed and maintained and be kept free from obstructions. There must be effective drainage.
- Windows and skylights must be safe to open and close and be clean.
- Doors and gates must be safe to operate.
- Escalators must be safe to use.

**Main aspects of the Workplace (Health, Safety and Welfare Regulations) 1992**
Continued

- There must be safeguards to prevent people or objects falling from a height or to prevent people from falling into containers of dangerous substances.

**Facilities**

- There must be sufficient lavatories and washing facilities.
- There must be an adequate supply of wholesome water.
- Suitable storage accommodation for clothing must be provided.
- There must be adequate seating for people at work.
- Rest areas should be provided, including provision for pregnant women or nursing mothers.
- Provision must be made for non-smokers in rest areas.
- There must be adequate facilities provided for people who eat meals at work.

**Housekeeping**

- All workplaces, equipment and facilities must be properly maintained.
- All workplaces must be kept clean.

**The Display Screen Equipment Regulations 1992 (as amended)**

These are likely to apply to virtually all administrators because they relate to anyone who uses a computer as part of his or her work. The main aspects of the regulations are shown in the table below. One important recommendation is that employees and safety representative should be encouraged to carry out their own risk assessments of their workstations. This can help to contribute to your evidence for this unit – as you will see on page 180.

**Main aspects of the Health and Safety (Display Screen Equipment) Regulations 1992 (as amended)**

These regulations relate to the use of VDUs and the design of workstations. A workstation relates to all the equipment, furniture and work environment of the person using the computer: desk, screen, keyboard, printer, chair, work surface, lighting, temperature, noise levels and space.

**Employers must:**

- Ensure all the workstations meet the minimum requirement as set out in the regulations (see below).

- Analyse workstations to reduce risks by examining the workstation and equipment and also the job being done and the special needs of individual staff. Employees and safety representatives should be encouraged to report any health problems. The employer must then take steps to reduce identified risks.
- Plan work so that there are frequent breaks or changes in activity. It is better if the user can choose when to take a break, but this is not a specific requirement.
- Arrange and pay for eye tests, on request, and provide special spectacles if the test shows these are needed.
- Provide users with relevant health and safety training and information.

**Workstations must conform to specific standards:**

- **Display screens** must have clear characters of adequate size, a stable image, adjustable brightness and contrast, be tiltable and swivel easily. There must be no reflective glare.
- **Keyboards** must be tiltable and separate from the screen with sufficient space in front to provide a 'rest' space. There should be a matt surface, the keyboard should be easy to use and the symbols must be clear on the keys.
- **Work surfaces** must be large enough to accommodate the work being done and must have a low reflective finish. It should be possible for users to rearrange the equipment to suit individual needs.
- **Work chairs** must be stable and allow easy movement and a comfortable position. The seat height and back must be adjustable and there must be good back support. A footrest must be provided if requested.
- **Working environments** should have satisfactory lighting with minimal glare. Windows should have blinds or workstations positioned to avoid reflections. Noise and heat levels should be comfortable. Radiation levels must be negligible and humidity controlled to a satisfactory level.
- **Software and systems** must be appropriate for the task, user-friendly and appropriate to the level of knowledge of the user.

# Hazards in your workplace

A **hazard** is anything that could cause you harm. Therefore many everyday objects are potential hazards – a computer, a car, a flight of stairs, a tiled floor. even the people you work with! A heavy box of paper is not a hazard in itself, but it becomes one if it's left where you could fall over it or if you lift it up wrongly.

The chance of an accident occurring or the likelihood of someone being hurt or injured is the **risk factor**. In most cases the risk factor from everyday items is quite low. A computer, safely positioned on a desk and with secure electrical connections, isn't a risk. One with frayed wires and a cracked plug most definitely is, so this is one reason why all electrical items are regularly checked for safety. Your colleagues are not normally a hazard, but if they are untrained, careless or silly then the risk factor is higher.

All employers must carry out regular **risk assessments**. This is a requirement of the Management of Health and Safety at Work Regulations and entails identifying risks and classifying them as high, medium or low. The risk must then be controlled. Ideally it should be eliminated or reduced. If this is impossible and there is still a significant risk then there must be suitable warning signs nearby, special precautions taken and, in some cases, appropriate training given to staff.

# Health and safety risks in your own job role and precautions to take

You may think that there a few risks if you work in a small office in a safe environment. Whilst this is generally true it is worth remembering that in 2003/4 two office workers were killed at work and thousands of people are injured every year. One administrator was killed when the stair-rail on which he was leaning broke and he plummeted to his death. The types of injury sustained by office workers who then needed more than three days off work to recover are shown in the table below. There may therefore be more health and safety risks in your job role than you first thought!

| | Type of accident | Number of occurrences |
|---|---|---|
| A | Contact with moving machine | 30 |
| B | Struck by moving object | 331 |
| C | Struck by moving vehicle | 54 |
| D | Strike against something fixed | 113 |
| E | Injured while handling, lifting or carrying | 867 |
| F | Slip or trip | 821 |
| G | Fall from a height | 128 |
| H | Trapped by something collapsing/overturning | 2 |

Injuries to office workers that caused an absence of more than three days in 2003/4

| Injuries to office workers that caused an absence of more than three days in 2003/4 Continued | | |
|---|---|---|
| | Type of accident | Number of occurrences |
| I | Harmful substance | 48 |
| J | Exposure to fire | 1 |
| K | Electricity | 18 |
| L | Injured by animal | 10 |
| M | Other kind of injury | 84 |
| N | Assault | 153 |
| O | Reason not known | 5 |

## Taking precautions

The specific precautions to take will obviously depend upon the exact hazard and the risk factor. Therefore highly toxic or dangerous substances must be kept locked away and handled only by trained staff, wearing appropriate protective clothing, to comply with the requirements of the COSHH Regulations (see page 164). The precautions to be taken with a bottle of liquid paper or a toner cartridge for the photocopier are less rigorous because the risk factor is less. Despite this there are some basic precautions to take. You should not inhale the fumes from correction fluid, and if you read the manufacturer's instructions you will find that there is a correct and an incorrect way to dispose of used toner cartridges.

**Did you know?**

The way people work with everyday objects is often referred to as **working practices**. If you still lick envelopes, handle paper carelessly or staple papers without watching then the item you are using is safe but your working practices are not.

### How to ... Take precautions

- Never attempt anything that is high risk, for any reason. Report it instead.
- Never guess how to operate equipment – read the instruction manual.
- Always report equipment problems unless you have been trained how to solve them.
- Obey all safety instructions, no matter how petty they may seem or how much you may be inconvenienced.
- Concentrate when you are working and only do one job at once.
- Never indulge in practical jokes that could result in an accident, or encourage anyone else to do so.

### Over to you

1  Hazards obviously vary depending on the type of workplace. Decide some of the main hazards that are likely to exist in each of the following types of workplace. If you have no idea then check out the websites below for inspiration. Some suggestions are given on the CD-ROM.

   a  a theme park like Alton Towers – see www.alton-towers.co.uk

   b  an offshore oil rig – see www.rigworker.com/industry.shtml

   c  a factory where glass is made – see www.pilkington.com

   d  a farm – see www.hse.gov.uk/agriculture/index.htm

   e  the police – see www.police.uk and find your local force.

2  Study the table on page 168–169 which shows the type of accidents that caused many office injuries in 2003/4.

   a  Rank the accidents to find the main reasons why injuries occur in an office.

   b  Calculate the total number of people who were injured.

   c  As a group, suggest what might have occurred to cause one accident for each type, bearing in mind that each of these occurred in an office. Compare your ideas with those of other people and/or the suggestions on the CD-ROM.

3  For your own workplace, decide the types of hazard that are most likely to harm yourself and others. Bear in mind this may depend on the type of organisation you work for. You can get ideas at a good website such as www.bbc.co.uk/health/healthy_living/health_at_work and www.tuc.org.uk/h_and_s. It will also help if you can obtain accident statistics for the previous year which show the types of accident that occurred in your workplace – and the reasons. Ask whether the person identified as being responsible for safety in your firm will help you (see page 178). Then keep your findings safe as you may be able to use these as evidence when you reach page 180.

# Remaining alert to hazards in the whole workplace

Knowing that there are regulations and being aware that your employer carries out regular risk assessments may be reassuring, but this does not mean hazards and risks can be ignored in the meantime. This is because the situation is constantly changing. Just because the photocopier or fax machine normally works reliably and safely doesn't mean that it will always do so. Equipment gets older and wears out or a fault may develop. A new member of staff may not use it properly or try to guess how to remedy a problem like

a paper jam – with disastrous results. Even if all staff are well trained, other more general problems can occur – from worn carpets or shelves becoming loose, to breakages and spillages or large deliveries of stationery piled in the middle of the floor. In all cases, if there is a significant risk factor, action must be taken immediately.

Some people have the mistaken idea that they need to take action only if the hazard is in their working area. This is incorrect. This does not just apply to your own working area but anywhere in your organisation. So if, on an icy morning, you are the first person to slither up to the main entrance of your building, it is up to you to take action, not put the kettle on and then watch to see whether anyone else does the same thing!

## The importance of dealing with or promptly reporting risks

If you spot a hazard that poses a risk then you have two choices. You can either deal with it yourself or report it. The difference will depend on:

- the type of hazard
- the training you have had
- the procedures that exist in your firm
- your own responsibility for putting right risks.

Therefore you would always report a broken window, but should be able to change a desk lamp bulb if you have been shown how to do this. Similarly, you would always (hopefully!) close an open drawer that posed a hazard, but whether you are expected to throw sand on an icy path will depend on the size of the organisation and your own job role.

## Risks you can deal with yourself

These usually include any risks related to cleanliness or tidiness in the office, including keeping walkways clear, repositioning small items of equipment to avoid trailing cables, picking up dropped paper, cleaning up small spillages, wrapping broken glass before disposing of it, closing doors and drawers properly, ensuring heavy items are stored safely, and keeping your own desk tidy.

Other risks you can put right yourself include those relating to your own working area – as you will see on page 185.

## Risks you should report

You should report all problems relating to office machinery and equipment and electrical items that you haven't been trained to put right yourself. You should also report any hazards related to the building or working environment – such as worn carpets or slippery floors, broken windows or furniture, and missing or faulty ceiling lights. It is also your responsibility to report risks you notice in other areas of the workplace, from a fire door that won't close to a faulty handrail on a flight of stairs.

### Snapshot – What bugs you at work?

If your list would include the person who keeps borrowing your stapler then you are on the wrong track. These bugs are living and are on your desk right now! According to research by Dr Charles Gerba in the microbiology department of Arizona University, the average office desk houses 20 961 bugs per square inch – far more than the average toilet! So next time you are tempted to lean on your desk, wipe your hand across it and then scratch your face you may hesitate a moment.

The reason why your desk is a pit-stop for germs is that is probably hasn't been cleaned properly for months. Very few employers pay their cleaners to give desks more than a superficial wipe – and that's if the surface is visible. Some are so full of papers, files, pens and personal debris that they are untouchable. Other workers use 'do not touch' notices to keep cleaners away, in case they disturb work in progress.

So, like your computer keyboard, your desk becomes a haven for everything from dead skin flakes to toast and biscuit crumbs. If you have a cold, and have spent most of the day sneezing as you go, then you can add airborne microbes to the list. And if you have recently spilt drops of milky coffee or yoghurt on your desk, and given it only a cursory wipe with a tissue, don't even think about what might now be breeding there!

The answer, of course, is to take action to improve your personal cleaning habits and mention Gerba's study to your colleagues. If they retort by arguing there is more toxic material emitted from the photocopier then buy a spider plant. Apparently, in 24 hours this can remove 87 per cent of pollution within 100 square feet. And perhaps the best place to put it would be on your desk!

## How to ... Keep your working area clean and tidy (and keep your germs to a minimum!)

- Don't leave food and drink leftovers or containers on your desk or in a desk drawer.

- Keep files in drawers and pens/paperclips in a desk tidy.

- Don't leave notes telling the office cleaner to ignore your desk.

- At the end of the day, tidy papers and files away so that you see the surface of your desktop before you go home!

- Clean your desk regularly with alcohol-based detergent wipes.

- Blast debris from your computer keyboard with a can of compressed air and wipe it with a multi-purpose cleaner.

- Use screen cleaner to keep your VDU spotless and reduce possible eyestrain and headaches at the same time.

- Use telephone wipes to keep the telephone receiver clean. Do this daily if you share your phone with other people.

**How to ... Continued**

- Don't open a window next to your desk on a windy day, particularly if your office is next to a main road.

- Don't put cups containing liquids or broken glass or crockery in your waste bin.

- Wash up cups you have used before you go home.

- Keep the area under your desk clear, so it can be cleaned easily.

- Wash your hands regularly throughout the day.

- Keep a box of tissues in your desk drawer in case you get an attack of the sneezes.

- Don't go to work with a heavy cold or sore throat.

# The requirements and guidance on the precautions

In some cases you have to use your common sense about the action to take. In others there is a written statement telling you what to do. For example, next time you pass underneath a railway bridge, look for a sign telling you exactly what to do if you see a vehicle hit the bridge. This explains who to contact so that the bridge can be assessed for safety. In this case you are specifically told the requirements.

Guidance on the precautions to take is also included in all manufacturer's handbooks and in all the health and safety documents in your workplace. These will have been specially written for the types of task carried out in your organisation. They are often contained in a health and safety manual that you can consult at any time.

## Over to you

1   A risk you may be reluctant to report is one caused by a colleague. Read the scenario below and then answer the questions that follow. Discuss your ideas with other members of your group or check them with the suggestions on the CD-ROM.

*Sara, who works in your office, seems to think health and safety is a joke. Her desk is a tip, she never takes her turn to tidy up the communal kitchen you share, she regularly leaves drawers open, and yesterday when it was raining you know she had a cigarette in the office despite the fact there is a strict 'no smoking' policy in your workplace. Today she wedged a fire door open when she was moving some equipment to another office and didn't bother to close it and then, during a fire drill, refused to leave her desk saying she was busy. At this point you lost it completely and told her she was a pest and a walking safety hazard. Her response was to shrug and tell you to get a life.*

**a** What main law is Sara contravening by her actions?

**b** If someone were hurt or injured by Sara's actions, what could be the consequences?

**c** If you report Sara to your boss, what action do you think should be taken?

**d** Do you feel you could do more to solve the problem yourself? Suggest anything else you could do to improve the situation.

2 Explain the action you would take (if any) to deal with each of the risks below. Discuss your ideas with your tutor or trainer or check them against those on the CD-ROM.

**a** When you visit the cloakroom this morning and wash your hands you discover the hot water is absolutely scalding.

**b** You are asked to take a laptop and projector to the meeting room for a presentation but the trolley that you normally use has broken.

**c** On a wet day, visitors to reception complain that the new floor tiles are very slippery.

**d** The lift lurches quite alarmingly when you are on your way out of the building one evening, but the entrance is deserted and there is no sign of the caretaker.

**e** You trip over a colleague's bag left on the floor next to his desk.

**f** As you are walking to the next office you see water dripping from the ceiling. You know that all the computer wires are in that area because you saw the technician working up there last week.

**g** The sink in the communal kitchen is filthy and dirty coffee cups are piled up everywhere.

**h** The window blind has jammed. Not that it matters very much because your office windows are so dirty the sun is just a blurry object in the sky.

# Identifying hazards and evaluating risks

You have now read about many of the main aspects of health and safety related to the workplace. In this section you will apply the knowledge you have learned to obtain evidence to show how you identify, evaluate and report high risks in your workplace and deal with low risks yourself, following workplace policies and legal requirements.

## Workplace policies relating to controlling health and safety risks

**Find out**

Your employer's safety policy should state the aims in relation to the health and safety of employees, the names of key members of staff and the arrangements for carrying out the policy. This is likely to include

- training and instruction
- company rules
- emergency arrangements
- the system for reporting accidents
- the identification of risk areas.

Unless there are fewer than five employees, this is a legal requirement. Find a copy of the policy that is in operation in your firm and examples of the procedures that you have to follow in an emergency.

To comply with the Health and Safety at Work etc. Act all businesses with more than five employees must have a written **safety policy**. The policy must be revised regularly to make sure it stays up to date.

The organisation will then decide its own **codes of practice** which state the procedures all employees must follow if there is an emergency, such as a fire, gas leak or bomb alert, or if an accident occurs. This will include how to contact a first-aider, where the medical room is situated, how to contact a doctor or send for an ambulance, and when an accident report must be completed.

Under the Management of Health and Safety at Work Regulations, all employers must also carry out **risk assessments** on the types of work activities that may have the potential to cause harm or ill-health. They must look carefully at what is going on in their workplace and check whether there are sufficient precautions in place.

Additional, specific risk assessments must be carried out in relation to the following:

- **fire risks** – to identify potential sources of ignition and evaluate existing fire precautions
- **first aid** – to check facilities, equipment and staff, based on the risk level of the working environment
- **young or inexperienced workers and students on work experience** – because both these groups are at increased risk and must receive proper training to minimise this
- **staff using VDUs and workstations** – to comply with the requirements of the Health and Safety (Display Screen Equipment) Regulations (see page166).

There will be specific workplace policies and procedures in place to make sure that all risk assessments are done regularly to comply with the law.

*A first aid box.*

*A fire extinguisher.*

# Your responsibility for health and safety related to your job description

As you already know, all employees have a legal responsibility to cooperate with their employer on health and safety matters. These may be listed in their job descriptions, which include a list of the tasks they routinely carry out as part of their jobs – but not always. If you have volunteered for additional duties, such as being a fire marshal, then this will not be in your job description because in this situation you have the right to change your mind. However, if you are responsible for certain health and safety duties in relation to a certain task or area, then you could find that these are included in your job description.

- You might have a specific duty at the end of each day to check that all computers are turned off, filing cabinets are locked, windows are closed and fire doors are kept clear.
- You might have the task of making regular checks of your immediate workplace for obvious hazards, such as trailing cables, broken furniture, faulty lightbulbs, equipment out of order, or heavy files on tops of cupboards.
- If you regularly use items of office equipment, such as a photocopier or franking machine, your job description may include a requirement that you use it safely, in accordance with company policies, and that you are responsible for reporting any problems and ensuring that it is serviced and repaired according to the supplier's agreement.
- You might attend meetings in your workplace on health and safety and represent your own area or department.

**Did you know?**

In many organisations staff have a general statement in their job descriptions that they must comply with the safety policy of the organisation, use recommended working practices, cooperate with their employer over risk assessments and report risks relating to their own job roles. Your contract of employment is also likely to refer to company policies on health and safety that you must follow.

### Over to you

1 Organisations have a legal responsibility to consult with their employees over health and safety matters, either through trade union safety reps or, if the workplace is not unionised, direct with their employees or through a nominated employee representative. Find out the system used in your organisation and how you could contribute to the process if you had useful suggestions to make.

2 You are approached by new colleagues with the following enquiries. In each case find out the information you should provide that is relevant to your own organisation. Then compare your answers with other people's to see how different organisations vary and how they are similar.

    **a** Jenny is interested in becoming a fire marshal and wants to know what it involves.

    **b** Salma wants to become a first-aider and asks how many there are and what qualification she would have to obtain.

    **c** Brian wants to know whether there is a recognised trade union and, if so, who the safety rep is.

    **d** Ashraf asks you to outline the procedure for reporting and recording accidents.

    **e** Judy wants to know if there is any guidance for an employee who is stressed and feels he or she can no longer cope with the job.

### Find out

Your organisation's safety policy will identify the people who have special responsibilities in relation to health and safety. Make sure you know who they are.

# Responsible persons to whom to report health and safety matters

If you work for a large organisation you will find that certain individuals have specific responsibilities for health and safety.

- A **qualified safety officer** or **safety adviser** may be responsible for the maintenance of health and safety in your workplace. This person is normally expected to tell senior managers about any changes in health and safety legislation, make sure that any changes relevant to the workplace are implemented, carry out safety inspections, investigate accidents, maintain and update the company's safety policy, and advise on and organise staff health and safety training.
- **Trade union safety representatives** may be appointed in each department to deal with staff concerns. This is the case when an organisation has a recognised trade union.
- **Staff representatives** may be nominated to take part in employer consultations about safety issues. This is the case in organisations where

there is no recognised trade union. This is because the law requires employers to consult all employees who are not already represented by trade union safety representatives.

In a large organisation, risks relating to a specific area are reported to the department responsible for that area, so that you may find:

- an estates or facilities management department that deals with general building improvements and repairs
- an electrical section that deals with electrical faults
- an IT department that deals with computer problems
- caretakers or janitors who will help if there is a leak or a breakage
- cleaners who remove rubbish and will help clear up a serious spillage or other problem
- security staff you can call on if you feel intimidated or threatened.

In a small business, overall responsibility for health and safety lies with the owner or the most senior manager. He or she may delegate the day-to-day issues, such as risk assessment, to a named 'competent person' but would still be ultimately responsible if there was a breach of health and safety law. There may be particular individuals who are responsible for specific areas, such as an IT specialist or a manager responsible for building repairs.

## How to ... Identify and evaluate risks

- Look for situations that are potentially harmful. These may relate to environmental factors, items of equipment or working practices that are part of your job role or in the workplace in general.
- In each case, decide who might be harmed and how serious the injury might be.

## How to ... Continued

- Decide whether the chance of this happening is high or low.
- Assess whether the existing precautions are adequate or more could be done.
- Report hazards with a high risk to the appropriate person.
- Deal with hazards with a low risk according to workplace policies and legal requirements.
- Review your assessment of that hazard regularly and revise it if necessary.

## Core unit link

Lots of the evidence you will collect for these questions can link back to your core units. The evidence for questions 1 and 2 may link to unit 201, performance indicators 4 and 5, as you will need to read written material and extract the main points.

For questions 3 and 5 again check whether this evidence links to unit 201 PIs 4 and 5, as well as unit 202, PIs 6–8, because health and safety is part of your employment rights and responsibilities.

Question 5 may link to unit 201, PIs 9 and 10, if you use your assessments to confirm effective working methods and if you identify and report problems when they arise. Because your written information should be accurate and clear and meet the needs of other people this should also link to unit 201, PIs 2 and 6.

Your evidence may also prove that you support diversity and link to unit 202, PI 11 – for example if you suggested that a warning notice should be translated into another language.

## Evidence collection

1 Make a list of workplace policies and other documents produced by your employer which relate to health and safety in your workplace. State also where they are kept. You may have been given some of these at induction, while others may be in a workplace manual for general reference.

2 Identify which policies directly affect you and are relevant to the way you do your work.

3 List the people who are responsible for health and safety in your workplace and say where they are located. Give examples of situations in which you would need to contact at least one of the people on your list.

4 Obtain a copy of your job description and highlight any specific health and safety duties you must carry out. Be prepared to discuss these in more detail with your assessor.

5 Assess your own workplace and your own method of working. Ideally you will do this on a regular basis and keep a written record that you can discuss with your assessor. During each assessment you should

   a Identify any working practices that you do – or which relate to your job – that could harm yourself or other people.

   b Identify any other aspects of the workplace that could harm yourself or other people – including visitors.

   c Decide which hazards have the highest risk and give reasons for your decisions.

   d Decide which hazards have low risk and explain how you must deal with these to comply with workplace policies and legal requirements.

   e Review your assessment after action has been taken.

# Reducing risks to health and safety

In this final section of the unit you will apply the knowledge you have learned to obtain evidence to show how you personally reduce risks by your own conduct, by personal presentation and by the actions you take.

## Working policies and your job role

Certain policies and procedures affect all staff. Others will relate only to certain job roles. All policies and procedures are regularly reviewed and updated, usually as a result of staff consultation. You should always ensure that you have the most recently issued policy. It is good practice to throw away the old one when it has been updated, to prevent confusion. You will normally be able to check the date of issue or the version number at the top or foot of the document.

Examples of policies and procedures likely to affect the working practices of administrators are shown in the table below.

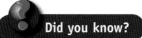

**Did you know?**

The **safety policy** states the arrangements for putting the policy into practice. **Procedures** state what you must do in a certain situation. These determine working practices in the workplace to ensure that the aims of the policy and the firm's legal responsibilities are met.

| Examples of health and safety policies and procedures | |
| --- | --- |
| **Area covered by policies** | **Examples** |
| Accidents and emergencies | • The procedures to follow in the case of a fire or other type of emergency evacuation (e.g. gas leak or bomb scare)<br>• What to do if an accident occurs and accident reporting<br>• First aid training, facilities and equipment |
| Employee health and welfare | • Smoking, alcohol and drugs in the workplace<br>• Workplace bullying, harassment and victimisation<br>• Maximum working hours, breaks and rest periods |
| Employee security | • Cash handling and banking procedures<br>• What to do if you feel threatened by a customer<br>• Security and protection for late night working |

| Examples of health and safety policies and procedures Continued | |
|---|---|
| **Area covered by policies** | **Examples** |
| Working practices | • The siting, use and maintenance of machinery and equipment<br>• General housekeeping and cleaning<br>• Use of computers and other IT-related equipment<br>• Hazard reporting |
| Legal compliance with specific Health and Safety Regulations | • Risk assessments<br>• Maintenance and checking of electrical equipment<br>• First-aid training, regular assessments of facilities and equipment<br>• Storage and handling of hazardous substances<br>• Use and storage of personal protective equipment<br>• Manual handling (includes lifting, moving and stacking of materials and equipment) |

# Suppliers' and manufacturers' instructions for the safe use of equipment, materials and products

As an administrator you will probably use all these items on a daily basis.

- **Equipment**. Many items will be electrical and there will be specific instructions for their use – photocopier, fax machine, electric stapler, VDU, printer, scanner, shredder, telephone, calculator etc.
- **Materials**. These are the consumable items you use – paper, envelopes, filing folders, sticky tape, Post-it notes etc.
- **Products**. These cover any other items you use as part of your job – liquid paper, scissors, hole punch, safety stool – as well as those that are not a fundamental part of your job (e.g. the office jug kettle and coffee percolator!).

Obviously trying to use a new photocopier or scanner is likely to cause more problems than switching on a new jug kettle if you can't be bothered to read the instructions. And you might think it is totally unnecessary to read instructions telling you how to use a pack of paper – until a paper jam

**Did you know?**

According to TV presenter Jeremy Clarkson, a recent manual for a mobile phone was longer than the one originally issued with the supersonic plane Concorde! This puts people off reading manuals, especially if they have to plough through 50 pages of information to find out how to do a basic operation. Instead they prefer to experiment by stabbing a few buttons to see what happens next!

indicates that something's wrong and you suddenly find that paper has a 'wrong' and a 'right' side!

This is the problem with ignoring instructions. Everything may go smoothly until the day you are frantically busy, with numerous deadlines to meet. That is the moment when the fax machine will whirr and die, the photocopier will jam and your VDU will blank out on you. And – because you've never looked at the manual – you won't have a clue what to do.

For that reason – and for others as you will see below – you are well advised to check the main points of the manufacturers instructions relating to equipment, materials and products you already use. Occasionally you may find that there is a slight discrepancy between the instructions in the manual and one of your workplace policies. In this case you should report the difference to your line manager or safety representative and ask for guidance on the correct action to take.

## Over to you

1 Answer the following statements as being True or False. In each case back up your answer with the reason or correct response. If you are stuck, the answers are given on the CD-ROM.

   a The new, large photocopier shouldn't be placed in the corner next to the wall.

   b You should switch off the fax machine if there is a thunderstorm.

   c Photocopier paper needs to be stored in a damp atmosphere.

**Over to you** Continued

**d** It is useful to have a photocopy of the 'troubleshooting' pages of each equipment manual stored in your desk or in a special file.

**e** If your printer jams, you release the paper by pulling and tugging it.

**f** If your manual goes missing, you solve the problem by asking your supervisor for help.

**g** Your photocopier should be serviced every week.

**h** Safety advice on how to use a shredder is essential reading.

**i** A telephone handset should be wiped with a damp cloth.

**j** You can refill an electric stapler safely without switching off the power.

**k** If your VDU doesn't work, ring your helpdesk or IT supplier immediately.

**l** You can safely use a red fire extinguisher on a fire involving electrical equipment.

**2** Bearing in mind your score for the previous question, list the equipment, materials and products you regularly use in your job and identify the manuals or instructions you need to obtain or check. Then state where each one is kept.

**3** Refer to the table on page 181–182 showing the type of policies most likely to affect administrators and identify those that relate to your own job role. Check whether there are any additional policies that relate to you but which are not mentioned in the table.

### Core unit link

Again your evidence collected here can link back to your core units. Evidence on your workplace policies should link to unit 202, performance indicator 2, and you can also link the procedures you follow to unit 201, PI 14. If you need to seek guidance because you are unsure about any aspect of the policy, say who helped you and link your evidence to unit 202, PI 5.

There is also the opportunity to obtain evidence on effective working methods and the identification and reporting of problems as they arise. This evidence links to unit 201, PIs 9 and 10.

### Evidence collection

**1** Obtain a copy of the most recent workplace policies for your job role and identify the procedures you follow. Write a brief summary stating how each of these affects your working practices.

**2** Obtain manufacturers' or suppliers' instructions you need or use as part of your work.

**a** Identify occasions when you have found these helpful and when you have used them – or might need to use them.

**b** Explain how you use them to make sure you use equipment, materials and products safely.

**c** Check whether there are any discrepancies between these and the working policies you must follow. List any that you find and report them, in writing, to your line manager or safety rep. Keep a copy of your document for your assessor.

### What if?

What should you do if there are no differences between workplace policies and suppliers' or manufacturers' instructions that you need to report? In this case your assessor can ask you 'what if?' questions to find out what you *would* do if this happened.

## Safe working practices for your own job role

**Remember**

Anyone can make a mistake, but this shouldn't be repeated time after time – especially if it could affect other people, too.

Adopting safe working practices means not only following workplace policies and manufacturer's instructions but also using your common sense and concentrating when you are working. Most people do this most of the time; but there are always days when we are rushing, stressed or distracted.

As you look down the following list, you may like to identify which actions would only hurt you and which would hurt your colleagues as well:

- not switching off equipment when you should do so
- not using appropriate equipment, such as a safety stool
- not reading or following instructions
- disregarding explicit safety procedures (e.g. by using the lift during an emergency evacuation)

- trying to repair a fault or problem you haven't been trained to do
- not using protective clothing when told to do so
- being careless and untidy (e.g. leaving desk drawers open and your personal belongings lying around).

Generally, safe working practices that will always minimise risks include:

- complying with instructions, regardless of what you feel or think you know
- walking around a building and up/down stairs, never running
- lifting only acceptable weights and bending your knees, not your back
- carrying only a small number of items so your view is never obscured
- closing drawers of cupboards, desks and filing cabinets immediately after use
- keeping your working area clean and tidy and putting your personal belongings away
- putting rubbish in the correct container
- stacking items safely
- using the correct equipment for the job
- only doing what you have been trained to do and asking for help when you need it
- carrying out a regular self-assessment in relation to your VDU and workstation (see below).

## Snapshot – A pain in the neck!

Martina Phillips is an Upper Limb Specialist Nurse at a large NHS hospital. Every week she sees numerous patients who have been referred to the clinic by their doctors because they have a musculoskeletal disorder (MSD). This term covers problems with muscles, joints and tendons all over your body. Martina specialises in upper-limb disorders (ULDs), such as stiff necks, swollen wrists and other problems with hands, wrists, arms and shoulders. These can occur if you sit at a computer for hours in a stooped position, repeatedly carrying out the same keyboard or mouse actions or continually trying to speak to someone with the telephone wedged between your shoulder and neck to keep your hands free!

The situation is made worse when job pressures mean that employees don't take sufficient breaks because they worry they won't complete their work. For the employer this is obviously self-defeating if the person is then ill and takes time of work. According to the HSE, each person suffering from MSD takes almost 18 days off work over a period of 12 months. In addition, 11 million working days a year are lost because of ULDs and bad backs caused by incorrect lifting.

How likely are you to suffer from MSD?

Do the quiz below to assess your personal level of risk in relation to MSD.

## Quiz

1 When you arrive at your desk do you:
   a Check your chair and VDU and, if necessary, adjust these to your personal needs
   b just start work?

2 The document you are currently using is:
   a alongside your keyboard on the workstation
   b some distance away, so you have to strain your neck to read it.

3 Your screen is:
   a clean and facing away from the window
   b a bit grubby and you can see your reflection.

4 Your feet are:
   a some distance from the floor
   b resting on the floor or a footrest.

5 When you are using your keyboard your forearms are:
   a roughly horizontal
   b angled downwards or upwards.

6 Your eyes are:
   a at about the same height as the top of the VDU
   b halfway up the VDU.

7 Your legs are:
   a able to move freely
   b restricted because of the clutter under your desk.

8 Your mouse is:
   a within easy reach
   b an arm's length away.

9 Your back is:
   a straight and supported by the chair back
   b hunched forward – you're slouching!

10 If a heavy box of paper is left next to your desk would you:
   a get a trolley or wait until someone can help you move it
   b lift it out of the way or bend down and push it.

11 If you are lifting something do you:
   a bend your knees and crouch down
   b bend your back and reach down.

**Over to you** Continued

12 At the end of the average day do you:
  a  feel great
  b  ache all over.

Each (a) option is the correct way to work. For each (b) you chose, change your habits before you find yourself with aches and pains every day!

# Personal presentation and health and safety

**Did you know?**

It is quite legal to have a dress code or guidelines on what to wear in the workplace provided this is not discriminatory. If you ignore the guidelines and subsequently have an accident, you might find that any compensation you could otherwise be entitled to would be drastically reduced.

Administrators may have to comply with dress code guidelines in the workplace but are less likely than some other employees to have to follow specific personal presentation requirements. If you handled food, for example, your employer would doubtless specify that you must wear special clothes, tie your hair back and wear a hat, hairnet or cap. If you refused then, quite legally, you could be dismissed.

The guidelines may include reference to the following issues:
- **Dangling chains or bracelets** could get caught in equipment or machinery. The same applies to scarves and neckties and can relate to equipment like a shredder just as easily as machinery in a workshop.
- **Inappropriate footwear**, such as very high-heeled shoes or sandals, would be a particular hazard if you frequently had to walk through workshop areas.
- **Very tight or short skirts** allow very little freedom of movement without becoming positively indecent. They may not distract you but they will certainly distract other people around you.
- **Low-cut, skimpy or crop tops** are inappropriate for much the same reason.
- **Distressed jeans** with frayed edges could easily catch on machinery or equipment, as could long flowing hair and large hooped ear-rings – particularly on male members of staff!

# Personal conduct and health and safety

Personal conduct relates to your behaviour, working habits and general attitude towards other people.

Behaving responsibly doesn't mean that you can't enjoy a joke. It means you know the types of thing that are genuinely funny and those that are not. Nothing is funny if it could, or will, endanger either you or someone else.

## How to ... Have impecable personal conduct

- Obey evacuation procedures promptly when you hear the alarm – even when it's raining and you were in the middle of an urgent task. (Think of it as a good excuse for a break – if you can!)

- Never work for too long at your computer without taking a break or changing your activity.

- Always consider the possible consequences of your actions before you decide to take a shortcut.

- Always tidy up after yourself and take your turn with the 'chores', such as making coffee and washing up the cups.

- Ask when you're not sure, and always say 'please' and 'thank you' when someone helps you.

- Never knowingly take actions that will endanger yourself and others – and apologise if you do so by mistake.

- Always report risks you notice to the correct person, if you can't deal with them yourself.

- The 'acid test' is that you would be described as thoughtful and considerate by your colleagues. If you are good fun as well, that's a real bonus!

## Evidence collection

1   Explain how you ensure that your personal conduct never endangers the health and safety of yourself or anyone else.

2   Describe how you make sure your personal presentation at work ensures the health and safety of yourself and others, meets any legal duties and is in accordance with workplace policies.

3   Obtain witness testimony from your line manager to confirm that your personal conduct and presentation is always appropriate and in accordance with all health and safety requirements, and that you are willing to make changes when these are necessary.

**Core unit link**

This evidence should link to unit 202, performance indicators 23–25, because you are behaving in a way that supports effective working.

## Case study A risky business

Kelly Sykes is an administrator in a large vehicle hire firm which rents out cars and vans. There is a workshop behind the office block where vehicles are serviced and valeted by a mechanic and his assistant. There is a temporary parking area in front of the office where customers leave or collect their vehicles. All the vehicles are kept in a parking bay at one side of the building which is locked at night with CCTV cameras for additional security.

Over the past few weeks there have been a number of minor accidents on the premises involving employees slipping or tripping. Kelly was asked to carry out a risk assessment and started by asking the staff who had already slipped where and how this happened. Then she walked around the buildings and noted any conditions that could contribute to a slip or trip. She noticed that part of the workshop was poorly lit and this was made worse because a bulb had failed, there was oil on the floor which made it slippery and several tools had been left lying around. There was also a discarded cigarette end on the floor, even though smoking is not allowed in the workshop.

In the narrow office corridor the cleaner had left the mop and bucket she had been using to clean the toilets. The floor in the toilets was still wet but there was no sign to alert anyone. Similarly a sign at the front of the building was missing. This used to alert visitors to a small step at the entrance and said that a portable ramp was available if required. In the office two waste-bins were overflowing and there were two large boxes of paper next to one desk.

### Questions

1   *Kelly started by talking to the staff who had already had an accident. Why did she do this?*

**Case study** Continued

2   What are the usual steps of identifying and evaluating risks in a risk assessment? Look back to page 179–180 if you are unsure.

3   List the hazards that Kelly found.

4   For each hazard on your list, decide whether the risk is high or low, bearing in mind the people who may be injured and the type of injury that could be caused.

5   Some of the hazards relate to working conditions that could be improved. Others related to working practices. Decide which are which and suggest recommendations for eliminating or reducing the risk in each case.

6   Why is it important that the firm has a portable ramp available if necessary? If you are stuck, look back at unit 202, page 141, for ideas.

7   Safety signs are erected when a risk cannot be eliminated. Suggest three signs that Kelly might recommend. If you are stuck for ideas go to www.safetyshop.com or www.seton.co.uk for inspiration!

Suggested answers are given on the CD-ROM.

# Your scope and responsibility for putting right risks

On page 172 you saw that there are two actions you can take if you are faced with a risk. You can report it or deal with it yourself. Normally you will be able to deal with risks relating to 'good housekeeping' and those relating to your own working area, such as:

- the way you have your workstation or working area organised
- your own behaviour and personal conduct
- your personal presentation
- your own working practices, from your posture to the way you use routine equipment.

You also saw that there are risks you should report – from broken furniture or damaged flooring to problems with equipment and machinery. Responsible employers will take action promptly, particularly if the risk factor is high. Unfortunately some employers do not take enough care and this can result in accidents that are serious enough to lead to prosecutions – as you will see below.

# Workplace procedures for handling risks

Your workplace policy will state the procedure for reporting risks, as you saw on page 176. It should also encourage you to make suggestions if you

**Remember**

There is a danger that as you become more familiar with dealing with health and safety issues you become complacent or over-confident. This is a risk in itself. It occurs when you think any new risk is a challenge you can cope with, regardless of whether you really can.

have good ideas for reducing risks to health and safety. You need to know the correct person to contact in each case. You also need to know the types of risk that are outside your responsibility and which you must report.

In a small organisation you will have to notify your supervisor or your manager who will decide whether the risk can be reduced easily or whether expert assistance is required.

## Changing places

*Your assessor may ask you how you would apply your knowledge of health and safety if you changed your job in the future. The examples below should give you some ideas, as each administrator is involved with different types of hazard and risk and has different responsibilities for putting them right.*

Elaine works as an administrator in a primary school. She is always on the lookout for risks that would affect the children and for hazards accidentally caused by them. Wherever possible she is expected to put these right herself.

Bryn works for a large chemical company. There are strict procedures all staff must follow if they enter restricted areas, because of the processes that are used and the substances produced. Any hazards in those areas must be immediately reported to a foreman or a security guard.

Tasnim works for an IT consultancy with offices on the third floor of a large building. The building itself and the entrance, lift, corridors and cloakrooms are communal areas that are kept clean and maintained by the management company responsible for the building, who also insist that they must be informed about any hazards that are identified.

Justine works for a firm of debt collectors. There is a specially toughened glass screen which separates the receptionist from the waiting area in case any callers are particularly angry or threatening. There is also a panic button to summon help if needed. Justine has been on a training course that helps her to deal with callers in a calm manner and to recognise signs of hostility that indicate she must get assistance.

Caroline works in a large hotel. She must note down any hazards reported by guests or her colleagues and ensure that these are followed up promptly, either by maintenance or the housekeeping staff. Staff are also encouraged to note any visitors who may be acting suspiciously or loitering in the area and report them to security.

1 For any *one* person listed above, identify the differences he or she would find if moving to your organisation and doing your job.

2 For any *one* person listed above, say how you would need to adapt your skills if you did his or her job rather than your own.

## Evidence collection

1 Carry out an assessment of a specific area linked to the types of accident that could occur in your workplace. Like Kelly, you could assess your workplace for risks related to slipping and tripping. Or, in agreement with your supervisor, you could choose a different area more relevant to your organisation's current needs.

2 Talk to relevant people and assess the area by observation. List all your findings. Decide which of these relate to working conditions and which to working practices.

3 Put right any risks that you can that are within the scope of your job responsibilities. Pass on your suggestions for reducing other risks to your line manager or other nominated person.

4 Summarise the activities you carried out as well as the outcome for your assessor.

## What if?

What should you do if either:

- there are no risks for you to put right whilst you are taking your award
- because there are no risks, there are no suggestions you can pass on for reducing these?

In both these cases your assessor can ask 'what if?' questions to check that you are competent in these areas. The practice work you have done in the 'Over to you' and case study sections of this unit should have given you the confidence to answer any questions you are asked.

## Core unit link

If you consult other people and question points you are unsure about, this will cross-reference to unit 201, performance indicator 1. If you contribute to discussions, remember to cross-reference this to unit 201, PI 3.

If you agree a realistic target and timescale for doing this work with your supervisor, plan how to make the best use of your time and other resources, keep him or her informed of your progress and meet your deadlines or take appropriate action, you can cross-reference this to unit 201, PIs 7, 8, 11 and 12. You should also take responsibility for your own work and follow the agreed procedures and therefore be able to link this to unit 201, PIs 13 and 14.

Both for this activity and others in this unit, you should be able to prove that you set high standards for your work, treat other people with honesty, respect and consideration, and help and support them when you can. If you can give examples to prove this then you can cross-reference these to unit 201, PIs 20, 24 and 25.

## Key skills reminder

If you are taking Key Skills awards, remember to discuss with your tutor or trainer how your evidence for this unit could also count towards those awards.

# Manage customer relations

### Unit summary and overview

This option unit has two sections:

- identify customer needs and expectations

- deliver services

The main role of all administrators is to provide support services. These may be provided direct to external customers who visit the business or make contact by telephone, email or fax. In many cases administrators provide services mainly, or exclusively, to internal customers. These are colleagues in the organisation who are dependent on the administrator for a service, such as providing information or carrying out a specific task. Both types of customer are important – as you will see as you progress through this unit.

In this unit you will learn how to build positive working relationships with customers and how to identify and confirm their needs. This will help you to provide services to meet both their needs and their expectations. You will also find out how to resolve or refer complaints if a problem does occur.

# Identify customer needs and expectations

To achieve this unit you need to be able to manage your customer relations. You 'manage' your relations only when you are in control of situations involving a customer; and this happens only when you can deal with the majority of customers you meet professionally and courteously. Of course, anyone can occasionally have a bad experience or a very difficult person to cope with, but you are less likely to have serious problems if you have the skills and the confidence to deal with all your customers helpfully and positively.

It also helps, of course, if you are one of those people who gets a 'buzz' from personally helping people, because then you will always put in the extra effort that often makes all the difference when you are dealing with a customer.

## Over to you

If you can, carry out this activity in a group, and then compare your findings.

Over the next week, on every occasion when you are a customer yourself, review what happened, how you felt afterwards and why you felt this way. Then decide whether the experience was 'excellent', 'dreadful' or 'average'. Your contacts may include:

- shop assistants

- anyone you telephone for information or assistance

- your colleagues at work, if you are asking for something

- anyone who provides you with a service – a bank cashier, dentist, doctor, hairdresser etc.

Perhaps over the week you will have at least one very good experience, possibly one terrible one and several that are 'average'. If all of them seem to be average at the moment then think back to experiences in the past when you have been really overjoyed or very disgruntled as a customer.

Aim to have three different experiences to discuss with other members of your group, or with your tutor or trainer. In each case give reasons for your judgements. Then decide the key factors that please and annoy you when you are a customer yourself.

## Did you know?

Managing your customers doesn't mean knowing the answer to every question you could be asked. It does mean giving every customer a good experience, whether you can do much for them or not.

# What is a 'customer' – and who are yours?

A customer is anyone who has the right to ask or expect you to provide a service. You may think that this can mean virtually everyone, but that is not quite true. Your internal customers are those people at work who can ask you to do something that is part of your job role or overall responsibilities. For that reason you can probably include your boss and the cleaner, too, if he or she asks you to tidy your desk so that it can be cleaned. Colleagues who ask you for a favour are not 'customers' – such as someone asking you to swop a day off – because you have the right to refuse a favour. With a customer's request, you normally don't have that right. If you are too busy to help then you should refer the request to someone else. The only time you should refuse is when, by meeting the request, you would have to do something that is not normally allowed or is outside your range of responsibilities.

# Why effective and efficient customer service is important

Businesses that pride themselves on superb customer service to their external customers are often said to be **customer-facing**. This is because they put the customer at the centre of everything they do. They consider the possible effect of every decision on the external customer – and this also includes the way the staff treat each other and respond to their internal customers. Staff are encouraged to respond rapidly to all enquiries and requests by colleagues because they know that this will always influence the quality of service being provided to an external customer. If Rashid, in Sales, rings Lucy – who works in Design – and asks for information he can expect a prompt response because she knows that he will need this for a reason, such as responding to a customer enquiry. So the way Lucy responds to Rashid directly affects that external customer's experience. If she takes two days to find the information, or gives it to Rashid with several pages missing, it is unlikely Rashid can respond efficiently. This could result in potential new business being lost. At

*A rapid response to colleague enquiries influences the quallity of service given to external customers.*

the end of the day, customer-facing organisations normally win more orders from external customers, and this is one of several reasons why businesses are so keen to provide superb customer service.

If you work in the private sector you should realise that your organisation will always be keen to increase the number of orders it receives because this directly affects profits. It is much cheaper to increase customers by encouraging repeat business and through recommendations than it is to keep advertising. And the main way to achieve this is to give the customer a superb experience. If you work in the public sector it is likely that your employer will have specific customer service standards to achieve – as you will know if you work for a hospital or your local council. All organisations also prefer to receive letters of praise than complaints, let alone read critical reviews about themselves in the press! So no matter which sector you work in, you can expect excellent customer service to be emphasised.

---

### Top ten benefits of effective and efficient customer service

1 All staff know that they can depend on their colleagues for prompt and accurate information.

2 Customer enquiries are handled quickly, accurately and professionally. This encourages customer loyalty, so repeat orders are gained.

3 Satisfied customers recommend the organisation to friends, relatives and other contacts, which results in even more orders.

4 Less time is spent by staff dealing with complaints and problems or having to soothe annoyed customers.

5 There is far less chance of damaging negative publicity.

6 Building a relationship with customers gives staff the opportunity to promote the company and its products or services. Listening to feedback gives them the chance to find out valuable information that can help the business.

7 The image and reputation of the business is constantly enhanced as word gets around.

8 The organisation flourishes as its profits and/or demand for its services increases, which results in better pay and promotion prospects for staff.

9 Individual staff have greater job satisfaction because they know they are doing a good job.

10 There is greater job security – companies with many satisfied customers are unlikely to go out of business.

---

**Did you know?**

There are many benefits of providing effective customer service. Check out the top ten opposite!

---

# The importance of positive working relationships with customers

A positive working relationship means that two people work together to find the best solution to meet their joint needs. They want to help each other to obtain the best possible result. This happens only in situations where the factors given below apply.

> **Key factors in a positive working relationship**
>
> ✓ Both people treat each other with respect.
> ✓ They recognise each other's needs, concerns and feelings.
> ✓ They focus on the situation and the facts.
> ✓ They trust each other.
> ✓ They look for ways to solve problems – they don't create them.
> ✓ They know they can rely on each other.
> ✓ They are honest yet tactful.
> ✓ They communicate!

Let's look at how this works in practice. Shahida works in a college office and carries out admin tasks for two section heads, Sara and Tom. She is currently involved in setting up interviews for prospective students to visit the college and meet members of staff.

Sara always seems to be rushing around and too busy to talk. Sometimes Shahida struggles to find her if she has a query or problem. Shahida is also a little frightened of Sara, who can be impatient and curt if she thinks a question is irrelevant. Sara puts her interview schedules in a basket in the office for Shahida to process, but her writing is difficult to read. Sometimes she changes her mind about dates at the last minute, which causes Shahida extra work if she has already prepared the interview letters.

Tom, on the other hand, tries to pop in to talk to Shahida every day. They discuss her workload and how long it will take to complete the outstanding letters, so the students are given enough warning about their interview dates.

*Some of your coustomers will be easier to deal with than others.*

Shahida likes dealing with Tom because he is often funny and she knows she can talk to him frankly if she has a problem.

It doesn't take a genius to decide which one of these working relationships is positive and which is not! On the basis that everyone gains in this situation you would think that everyone would aim to be a Tom and no one would want to be a Sara, but – as you will know yourself – life isn't like that.

## How to ... Build positive working relationships with (most!) customers

- Always give the impression that you are delighted to be dealing with them (whether you are or not) and want to help.

- Treat each person as an individual. With a new external customer find out his or her name as soon as you can. Using it in the conversation makes the discussion more personal and helps you to remember the name. Then if external customers become 'regulars' you can impress them by immediately proving you remember them.

- Make sure you understand exactly what you are being asked to do by taking notes and checking that the details are correct.

- If you cannot carry out the request then always explain why this is the case and suggest an alternative.

- Focus on trying to meet your customer's needs, even if this means being quite inventive or doing something differently. So long as you don't overstep your area of responsibility, this is fine. If you are not sure, check with your boss first.

- Never promise something you cannot deliver.

- Never let your customer down. If there is an unexpected problem or difficulty then let the customer know as soon as possible, and suggest a solution if possible.

- Keep customers informed if a situation is ongoing. You are better communicating too often than too little.

- Take pride in building up your contacts and keeping them happy.

## Different types of customer

Tom is an ideal internal customer. He is reasonable, nice, calm and courteous. Unfortunately it does not follow that ideal customers always have their needs met. Nor is it the case that you will always deal with this type of person. So how do you build a positive working relationship with someone who is rather less than your ideal choice?

First, it helps if you can see this as a challenge, rather than a problem. This affects your own state of mind and changes your attitude. Second, you have to decide where the boundaries lie. It is one thing to be treated rather dismissively, it is quite another to be openly insulted. You should never expect to have to deal with open aggression or threats by anyone – and most organisations will have specific policies that state this.

But some customers are just hard work rather than openly hostile. In fact, they may think they are being perfectly reasonable and be amazed if anyone told them otherwise. So how do you cope with this type of person? There is no magic solution because each person is different, but the following techniques normally help.

● People are often less reasonable because they are totally focused on their own needs, rather than anyone else's. We all tend to do this if we are in a panic, frantically busy or having a really bad day. You might like to think back to the occasions when you have been less than reasonable about something and consider why that was.

● It can help to look at the issue from the customer's point of view. If you focus on that person's particular needs and try to analyse why he or she behaves in a certain way, you may respond to the person more appropriately. Sometimes acknowledging that you recognise his or her concern helps enormously, as some people simply need lots of reassurance.

● Always remember that you cannot change the way another person reacts to a situation, you can only change the way *you* respond.

This may help you the next time you deal with any customer who is overly fussy, a bit bossy, is panicking about something or checking every detail three times. In any of these cases, being understanding and providing reassurance is just as valuable as proving you are efficient. If this doesn't work then you may have to be more assertive – to make it quite clear, politely, what you can and cannot do (see unit 201, page 68).

With an internal customer, when you are satisfied you have tried everything possible to identify and meet the person's needs, and worked to build a positive relationship, then the final step may be to have a quiet word with that person (or your supervisor) to discuss how *your* needs also need to be recognised for the relationship to work.

**Snapshot – Getting off on the right foot**

It is hard to build a positive working relationship with customers who are irritable because they have waited a long time for attention. A useful tip is to acknowledge a new arrival by smiling and nodding 'Hello', but organisations that deal with large numbers of customers often use more sophisticated methods. If you have picked out a numbered ticket to join a queue, seen your name appear on an LCD display when your turn is due or heard a computerised voice telling you 'Cashier number 3 please' then you are being 'handled' by an automated queue management system. Other tactics involve distractions such as advertising screens, music and television.

Some companies are going even further. In June 2005, HSBC introduced its own in-house radio station, HSBC Live, in 400 of its busiest branches. This plays a mixture of popular music, news, sport and weather forecasts as well as providing information on products and services. The programmes will be produced by Immedia Broadcasting, run by former Radio 1 DJ Bruno Brookes. The bank says that an added benefit is that the noise masks personal information exchanged between bank customers and staff.

The Independent Banking Advisory Service has criticised the idea, arguing that it is more important to reduce queues than play music. At May's annual general meeting several customers complained to the HSBC chairman about long queues, particularly at busy lunchtimes. Since then the bank says it has recruited an extra 1000 staff to help customers.

Certainly HSBC is not the first organisation to introduce its own radio station. Dixons, Spar, Iceland and Lloyds Pharmacy also operate their own live radio stations, courtesy of Immedia Broadcasting. How effective this is when you are in a rush and there are no staff available to help you is another matter!

# Identifying and confirming customer needs

Many organisations have specific procedures for identifying customer needs. As an obvious example, if you visit a restaurant you will normally be given a menu or shown a list of dishes that are on offer. You can then choose what you want. The person who serves you will answer any queries you have and confirm your order. It is as simple as that.

Organisations that sell complex products or services normally train their sales staff in the best questions to ask to establish a customer's needs. They then aim to meet these, wherever possible, from the range on offer. If a product or service is highly technical, in-depth questioning will not normally be your job, as an administrator, even though you may be a key point of contact whenever a specialist is not available. Quickly establishing and confirming any customer's needs – whether internal or external – means that you are far more likely to respond appropriately and quickly to the request. Your customer will also be more confident that his or her needs will be met. It is therefore useful to have a few techniques up your sleeve to enable you to do this with ease.

## Stage 1: Identify your customer

Customers vary in terms of:
- the degree to which they know what they want or need
- their ability to communicate this information to you
- their manner and attitude
- their status or importance.

Some customers will be well-informed and have specific requirements. Others may not have a clue and expect you to guide or advise them. In between are those customers who have a good basic knowledge but expect you to make suggestions and recommendations.

Obviously all customers are important but it is sensible to realise that those with VIP status should be given top priority!

## Stage 2: Respond accordingly

### Find out

Your customers will all want prompt and top-quality service. How would you summarise the other main needs of your customers?

The first step is to establish whether your customer is already well-informed and knows exactly what he or she needs. You can do this by careful questioning. If you have forgotten about this, then turn back to unit 201 and re-read pages 8–9. Remember that questioning isn't an inquisition. Ask only questions that are relevant and suggest appropriate alternatives if these would be better than the customer's original ideas.

Questioning becomes even more important if you are dealing with a customer who struggles to communicate his or her needs to you. Experience helps as you will be more practised at identifying key areas related to your job or the service that your customers often don't know. In this case it is useful to draw up a quick checklist of questions if one doesn't exist already.

When you have identified the customer's needs then confirming them is absolutely essential. This means going through your list to make sure there are no misunderstandings and nothing has been forgotten. It is always better to confirm what is required in writing and email is often ideal for this. Keep any written records safely. These are especially valuable if there are any problems later (see page 213).

Whereas a pleasant, friendly customer is always better to deal with, generally if you treat all customers courteously and show them that you are dealing with the situation professionally you will have few problems with manner and attitude. If you do, then refer to the notes on page 199. If this fails, ask your supervisor for help.

# Types of quality standards that are appropriate to your responsibilities

In May 2005, the Royal Mail was pleased to announce that it was meeting its target level for first class mail of 92.8 per cent next-day delivery. It was so delighted that it took out full-page advertisements in many national newspapers to thank its customers and its staff who, it claimed, were now delivering a first-class service.

For all Royal Mail employees these targets are part of their quality standards. To achieve quality targets mail needs to be delivered quickly and also needs to be delivered to the correct address. Many people work to meet advertised targets and quality standards – train drivers aim to get you to your destination quickly and safely; health service workers aim to treat

you effectively within specific waiting times; all educational and training establishments are checked to see whether they are meeting targets and quality standards – as you will know if you have ever been in a class that is visited by an Ofsted or ALI inspector who is checking and assessing the overall performance of the organisation.

As an administrator, your targets will depend on the type of organisation that employs you and your own job role.

## Organisational aims and quality standards

In this case the standards directly relate to the aims of the organisation and you are responsible for contributing to their achievement. For example, if you worked for the AA your targets would relate to helping stranded motorists quickly. If you worked in the health service they would involve meeting waiting-list targets and providing information to patients. If you worked for a college or training organisation then they would involve providing accurate and timely information to learners, trainees, employers and parents and preparing for any Ofsted or ALI inspections.

## Service standard targets

You may have specific service standard targets to meet – such as answering the telephone within six rings or completing photocopying requests within 24 hours. Even if these are not set down in writing, there will obviously be certain minimum expectations you must meet – such as obtaining the relevant information when you take a message and passing it on promptly; photocopying and collating documents correctly so that all pages are clear and readable; or delivering internal mail quickly and to the correct desk. For any task you do, for both internal and external customers, you should be able to identify appropriate quality standards without too much prompting!

# The role of procedures

Some organisations have procedures that set down exactly how staff should deal with customers. The aim is to ensure that all staff respond to common situations in the same way. In some companies, such as call centres, staff may even have a script they have to follow over the telephone, with a standard greeting and ending.

In most other organisations you have more flexibility, but there may still be procedures to ensure that all staff:

- respond to customers promptly
- greet and address them properly
- deal with complaints in the correct way
- keep company information confidential
- process returned goods appropriately.

## Responding to customers promptly

Customer service standards often include target response times. Here are some examples:

- All telephone calls must be answered within six rings.
- All telephone messages must be actioned within 24 hours.
- All letters must be acknowledged within four working days.
- All visitors to reception must be acknowledged immediately on arrival.
- No visitor with an appointment should have to wait more then ten minutes to be seen.

The aim, of course, is to minimise delays for customers – linked to preventing queuing problems you read about in the Snapshot on page 200–201. On a normal day, the targets should be quite achievable but difficulties may occur on other days, especially if you are very busy, short-staffed or trying to do several jobs at the same time. What can you do if three people are waiting to speak to you, the telephone is ringing and your boss signals he wants to speak to you? The tips in the box below may help you!

### How to ... Provide prompt attention to customers even on busy days

- Try not to panic. That never helped anyone!

- Deal with external customers before internal – unless your internal is both high-ranking and unreasonable! Most bosses would expect you to look after external customers first.

- Acknowledge customers who are waiting by looking at them and smiling, rather than pretending they don't exist. There is nothing worse than being totally ignored.

- If there is a delay, apologise and give a time estimate: 'I'm sorry to keep you, I'll be with you in five minutes.' Always over-estimate the delay – then you give the customer a pleasant surprise when you are free sooner than expected, rather than later.

- If the telephone rings, apologise to your customer, answer the call and keep it short. If necessary, arrange to call back. Even better, if you are busy dealing with several customers face-to-face then ask someone else to take the call.

- Start a conversation with a customer who has waited by apologising. 'I'm sorry to have kept you waiting' is normally enough – it recognises there has been a delay and your customer has been patient.

- Don't be too proud to ask for help on a very busy day if you are struggling to cope.

## Greeting and addressing customers

**Did you know?**

Some organisations prevent staff saying 'Can I help you?' because an awkward customer can answer 'How do I know?' 'May I help you?' is also disliked because the customer can answer 'No, you may not.' Theoretically, 'How may I help you?' means the customer has to give a positive response!

Many businesses have a 'corporate style' that they train staff to use, along with certain words and phrases. For example, you might be told to answer the telephone with a specific greeting, identify yourself by your first name and ask how you can help: 'Hello, Software Solutions, Jenny speaking, how may I help you?' You may also have to close the conversation in a standard way, such as 'Thank you for calling Software Solutions.'

Even if the script is less rigid, you may be told that it is important you give your name in a conversation with a customer. This makes the call more personal but also means that you have identified yourself in case the customer later wants to make a complaint!

Useful tips if there are no specific rules to follow are:
- Be formal rather than informal. No one is ever insulted by being called 'Sir' or 'Madam', no matter how old or young they are!
- Use a customer's name if you know it.
- Remember that 'Good morning' (or afternoon) is more formal than 'Hello' which is more formal than 'Hi'.
- Saying 'Goodbye, thank you for calling' is usually the best way of ending a telephone call with an external customer who called you. If your caller was internal, say 'goodbye' to senior or much older staff, rather than 'bye' – which is better kept for colleagues of your own age.

## Procedures for dealing with complaints

**Find out**

- What procedures do you have to follow in your job that relate to customer service?
- What are your company policies on dealing with complaints?

You can read about these later on page 216.

## Procedures for protecting confidential company information

You can read about these on in unit 202 on page 151–156. Turn back to refresh your memory.

## Procedures for processing returned goods

A specific procedure is essential for all customers to be treated fairly and equitably. It would obviously be unfair if one customer was given a full refund and the next one was refused, just because a different member of staff was on duty. It would also be illegal because all customers have the same protection in law. Under the Sale of Goods Acts 1979 and 1995 all goods sold must be:
- as described (e.g. if a bag is described as leather, it must be so)
- of satisfactory quality, in relation to the price paid, the description and its age
- fit for the purpose for which it is intended (e.g. an umbrella must open and be waterproof).

*Even sale goods must be fit for the intended purpose.*

If any of these terms are breached then the customer is entitled to a full refund and does not have to accept a voucher or credit note.

There is no obligation for businesses to accept returns because customers have simply changed their minds, but many do, provided that the goods are returned within a specific time (e.g. 28 days).

# Agreeing timescales, quality standards or procedures to follow

**Did you know?**

Text messages to customers rose by 37 per cent between 2004 and 2005 according to one survey. They are ideal for keeping customer updated about sale or service situations, such as offers to buy a house or when an engineer can visit.

Sometimes you will have no option about any of these.

- If there is a fixed, advertised timescale or quality standard then it is up to you to meet it. It is not normally negotiable without the express agreement of your boss or supervisor.
- The same applies to written procedures that all staff must follow.

However, there are obviously many situations when you have to use your own initiative. Examples are:

- You agree to find out information and call your customer back.
- You agree to send information through the post or email a customer.
- You agree to do a specific admin task for a customer, such as producing or photocopying a document.

## Deciding on a timescale

In this case you will normally try to negotiate a timescale for completion that meets the customer's needs and fits with your workload. The key word here is 'negotiate'. This means that you listen to what the customer wants and make positive suggestions, based on the urgency of the task, your existing workload and what needs to be done. Ideally, your customer should also listen to you and take your views on board so that a mutually convenient timescale is agreed. However, there are some hints and tips that might help you to achieve this, as you will see below.

## How to ... Negotiate a timescale

- Always start by finding out the timescale your customer expects. This may give you more time than you would have expected or allowed yourself!

- Be prepared to drop everything if the task is urgent and important and/or the customer is a VIP.

- Allow sufficient time to do the task properly and conscientiously when you are calculating how long it will take.

- Normally most customers are reasonable and appreciate that it takes time to do a job properly. It therefore helps if you explain the reason for the timescale you have suggested.

- Always remember that it is better to under-promise and over-deliver, rather than to make promises and fail to meet them.

- Try to make positive suggestions, rather than negative ones. For example, say 'If I receive the information by 10 a.m. tomorrow I can prepare the draft document by lunchtime', not 'I won't be able to do it until tomorrow lunchtime at the earliest' or 'I'm too busy to do it today.'

- If a customer continues to insist on a faster timescale than you can cope with, ask your supervisor for help. If the customer (or task) is very important, then your supervisor may arrange for other people to help or other work to be taken off you so that you can meet the request.

## Agreeing quality standards

High-quality work takes time. So, for example, it will take you longer to produce an error-free, perfect, final version of a document than a draft that your supervisor is going to read and amend. It is therefore important that you understand exactly what you are being asked to do, why you are being asked to do it and who it is for – otherwise there are two possible dangers:

- You can spend longer than is needed, either preparing something in more detail or to a higher quality standard than is required.
- You do the job too quickly, thinking that quality is not an essential issue, and are then criticised for sloppy work.

Despite this, always remember that there are certain minimum standards you should set yourself. *All* your work should be usable, first time round. If work comes back to you to be redone, then this should only be because the originator has changed his or her mind, not because you made a mess of it or didn't understand what was required.

## Deciding on procedures to follow

You will always be expected to follow formal written procedures. However, these are more a feature of large organisations and those in the public sector than small private businesses. If there are no formal procedures in your workplace that relate to a customer's request, and you are unsure what to do, your best strategy is to ask a more senior member of staff or your supervisor for advice.

**Remember**

Never be casual about a customer's name and title. Incorrect spelling and titles annoy most people. If you don't know whether a woman is married or single, leave out the title altogether or put 'Ms'.

### Over to you

1 Who are your customers? Make a list of the types of internal and external customers you deal with and the typical issues they contact you about. Then suggest three ways in which you can try to build a positive working relationship with them.

2 Find out more about queue management – which is commonly used by hospitals, health centres, local councils, benefit offices, banks and retailers – by checking out the following websites: www.postfield.co.uk (where you can take a quick tour of their Intelligent Queueing System), www.scancoin.co.uk, www.q-matic.co.uk and www.qmgroup.com.

3 If you work for a large organisation that uses such a system, identify the benefits both for customers and for staff. If you work for a small business, explain what action you take if you are busy and several people want to speak to you at once, to ensure that your customers are happy to see you.

4 Suggest four reasons why effective and efficient customer service is important to your employer.

5 The Department for Education and Skills (DfES) is keen to offer a good service to schools, colleges and all other types of learning institutions. It publishes its service standards online at www.dfes.gov.uk/cust_serv_standards. Access these and see how long you could expect to wait if you wrote to them or visited them about your own studies!

6 Check out online the service standards of at least two other organisations by entering the words 'service standards' or 'customer service standards' into a search engine such as Google.

7 Decide what you would do in each of the following situations and share your ideas with other members of your group or your tutor or trainer.

Some suggested responses are given on the CD-ROM.

**Over to you** Continued

**a** An internal customer of yours is always claiming that his requests are very urgent and that you should drop everything to do them.

**b** An internal customer always insists that her documents are not drafts so you take your time to make sure they are perfect. She then routinely changes them, so that you have several alterations to make.

**c** You are just about to leave for an urgent appointment when you take a call from an elderly customer who wants information. The more you try to rush the conversation the more confused the customer becomes.

## Core unit link

Analyse your log to see whether you have evidence to cross-reference to supporting diversity in unit 202, performance indicators 10–12. The reason for contact, the action you took and the tasks you have undertaken should also provide evidence that you help your organisation to achieve its purposes and values, and will therefore link to unit 202, PIs 1–4.

The evidence for question 3 should link to unit 201, PI 1–6, depending on the exact types of communication you have with your customers.

You should be able to link evidence relating to targets, guidelines and timescales and how these affect your working methods and performance to unit 201, PIs 7, 9, 12, 13 and 14.

Evidence on guidelines and procedures and employment legislation will link to unit 202, PIs 2, 6 and 7, as well as unit 201, PI 14.

## Evidence collection

1 Keep a log or work diary of customers you deal with over the next few weeks. Suggested headings are

- *Name of customer*
- *Internal or external*
- *Reason for contact*
- *Method of contact (phone, visit, email etc.)*
- *Service provided*
- *Other relevant comments*

Use the final column to record any special circumstances that applied, such as whether the task was very urgent or complex or whether there were any problems you had to resolve.

Be prepared to describe some of your encounters in more detail with your assessor. You will also find this information invaluable when you want to find examples of situations you have experienced.

2 Keep a detailed record of tasks you are asked to carry out by your internal customers, linked to your log above. You can do this by copying formal job request forms or by making your own notes. In each case say how you identified and confirmed your customer's needs and expectations.

3 Keep a record or a copy of any communications you have had with your customers, either internal or external. These can include emails, telephone messages, memos or other documents. Select three or four of these and describe how, in each case, you identified and confirmed the customer's needs and expectations.

4 List any customer service policies or standards with which you must comply when dealing with external customers and any targets that relate to

your job. State where they are usually kept. Attach to this list a description of how you used them to agree quality standards or timescales for two or three of your customers.

5 Find out any other guidelines or procedures you must follow when you are dealing with customers and any industry-specific legislation or regulations that relate to your role. List these in a short personal statement, countersigned by your supervisor.

# Deliver services

Even if you prove you can identify and confirm your customers' needs and expectations and agree the timescales, quality standards and procedures to follow, you now have to deliver the service. In most cases this will be straightforward and you will simply carry out the work you have been asked to do. Occasionally, though, you may experience problems – and so might your customers. Being able to deal with these and any complaints you receive both promptly and professionally is a key part of managing your customer relations.

## Providing the services you have agreed and meeting timescales and quality standards

On most occasions you will agree to do something, do it and then get on with your next job. Sometimes there may be problems – as you will see below – but hopefully this will only happen on isolated occasions. The majority of the time your customers will be pleased – if not delighted – with the work you have done. Or are they? Many people believe that you can't assume this unless you are told – and for that reason they make 'Customer Happy Calls' to find out!

As an example, Beverley works as an administrator for a local car dealership. Every time a vehicle is serviced or repaired it is logged in and out. A week after the vehicle has left the workshop Beverley rings the customer to check there are no problems, that the work was done promptly and that the customer is completely satisfied.

Sometimes, however, it may not be possible to provide a service that you agreed to perform. The reasons may include any of the following:

- The work or service was outside your area of responsibility, so you should never have agreed to do it in the first place.

**Find out**

Many firms routinely make **Customer Happy Calls** to external customers after a sale or service was provided, to check that the customer's needs and expectations were met.

You can also make them to your internal customers to find out what they thought of the job you did for them, obtain feedback on your performance and link this to your evidence for unit 201.

- You agreed to unrealistic timescales or quality standards that are unachievable with the resources, materials and skills you have.
- You need help from someone else who has let you down.
- An unexpected crisis has occurred – such as your computer has crashed, the photocopier has broken down, the Royal Mail is on strike or you have caught 'flu!

In the first two cases you have contributed to the problem by agreeing to provide a service that you cannot perform. You may have done this in good faith, to be helpful, and only later find that there is a problem. If you are dealing with an internal customer it is usually better to be honest and apologetic. If your customer is external you may have to be more diplomatic. You can hardly say that your sales staff are so disorganised it will take at least another week before anyone can make a visit. If you are stuck, you would be wise to explain the situation to your supervisor and ask for advice. This is far better than trying to bluff your way out of the situation.

If other people have let you down, then you still need to be diplomatic, particularly to your external customers. *Never* 'rubbish' your colleagues in public to get your own back no matter how annoyed you may be. Instead focus on finding a solution by using your common sense, imagination and ingenuity to remedy the problem. If you are ill, then you should tell your supervisor about any outstanding work you have to do, so that it can be given to someone else. The same applies if you are overwhelmed with jobs and feel that you cannot cope. If equipment breaks down or there is some other reason outside your control preventing you from providing a service as agreed, then try to find an alternative solution and keep any customers informed if there is a problem or delay that affects them. They may also suggest ways of getting round the problem.

**Remember**

Most customers are far more interested in what you are going to do to put a problem right than why it occurred in the first place.

Anyone who dials 999 to obtain police assistance in an emergency expects prompt and efficient service. Indeed, their life may depend on it. But the police receive many other calls to their communication centres or helpdesks that aren't necessarily an emergency. Lancashire police now grade all calls so that the response will be targeted to more precisely meet the needs of the caller.

Under the PASS (Public Assistance and Service Standards) scheme, calls are graded from 1 to 5 based on the type of incident and the vulnerability of the caller. A grade 1 call is an emergency with a target response time by a police officer of 15 minutes. At the other end of the scale a grade 5 is allocated to calls that can be dealt with by the communications centre or helpdesk without any need to involve a police officer.

The aim of the system it to provide a better quality of service to customers. This is particularly important given the number of calls handled by the police. In Lancashire alone over 800 000 incidents are recorded a year and it is important that resources be used as effectively as possible. No one wants police officers diverted on a non-essential errand when they are urgently needed elsewhere. The aim of PASS is to improve performance and provide a better service to the community.

# Problems customers may experience and who to report them to

Basically customers experience a problem if their needs and expectations are not met. Some types of problems you can try to solve yourself, others must be reported to your supervisor or the person responsible for a particular area in your organisation – such as the Sales Manager or Customer Service Manager.

Use the table below to identify the most usual type of response that can help to solve some common problems you may experience.

| Type of problem | Suggested response |
|---|---|
| Customer wants a product or service your organisation doesn't provide | Suggest appropriate substitutes/ refer to sales manager or sales staff/ suggest nearest outlet where item is available (builds good relationship even if a sale not made) |
| Customer wants technical details on a product or service | Refer to sales or technical person who can help and/or arrange to send literature |

| Type of problem | Suggested response |
|---|---|
| Customer asks for advice on the best product or service to buy | Unless you have an in-depth knowledge about your products/services, refer to a member of staff who can give personal assistance |
| Customer's requirements have changed since an order was placed | Take down the details and check whether the customer's request can be met<br>Refer the request to your supervisor if you are unsure |
| Customer is returning a faulty product | Under the Sale of Goods Acts, if the product is faulty then a full refund must be given (see page 206) |
| Customer is returning a product because it is no longer suitable/the customer has changed his/her mind | You are under no legal obligation to give a refund or exchange<br>Refer to your organisation's procedures for dealing with returns, or ask your supervisor |
| Customer has a very minor grumble or complaint | Apologise on behalf of your employer<br>Make a note of the complaint and tell your supervisor<br>If you can, put the problem right on your own |
| Customer is making a formal complaint | Refer to your company's complaints procedures (see next section) |

## Snapshot – Online customer service

Many businesses use their websites to provide customer services. This enables anyone with Internet access to get help or find information at any time. For example, on the Royal Mail website you can look up postcodes and track packages sent by Recorded Delivery or Special Delivery services.

Online information and assistance is obviously essential for businesses that have only an website presence, such as Amazon and Dell. If you buy a computer from Dell then you can track the delivery online and contact them online if you have a technical problem. The Amazon site also tells you what to do if you change your mind about an order or if you want to return a purchase. Apple is another company that effectively utilises online customer service.

If you own an Apple i-Pod and it breaks down, the instruction manual tells you to go to Service and Repairs on the Apple website. When you enter the place of purchase and the serial number of your i-Pod the system checks that your warranty (for a free repair) is still valid.

If your i-Pod passes this check you are then prompted to enter details about your name and address and, a few days later, you receive a special mailing box. You return your i-Pod in this box (post free) and then wait for it to be repaired and returned. Apple will email to say the package has been received, then to confirm they have identified the problem and finally to say that the package has been despatched back to you.

This procedure means that customer needs and expectations can be met as promptly and efficiently as possible. If you work for a business that deals with customers online, you may find it useful to check your website to find out what online information is provided for customers who have a query or experience a problem.

# Resolve or refer complaints in a professional manner and to a given timescale

There are two skills involved in handling complaints professionally. The first relates to the way you deal with the complaint; the second concerns the way you handle the person. For this reason, many organisations issue staff guidelines and procedures so that all complaints are dealt with in the same way.

## Procedures for dealing with customer complaints

Procedures tell you the action to take if you receive a complaint. Normally procedures for dealing with internal and external customer complaints are rather different.

- **Internal complaints**. If you receive a complaint from an internal customer then do the following:
  - ■ Write down the details, unless the matter is very trivial.
  - ■ Apologise and take personal action to put matters right, particularly if you contributed towards causing the problem.
  - ■ If the matter is minor and relates to one of your colleagues, pass the message on promptly to that person so that the problem can be rectified.
  - ■ If the matter is more serious, pass on the information to your supervisor in private. Do not discuss the issue with anyone else.
- **External complaints**. You should refer to your organisation's complaints procedure before you take action. You should be able to find guidance that covers issues such as those listed below, otherwise ask your supervisor about the action you should take.
  - ■ Customers making a serious complaint may be asked to put it in writing and address it to a specific manager. Alternatively there may be a complaints form that they can complete. This ensures that all the key information is obtained.
  - ■ There may be a target date for resolving minor complaints (e.g. five working days) and staff will be encouraged to use their initiative to solve these immediately wherever possible.

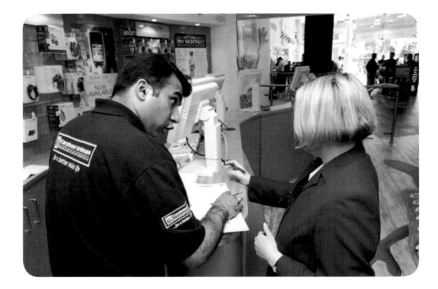

- Serious complaints are normally acknowledged promptly and then investigated by a senior manager.
- All complaints are often recorded in a complaints log. These are analysed at intervals to check whether there are any common problem areas needing attention and to see whether the overall situation is improving or getting worse.

## Dealing with a customer who has a complaint

Many customers with a complaint are calm and reasonable and just want the matter put right. Others may be more excitable or even angry – particularly if they have been severely inconvenienced. You can normally tell immediately by the customer's body language and tone of voice. The trick is for you to stay calm and positive – as you will see below.

> **Remember**
>
> If you receive a complaint, take down the details. *Never* admit liability or promise compensation. This can result in serious problems if the customer's allegation is found to be incorrect.

### How to ... Handle someone making a complaint

- Stay calm yourself. Take a few deep breaths if necessary.
- Listen carefully and *don't* interrupt.
- Don't take the complaint personally. Think of it as a problem you may be able to solve.
- Look sympathetic and interested so that the customer knows you want to help.
- Make notes if the matter is detailed or complicated.
- Don't contradict or insult the customer by saying 'You must be mistaken' or 'You are obviously confused'.
- Apologise on behalf of your organisation for the problem. This is *not* the same as admitting responsibility.
- Don't make any judgements about who is right or wrong and *never* say your organisation is at fault.
- Use careful questioning to find out what action the customer wants you to take. Some customers may not want you to do anything except listen and pass on their concerns to a manager.
- If you can solve the problem without exceeding your job role then do so.
- Never promise anything that is outside of your area of responsibility.
- Get help immediately if the customer threatens you or if you are losing control of the situation.

All organisations have a responsibility to protect staff who may be verbally abused or threatened by customers or visitors. It also helps if staff have been trained how to deal with difficult people, know how to try to diffuse a potential conflict, and don't consider asking for help equals personal failure. You can find out more in option unit 206 on page 290–291.

### Case study  We know where you're going!

*Read the case study below and then answer the questions that follow.*

Aisha works for HouseMove, a local estate agency. As well as her admin duties she also deals with customers who call in or phone, especially when her manager is out of the office.

When people want to buy a property Aisha works through a checklist to make sure they have thought of everything. This includes: price range, location, number of bedrooms, garden, garage and type of property (house, bungalow, flat) and whether the buyers want something new or old – which may need renovating. She transfers their requirements to a printed sheet and checks it with the customer and then files it in her mailing register file. If a property comes up for sale that matches this description, Aisha telephones the customers to see whether they are interested. If they are, she sends out a sales brochure or refers them to details on the website. She also checks that their requirements haven't changed since she last spoke to them.

When customers want to sell a property, Aisha arranges for her manager to visit to give a free valuation. If this is accepted and the customer wants to go ahead, Aisha orders a 'For sale' board from an external company that puts up the board and is responsible for safety issues relating to it. She prepares the sales brochure and advertises the property in the local paper. She knows the property must be described accurately because under the Property Misdescriptions Act it is an offence for an estate agent or property developer to make a false or misleading statement about land or buildings.

Problems can occur when customers arrange to visit a property and fail to turn up, especially if a seller has waited in for them. Or a seller may complain the property hasn't been advertised enough or the description isn't accurate. If a complaint is serious Aisha asks the customer to put it in writing for her manager. However, HouseMove believes that if communications with customers are good, problems are usually avoided. They therefore contact customers to give advance warnings of viewings and make regular courtesy calls to sellers to give feedback after each visit. If the feedback is critical Aisha has to be tactful, but she believes that keeping customers informed is important, particularly as some properties take a while to sell. Satisfied customers recommend the agency to their friends and this frequently results in new business.

## Questions

1   *How does Aisha identify and confirm her customers' needs?*

2   *Identify two benefits of employing an outside company to put up the 'For sale' boards.*

3   *An estate agent describes a property as 'fully double-glazed' when this applies only to the front windows. Does this matter? Give a reason for your answer.*

4   *Explain the methods Aisha uses to build positive working relationships with her customers.*

5   *Suggest two reasons why Aisha doesn't send out sales brochures on properties to customers without phoning them first.*

6   *How do you think Aisha would respond to the following customer queries?*

   **a**   *Can you make sure our house is advertised in the next two weeks because we want a quick sale?*

   **b**   *Can you guarantee our house will be sold within a month?*

   **c**   *We have a house like that, how much is it worth?*

   **d**   *I live alone and would like all viewers to be accompanied by someone from your office. Is that possible?*

Suggested answers are given on the CD-ROM.

## Changing places

*Your assessor will ask you how you will adapt your customer skills if you change your job in the future. You will need to think about the way in which your customer's needs would change if you worked for a different organisation, in addition to the type of problems you might encounter.*

Simon works as administrator in a computer services department. His customers are all internal as he logs queries and problems for the technical staff and also issues computer supplies on request. He needs to be able to question staff carefully to find out what the fault is and solve simple user problems himself.

Noreen works in an insurance office. Most of her customers are external and usually contact her by telephone. If an enquiry is technical then she passes it on to one of the specialist staff but has learned to answer routine queries herself. She keeps a list of all claims forms that are requested and the date she has posted these to customers, in case there are any queries.

Claire is administrator for a firm of graphic designers and printers. She deals mainly with business customers who are enquiring about work or work in progress. Occasionally problems occur in the printing process or if goods are damaged on delivery. Claire prides herself on solving most problems quickly, using her own initiative.

Nasreen works as an administrator for a housing association that provides houses to rent or buy and also helps vulnerable people who would not normally be able to rent or buy property. The local area is both culturally and ethnically diverse and Nasreen enjoys dealing with a wide variety of customers, all with individual needs. To ensure fairness, the association has strict procedures for dealing with enquiries and complaints which Nasreen always follows.

1 For any *one* person listed above, identify the differences he or she would find if moving to your organisation and doing your job.

2 For any *one* person listed above, say how you would need to adapt your skills if you did his or her job rather than your own.

## Over to you

1 Try to solve each of the following problems as imaginatively as you can. Some suggested answers are given on the CD-ROM.

   a You promised to send an urgent document to a customer but the local Royal Mail sorting office is on strike.

    **b** You urgently need to give a customer a message about a confidential matter but you are unsure whether you should ring him with this information at work.

    **c** A customer needs to complete a complaints form but is only partially sighted and is having difficulties.

    **d** The photocopier breaks down as you are in the middle of copying a spreadsheet you prepared for an internal customer.

    **e** A customer rings to say that he has a problem calling in to your offices to see your sales staff as agreed because he has hurt his ankle.

**2** Suggest the action you would take if you received each of the following complaints. Compare your ideas with other members of your group, your tutor or trainer.

    **a** 'I was promised a booklet by one of your colleagues. That was a week ago and nothing has arrived yet.'

    **b** 'Someone has dropped a big bag of rubbish outside your door. Did you know?'

    **c** 'I can never read your writing on the messages you take – can you do something about it please.'

    **d** 'The photocopying you did yesterday is unusable. All the pages are crooked and three of them are missing entirely.'

    **e** 'It's impossible to find this office, you know. You could do with some proper signs leading from reception.'

    **f** 'Your representative told deliberate lies. I'm going to see my solicitor.'

## Evidence collection

**1** Ask two or three of your internal customers for witness testimony which gives examples of the type of requests they regularly make and in which they describe your working relationship with them. It is helpful if they can confirm that you always identify and confirm their needs, agree timescales, quality standards or the procedures you must follow, deliver services as promised and solve any problems as and when they occur. Your witnesses need to give specific examples of services you have provided or problems you have solved rather than just make general statements about you.

Note that you should not ask external customers for witness testimony without the specific agreement of your supervisor. However, should you

### Core unit link

This evidence should link to unit 201, performance indicators 20, 24 and 25, because you are supporting effective working. If any of the information you deal with is confidential this will link to unit 202, PI 14.

**Core unit link**

You should be able to cross-reference the evidence from question 2 to unit 201, performance indicators 1 and 2, as well as unit 202 PIs 1–4.

If you use feedback from any of your customers to look at how you can improve your own work, cross reference your evidence to unit 201, PIs 15–17.

**Evidence collection** Continued

receive a thank-you letter or card, discuss this with your assessor who may agree that you can use it as evidence.

2  Keep a log of Customer Happy Calls or courtesy calls you make and the responses you receive. If it is not organisational policy to make these to external customers then you should still be able to make them to your internal customers. Check with your supervisor.

3  If you deal with customer problems or complaints you may have to log these as part of your organisational procedures. In this case copies of these documents can be included as evidence. You should also keep copies of written notes you have made in response to any complaints or copies of any complaints forms you have completed. Attach details of what you did after you received the complaint or found out about the problem (e.g. how you solved it or who you passed it to).

## What if?

What should you do if no complaints occur within the time you are being assessed? In this case your assessor will look for records of previous complaints you have dealt with. If there are none, then you will be asked what you *would* do in this situation.

## Key skills reminder

If you are taking Key Skills awards. remember to discuss with your tutor or trainer how your evidence for this unit could also count towards those awards.

# Manage diary systems

## Unit summary and overview

This option unit covers all the main aspects of managing a diary system, whether paper-based or electronic. The diary is the most commonly used method for planning and coordinating activities in any office. You may keep a diary yourself to schedule arrangements for certain days or tasks you have to do. Or you may be responsible for looking after the office diary or your boss's, either on your own or as a member of a team. In that case this unit would be suitable for you. When you manage a diary system you have the ability to ensure life runs relatively smoothly for everyone. You also have the ability to cause chaos for your colleagues and for your customers!

As you work through this unit you will find tips to enable you to do this job efficiently, so that you can help to prevent and solve any problems that might occur, especially when conflicting requests are made.

**Link to option units**

As you gather your evidence for this unit you should also obtain evidence for your core units. Watch for the CU link logo which suggests how the evidence you may collect may count towards both this unit and your core units.

Remember that you might be able to identify other links yourself, because of your own job role and the evidence you have obtained.

Talk to your assessor if you need further guidance on how your evidence should be cross-referenced.

**Did you know?**

Staff holiday leave can be recorded in a diary system to ensure that too many people are never absent at any one time.

# The importance of using diary systems

For one moment, imagine the havoc if every employee made his or her own arrangements but never wrote them down or told anyone else. Even in the smallest firm it would be chaotic. People would be out of the building, but no one would know where they were. Meetings would be impossible to plan and arrange. The administrator would be unable to arrange appointments for customers on behalf of a colleague. Staff would make arrangements but possibly forget some of them. Before too long it is likely that all but the most patient customers would have gone elsewhere. In that case, of course, the business would be forced to close.

While that is an extreme example, it shows how important it is for every business to have a sensible system of planning and recording activities and resources which everyone knows and uses. A diary system:

- **Records scheduled and planned activities** such as business meetings, appointments with customers, training events, dates of sales trips, interview arrangements and many others. In your own diary you can include tasks to do such as ordering stock, making a phone call, collecting tickets and so on.
- **Schedules the use of shared resources**, such as a meeting room, special equipment (e.g. a laptop and projector for PowerPoint presentations) or company vehicles. The time slots show who has booked the item and for how long.

*Diaries prevent squabbles over shared resources.*

# Benefits of using diary systems

Many benefits come from using any type of diary system, provided it is used properly. This will become apparent as you progress through this unit. Some of the main ones are identified in this section.

## Keeping a diary yourself

- You can enter all your commitments for each day so that you don't forget anything. This can include meetings, appointments, other events and tasks you have to do.
- You can manage your time better if you can picture your whole day in advance and know what you are doing, rather than be constantly surprised! (See also the information on time management in unit 201, page 40.)
- You can put top-priority tasks – those that are both urgent and important – at the top of your task list for the day to make sure that these are done first. (See also the information on how to prioritise in unit 201, page 39).
- You can tick off tasks you complete, and carry forward any that remain to the next day.
- If you are unexpectedly absent, people can check your commitments and work outstanding by looking at your diary.
- If you have an important task to complete you can schedule time for this, in agreement with your supervisor, so that you won't be disturbed.
- If you are very busy and arrangements and commitments are constantly changing, having a diary means you are far less likely to get confused or forget anything.

**Remember**

Many of the benefits of keeping a diary yourself link with the methods of planning and being accountable for your work that you met in core unit 201, on pages 35–54.

## Managing an office diary system

- Information on activities, staff availability and customer appointments is always available.
- It is easy to check whether a member of staff is supposed to be in the office. This means you don't waste time trying to contact someone who is away or otherwise not available.
- Because you can check the future plans of staff you can often answer queries quickly and easily just by referring to the diary.
- You can arrange meetings even when some of the participants are away from the office, simply by looking for the next date when everyone is free.
- Resources can be used efficiently and fairly as they can be allocated throughout the day using a booking system.

- There are fewer dangers of problems through forgotten appointments or double-bookings.
- Important information about an activity (or resource) can be entered in the diary for ease of reference, such as the contact number of a customer or the location of a meeting.
- The diary can act as an important reminder system, as you can see in the snapshot on Althams Travel Service.

## Snapshot – Super service – thanks to the diary

Althams Travel Service Ltd is a large independent travel agency with over 30 branches in the north of England. Within each branch a diary is kept to remind staff of the important checks that must be made for each holiday that is booked.

Each time a holiday booking is made an entry is put in the diary for two weeks ahead, for ten weeks before the date of departure, and for two weeks before the date of departure. The first entry reminds staff to check that confirmation has been received from the tour operator. If not, the tour operator is reminded and a further note put in the diary to check again that it has been received. The second entry reminds staff to check that the customer has paid the balance on the holiday as agreed at the time of booking. The third entry reminds staff to check that the tickets have been received. Obviously, if people are going away soon after making the booking then the gaps between the entries are less.

The branch administrator checks the diary every day and follows up any outstanding items. The system acts as a vital reminder to all the staff and helps them to ensure that no one's holiday is ruined because of forgotten or missing documents.

You can find out more about the company at www.althams.co.uk.

# Types of diary systems

A diary system is any method of planning and scheduling future events. These can be divided into two different types.

- **traditional paper-based systems**, such as pre-printed desk or pocket diaries, wall-planners or appointment books
- **electronic systems**, such as diary or calendar software, PDAs (personal digital assistants) and electronic appointment systems.

Today many businesses prefer the flexibility and ease of an electronic system – but not all of them! Some businesses still prefer to retain a paper-based system. Each system has its advantages and disadvantages, as shown in the table below, and the choice will depend on the situation and the reason for its use.

**Find out**

How many of your colleagues use electronic diaries and paper diaries? Do some people use both? Think about why some people feel they need to use both types of diaries.

## Traditional diary systems

| System | Advantages | Disadvantages |
|---|---|---|
| **Pre-printed desk diary** | Portable<br>Easy to find and enter information by date/time<br>Useful supplementary information (e.g. holiday dates)<br>Specialist versions available, e.g. academic year diaries | Easily lost<br>Difficult to read if too many entries per day or writing is poor<br>Movements of manager not known if each takes own diary out of office<br>Pre-printed time slots may not match requirements<br>Time-consuming to search for information if date of activity not known.<br>Not easy to edit entries neatly |
| **Wall charts, calendars and planners** | Special designs are available to suit different purposes<br>Entries can be written or identified by colour symbols<br>Wall mounted = highly visible<br>Can show activities planned for up to a year in advance | Keeping a chart up to date can be time-consuming<br>Too many symbols or entries are confusing<br>Coloured sticky symbols mean planner is not reusable<br>Magnetic strips sometimes fall off |
| **Appointment book** | Pre-printed with dates and times<br>Easy to enter customer/client bookings | Some written entries may be hard to read<br>Serious problems if misplaced or 'borrowed' from reception |

## Paper-based systems

### Pre-printed desk diaries

This is the traditional method used by managers and office staff to record business appointments and activities. They are also used by many administrators to record their own and their boss's commitments as well as jobs they have to do on certain dates.

### Wall-mounted wallcharts and planners

Some are designed for specific purposes whereas others are more general. A perpetual planner has no fixed dates and can be used every year. On some boards you write on the information with a 'wipe-off' pen, on others you stick magnetic symbols and shapes to signify different events.

This system is used for planning/scheduling activities or commitments that affect many staff over quite a long period – monthly meetings, trade fairs or exhibitions, staff holiday leave, staff training and development events etc.

### An appointments book

This is divided into time slots for customer appointments to be recorded. Some have sufficient space for more detailed information to be kept on clients or customers and there are a variety of different designs.

This system is used by many small businesses to record client bookings – hairdressers, dentists, doctors, vets etc.

## Electronic systems

Today more and more businesses are replacing their paper-based systems and recording the information on computer, mainly because of the advantages of using an electronic system. These are listed in the chart opposite, and as you will see there are more advantages to this type of system than disadvantages.

### Electronic diary programs

The best known program that incorporates a diary or calendar is Microsoft Outlook. There are alternatives, such as Lotus Organiser. Most diary programs enable users to keep their diary and schedule their activities (or resources) on computer, organise and manage lists of tasks and keep an address of contacts. Microsoft Outlook also has an email function.

In most programs the calendar on screen looks like a 'paper diary' page. The current date is shown at the top with hourly slots into which entries are made. Other dates are selected using the small calendar on the screen. In Microsoft Outlook the diary also updates as meetings are arranged and shows details about the meeting, such as the agenda and a list of those who have agreed to attend.

Electronic systems are used by businesses that prefer to schedule activities and resources by computer rather than use traditional paper-based diaries.

## Electronic diary systems

| System | Advantages | Disadvantages |
|--------|-----------|---------------|
| Electronic diary or calendar software (e.g. Microsoft Outlook) | Information can easily be shared over a computer network<br>Entries are not restricted in length and can be viewed by day, week, month or year<br>Entries can be searched for and edited easily<br>Automatic reminders can be set to give alerts ahead of an activity<br>The diary can be uploaded on to some PDAs and/or pages printed out<br>The diary can not be lost<br>Pre-programmed features prevent basic errors being made (e.g. making an appointment for a past date)<br>If accessible over the Internet, users can view it when away from the office<br>Access can be restricted so only free time slots are visible, not activities<br>Meetings can be booked electronically be using the diary to find a free time for attendees and sending invitations by email<br>Resources can be set up in the system and booked by users online or by an administrator who controls which requests are acceptable | Computer failure means diary not available<br>Possible data corruption means back-up copy essential<br>If stored on office PC, not portable unless user has online access from laptop or PDA<br>To work effectively as a shared facility, all members of staff need to use the system<br>Mistakes and out-of-date information is on view to all who can access the system<br>May be some resistance from staff not used to using computers or who do not have regular access to a computer |
| PDA (personal digital assistant) | Portable so entries can be made whilst travelling<br>Diary entries can be uploaded from and downloaded to the office PC<br>Buzzers and alarms can be set to give reminders<br>Most have touch screen and incorporate handwriting recognition | Entries not downloaded on main system would be known only by user<br>Loss can be disastrous unless key information is backed up<br>Some are easier to use than others<br>Must be kept up to date with information in main office diary |
| Electronic appointment software | Shared system provides all users with key information<br>Easy to enter/retrieve information<br>Buzzers or graphic alerts tell staff when visitor has arrived/how long they have been waiting<br>Safeguards to reduce problems (e.g. double-booking warnings)<br>Can be set to send automated email or text messages to remind client about appointment, which reduces number who fail to attend | Need computer access to view system<br>Not accessible if there is computer failure<br>If client information stored, confidentiality must be considered<br>Email reminders or text messages may annoy some clients |

**Find out**

If your workplace still uses a paper-based system, find out whether there are any plans to convert to an electronic system in the near future.

*Microsoft Outlook – a popular electronic diary and e-mail package.*

As you will see from the list of advantages, they are ideal on a network system because information can easily be shared between computer users.

### Electronic appointments system

These are used to record pre-arranged visits by customers or clients. Whilst a diary program such as Microsoft Outlook can be used for this purpose, many organisations prefer specific, customised systems. In many cases the appointments system is part of a professional software package that has been developed for a particular industry, as you will see from the later snapshot on the Malt House.

### Personal digital assistants (PDAs)

These all contain electronic diary programs as well as a 'To do' list, an address book, calculator and memo pad. Virtually all have a touch screen and most

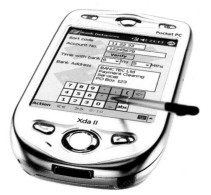

### Did you know?

Many electronic appointments systems have the option to send clients a text reminder a few hours before. This is useful in businesses when non-attendance is costly and inconvenient for professionals, such as doctors and dentists.

incorporate handwriting recognition. They are also PC-compatible so that information users enter when they are away from the office can easily be downloaded into the main system on their return.

PDAs are used by managers and executives who regularly travel on business and want to be able to schedule meetings and commitments at any time.

**Find out**

Does anyone in your organisation use a PDA? If so, find out more about its features and whether the user can automatically upload information into his or her office computer.

## Snapshot – Time to open wide!

The Malt House is a specialist dental treatment centre in Manchester. Although it is only small, it uses state-of-the art equipment and software that includes an electronic diary and appointment system. This is part of a specialist software package for dentists called EXACT Professional, produced by Software of Excellence, a New Zealand company.

Each dentist or hygienists' appointments are colour-coded and listed on screen for each day in time order. The system also records the availability of each member of staff on a horizontal coloured bar so that appointments won't be made when someone will be away on holiday or even out at lunch.

When a patient's arrival is logged by reception a small figure appears on the screen. As the patient waits, the graphical figure plays with a yoyo. The longer the wait the more exhausted the figure becomes until it collapses in a heap after ten minutes! The aim is to encourage staff to see patients promptly, although they argue that anyone who arrives 15 minutes late will, on this system, actually be dead on arrival!

##  Over to you

You will find these activities particularly valuable if you use only a paper-based system where you work and would like to know more about electronic systems. If you use Microsoft Outlook you might also find them useful, because it will give you a greater appreciation of other systems in operation in different types of business.

1  Your brother is a physiotherapist and is considering changing the paper-based diary system at his practice to an electronic system. Each of the following is an example of a software package that he could use. Investigate at least two online and then decide which one you think he should use, with reasons.

   **a**  Niche appointments at www.niche-technologies.co.uk – then click on 'Products'

   **b**  Padtech at www.padtech.co.uk

   **c**  Multicalendar at www.multicalendar.com

   **d**  Athyrium at www.athyrium.com.

**Over to you** Continued

2   Your boss has recently heard about the MyOffice shared diary service and wants to know what this is. She has asked you to find out more from their website at www.myoffice.net/diaryfeatures.htm. Go to the site and list four key features of MyOffice.

### Core unit link

If you can link the reason why the diary (or diaries) are kept to your organisation's mission and objectives, you can cross-reference your evidence to unit 202, performance indicator 1.

### Evidence collection

Your evidence for this unit must show that you understand the diary system in your workplace and why it is appropriate for your employer's business.

Start by writing a personal statement describing your diary system and why it is used. Remember to include:

● the type of system you use (paper-based or electronic)

● why each diary is kept (e.g. to track resources or activities or both)

● your own involvement – you may be personally responsible for keeping a diary or share this responsibility with other people

● the training you received before you were allowed to use the diary.

Sign your statement and ask your supervisor or line manager to countersign and date it to confirm its accuracy.

### Did you know?

In health centres and doctors' practices, space is usually left in the diary each day for emergency appointments. These time slots cannot be given to a patient unless someone senior has agreed that their symptoms require urgent attention.

# Using different types of diary system

There is a skill to using any type of diary system. No matter how many features it has, or how good the supplier says it is, it will be effective only if you use it properly. As a first step, this means that you must be able to enter information so that it is accurate, complete and – in the case of a paper-based system – easy to read.

You also need to comply with any rules relating to the way entries can be made or changed.

### How to ... Make entries in a paper-based diary system

● Enter all appointments as soon as possible. If you are making an appointment for someone, write it in as you are speaking and then read the entry back to the person as a double check.

- Use clear handwriting.

- Write unusual or important names in capitals.

- Write provisional appointments in pencil, until they are confirmed.

- Take down all important appointment information you need – name, address, location, telephone number and reason for appointment. A telephone number is essential if a meeting has to be cancelled at the last minute.

- Do not write confidential information about a client or an appointment in the diary.

- Enter regular appointments and meetings throughout the year.

- Tick or cross off appointments when they have taken place – then it's easy to check whether any have been postponed and must be rearranged.

- If an appointment is cancelled, cross it out completely and write 'Cancelled' after it, so that there is no chance of misunderstanding.

- Don't mix appointments and reminders of jobs you have to do on the same page of the diary. Use facing pages or rule a line across the page.

- If you keep a large office diary for two or three people, divide it into a column per person. Contrasting coloured inks for each person will make the entries even easier to identify quickly.

If you are using an electronic system, you must know how to operate the system and this will usually involve a short training session. No matter which type of electronic system you use, check that your skills match those given in the 'How to ...' box below.

**Did you know?**

If you are using the diary system in Microsoft Outlook you can gain help and training online at http://office.microsoft.com/training.

**How to ...** Make entries in an electronic diary system

- Ensure that you can carry out routine operations easily, such as

  - making a new appointment

  - setting up a repeat appointment

  - setting up or agreeing a meeting

  - setting an alarm or other special features

  - finding an entry

  - changing or amending an entry

**How to ...** Continued

- deleting an entry

- viewing entries in different ways (e.g. by day, week or month)

- taking a printout.

- Check that you can move to any date you want to view. In Microsoft Outlook use the small calendar at one side of the screen and the task bar above to access dates that are further back or into the future.

- Check that you know the significance of different coloured entries or symbols so that you can interpret a diary entry quickly and accurately.

- If you manage several diaries (e.g. to book activities for different people or to control several different resources), always check you are in the right diary before you start!

- Check that you have all the essential information you need to make the entry (e.g. start time, end time, location, name of person, reason for the appointment or meeting). If any information is missing, 'flag' or colour the entry as a reminder that you need to obtain this.

- Set the alarm and any other special features, if required.

- Check that the entry is correct and save it.

- Double-check that the entry is displayed correctly on the correct date. Remember to check both month and year!

### Core unit link

If you can include information on policies, systems or procedures that you follow, and say how the diary system helps to protect and improve the image of the business to outside organisations, then you can cross-reference your evidence to unit 101, performance indicators 2–4.

### Evidence collection

1 Prepare a summary of the way in which you make entries in your diary system. Then attach a photocopy or printout of a few diary pages you have prepared. If the responsibility for keeping the diary is shared, highlight the entries you have made.

2 List any rules that apply to your diary system that users must follow. If there are no specific rules, suggest occasions when you would be likely to refer a query to your boss, rather than enter it on your own.

## Making changes to entries

Whatever type of system you use, it is often necessary to make changes to entries that have been made previously. You may be expected to:

*Making an appointment using Microsoft Outlook.*

- add further information
- amend the existing information
- change the date and/or time
- delete an entry.

Most changes will be straightforward. If your boss tells you that the time and date she will be visiting a customer has changed, then in a paper-based diary you will cross out one entry clearly and re-enter the information under the new date. In an electronic system, you can usually double-click on the entry to bring up the associated appointment card, change the date and click on the Save icon or button.

In some cases, however, you may not be able to make the requested change. For example, when you try to change the time and date of a meeting between two people to suit one of them you might find that another person is already booked at that time or has arranged to be out of the office. This obviously causes complications as you would only be able to make the change if you altered the existing entry, which may not be possible. You will see how to solve problems like this as you progress through this unit. In the meantime remember that you ought not to confirm a change is possible until you have obtained all the relevant information you need and checked the implications for existing entries.

# Types of information to obtain

The information you must obtain will depend on the type of change you need to make and the type of activity or resource involved:

**Remember**

If you are amending an entry *always* double-check that you are *changing* an existing entry, not adding another one – otherwise you are in danger of duplicating the appointment or booking.

### Remember

Write down information you receive verbally so that you don't forget it. If you receive information in writing then you may have to read the document carefully to find what you need.

- *For a rearranged activity* such as a meeting or appointment you need to know the new date, time and duration and whether or not the location is the same.
- *For a rearranged meeting* you also need to know whether you must notify the participants about the changes. You will be able to do this automatically if your diary package is linked to your email system.
- *If you are scheduling resources*, such as specialist equipment or rooms, you need to know the new date and time, the person requesting the change and the reason for the booking. This will prove very useful if you have multiple requests and have to prioritise them – as you will see later.

### Core unit link

If you are given information verbally and question points you are unsure about, then you may be able to cross-reference your evidence to unit 201, performance indicator 1. If you have to read written material that contains information you need and then extract the main points, this will cross-reference to unit 201, PIs 4 and 5.

### Evidence collection

Keep a written log of the changes you are asked to make over a period of time, until you have a list that will give your assessor an accurate idea of the type of changes you make as part of your job. Note down the type of change, the information you were given and how you obtained it.

For each change you list, identify whether or not the change could be made easily. In each case where there was a problem, you will need to describe this and say what you did to solve it (see page 238 and 241).

When you have completed your log, ask your supervisor or line manager to countersign and date it to confirm that its accuracy.

# The importance of prioritising requests

If you prioritise requests then there are two main benefits:

- You will give precedence to the most urgent and important requests that are made.
- You will usually upset fewer people!

However, this isn't always easy, as you will see below!

### Over to you

*Read what happened when Salma tried to juggle conflicting demands and then see whether you could do any better by answering the questions that follow.*

Salma keeps a diary to schedule the use of two meeting rooms. These can be booked by anyone in the company. One is a quite spacious, well-furnished room that can hold 25 people and has an integrated presentation system. It overlooks a small garden. The other room holds 10 people, needs decorating and overlooks the staff car park. The furnishings are fairly basic and it has no integrated presentation system, although a portable system can be used in the room.

One of the sales staff, Rob, booked the larger room to give a presentation to an important customer next Tuesday. The customer has now said he can visit only on Wednesday so Rob needs to change the room booking. Salma says Rob can use only the smaller room on Wednesday because the large one is already booked for a staff training event. Rob says this is completely unacceptable and a row ensues.

1 What *precise* information should Salma have obtained from Rob?

2 What *precise* information should Salma have already obtained about the staff training event?

3 In what way(s) could examining the detailed information help Salma to come to a decision?

4 In your opinion, which event should generally be given top priority – and why?

5 If the sales manager insists the training event is moved, should this influence Salma's actions – and if so, why?

6 If the training manager says the training event must stay where it is, what should Salma do?

7 If the decision is up to Salma, and you were in her shoes, what would you do?

If possible, discuss your ideas as a group or check your ideas with the suggestions on the CD-ROM.

## How to ... Prioritise requests

Use a three-stage approach.

- *Stage 1*: Consider the type of event or activity and its urgency or importance. In most businesses events involving external people – especially customers – are given priority over internal events. This is because increasing sales/meeting customer targets is an important aim of all businesses.

- *Stage 2*: Look at the status of the person making the request. A senior manager will normally outrank a more junior employee. If both people have equal status ask them, politely, to decide between them or ask your boss for guidance. Another solution is to move to stage 3.

**How to ... Continued**

- *Stage 3*: Look at the order in which you received the requests. If both the events and the people making the request are 'equal' in terms of importance and status, then the general rule is 'first come, first served'. This normally saves any further arguments.

BUT ... always remember that there is often room for negotiation and common sense. This means thinking of ways in which the problem can be solved and suggesting it to those involved.

## Problems related to new requests

In April 2005, Pope John Paul II died. Prince Charles had to attend the funeral in Rome on behalf of the Queen and, to do this, he had to reschedule his wedding from Friday to Saturday. This meant changing the date of his civil ceremony at Windsor register office – and this caused a problem. Three other couples had booked weddings for that day, and the times of their ceremonies had to be changed to accommodate Prince Charles and his bride. Normally this would not even be considered but, because of the importance of the event and the status of the people involved, the register office staff contacted the other couples to see whether they would be willing to change their times. They agreed so the problem was solved.

This is a typical example of the type of 'knock-on' problem that can occur. In other words, to meet one request you have to make adjustments or amendments that will affect other people. Before you know it, what seems to be a simple request starts to look awfully complicated.

Here are some other types of problem you might meet:

- Essential resources are already booked for the time or date requested (e.g. a room or equipment).
- A room is available but is unsuitable because of size, location or facilities (as you saw with Salma's problem).
- Key people are not available.
- There is insufficient free time to schedule a new activity.
- You need to have special permission before you can make other, related changes.
- If you agree you would be breaking a rule about the way in which diaries and appointments are made.

# Solving problems related to new requests

In the case of Prince Charles' wedding, the problem was solved because the register office staff were prepared to contact other couples and the other couples were prepared to be flexible. This is an excellent example because it shows the action to take in this situation:

- Check the effect of any new request or change on other people or resources.
- Contact those who are affected.
- Explore and negotiate alternative arrangements.

If the situation is very complicated, or if senior members of your organisation are involved, then it is sensible to talk through options with your boss. You should always do this, of course, if you would not be authorised to make changes to other arrangements without permission.

It is also useful to be able to make suggestions that most reasonable people would accept. Salma could have suggested that the 'best' room could perhaps be used for both the customer *and* the training event with a bit of careful arranging, such as the customer arriving at lunchtime when staff on the training event were on their break. However, it would be important to allow time for someone to ensure the room was left clean and tidy after the morning training session.

**Remember**

Often, being creative and imaginative can help you overcome problems – and your colleagues will normally be grateful. But if you have a really tricky problem or are struggling to deal with someone, don't argue. Simply say that you will refer the matter to your boss for his or her decision.

# Balancing the needs of those involved

You have already seen how Windsor register office staff tried to balance the needs of royalty with those of the other couples booked for the same day. You have also seen how, in the case of Salma's dilemma, it was important to consider the needs of all those involved.

When you 'balance' people's needs this means you are treating each person as an individual and trying to be fair to everyone. You are not *automatically* treating someone more favourably just because they are important (even though you may have to bear this in mind on some occasions). Instead you are looking at their reasons for making a request and giving priority to those people with the most urgent need. Sometimes you will have rules to help with this, but at other times you will have to use discretion and common sense. A good rule of thumb is always to treat people as you would like to be treated yourself! You can test your ideas here by doing the activity below.

## Over to you

In each of the following situations:

**a** identify the people involved

**b** for each person, state what their needs are

**c** state what action you would take, and why.

If possible, compare your ideas with others in your group and with the suggestions on the CD-ROM.

**1** Maria works on reception at a veterinary practice. Tonight is her late shift and both she and the vet on duty won't finish until 7.30 p.m. as the diary is already full. Around 7 p.m. she receives two calls. The first is from a customer who is frantic as her cat has just returned home covered in blood and limping. The second is from a customer who urgently wants to pick up some dog food and can't get to the surgery until 7.45 p.m.

**2** Your boss asks you to schedule a meeting with an important customer for 2 p.m. on Wednesday. He tells you to tell the graphics designer, Kate, to be there. When you check the diary Kate has a half day holiday booked for that Wednesday.

**3** The MD of your company wants one member of your department to go to his office at 1 p.m. tomorrow to give technical information to a customer. The diaries of the staff show that Imtiaz is visiting another customer, Ken has to attend a safety meeting from twelve until one and is then at lunch, and Cath will be interviewing a job applicant. The only person free is Becky who started just two weeks ago and doesn't really have enough experience. However, she has said she will do anything else you want her to do.

# Recording and communicating changes

When an acceptable or agreed change is made in a diary there are two stages in the process:
- The change must be recorded properly in the diary.
- All those involved must be informed.

The danger areas are when there are several people involved and you can't get hold of everyone immediately – so here are some golden rules:
- Make a list of everyone who is affected.
- Select the most appropriate method of communication depending on the urgency of the situation. It is no use notifying someone by email that their appointment in one hour has been changed – they may not access their email in that time. In this case you need to ring the person or find him or her.
- Tick off the names on your list only when you know each person has received your message.

# Keeping the diary up to date

You may be asked to record new entries and make changes throughout the day. If you are sitting at your desk or the diary is instantly available then there are usually few problems – unless you are trying to do two things at once! You also need to know what to do if you aren't at your desk, the diary isn't available or – even worse – several members of your team make diary entries in their pocket diaries or on their PDAs and don't always remember to tell you. Here are some useful strategies:

- Always writing down in a notepad entries you are given or changes you must make. This also enables you to query any information you are given that is incomplete.
- Carry your notepad with you, so that you can write down a request when you are away from your desk or if the diary is missing or unavailable, for some reason.
- Tick off each entry or change as you make it in the diary.
- Have a fixed routine for liaising with colleagues who make appointments when they are out of the office, so that you can obtain information from their pocket diaries or PDAs. This isn't necessary if they own PDAs that will also upload information into your main computer system, but many won't!

### Core unit link

If your evidence includes written information, this should cross-reference to unit 201, performance indicator 6.

### Evidence collection

Keep safely all the notes you write. They are excellent evidence of your communication skills and prove your organisational abilities. Similarly, if you notify anyone in writing about a change you have made, keep a copy for your evidence file. If you normally tell people about changes over the telephone, you can ask for witness testimony as proof. Witness testimony from your boss, to confirm that you always keep the diary up to date, is also valuable.

### Case study Could you be jilted by a registrar?

*Read the case study below and then answer the questions that follow. Check your answers with those on the CD-ROM.*

Anyone who wants to get married in the UK has to comply with a number of legal formalities. For many people this involves contacting the register office in the district in which they wish to marry. The main exception to this requirement is when couples want to be married by the Church of England, as the vicar can make all the arrangements and register the marriage. In most other cases, a registrar must attend the ceremony, record the details in a special register and issue a marriage certificate.

For that reason, in every register office in the land there is a special diary kept to record planned weddings that will be held in their district. And making sure that all the entries are made correctly is very important. No one wants a bride in her finery, surrounded by guests, but with the registrar nowhere to be found!

To prevent this happening a number of safeguards are in place. These involve special checks and procedures when entries are made into the diary.

The first step is for the couple to contact the register office in the district where they wish to marry – not where they live. First some basic checks are made to ensure the time, date and venue meet legal requirements. In addition, there must be sufficient travelling time allowed to enable the registrar to arrive at the ceremony with ease. In some districts a minimum of 1.5 hours (or more) is always allowed between weddings to prevent potential problems, regardless of the actual location. Assuming the couple's plans are agreed, their wedding is now entered in the diary.

The entry is made in pencil when the time, date and venue are agreed and a letter is sent to the couple telling them they must now give formal notice of their wedding.

The entry is made in ink when the couple have given formal notice and all the identification and other checks have been made. The couple do this by each visiting the register office nearest to where they live. This office will fax a copy of the notice to the register office in the district in which the ceremony will take place, if this is different.

The entry is highlighted in coloured pen once the formal authority to marry is produced after a further 15 clear days. This is the legal document the registrar takes to the wedding.

The diary is updated every day and kept in a fireproof vault for security. There is restricted access on use by register office staff and no details are ever discussed with other people, no matter what reason might be given.

Changes can be requested – as Prince Charles proved. Normally these relate to times and dates. If a change of venue is required, the couple must give notice all over again.

Since June 2005 each district has had the option to convert to an electronic diary system. This provides a number of safeguards. Double bookings are no longer possible and automatic prompts cover all the checks that need to be made. However, back-up disks and a paper copy will be essential in case the system fails unexpectedly.

### Questions

1 *Suggest two benefits to register office staff of the three-stage process of making diary entries.*

2 *Suggest two reasons why confidentiality and security are so important.*

**3** Identify four benefits of using an electronic system, rather than a paper-based diary.

**4** What do you think would be the consequences if each of the following errors was made. Discuss your ideas with other members of your group or check the answers on the CD-ROM.

**a** A couple change the date of their wedding. The new entry is made but the old one is not deleted.

**b** Two weddings are booked too close together by mistake.

**c** A couple cancel their wedding at the last minute but the wrong ceremony is deleted from the diary.

# Security and confidentiality issues

As you saw in the case study above, many diaries contain information that must be kept confidential. If you use a paper-based system, then it is sensible not to include information that is very sensitive. If you use an electronic diary system which is shared, then the usual way of dealing with this is to allocate different access privileges to people. These control:

- the type of information people can view (e.g. 'free' and 'busy' slots only or the details of each appointment)
- the actions people can take (i.e. whether they can only read the diary information or also make and change entries).

There are obvious reasons for these differences. It is doubtful whether many senior managers would want full details of their diaries to be on show to all the workforce, let alone to people outside the company. They would certainly not want their competitors to know what they were doing. So there are good reasons for keeping the details of many appointments confidential. You would also find that if you worked for a doctor or solicitor, for example, both of whom are constrained by professional responsibilities, you would have to agree never to disclose information about a patient or client. For the same reason, details relating to the reason for a visit are not usually entered into an open diary or appointment book system.

Diaries also need to be kept safely. If a paper-based diary goes missing it is at best inconvenient and at worst disastrous – as you saw with the register office diaries. In the case of electronic diaries this means having a back-up kept in a safe place – or a printout of the next day's appointments as a safeguard in case there is a system problem.

*Make sure your diary stays confidential!*

## How to ... Manage security and confidentiality issues

- Never leave a diary or appointment book open where it can be read by visitors to your office.

- If you leave your desk then either take the diary with you or put it away in a desk drawer. Lock the drawer if the diary contains confidential information.

- Always store a paper-based diary or appointment book in a locked drawer or cupboard at the end of each working day.

- If you use an electronic system, angle the screen away from external visitors when you are making or changing entries in their presence.

- Make sure you have a back-up disk or a hard copy of the next day's appointments stored in a safe place.

- Never leave the system logged on when you are away from your desk.

- Don't answer questions relating to appointments or arrangements unless you know for certain that the questioner has the right to know. Don't enter into a discussion, simply refer the person to your boss for information. This is particularly important if someone is trying to find out information over the phone.

- Abide by any other rules relating to confidentiality and security that apply in your particular workplace.

## Changing places

*Your assessor will ask you how you would apply your skills if you changed your job in the future. Although diary systems are used by most businesses, the type of system and reason for use may vary, as you can see below.*

Diana works in an estate agency. She uses a paper-based office diary to book and record appointments for the sales negotiators and valuers who visit properties that are on the market.

Wendy works for a local veterinary practice. She uses an electronic system to record pet owners' appointments to see different vets and to schedule operations. The system also shows when an individual vet will be away from the practice, either on holiday or to attend a conference or meeting.

Jonnie works for a solicitors' practice where appointments are scheduled electronically, per solicitor. They may be made by the solicitors themselves or their administrators. A buzzer system warns each solicitor ten minutes before each appointment.

Petra works for the marketing department of a large national retailer and frequently travels on business. She always carries a PDA and records appointments she makes while she is out of the office. She then downloads this information into the office computer system so that her colleagues always know her movements and her availability.

Liane works for a luxury hire car business. The firm has six rare classic cars, three high-performance sports cars and three stretch limousines. Liane is responsible for recording all bookings on an electronic diary package.

1 For any *one* person listed above, identify the differences he or she would find if moving to your organisation and doing your job.

2 For any *one* person listed above, say how you would need to adapt your skills if you did their job, rather than your own.

## Evidence collection

1 Write a brief account explaining the security and confidentiality issues that relate to your own diary systems and how you manage these.

2 Finally, review your own performance of using a diary. Explain how the methods you use to keep the diary enable you to do the job effectively. Then identify how you have used feedback from other people to improve your work. If you have made mistakes in the past, then say what these were and explain how you corrected them or what you have done to improve your performance.

## Core unit link

You can cross-reference this evidence to unit 202, performance indicator 14. If you have had any concerns about security or confidentiality that you have reported to an appropriate person, then you can cross-reference that evidence to unit 202, PI 15.

Check the statements you have written and then cross-reference these, as appropriate, to unit 201, PIs 9, 13, 15, 16 and 20.

## Key skills reminder

If you are taking Key Skills awards, remember to discuss with your tutor or trainer how your evidence for this unit could also count towards those awards.

# Organise business travel and accommodation

### Unit summary and overview

This option unit covers all the main aspects of making travel and accommodation arrangements for colleagues who are planning business trips. This is a very responsible job because no one wants to experience problems when they are away – especially easily avoidable ones caused by sloppy administration. From planning a one-day visit to a nearby city to organising a major business trip abroad, the more you know about the best ways to go about the task, the more options you can often suggest. You will also avoid some of the major pitfalls lying in wait for the unwary!

In this unit you will find hints and tips to help you to advise any colleague of suitable options, and this will also be of value if you need to discuss proposed plans and preferences with your firm's travel agent.

# Organising business travel and accommodation effectively and efficiently

Many business people travel regularly as part of their jobs and the vast majority rely on their administrative staff to make arrangements for them. If this is part of your job, then you will be expected to do an efficient and effective job, mainly because mistakes can be very costly, inconvenient and make your organisation look very foolish. So don't copy the administrator who booked a plane ticket to Amman (in Jordan) when she should have been arranging a trip to Oman some 1500 miles away, or the one who sent her boss to Stuttgart – unknowingly on a public holiday – and for good measure booked a hotel in the middle of the red-light district!

Arranging business travel and accommodation is a skilled job. The longer you do it the more you learn, but even at the outset you need to be aware of certain essential facts and key skills you need.

## Link to option units

As you gather your evidence for this unit you should also obtain evidence for your core units. Watch for the CU link logo which suggests how the evidence you may collect may count towards both this unit and your core units.

Remember that you might be able to identify other links yourself, because of your own job role and the evidence you have obtained.

Talk to your assessor if you need further guidance on how your evidence should be cross-referenced.

## How to ... Organise travel and accommodation effectively and efficiently

- Know and understand the organisational rules and procedures you must follow when you are making any travel arrangements, such as whether you need to use preferred travel companies or hotels.

- Make sure you have all the facts relating to a trip before you start. These include the preferences of the person travelling and the budget.

- Find out the options and get the traveller's agreement before you make any reservations.

- Pay close attention to detail. Checking a ticket or a reservation form means you must be able to read – word by word – very carefully.

- Never assume or guess anything. Take action only when you have the facts.

- Keep a written record of everything you research or reserve.

- Check, double-check and triple-check the details of a trip – even if it's only a train journey to Glasgow.

- Keep your paperwork neat and tidy, so you can find anything in a matter of seconds.

- Consult experts when you need them and always be willing to listen and learn.

- Learn to enjoy finding out new things about people and places – if you don't do so already!

## Did you know?

A good tip is to keep a record for each person in your firm who travels. Include key personal information such as seating preferences, favourite airlines, diet specifications, frequent-flyer number (see page 251 for an explanation) and the date his or her passport must be renewed.

# Main types of travel and accommodation arrangements and the procedures to follow

**Find out**

Most organisations whose staff travel frequently have company travel insurance to cover the risks of travel. Otherwise anyone travelling abroad will need his or her own policy. Find out which applies in your organisation.

The types of travel and accommodation arrangement you make will depend very much on the type of work undertaken by your employer and the scope of its operations. Some executives travel extensively in the UK but rarely outside it. Some organisations have mainly European contacts while others operate on a global basis, sending executives all over the world.

On this basis you may be regularly booking air tickets and making reservations at hotels in different countries, or most of the trips you organise may involve train travel to a range of UK cities and occasional overnight accommodation. The skills you need to book both kinds of trip aren't very different, although there is more to think about if the trip involves ten days in the Middle East rather than two days in Dublin, simply because there is the potential for more to go wrong. This is when expert help is invaluable, so hopefully your procedures include reference to the travel agents in your area that you can use.

## Organisational procedures

**Did you know?**

Organisational rules often include restrictions on the class of travel (e.g. first class, club class or economy) you can book for employees, depending on their seniority.

Many organisations have rules and procedures that cover the following aspects:

- the travel agent, travel company or hotel booking agencies that can be used
- the amount of money that can be spent per night on accommodation (often depending on the status of the person travelling)
- the class of travel that is allowed – first or standard on the rail network, economy or club/business class for air travel

*If your organisation isn't right, your traveller could pay the price!*

- the mileage allowance permitted if a car is used
- whether hire cars are allowed and, if so, the budget for these
- the distance to be travelled before overnight accommodation is allowed
- the subsistence allowance or expenses that are allowed for the business traveller to pay for meals, snacks, taxi fares and other items during the trip
- how payment is to be made.

Executives may have corporate credit cards, otherwise they may pay the amount personally and then be reimbursed through an expenses claim. Foreign expenses are rarely paid direct by organisations unless there is a branch office in that part of the world.

# Confirming the travel and accommodation brief and budget

If you are new to making travel and accommodation arrangements then you may think it would be simpler to simply phone the local travel agent as this would save a lot of work for everyone. Sometimes this is true but there are often other aspects of the trip to consider – and some preparatory work to be done – before you can talk to anyone. In addition, some of the queries that arise may be better researched online or referred to other types of travel specialists, as you will see.

## Factors to consider

For any trip, there are several aspects to think about:
- the method of travel (e.g. rail, air, road, sea)
- the type of accommodation required
- the dates and preferred times of outward and return travel

*Arriving on a public holiday isn't always a good idea!*

- meetings and other business commitments during the visit
- essential documentation
- the cost of the trip and the budget allowed
- payment and money issues.

If the trip is outside the UK, then additional factors include:

- passport and visa requirements
- other considerations – such as health precautions, climate, business customs and public holidays.

## The travel and accommodation brief

This brief refers to the instructions that you are given, based on the proposed trip. In some organisations, a travel form is issued to anyone who wants a booking made. This is useful because it helps to identify all the possible options at the start and is particularly invaluable if you are given instructions over the telephone. If your organisation doesn't have a briefing form, perhaps you could design your own to make sure you always obtain all the important information you need at the outset. This should include:

- full name(s) of all the travellers and, preferably, date of birth
- requested date of departure and return
- preferred method of travel and any individual preferences, such as a particular airline or route
- other requirements – such as transport on arrival, currency requirements or visa check
- any specific budget requirements you must take into account.

The contents of the form are invaluable because it should provide:

- enough personal information on those travelling to enable you to give sufficient information to a travel agent or airline for ticketing purposes
- information on individual preferences to save you from having to ask about minor details
- information on other requirements associated with the trip (such as possible visas or currency requirements) to enable you to make out a checklist of jobs you must do now.

Ideally your form will include an action column in which you can record the information you obtain alongside each request and tick off items as reservations are made. An example of this type of travel form is shown below.

## Travel form

Name: Sue Kemp    Department: Sales

**TRAVELLER DETAILS**

| Title | Surname | First name(s) | DOB |
|-------|---------|---------------|-----|
| Miss | Kemp | Susan Jane | 24.10.76 |
| Miss | Bryant | Polly | 5.3.79 |

| TRAVEL REQUIREMENTS | ACTION TAKEN: |
|---|---|
| From:  Birmingham         To:   Barcelona<br><br>**Departure date:**   15 October<br>Preferred time:   Morning<br><br>**Return date:**   17 October<br>Preferred time:   Afternoon<br><br>Method of travel:  Air         Preferences:   None | |
| **ACCOMMODATION REQUIREMENTS**<br><br>Location      Dates of stay      No. of nights<br><br>Barcelona      15 – 16 October      2<br><br>Preferences:  2 single rooms, central hotel, min 3. | |
| **OTHER REQUIREMENTS**<br><br>Visa check:  No    Vaccinations check:  No<br><br>Transport:         Taxi from home to airport and return.<br>Juan Cortez from the Barcelona office is meeting us on arrival and will arrange a taxi for our return to the airport.<br><br>Currency:   £50 in euros | |
| **Estimated cost:**     Please supply<br>**Budget approved:**   £800<br><br><br><br>Signed ........ *S Kemp* ...................................................... | |

## The budget

This limits the amount that can be spent on a trip. As you will see in the case study on page 266, there may be a maximum amount that can be spent on accommodation, or the organisation may have negotiated special rates with a hotel chain or booking agency that it uses regularly.

If you are asked to cost out a trip, then you need to check the price of each option you research. Many websites will search for cheap flights across a range of airlines and will also offer you a variety of hotels at different prices (see page 255 for more information).

No-frills' airlines such as easyJet, Ryanair, Flybe and bmibaby are often welcomed by businesses as a way of saving money on travel. Be aware that bookings must usually be made online, there are no free meals and little flexibility about dates or times. Budget hotels, such as Travelodge and Premierlodge, are popular for the same reason.

Finally, check the options possible within the budget with the traveller before you make any reservations.

## The travel file and checklist

Each completed travel form should act as the basis of a specific travel file for that particular trip. It is sensible to open a new travel file immediately after you receive a request so that you have somewhere to keep all the documents and information you are likely to collect.

Label the file clearly with the date of travel and the name of the first person on the list of travellers. Keep your files stored in date order, so that you can quickly find the correct one. This also acts as a useful reminder because the files on the top of your pile are always the most urgent ones.

If your travel forms don't include an action column – or if the trip is very complex and there isn't enough room to list everything you need to do – then you may prefer to make out your own checklist. You can then organise the tasks you must do under headings and leave enough space to make notes.

The form or your checklist should be clipped to the front of the travel file and checked daily, to make sure you are up to date with jobs to be done. Arranging travel is one job that must not be delayed, particularly if someone wants a reservation on a busy day at a peak time. Forgetting to make a reservation promptly can result in having to pay more money or having to accept an indirect travel route or a less convenient time option. Forgetting to make it altogether would be disastrous!

If you had to draw up a checklist to accompany the travel form for Sue Kemp and her colleague, it may look similar to the example opposite.

**Did you know?**

Senior members of staff may not put the budget requirements for a trip on a travel form. Instead they may ask for the estimated travel cost and then initial this as being acceptable.

**Remember**

The 24-hour clock is always used for travel reservations to avoid confusion, so instead of saying 11 a.m. and 5 p.m. you would say 1100 hours and 1700 hours. You also need to take account of time differences – see page 263 for information.

## Travel checklist

Passengers  Sue Kemp x 2          Date of travel 15 October

**Travel**

Birmingham – Barcelona by air (no preferred airline)

Outward: 15 October a.m. flight

Return: 17 October p.m. flight

Check flight times and prices

**Accommodation**

2 x single rooms – check 3 or 4 star hotels, centrally located.

Obtain information on suitable hotels

**Currency**

£50 in euros

Order from travel agent

**Other**

Book 2 taxis from home addresses to Birmingham airport and for return.

Check and supply estimated cost for trip

# Sources of information and facilities for making travel and accommodation arrangements

Many travel organisers find the Internet invaluable when booking travel. All major airlines, rail companies, ferry companies, hotel groups and booking agencies have websites. You can look up timetables online, either through individual companies or through travel companies such as OAG (see the snapshot on the next page). This can be easier because you can compare the timetables of many providers at the same time. A good example of this is www.thetrainline.com which provides timetables for all rail providers in the UK.

You can also investigate other online travel providers, such as Expedia.com, Opodo.com and Orbitz.com where you can build a trip comprising separate components, such as transport and accommodation. Lastminute.com is also useful if you need to make an urgent booking because it specialises in short-notice reservations. At www.travelocity.co.uk/theknowledge you can view an advanced range of services specifically developed for business travellers. These include access to hand-picked hotels with photos, location maps and reviews, anywhere-to-anywhere bookings, 24-hour hold for eligible airline reservations and e-ticketing for many airlines, a fare watcher service to help travellers stay within budget, and graphical seat maps to pre-select seating.

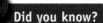

**Did you know?**

If your business traveller uses a car in the UK, satellite navigation will help him or her to find the way. Or you can check routes and places at www.multimap.com and www.streetfinder.com – and by using a package like Microsoft's Autoroute.

You can also obtain information on any foreign country either through the OAG site (see below) or from the website of the Foreign and Commonwealth Office. This is particularly useful if your colleagues are considering visiting a country where there may be particular problems as security alerts and advice on travelling is regularly posted on the site. The Department of Health provides useful travel advice on its website, included essential and recommended vaccinations for foreign trips.

There are one or two dangers with making reservations online unless you have received special training. First, it is often very difficult to work out which is the cheapest travel option, particularly for flights. Second, you may not have the authority to make bookings and payments online for your firm. Third, if you make a mistake you might create serious problems – such as an unsuitable booking that you cannot cancel! For that reason, after you have found out the basic information, you may feel safer making the reservations through a specialist travel agent.

## Snapshot – The value of OAG online

Not very long ago, no one working in a company's travel office would have lasted five minutes without their blue and white OAG (Official Airline Guide) books. These were bulky blue and white books containing a fascinating amount of detail about virtually every flight in the world. On a rainy Monday morning, you could flip through the pages, imagining yourself flying from one Pacific island to another – even looking up the departure and arrival times. The official reason for their purchase was, of course, to research flight options for your business travellers and find out which were preferred before you contacted the airline or your local travel agent to make a booking – from a choice of over half a million, from every commercial airport in the world.

In the 1990s things changed. The growth and popularity of the Internet meant most airlines had put their timetables online. No longer were OAG guides needed because travel organisers and agents could find all they needed without having to pore over flight lists in books.

So OAG reinvented itself by launching online, using its experience, expertise and information to provide one of the best travel information sites on the Net. Free information is given on a wide variety of topics – such as all the places you can fly to from Manchester, whether you need a visa to enter Japan, what inoculations are required for Egypt and what the climate and customs are in Fiji or Sumatra. For an additional small charge you can also have access to *OAG Flights* which provides the vast range of timetables that were originally available in the blue and white books. If you aren't sure whether your boss would think this is worth the money, take advantage of the free trial period to find out. You can find out more at www.oag.com/oag/website/com/en/home.

*Allow enough time for business travellers to make connections!*

## Itineraries and schedules

When you find out the information you need, it is important to talk this through with the traveller before you make any reservations. It is also important to double-check that the schedule is manageable. Your travel agent should stop you making basic mistakes with connection times, but there are still many other pitfalls to be aware of. Here are some:

- Don't assume that someone can travel from a city train station to an airport in five minutes flat.
- Don't forget to allow for checking-in time at airports and the collection of any baggage on arrival.
- Don't assume that it is possible to attend a meeting within ten minutes of arriving in a city.
- Remember that many cities have more than one airport and several train stations!

Often the easiest way to judge whether the schedule is manageable is to make out a draft itinerary (see page 263–264). You will need to ensure that spaces are left in the schedule for any meetings that still need to be arranged.

## Arranging meetings necessary during the trip

Many business travellers arrange their own meetings. The whole purpose of the trip may be to attend a previously arranged event – from a meeting to a conference or exhibition. In other cases you may be expected to make or confirm arrangements, particularly with branch offices being visited or with your opposite number in a firm that your organisation regularly contacts.

The most usual method of doing this is by email. This is better than the telephone, especially as you are dealing with someone abroad, as there is less chance of confusion and once the date and time have been confirmed you have the proof, in writing, for the travel file.

It is easier if you can offer several dates when you first make contact. You will have less flexibility if the traveller is trying to fit this in as an extra meeting during a pre-arranged trip and the date(s) or time(s) are restricted.

After you have arranged the meeting it is useful to note any documentation that needs to be taken, so that this can be included on the final itinerary.

## Making the reservations

You will need to make any 'no-frills' airline booking online. Otherwise, the safest route is to contact your firm's travel agent unless you have been trained how to make reservations online with your organisation's preferred carriers.

You can book train tickets in several ways. You can make a reservation on Eurostar by telephone, online or through your travel agent. Some travel agents, but not all, deal with ordinary train reservations so check with yours. Reservations are essential, however, for intercity trains, particularly at busy times, and it is important to reserve a seat as well. It is not possible to book a seat on regional services. If you can't use your local travel agent then reservations can be made at www.thetrainline.com, by going to the train operators' website or phoning the train operating company for the mainline service you want to use or by visiting your nearest mainline station.

You can make a hotel reservation direct with the hotel, or through your travel agent or a hotel reservations agency. Many large international chains, such as Holiday Inn, Hilton and Marriott, have a central reservations number/website for making bookings at their hotels all over the world. This is far easier than trying to phone an overseas hotel, particularly if English is not their first language.

### Find out

You can choose train seats that face forwards or backwards on many trains. Find out your traveller's preferences. If you normally buy standard class tickets to save money, and travel is during a weekend, check whether any cheap upgrades to first class are available.

### Did you know?

If you make hotel bookings for female executives in London, check out the five-star Grange City hotel that has a wing catering only for women. The 68 rooms in this wing are specially designed with women's needs in mind. The aim is to lessen security worries for women travelling alone.

## How to ... Book hotel accommodation as agreed

- Make sure you have all your requirements in front of you before you start. These should include:

  - the date and day of arrival, the date and day of departure and the number of nights

  - the estimated time of arrival (you should always notify the hotel in advance if this is likely to be later than 6 p.m. so there is no danger of your traveller being considered a 'no show' and the room being re-let)

  - whether breakfast is required (this is not an option in many countries where bookings are for room only)

  - the type of accommodation required (single, twin, double, ordinary, executive, deluxe etc.).

- On the telephone, ask the reservations clerk to repeat back the information to you so that you can be satisfied you have been understood correctly. Then check how you will receive written confirmation. If it is not usual for the hotel to send a letter of confirmation, agree to exchange emails instead.

- On the Internet, read any online booking forms carefully. Remember you may have a choice of types of accommodation so check that you stay within budget and stick to the type agreed with your traveller. Print out a copy of the form when you have completed it. You will normally receive an automatic email confirmation as well.

- Keep a copy of all accommodation emails or forms in the travel file.

### Remember

There is less chance of confusion if you always confirm the number of nights when you book accommodation. For example, arriving 4 June and departing 9 June involves five nights.

### Over to you

1 Use the OAG website to find the answers to the following questions.

  a Do the motorists drive on the left or the right in Japan?

  b Is there a national holiday in Canada in September?

  c Can one fly direct from Leeds Bradford airport (LBA) to Amsterdam?

  d Can one fly direct from Leeds Bradford airport to Toronto?

  e How many terminals are there at Bournemouth airport?

  f Is a visa needed by a British person to visit Egypt?

  g What currency is used in Iceland?

  h What is the direct dialling code for Iceland?

**Over to you** Continued

2 If you are visiting a hotel on holiday, you may want to know whether it has a large pool or a spa. Business travellers, however, often have other needs.

   **a** Imagine you are travelling on business to an important meeting. What facilities would you like the hotel to have? Suggest six you would consider essential.

   **b** Then suggest an additional three facilities you think female executives, such as those visiting the new wing at Grange City, would want.

Compare your lists with other people or your colleagues and then check your ideas with the suggestions given on the CD-ROM.

3 Your boss phones you and says he urgently needs you to find out how he can get to Dublin tomorrow morning, returning two days later. He will also need a four-star hotel in the city for two nights at a reasonable price.

   **a** Identify two ways to obtain this information.

   **b** Using your own town as a base, find out the travel information that is required.

   **c** Find the names of three hotels he could stay in that meet his requirements.

Check your answers with your tutor or trainer.

4 Practise researching online by deciding on three places you would like to visit if you had a choice. Then use one or more of the websites mentioned on page 255 to build your trip and find out the cost.

## Core unit link

Obviously you will communicate with travellers and will discuss their needs. You will have to read written material and provide written information to people, so it is likely that your evidence for question one will link to unit 201, performannce indicators 1–6.

You should keep your traveller informed of your progress because you will be working to a deadline. Check how your evidence for question two links to unit 201, PIs 7–12.

Because you are working with outside organisations and individuals, check whether you can cross-reference your evidence to unit 202, PI 4, as well as to Unit 201, PIs 1–6.

Question three's evidence should link to unit 201, PI 14, because you have to follow agreed procedures, in addition to unit 202, PIs 1–3.

## Evidence collection

1 Keep copies of travel forms you receive or other notes you make when you are confirming the travel, accommodation and budget requirements with a traveller. Ask the traveller to countersign these to confirm the discussion. Discuss with your assessor which of the forms should go into your portfolio.

2 Keep copies of your checklists and the notes you make, as well as emails or faxes that confirm meetings or reservations or which answer travel enquiries. In addition keep copies of all draft itineraries and schedules and ask the traveller who agreed them to make a note on them to confirm this. Again discuss with your assessor which documents should go into your portfolio.

3 Make a note of the location of your organisation's travel policy and any specific procedures you must follow when you are making travel and accommodation arrangements. Be prepared to talk about them in a professional discussion with your assessor.

# Procedures to make credit and payment arrangements

Your organisation's procedures will include the steps you must take to obtain finance for anyone travelling on behalf of the firm. There are various payment options.

- Company (corporate) credit cards can be issued to staff who travel on business. These are used to pay for most expenses at home and abroad.
- The traveller can be given cash, in foreign or English currency, to pay for expenses such as taxi or tube fares.
- Travellers' cheques are useful for taking spare cash abroad safely. In this case the numbers of the cheques need recording and kept separately from the cheques themselves. You will also receive a list of the banks in different countries to be informed of any loss.

Alternatively, the traveller may pay his or her own expenses and reclaim them on return. In this case the person may use a personal debit or credit card to obtain cash or settle any bills.

If you have to obtain foreign currency then the procedure may be different if you work for a large company, where many people routinely travel abroad on business. In this case you may be able to obtain common foreign currencies, such as the euro, from your finance office. If you work for a small firm, you will need to obtain foreign currency from your bank or travel agent. Common currencies will be kept in stock but you will have to order any unusual ones. Your bank or travel agent will also supply any travellers' cheques you need. It is normal to ask for sterling travellers' cheques as these can be converted in any country, although it is wise to check which your executive prefers. In some countries of the world, US dollar cheques may be preferred.

**Did you know?**

Some countries (e.g. Russia and Morocco) have currency regulations that prevent local currency being taken out of the country, so your traveller has to obtain this on arrival. You can find out from your firm's bank or travel agent which countries have these restrictions.

# Information to provide to the person travelling

You can expect the person who is travelling to require the following documents and information and it will be your job to obtain and collate these:

### Basic documentation

- air, rail or other travel tickets
- hotel reservation confirmation or vouchers
- relevant timetables and maps
- copies of any essential travel insurance documents
- current vaccination certificates.

### Documents you may need to prepare

- a travel folder containing all the relevant information for the trip
- two itineraries – one detailed and one summarised and attached to the front of the folder
- emails or other confirmation documents for hotels
- business documents related to visits being made or meetings to attend
- a contact list (see page 268): travel company, 24-hour helplines, hotel number, transport operators (e.g. airline, rail company), colleagues or local offices, clients being visited etc.
- a currency receipt.

The documents need to be collated into a sensible order, so that all documents on one topic are clipped together. It is normal to put documents relating to the trip as a whole into date order, so that confirmation relating for a meeting on the 16th, for example, would be placed in the file before an email relating to a meeting on the 20th.

## Maintain your own records

You will obviously be handing over a considerable amount of information to the traveller but this shouldn't mean you have no record yourself. Imagine how it would look if someone asked you which hotel had been reserved or on

*Be realistic about the amount of information your traveller can deal with!*

which date the traveller returned – and you had no idea! You need records for three main reasons.

- You have to be able to answer any queries relating to the trip while the traveller is away.
- You have to keep a record of what was arranged in case there are any queries when the bills are received.
- You can build up your own reference files relating to travel and accommodation options. As you will see on page 269 if you use feedback from the traveller to evaluate these you can identify the best choices and this can save you a considerable amount of time if you are involved in making arrangements for the same destination in the future.

## Provide the information and documents in good time

The information and documents will be collected over a period of time and it is essential that everything is placed promptly in the travel file. It is wise to check off all the relevant documents against a master checklist as you receive them – and as you check them. This avoids a last-minute panic because something hasn't been received yet.

It is imperative that you check key documents as soon as they are received. Any tickets must be checked to confirm that the name of the passenger, date of travel, time of departure and other details are as specified. For accommodation, the date of arrival and departure is critical, as well as the type of room and quoted room rate. If you receive any currency, check that the amount you have matches the amount on the attached receipt.

**Remember**

It is useful to check that your traveller has a good supply of business cards to take on a trip – or put a few spare cards in the travel folder.

## Confirm that the itinerary and documents meet requirements

The next stage is to draw up the itinerary. This will be relatively easy if you have kept your checklist up to date and filed papers in your travel file neatly, as you are simply extracting the key information. The itinerary is a list of all the travel and accommodation arrangements for the trip, from leaving home to returning home. Many executives prefer a comprehensive version to include all the visits arranged, stating where they will take place, when and with whom – giving a contact name and number – and including any social functions they must attend. It is often useful to clip or staple this longer version to the front of the travel file and to provide a shorter version of essential travel details and the hotel name for reference that can be carried in a pocket.

**Remember**

Flight arrival times are always shown in the local time of the destination and take account of any time differences. You can check these online at www.timeanddate.com/worldclock.

An example of a full itinerary for Sue Kemp is shown on the next page. Observe the following elements:

- **The point of departure and return** – and whether this is home or office. Always check with the traveller, but generally the earlier the start, the later the return and the longer the trip then the more likely it will start and end from home.

- **The travel arrangements that have been made.** Ideally an itinerary should have no travel gaps, so you may need to check the arrangements that are needed to get your traveller to and from the airport or train station both here and abroad.
- **Sufficient time for check-in** at the airport to conform to the airline rules. This will be stated on the ticket or you can always check with the airline or your travel agent.
- **Telephone numbers** – the number of the taxi firm and the mobile number of the colleague that Sue Kemp is due to meet, so that if there is a travel problem it can be sorted out easily
- **Hotel details** – hotel name, address and telephone number.
- **Appointments** – details of appointments and/or social arrangements, including the name of the person being met, the address and telephone number together with details of the files containing any relevant papers.

Reference should be made also to the currency being taken.

---

### Itinerary for Sue Kemp and Polly Bryant

**VISIT TO BARCELONA, 15 – 17 OCTOBER**

**Monday 15 October**

| | |
|---|---|
| 0720 | Taxi from home to airport (J L Supercars – Tel: 061 392 4990) |
| 0820 | Check in at airport |
| 1020 | Depart flight IB 7590 |
| 1350 | Arrive Barcelona (to be met by Juan Cortez – mobile 0034320938499) |
| | Accommodation reserved at Hotel Amrey Diagonal, Avinguda Diagonal 161-163, 08018 Barcelona, Tel: (34-93) 4868800 |
| | Confirmatory email attached |

**Tuesday 16 October**

| | |
|---|---|
| 0900 | Meeting at Barcelona office |
| | For relevant papers see folder 1 |
| 1400 | Meeting with Isabel Pilar at El Corte Ingles |
| | For relevant papers and fabric samples see folder 2 |
| 2000 | Dinner with Manuel Burgos and Juan Cortez |
| | Table reservation being made by Barcelona office |

**Wednesday 17 October**

| | |
|---|---|
| 0900 | Meeting in Barcelona office |
| 1130 | Depart airport (taxi to be arranged by Barcelona office) |
| 1230 | Check in at airport |
| 1430 | Depart flight IB 7591 |
| 1600 | Arrive Birmingham. Taxi booked with J L Supercars for transport to home or office (Tel: 061 392 4990) |

**Currency**

£50 in Euros

*Knowing what to wear can save a lot of embarrassment!*

The itinerary provides a useful guide when you are assembling the documents because you can check, item by item, that nothing is missing – from tickets and accommodation confirmations to documents relating to forthcoming business meetings and visits. These should be numbered separately for each meeting and a cross-reference entered in the itinerary. A final category is 'miscellaneous documents', including invitations to events and any information you have obtained on social customs or public holidays that would be useful.

Currency or travellers' cheques should be handed over separately and not put in with the travel documents.

## Final checks

As you become more experienced you will automatically run through a final checklist in your mind as you confirm that everything is correct and complete. This should include:

- tickets, passport and visa (if needed) *checked*
- all confirmation documents in the right order and *checked*
- all meetings documents *checked*
- enough time allowed to get to and from all meetings and travel points *checked*
- no travel gaps or missing information *checked*.

### Case study A trip to the Big Apple!

*Read the case study below and then answer the questions that follow. Check your answers with those on the CD-ROM.*

Julie Mitchell is a Bid Manager for Bower Auction Houses. She leads a team that writes and designs documents which convince clients to sell their property – such as fine paintings and furniture – through Bower rather than their competitors. Julie regularly travels to meet and exchange ideas with her opposite numbers in Paris, Zurich, Melbourne and New York and has just returned from a trip to the Big Apple – as New York is often known.

Bower Auction Houses use the services of a local high street travel agent. Tilly, one of the firm's administrators, made all the travel arrangements for Julie's trip, including booking the flights and the hotel the firm uses in New York, arranging a cash advance of $500 and an extension on Julie's corporate credit card from £1000 to £4000.

Tilly had to take account of Bowers' rules and procedures when she made the booking. The travel policy is listed on the company's intranet – an information area on the computer system restricted to employees only. This means that employees can refer to it at any time. All Bid Managers must fly economy whereas the CEO and Chairman fly business class. For accommodation, the firm has several deals with hotel chains that mean whichever country they are in they get a fixed corporate rate that has been pre-agreed. Julie stayed at a four-star hotel near Central Park. There is also a food budget. For Julie, this was $15 for breakfast, $20 for lunch and $40 for dinner. Julie had to keep all receipts for cash purchases to claim them back and all receipts for card purchases to attach to the bill at the end of the month.

Other allowable expenses included taxis to business meetings and to/from the airport and any art-related books or publishing materials she wanted to buy in New York.

Julie settled the hotel bill with her corporate credit card. The cost was $200 dollars a night for five nights. Julie paid for both herself and her graphic designer on the trip. In case of emergency she had her New York line manager's home, work and cellphone number but, thankfully, didn't encounter any problems.

**Questions**

1  Why is it useful to put a company's travel policy on the firm's intranet?

2  Suggest two reasons why the firm uses a local travel agent to make the reservations.

3  Suggest two reasons why Julie's corporate credit card limit was extended for the trip.

4  What was the total cost of accommodation on the trip, in dollars?

5  Explain how Bower controls the cost of accommodation for its employees.

6  Suggest two costs Julie would have paid in cash.

7  Why do you think only senior employees are allowed to travel business class?

8  Why was Julie given her New York line manager's home and cellphone number?

# Problems with arrangements and how to deal with them

There are too many different types of problem that can occur with business trips to list in a book! However, they can be sub-divided into different groups. Problems can arise because of:

- missing, incomplete, incorrect or late travel documentation from the travel agent
- a misunderstanding over a booking or reservation
- sudden changes to schedules
- accidents, mishaps and loss
- traffic delays and flight delays (often because of poor weather).

There are four ways in which you can minimise the effect of problems outside your control:

- Take steps to ensure that problems that occur during a trip can, so far as is possible, be solved on the spot by the traveller. This is best done through a comprehensive contact list that give the names, addresses and telephone numbers that could be needed.

**Remember**

Don't cause problems yourself! Keep documents in order and in a safe place, check them thoroughly and prepare for a trip as far in advance as possible.

- Keep a similar list yourself with key sources of advice you may need (see the list below). Don't just rely on one stored on your computer, keep a hard copy in your desk drawer.
- Make sure you and your travellers know the action to take if there is a problem. Missing luggage must be reported at the time, before the traveller leaves the airport. To qualify for an insurance claim any losses or accidents must normally be reported immediately. If an airline passenger is inconvenienced by cancellations, overbooking or lengthy delays then, according to European Commission rules, they must be paid compensation up to £420 (at the time of writing).
- Make sure you and the person travelling know how to contact each other at all stages of the trip in an emergency. Mobile phones and laptops that can receive email anywhere have improved communications enormously. In a crisis, the last thing you need is to find that you have no contact number for the person travelling.
- Keep a spare set of contact details for the trip in case your traveller loses the list or, even worse, loses his or her mobile phone!

## Emergency contact lists

### The traveller's contacts

- Details of any company branch offices and mobile number(s) of person in charge/key staff
- Details of other customers in the area who could be visited if there is time to spare or an appointment is cancelled
- Details of a reputable car hire firm in the area
- Contact details of travel agent and airline
- UK code for making calls from country being visited
- Phone numbers/addresses of:
  - local bank for reporting lost travellers' cheques
  - British embassy or consulate in the region
  - insurers' 24-hour helpline (or other number to which any claims must be reported immediately)
  - card protection agency (in case credit cards are stolen)

### Your list

- Your travel agent (for travel rearrangements and problems)
- Your travel insurance company (for accidents and loss)
- The British Embassy in the country concerned (for loss of passport)
- The Foreign and Commonwealth office (for serious incidents abroad)
- Other embassies and consulates (for direct advice on visas etc.)
- Your organisation's bank (for problems/advice on money abroad)
- An international hotel booking agency (in case of an accommodation crisis)
- An international car hire firm (in case of serious transport difficulties)
- An experienced colleague – in case you are completely stuck!

# Evaluating the travel and accommodation used and recording the evaluation

Many organisations issue review forms to business travellers asking them to evaluate the services used. These are very similar to the ones you may have filled in at the end of a holiday, either just before you left a hotel or when you were on the plane or coach home.

The survey should include sections related to:

- **the departure experience** – in case an alternative point of departure could be selected to improve matters
- **the journey, related services and cost** – in case an alternative provider would provide better service/value for money
- **the overall journey** – in terms of speed and service
- **the accommodation** – in terms of cleanliness, service and cost
- **any problems experienced** – and how these were resolved/whether they could be prevented in the future
- **any other relevant comments** that may be helpful for future travellers.

There is no point issuing this type of questionnaire and then putting the responses in a file to gather dust! You need to analyse the answers and use them to modify your records and files. You could, for example, give your own star rating to hotels, based on feedback from your colleagues. You could identify preferred airlines and train operators in terms of pitch (the space between your knees and the seat in front), food and service. You could identify the best routes to travel to different destinations, particularly for long-haul journeys. You can also include your own comments relating to whether you receive good or bad service from external organisations you contact. You can then update your records so that you always opt for the best quality option for future trips given the budget agreed.

## Changing places

*Your assessor will ask you how you will adapt your skills if you change your job in the future. You will need to think about the way in which your role might change if you worked for a different organisation.*

Dawn works for a large machine manufacturing company that sells all over the world. She arranges travel for the directors, the sales representatives and technicians who repair equipment if it goes faulty. The directors fly business class and stay in four-star hotels. The sales reps fly economy and so do the technicians, who must also stay in three-star accommodation.

Sonia works as administrator for a member of the European Parliament who lives in England but works in Brussels. He sometimes travels by air but more

**Changing places** Continued

often travels on Eurostar. Sonia keeps a careful record of all his expenditure on travel so that he can reclaim it as expenses.

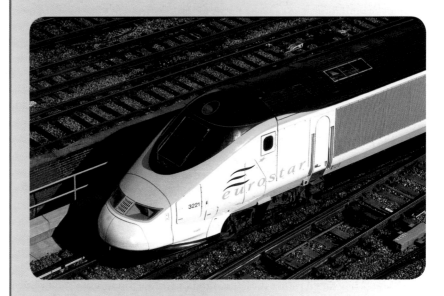

Jamilla works for her local college. She arranges travel for staff who need to attend meetings and other events, mainly in the UK. Most of them prefer to travel by train rather than drive. Overnight stays are not allowed if the traveller could return that night. Occasionally she arranges student trips, normally by contacting a specialist student travel firm.

Jack arranges travel for the staff who work for a production company specialising in 3D graphics effects for films and television. The designers and technical staff often need to travel to proposed programme locations, all over the UK, to assess these. This sometimes means finding overnight accommodation in quite remote areas. The technical director regularly travels between her offices in Edinburgh, Leeds and London and usually prefers to go by air.

John has a high powered job as a management consultant and relies on his administrator, Penny, to arrange meetings for him and make all his travel arrangements. He regularly flies to Germany and Scandinavian countries where he has several clients. Penny books his flights through a travel agent but makes hotel bookings direct. John frequently entertains clients in the hotel so needs to stay somewhere that gives high quality service.

1  For any *one* person listed above, identify the differences he or she would find if moving to your organisation and doing your job.

2  For any *one* person listed above, say how you would need to adapt your skills if you did his or her job rather than your own.

1  Sue Kemp has asked you for a summary itinerary, printed on a small card that she can keep in her bag. She wants it to contain essential travel information and the details of the hotel. Look back at the itinerary for Sue Kemp on page 264 and use this to extract the information required in a clear, easy-to-read format. Check this against the one shown on the CD-ROM.

2  Say what you would do if each of the following problems occurred when your boss is on a business trip to Nice in France. Then check your ideas with the suggestions on the CD-ROM.

   a  The plane is delayed for three hours so she will miss her first appointment.

   b  She leaves her travel folder on the plane and rings you in a panic.

   c  The day before she is due to fly on to Frankfurt in Germany, there is a strike of French baggage handlers and no planes are flying from Nice airport.

   d  She has her passport stolen in Frankfurt.

3  Time zones can cause a lot of problems! Check you understand how these work by answering the following questions. Remember that Britain is on GMT in the winter and BST (GMT +1 hour) in the summer. But many other countries have summer systems, too, like Daylight Saving Time, so the time difference stays about the same all year round.

   a  If it is 12 o'clock in London in December, what time is it in the following places. Use the 24-hour clock for your answers.

      ● New York (GMT – 5)

      ● Tokyo (GMT + 9)

      ● Sydney (GMT + 11)

      ● Vancouver (GMT – 8).

   b  Check your answers online at www.timeanddate.com/worldclock as well as on the CD-ROM. If you do this activity in summer, bear in mind you must allow for the difference.

   c  I leave London at 1330 and arrive in New York at 1600 *local time*. Explain why the flight seems only to take two and a half hours.

   d  I return to London four days later. I leave New York at 2130. Explain why my arrival time is 0915 the following day.

   e  Look back at Sue Kemp's itinerary. Now check the duration of her journeys to and from Barcelona in Spain. What does this tell you about the time difference?

   f  Your boss is staying in Wellington, New Zealand. You have a crisis in the office at 4 p.m. Would you ring him immediately? If you are not sure, check www.timeanddate.com/worldclock to find out!

## Core unit link

Question one's evidence should also prove that you behave in a way that supports effective working and link to unit 201, performance indicators 20 and 25.

The evidence for question two should link to unit 201, PIs 12 and 14. Check too, whether you can link this to security and confidentiality requirements in unit 202, PIs 13 and 14.

If your travellers also confirm that you treat them with honesty, respect and consideration, enjoy new challenges and are helpful and supportive, then your evidence for question three will link to unit 201, PIs 20, 22, 24 and 25.

In question four if any problems were caused by a mistake you made, then this will link to unit 201, PI 13. Similarly, feedback from other people will link to unit 201, PIs 15 and 16.

If you also use this information to improve your own performance, then your question five evidence should link to unit 201, PI 16.

## Evidence collection

1   Make sure that the copies of your completed travel files are available to show to your assessor. These can cover past trips and future trips where you have already received and checked the tickets. They should include a copy of the finalised itinerary for the trip, agreed with and countersigned by the traveller. Be prepared to explain how you collate the documents and to show the records that you keep.

2   Keep records of any credit and payment facilities you have obtained and any payments you have made and note down the location of the procedures you have to follow for these.

3   Ask two or three of your regular travellers to provide witness testimony to confirm that you have met their needs, made the necessary arrangements and provided the information and documents in good time. Alternatively, if your organisation issues a review form to assess the trip afterwards, make a copy and ask your traveller(s) to add an extra comment about your role in making the reservations.

4   If you deal with problems relating to a trip, you can either write a personal statement about this, discuss it with your assessor or ask the traveller who was involved to make an additional comment on the review form or provide witness testimony for you.

5   Be prepared to have a professional discussion with your assessor about the ways in which you evaluate the external services you use, such as airlines, train companies and hotels, and how this has influenced the bookings you now make. Support your claims by showing records relating to evaluations – such as travel review forms, formal or informal feedback from your travellers or your own notes.

## What if?

What should you do if no problems arise during the time you are being assessed? In this case your assessor will ask 'what if?' questions to check what you *would* do if a problem occurred.

## Key skills reminder

If you are taking Key Skills awards, remember to discuss with your tutor or trainer how your evidence for this unit could also count towards those awards.

# Deal with visitors

## Unit summary and overview

This option unit covers all the main aspects of meeting visitors' needs at reception. The receptionist is often the first point of contact for visitors to an organisation and can therefore influence their judgement of the whole business. In this unit you will learn about the skills required to give a professional image as well as how to cope with the type of queries or problems you might have to deal with.

Many people who are new to reception work often struggle to balance efficiency with being friendly and helpful, particularly when they are very busy. By the time you have completed this unit and obtained your evidence, you should feel far more confident about your ability to do this, even in some quite difficult situations.

### Link to option units

As you gather your evidence for this unit you should also obtain evidence for your core units. Watch for the Core unit link logo which suggests how the evidence you may collect may count towards both this unit and your core units.

Remember that you might be able to identify other links yourself, because of your own job role and the evidence you have obtained.

Talk to your assessor if you need further guidance on how your evidence should be cross-referenced.

### Did you know?

Statistics show that we assess someone new within three seconds of meeting them, whether we are looking at them or speaking to them over the phone. A professional reception service immediately reassures new callers and gives the message that the organisation is efficient and cares for the people it deals with.

### Find out

Check out the different duties undertaken by receptionists, skills required and current salary levels in your area online at a recruitment firm such as www.reed.co.uk or www.totaljobs.com.

# The importance of a friendly and efficient reception service

We are all influenced by first impressions. While many of your school days might now just seem a blur, you may still remember your first day at a new school or in a new class. The same applies to any occasion when you have been somewhere for the first time – a holiday resort, a concert, a hospital or a college or workplace for an interview. If it is a new experience you may be rather apprehensive. Your immediate first impression will then be influenced by the way you are treated. If you are greeted with a smile and made to feel welcome then you will start to feel better. If the service is efficient, too, then you are likely to have a good opinion of the whole organisation.

It is for this reason that reception is often called the public face of the organisation, and this is why some organisations will spend large sums of money to ensure that the reception area is as welcoming as possible – with customised furniture and other facilities, such as daily newspapers and a coffee machine. The aim is to give all visitors a good first impression. Obviously there is little point in doing this if the receptionist is surly or unkempt as this ruins the whole effect.

If you work in reception then you have a very responsible job, because you can personally influence many of your visitors. If they are very impressed they are likely to recommend your organisation to other people. If they have a bad experience then they are not only likely to go elsewhere themselves in future, but may tell their friends to do the same!

# The role of the receptionist

Businesses that have a constant stream of visitors often have receptionists. Examples include large hotels, hospitals, health centres, solicitors and many commercial organisations, such as the BBC. In these cases the receptionist(s) may be fully occupied ensuring that each and every visitor is dealt with promptly and properly.

Smaller organisations and businesses that have fewer personal callers will normally expect their receptionists to do other administrative duties as well, such as maintaining the office diary and/or appointments book, answering the telephone and responding to email enquiries.

However, for anyone working on reception the key area of the work relates to dealing with visitors promptly and efficiently. The person's overall role is therefore likely to include:

- welcoming visitors in a friendly, professional and helpful manner to create a good first impression of the organisation
- greeting visitors on arrival and meeting their needs
- handling enquiries from callers

- providing information related to the organisation
- maintaining the reception area and ensuring it is kept tidy
- keeping visitor records
- monitoring access to the building by visitors
- carrying out day-to-day administration duties related to reception, including answering telephones and emails
- liaising with other departments in the organisation about visitor needs and related matters
- dealing with any visitor problems promptly and efficiently.

## How to ... Help visitors feel welcome

- Make eye contact and smile when a visitor arrives, even if you are dealing with someone else or are on the telephone at the time.

- Greet the person by saying 'Hello', 'Good morning' or 'Good afternoon' and ask how you can help.

- Greet regular visitors by name, whenever you can.

- Find out a new visitor's name tactfully. Say 'Could you give me your name, please', not 'What are you called?'

- If the visitor needs to record his or her arrival in a visitor log, have a pen available and show the visitor the information you need.

- If required, notify the appropriate colleague(s) promptly of the visitor's arrival (see page 286).

**Did you know?**

If visitors will have to wait, it is better to warn them than to say nothing. When you estimate the wait, under-promise and over-deliver. This means suggesting a longer delay than is likely, simply because it is better to be told the wait may be 15 minutes – when it is really 10 minutes – and then be pleasantly surprised, rather than the reverse.

**How to ... Continued**

- Remember that talking about neutral topics, such as the weather or the journey, often breaks the ice and helps a visitor to relax.

- If there is likely to be a short wait, make sure the visitor knows the facilities that are available such as newspapers, magazines, water cooler or coffee machine.

- If the visitor has travelled some distance, be prepared to point out where the toilets are situated.

- Don't 'blank out' visitors who are sitting and waiting. Monitor how long they have been there and reassure them you haven't forgotten about them. See also page 279 for more information.

# The importance of providing a positive image

On a sunny morning, when you are wearing a favourite outfit, having a 'good hair day' and the world is treating you well, it is easy to smile at everyone you meet and want to help them. This isn't as easy on a day when you arrived dripping wet, ten minutes late, depressed after a major row with a friend last night and then spilt coffee down yourself! The image you are now in danger of giving is rather different unless you can arrange for someone to cover for you while you freshen up and cheer up!

Similarly, it is easy to present a positive image of your organisation when work is fine and you are doing well. But if you have problems with a colleague or are under pressure with lots to do and no time to do it, you may be far more grumpy and even terse with visitors.

At the opposite extreme, there is also the danger that you say too much in your urge to appear friendly. Chatting to visitors about your workload and the difficulties of finding anyone quickly in Sales may seem quite harmless and even be welcomed by one or two visitors, but most people – including your boss – would consider this unprofessional. Some visitors might even be embarrassed. Always remember that a good receptionist is welcoming and articulate – but is also tactful and discrete.

## How to ... Present a positive image of yourself and your organisation

- Wear clothes that reflect the image your organisation wants to portray – whether formal or informal.

- Be well groomed at all times.

- Look pleasant, cheerful and welcoming

- Smile when you greet people and make eye contact

- Be prepared to mention a 'neutral' topic in a friendly way, such as the weather, parking, journey or distance travelled.

- Keep visitors informed if they will have a short wait, so they know you haven't forgotten them.

- Always be polite and courteous, no matter how busy you are.

- Treat everyone the same regardless of their appearance.

- Never make witticisms or tactless comments about your employer, your boss or your colleagues.

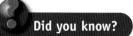

### Did you know?

There are lots of reception scare stories about people being treated badly because they looked a bit scruffy – and the receptionist later finding out how important they were. These days you can't assume all VIPs will be dressed formally, so beware!

That's the Chairman, you know

# Your visitors, their requirements and needs

The visitors you deal with, and their needs, will largely depend on the type of organisation you work for and the goods or services it offers. The main factors that influence a visitor's needs are shown in the diagram below.

**Types of visitors**

Visitors can be categorised in various ways, such as:
- whether they are private individuals or business contacts
- their personal characteristics (age, ethnicity, gender etc.)
- how often they visit
- the distance they travel.

Visitors to a large commercial organisation are most likely to be business contacts who have regular contact with the firm. They will mainly be suppliers, potential suppliers, customers or potential customers. The scope of the company's operations will affect how far they have travelled – from within the region, another part of the UK or from abroad.

Visitors to public sector organisations, such as your local council, hospital or college, are more likely to be private individuals who live in the area. Their personal characteristics will depend on the profile of the local community.

This type of information can often be found by looking in the visitors book or appointment system. The visitors book will normally give the name and address of each person and, if they are visiting on business, identify the company they represent. More detailed personal information will be available if the appointments or recording system is linked to a client or customer database.

**Remember**

In unit 202 you saw how you should support diversity. This links with the type of visitors you deal with and how you help to meet their individual needs.

Type of visitor

Their state of mind

Reason for visit

Any additional needs they have

The type of visitors will influence the facilities available.

- Business people who have travelled some distance may want to freshen up. Many organisations ensure that overcoats and wet umbrellas can be left in a coat stand or cloakroom. Someone who has come straight from the airport may need to leave luggage in a secure place. Newspapers in reception will probably be titles like *The Financial Times* or *The Times*, and magazines may include *The Economist*. If there is a plasma television it will probably be tuned to a news programme.
- Amenities and distractions for family groups, young adults or children include a toybox in a corner and/or a fish tank, newspapers and magazines such as *The Daily Mail*, *Hello* and *Cosmopolitan* and a television tuned to standard daytime programmes or children's TV. Easy access to a toilet area is essential for young children.

**Reason for visit**

Visitors arrive in reception for various reasons. They may be attending or making an appointment, leaving a package, making an enquiry or a booking, checking in, buying a ticket, asking for information, paying a bill or arriving for an interview – to name but a few! The reasons vary depending on the type of organisation you work for.

The main reason why visitors come to your organisation, and the amount of time they might have to wait, will affect:

- the type of queries you can expect to answer on a routine basis
- the information you need to have available to give to visitors
- the number of distractions that are available
- the action you are expected to take on their arrival.

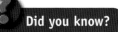

For this reason a hotel is likely to have leaflets and timetables on local services and attractions and receptionists will be trained to check (or make) a booking, register the guest and process payments when required. A health centre will have advice leaflets on diet, inoculations and common ailments, facilities for babies and young children, and receptionists will log arrivals against the appointment system and ensure health professionals have the patient records they require.

### The visitor's state of mind

People can arrive in reception in a variety of different moods. Some will be relaxed and happy, others may be anxious or nervous, a few may be tetchy or impatient.

In some cases the reasons for this may be nothing to do with their visit. Anyone who has spent ten minutes looking for a parking space after being in a traffic queue for 20 minutes and who is now late for the appointment is likely to arrive in quite a state. It is the receptionist's job to deal with this calmly and reassure the visitor that, so far as is possible, everything will be done to ensure their needs will still be met.

In other organisations, receptionists have to be prepared to deal with people who are anxious or upset because of the nature of their visit. This may be the case, for example, if you work for a medical specialist, a solicitor or a vet – where owners may be very distressed if their pet is seriously ill or has had to be put down. In this case a visitor may be distracted and need to be handled gently and tactfully. A visitor who is very upset may need to be offered the option of going to a private area for a while to recover.

Sometimes impatience, anxiety or irritation can make people aggressive, rather than upset. There is no reason why anyone should have to tolerate verbal insults or aggressive behaviour in reception, and anyone who works on reception should be aware of their employer's policies for dealing with this situation and know how to get help. You will learn more about this on page 289–290.

**Additional needs**

Your visitors may have additional needs, particularly if they have arrived from abroad and don't speak English very well or if they have a disability. You will always do better dealing with people who are different from you if you are a natural 'people-person' and enjoy trying to understand and help other people. If you find this quite difficult at times, the tips in the table below might help.

**Remember**

Dealing with a variety of visitors may link to both diversity and discrimination issues covered in unit 202.

| The additional needs of visitors | |
| --- | --- |
| **Type of visitor** | **Suggested action** |
| **Foreign visitors** | *It may only become obvious that someone cannot speak English very well when you try to explain something to him/her. So:*<br>Speak relatively slowly<br>Use simple English words (and no slang or local expressions!)<br>Use short sentences<br>Write it down – the person's reading skills may be better than his/her listening skills<br>Don't shout, be embarrassed, laugh or show impatience<br>Know which of your colleagues speak other languages<br>Ask for help if you need it |
| **Visitors who are deaf or hard of hearing** | *You cannot tell if someone is deaf by looking, but most deaf people can lip read. So:*<br>Look at the person when you are speaking<br>Don't speak too quickly<br>If asked to do so, write down what you want to say<br>Don't shout!<br>Know whether your organisation offers the TypeTalk service to deaf people who make contact by phone |
| **Visitors who are blind or visually impaired** | *Not all blind people wear dark glasses or carry white sticks, but someone with a severe visual impairment may tell you this as he/she arrives. So:*<br>Speak to the person so that your voice will act as a guide |

**Did you know?**

You will empathise more with someone who is struggling to communicate with you if you think how you feel if you are abroad, don't speak the language and are trying to make yourself understood!

| The additional needs of visitors Continued | |
|---|---|
| | Unless the person asks for assistance, don't grab hold of him/her<br>If you are asked for help, lead gently<br>Warn of obstacles and stairs – say how many steps there are and whether these are up or down<br>Tell the person if there are Braille buttons on the lift or on other signs |
| **Visitors who have mobility problems** | *Under the Disability Discrimination Act, all organisations must provide appropriate access and facilities for visitors. So:*<br>Know the facilities that exist in your organisation, such as wheelchair access, disabled toilets and disabled parking spaces<br>Be ready to hold open doors<br>Don't try to rush someone or appear impatient because he/she is on crutches or in a wheelchair |

## Snapshot – Receptionist of the year

In 2005, Jayne Backhouse of the Pearl Veterinary Group in Shrewsbury was named Vet Receptionist of the Year at the annual Petplan Veterinary Awards. She beat over 100 other competitors to win the trophy and £1000 in Virgin vouchers.

Jayne was nominated by both clients and colleagues for her incredible dedication to the job. She often picks up clients and their pets if a vet cannot visit, drops off prescriptions and calls to check that disabled and elderly clients have arrived home safely after visiting the surgery.

Jayne's job involves controlling the appointments system, sending in drug orders and answering the telephone. Previously she was an NHS nurse and this has helped her to offer advice easily and give worried clients an accurate update on their pet. According to her colleagues, much of the success and the reputation of the practice is due to Jayne, who often works long after her shift has ended and volunteers to come in when the practice is short-staffed.

Petplan, the leading UK pet insurance provider, searches nationwide for the best vet, vet nurse, vet receptionist and vet practice. It donates £1 to Petsavers, the charity of the veterinary profession, for every nomination received. So if you are impressed with someone at your vet's, why don't you nominate him or her for an award? Or you can go to www.pearlvetgroup.co.uk to check out the practice Jayne works in, take a virtual tour of the reception area and look at the facilities offered to clients.

1 Suggest the facilities and the types of information available for visitors that you would expect to see in each of the following reception areas:

   **a** a large college

   **b** a dental practice

   **c** a manufacturing organisation that exports all over the world

   **d** a children's clinic

   **e** a recruitment agency.

2 Identify the main need of each of the following visitors and suggest the best action to take in each case:

   **a** Two elderly visitors arrive in the middle of a cloudburst. They are shivering and soaking wet.

   **b** A visitor arrives in reception obviously distressed and tearful. You know she will have to wait at least five minutes to see the person she wants.

   **c** A visitor dashes in to say that his car is on double yellow lines outside your building, he can't find a parking space anywhere and he had an appointment to see your sales manager ten minutes ago.

   **d** A young mother with a toddler son has already been waiting 15 minutes. The child is getting fractious and this is irritating other people who are waiting.

   **e** A young woman arrives for an interview. She is obviously nervous and upset that, as it's a very stormy day, she is windblown and doesn't look her best.

## Evidence collection

1 From entries in your visitors' book or appointments book, or from your own experience, write a brief personal statement which identifies:

   **a** the main types of visitors you deal with

   **b** the main reasons they visit your organisation

   **c** your visitors' usual requirements

   **d** the steps you take to try to ensure their needs are met.

2 Keep a log (or photocopy your visitors or appointments book) to identify the visitors you have dealt with recently. In a professional discussion with your assessor, be prepared to talk about the needs of some of these visitors, how you communicated with them and what you did to help them.

### Core unit link

Your work should link to unit 202, because you will be working to achieve your organisation's purpose when you deal with visitors – so check your evidence against performance indicators 1–4. You may also be supporting diversity, so your evidence should link to unit 202, PIs 10 and 11.

With question two, when you communicate with visitors this is likely to link to unit 201, PIs 1 and 2.

**Core unit link**

If your suggestions from question three are based on feedback from visitors and you use this to improve your own work and suggest improvements, your evidence may link to unit 201, performance indicators 15 and 16.

If you set yourself high standards, treat other people with respect and help and support them, you should also be able to link your question four evidence to unit 201, PIs 20, 24 and 25.

If you have to extract and explain points from written material, as in question five, remember that this links to unit 201, PI 5.

**Evidence collection** Continued

3 Critically analyse your reception area together with the facilities available to visitors. What makes the area welcoming? To what extent do the facilities meet the visitors' needs? Are there any improvements you could recommend? Write your views in a brief statement that also identifies how you make the most of the facilities that exist or how you try to compensate for those that are lacking.

4 Obtain a copy of your job description that includes your reception duties, or any document you have been given that summarises your role on reception. Alternatively you can write a brief description of your role. Use this as a basis for a professional discussion with your assessor about your work and be prepared to explain why you think it is important that you present a positive image of yourself and your organisation.

5 List the type of information you have available for visitors and, in each case, include the reason for keeping this.

# Organisational and security procedures

In most large organisations the reception area is at the front of the building and is adjacent to the car park, assuming there is one. It should be impossible to enter the building without going through reception. If the work carried out by the organisation means it must be very security conscious, there

*An organisation within an office block will have a deferred reception.*

may be a separate gatehouse, manned by security, before visitors ever reach reception.

A smaller organisation in a large office block may have a **deferred reception**. This means that visitors will enter the building, check the building directory for the firm they want – go to the one they want – and enter a suite of offices. The first person they will see is the receptionist.

Obviously the size and type of organisation will determine the security procedures in force. However, it is very unusual to work for a firm that has no procedures at all, otherwise it would be open to random acts of violence and theft, quite apart from problems relating to confidentiality.

Receptionists fulfil a security role by ensuring that casual callers don't have access to the building. They have a responsibility to follow the procedures that have been devised and to report anything suspicious or unusual. You may have to follow several procedures yourself but may not have thought about the reasons behind them. The chart below should make these clear.

**Find out**

What are your organisation's procedures that you must follow when you are dealing with visitors? Write these down as a list of Do's and Don'ts for yourself.

**Remember**

Your role in relation to security links to core unit 202, where you learned about maintaining security and confidentiality.

## Organisational and security procedures to follow and the reasons for these

| Reception procedure | Reason |
|---|---|
| The reception must never be left unattended | Visitors could gain unauthorised access to the building – or to documents on reception |
| The arrivals of all visitors are recorded, as well as their times of departure | In an emergency, the number of visitors in the building is known |
| Visitors are asked for details of their name, address and reason for the visit | Only visitors with an appointment may be allowed to see members of staff. In an emergency the name and whereabouts of all visitors is known |
| Visitors are asked if they have arrived by car, where they have parked and for their car registration number | If a car needs to be moved for any reason, the owner can be found quickly |
| All visitors are issued with a visitor badge on arrival – this shows the date and time of the visit | Only staff and authorised visitors are allowed to enter the offices or workshop areas |
| Important information, such as the action to take in an emergency, is given to visitors – this is often printed on the reverse of the badge | Visitors know what to do if there is an emergency evacuation |
| The person the visitor has arranged to see is contacted by the receptionist promptly | This validates the appointment as well as making sure the visitor is dealt with |

| Organisational and secrity procedures to follow and the reasons for these Continued | |
| --- | --- |
| **Reception procedure** | **Reason** |
| Visitor badges are collected on departure | Visitors cannot return on another day and use the badge |
| Visitors are escorted in certain areas | To ensure visitors do not enter restricted areas where they may have access to confidential information or development work |
| Some types of paperwork must not be taken into the reception area | Sensitive or confidential information may be seen by visitors |
| Visitors must take belongings with them when they leave reception | Unattended items may cause a security scare |

One part of the normal procedure is to notify colleagues of a visitor's arrival as required. This is obviously unnecessary if you work in a hotel or a tourist attraction where anyone can call in. It is essential, however, if you work for an organisation where visitors are seen only by appointment.

### How to ... Inform colleagues of a visitor's arrival

- Greet the visitor and check the appointment on the system you use.

- Complete any required logs or the visitor book before you notify your colleague.

- Depending on the system in use, you may simply record the visitor's arrival on the computer system (see page 208 and snapshot on page 231) or you may phone your colleague.

- It is normally wiser to phone your colleague when a visitor is seated and not standing close to you – in case your colleague makes any comment you wouldn't want the visitor to hear!

- If your colleague can't be found immediately, don't panic. Give a message to someone in the department that you need the person to phone urgently, or use the tannoy or bleeper system.

- Always be prepared for some colleagues to make remarks to you, over the phone, that you are not expected to repeat to the visitor!

- A standard response may be 'Tell them to wait a moment, will you?' Agree to this but be prepared to phone again with a reminder if your colleague hasn't put in an appearance after five minutes.

# Problems that may occur with visitors and how to deal with these

Because the receptionist is the first point of contact for virtually everyone visiting the organisation, he or she needs to be well-trained, calm, positive and knowledgeable. This may sound a long list, but is important because it will mean that any problems are dealt with relatively smoothly.

- **Well-trained** means that the receptionist knows what to do if a visitor is aggressive and the best way to react to diffuse a difficult situation.
- **Calm** means that crises aren't made worse or exaggerated by anyone panicking.
- **Positive** means that the receptionist will always want to find a solution to a problem.
- **Knowledgeable** means that the receptionist will know who to contact and what to do if a serious problem occurs – as well as recognising situations where assistance is required.

Problems occur for a variety of reasons that can broadly be divided into four main categories, as you can see in the table below.

| Problem types | Examples |
|---|---|
| With the appointment | A mistake about the time or date<br>No record of the appointment<br>The person to be seen isn't available<br>The visitor has arrived very late or very early |
| With meeting the visitor's needs | There is a long delay (especially if the visitor is in a rush)<br>There is nowhere to park<br>No-one can answer the visitor's queries<br>There isn't information available to give to the visitor<br>The visitor wants something your organisation cannot/does not provide<br>Computer failure means you cannot process a request or transaction |
| With the visitor's behaviour | A visitor won't accept an explanation you give<br>The visitor is asking you to break organisational rules<br>A visitor is angry about having to wait or wants to complain about the organisation |
| Emergency situations | There is a sudden evacuation<br>A visitor is suddenly taken ill<br>A visitor has an accident |

**Find out**

What are your organisational procedures for dealing with problems? Check that you know what these are and the help and guidance they provide.

## Solving problems

There is rarely one simple answer for solving a problem. Much will depend on what has gone wrong (and why) and the procedures you must follow. It normally helps if you are a positive person who likes to think creatively. If you are someone who enjoys saying 'No' then you can expect to exasperate your visitors and your colleagues on a regular basis!

### Appointments and associated problems

There is normally a standard series of actions you will take when someone arrives for an appointment. This involves:

- checking the appointment against your internal system or diary
- making a note that the person has arrived
- notifying the colleague the visitor is about to see of his or her arrival.

In most cases you can expect this to go smoothly, but on some occasions it won't – for all the reasons shown in the table above. In this case you need to take further action.

- If there is no record of the appointment, don't panic. Ask the visitor for more information, such as the name of the person he or she is to see and when/how the appointment was arranged. It may be that your colleague forgot to put the appointment in the system. Ask the visitor to take a seat while you ring your colleague to find out.
- At the same time, check your system for alternatives. Is the visitor booked in for a different time or date?
- In the worst-case scenario, the person you need isn't available. In this case find someone else in the same department and explain the problem. Say you need someone to come to reception to see the visitor.
- If you simply find the visitor has arrived very early, make sure you point out the facilities on offer, such as reading materials and drinks. Few visitors would expect to be seen before the pre-arranged time.
- Don't try to hide serious problems – like the fact the appointment was actually for tomorrow or yesterday. The best strategy is to be tactfully honest! Check to see whether someone can see the visitor today. If not, you may have to offer a new appointment.
- If the visitor is late then your ability to help will depend on the organisation you work for and its procedures. If your visitor was seeing a specialist or consultant then that person may have left or now be seeing another person, in which case you will have to offer an alternative date and time. If possible, a more acceptable alternative is for the visitor to see someone else. At least their journey will not have been wasted.

### Problems meeting the visitor's needs

Any visitor starts to have a bad experience the moment that plans begin to go awry. If you can take action to try to rescue the situation – or at

**Did you know?**

In some organisations visitors now log their own arrival. They enter the time of their appointment in a small display unit. This is compared with the electronic appointments system and the visitor is asked to confirm his or her name. The person the visitor has come to see is then notified electronically. The receptionist is needed only if there is a problem.

**Did you know?**

Normally, when there is a problem, the best thing to do is to apologise for the inconvenience on behalf of your organisation. Even if it is not your fault, the visitor is having a bad experience and your sympathy will be appreciated.

the very least lend a sympathetic ear – there is less chance of the problem escalating.

- If there is a long delay, apologise immediately. While it can be useful to slightly over-estimate the waiting time this isn't always advisable if the appointments are running very late! Offer refreshments and be prepared to offer a new time/date if the visitor genuinely cannot wait. If this is unacceptable, ask your supervisor for advice.
- Parking difficulties are common with many organisations. It helps if visitors have been told about nearby public car parks and/or if spaces can be reserved for visitors who have travelled a long distance by car. If you are desperate to help an important visitor, find out whether a colleague could move his or her car to make space.
- In any situation where you cannot provide something immediately for the visitor, this does not mean you can't provide it at all! Make a note of any outstanding query or information request and arrange to get in touch by post or email as soon as you can. Similarly if you have computer problems then post or email the document when you can. If your organisation doesn't provide a particular service then simply say so. If you know an alternative source of supply then suggest this.

---

**Organisational policy statement relating to aggressive behaviour**

### WELCOME TO WESTVIEW HOSPITAL

### TO ALL PATIENTS AND VISITORS

Please help our staff to give you a consistently high level of service by respecting their needs and rights as well as your own.

**Our staff have been trained to:**
- Always treat you with courtesy and respect
- Do their best to ensure you are in a safe environment
- Defuse and deflect aggressive behaviour and report any incidents that occur.

**We ask you to:**
- Treat our staff with courtesy and respect
- Respect their right to work in a safe environment
- Be aware of the consequences of indulging in verbal or physical abuse. This may mean
  - being asked to leave the premises immediately
  - a criminal prosecution for alleged assault
  - the refusal of any further treatment at this hospital

*Thank you for your cooperation*

Simon Parkes
Chief Executive

## Problems with the visitor's behaviour

Most people become annoyed when they encounter unexpected problems or delays. You know this yourself! If this happens on a day when everything

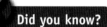

*Conflict situations can take many different forms.*

seems to be going wrong, and especially if the person is rather fiery to begin with, you can expect them to become really cross. This does not mean that you are expected to tolerate verbal abuse. It does mean that you need know two things:

- how to diffuse conflict situations so that you make things better, not worse
- when to recognise that you are out of your depth and need help.

Most conflict situations occur because someone is being prevented from getting something they want. In most cases, if you give a calm explanation and are obviously trying to do your best to help, most visitors will calm down, even if they were irate to start with. In some cases other people may be more difficult to deal with. This doesn't mean you should change what you are saying, but you may have to change your behaviour. If you are seen as part of the problem then things can only get worse. Check the 'How to ...' box to see what you should do instead.

## How to ... Respond in a conflict situation

- Know your organisation's policies so that you know where and how to get help if you need it. This will help you to feel more secure.

- Don't think that everyone who gets annoyed is a threat. Many people just get cross and frustrated if things go wrong and feel better for talking about it.

- If someone is complaining or fed up then listen. Don't interrupt or – even worse – contradict. Sympathise and make it obvious you appreciate their difficulties.

- Studies show that most people who are being difficult don't see themselves like this! Basically they want something and see you (or your organisation) as the barrier to achieving this. One way to solve the problem is to try to remove the barrier, if you can.

- If you listen, acknowledge what someone is saying and try to identify exactly what they want – and then suggest a solution. The problem may end immediately.

- If any solution is out of your hands, tell the visitor that you are referring the matter to your supervisor immediately – and do so.

- If the visitor is shouting, upsetting other people, swearing, appears to be under the influence of drink or drugs, calling you names or scaring you then don't hesitate. Get help immediately. Press the panic button if you have one.

### Emergency situations

In an emergency, visitors in the reception area will expect the receptionist to take the lead. Actions include the following:

- Ensure people waiting in reception promptly evacuate the building and go to the correct assembly point. Tell visitors when they can re-enter.
- Check any public toilets.
- Contact a first-aider immediately to attend to a visitor who feels ill or has an accident in reception.
- Make a note of what happened if an accident occurred so that the accident report can be completed.

### Case study Do as I say, not as I do!

*Read the case study below and then answer the questions that follow.*

The patients of one dental surgery were pleased when the little practice moved to new premises that were light, airy and modern; and where parking was easier. They liked the fact that Lisa was facing them at a curved wooden reception desk as they arrived, and they no longer had to peer at her through a little glass window. Most said how much they welcomed the change, and how much they appreciated the new features and amenities, such as the water cooler, children's play area and little TV in the corner.

Lisa and her boss were equally pleased with their new working environment – and determined that standards wouldn't slip. To ensure this, they decided to communicate their main concerns to patients by producing a series of notices. Lisa created these on her computer, printed them out in large type on A4 paper and pinned them on the walls. By the end of the second week she had prepared 12 notices, and had plans for many more.

She was rather surprised when she overheard one or two patients grumbling about this approach. When some started to complain, Lisa added another notice that complaints must be in writing and addressed to the dentist.

A week later she had a bad experience when one patient who arrived five minutes late was told he had missed his appointment. When he argued Lisa just pointed at the notice. The dentist had to be called to calm down the situation.

Some time later Lisa changed her job and started work for a larger practice where a completely different system was used. Here every patient was greeted by name, told how long they might have to wait if there were any delays, and given a card that included emergency telephone numbers and other practice details. There didn't seem to be any notices at all. Lisa also found that patients didn't get annoyed or angry as much here, so she had fewer problems dealing with difficult people.

**Questions**

1   a   *Identify four improvements to the facilities when the practice moved.*

    b   *Explain how each of these would help to meet the visitors' needs.*

2   a   *Why did Lisa and her boss decide to produce the notices?*

    b   *Why do you think the patients disliked them?*

    c   *How do you think the notices would have affected the appearance of the reception area?*

    d   *How might the notices affect visitor behaviour?*

3   *What is your opinion of Lisa's ability to manage conflict? Give a reason for your answer.*

4   *From Lisa's experience in her new job, suggest alternative and better ways of communicating organisational requirements to visitors.*

5   *If you could keep four notices only, which would these be? For each one you choose suggest how it might be more tactfully worded.*

# Organisational structures and communications channels

Working in reception is always very difficult to anyone new to an organisation. This is because they do not understand how the firm operates. This means that they struggle to answer questions and don't know who to contact if there is a problem.

Quite simply, the better you know how the organisation operates, and who does what, the quicker and more efficiently you can deal with any visitor and the more likely you are to meet their needs. Ideally you should know these things:

- **The organisation's structure**. This includes its size, how many branches or departments there are, where they are located, who is employed in each one and what they do. You should also be aware of the quickest ways to contact all these people.
- **The organisation's policies and procedures**. These include the main methods of communicating both between and among staff, policies relating to making and cancelling appointments, seeing people without an appointment, late arrivals, and giving charitable donations to people who call in reception. You should also be aware of the actions you can take yourself to solve a visitor's problem and those you can't.
- **The products/services offered**. Even if you can't understand all the details you should have a broad appreciation of what your organisation offers and what it doesn't. Otherwise you look silly if you can't answer even the most basic query. The easy way is to keep a catalogue, prospectus, set of leaflets or company brochure in your desk and read them!
- **The staff employed by your organisation**. People leave, are transferred, promoted or take on different responsibilities. You need to keep up to date with changes so that you can refer difficult enquiries promptly to the correct person.

# Making sure visitors' needs are met

You make sure your visitors' needs are met if you:

- know that the facilities and amenities are available that your visitors are likely to need
- are well informed yourself and can answer most enquiries with ease
- have the information available your visitors are likely to need
- can cope if there is a problem, such as a delay or misunderstanding
- are aware that, by their body language, most visitors leave reception in a positive frame of mind
- routinely check with visitors informally that their needs have been met (e.g. 'Is that what you were looking for?', 'Is that ok?').
- report back to your supervisor if you are starting to experience a problem because visitors are unhappy or complaining, so that something can be done about it.

If you work in reception in the leisure industry – such as at a hotel or visitor centre – then you are likely to find that your organisation issues feedback forms to all visitors for completion. One section will be devoted to the visitor's experience on arrival and whether he or she was dealt with promptly and politely and was given all the information required. The organisation will analyse these forms regularly to check that visitors' needs are being met.

Local councils, hospitals, colleges and other public sector organisations may also issue visitor satisfaction forms so that they can formally obtain feedback on the services they offer and try to improve these.

Formal written feedback is less likely to be requested by business organisations or small service industries, such as a doctor's or dentist's practice, although there should be a system for recording and acting on any complaints that are received and these should be analysed, regularly, to see if action is needed. In other cases, organisations invite comments by putting up notices – but don't overdo this and fall into the same trap that Lisa did in the case study!

## Changing places

*Your assessor will ask you how you will adapt your skills if you change your job in the future. You will need to think about the way in which your visitor's needs would change if you worked for a different organisation, in addition to the type of problems you might encounter.*

Gemma works in a conference centre. She regularly has to give people directions to different lecture theatres and tell people where refreshments are being served and where to leave their coats. Problems can occur when a speaker or group of visitors are delayed or if someone is taken ill during an event.

Ashraf works for a government department. All visitors attend by appointment. These have been made in advance with various officials in the building. All appointments are logged on to the computer system. Ashraf must check the system when each visitor arrives and issue a visitor badge before directing the visitor to the correct floor where the official can be found. If he is very busy and a problem occurs, he asks the visitor to wait and refers the query to one of his colleagues, so that he doesn't hold up other people who are arriving.

Justin works for a large chemical company. Security procedures are very strict and no one is allowed in reception until they have been vetted by the security staff at the gatehouse. Many visitors are important customers, some of whom have travelled long distances to attend meetings or be shown around the plant. Justin sometimes has the job of escorting them as well as ensuring that refreshments are provided promptly.

Danielle works in a health spa. She greets all visitors as they arrive and makes sure that new visitors complete a registration form. She shows them

**Changing places** Continued

around, giving an explanation of all the facilities before she contacts one of the consultants. The whole area is relaxed yet professional and Danielle has to take particular care of her appearance and manner to reflect this.

Samina works for a local accountant. Nearly all visitors arrive by appointment although sometimes clients call in to leave documents for some of the staff. Because many of these documents are important and/or confidential, Samma makes certain they are taken promptly to the right office. If visitors have to wait, Samma always offers them a hot or cold drink. She also makes sure they have a copy of that day's papers to read.

1 For any *one* person listed above, identify the differences he or she would find if moving to your organisation and doing your job.

2 For any *one* person listed above, say how you would need to adapt your skills if you did their job rather than your own.

### Over to you

1 Many visitors need to be given directions – to a nearby car park, another office or a different part of the building. For one enquiry about directions you regularly receive, work out the best way to answer the request. Check your final explanation with your tutor or trainer to see if it is clear.

2 Your organisation is expecting three important visitors from Japan this week.

   a Suggest three specific needs that these visitors may have on arrival.

**b** Your boss thinks that a special flower display may look nice in reception but has read somewhere that, to the Japanese, different flowers and types of display have special significance.

    i   Do you think this matters or is unimportant?

    ii  What ideas do you have for finding out more?

**c** You are aware this is a top-priority visit. What steps would you take to ensure you give a positive image of yourself and your organisation?

**3** You work in a large legal practice as administrator/receptionist. Decide what you would do if each of the following problems occurred.

**a** A representative calls and refuses to leave until he can talk to one of the partners. You know the partners won't see him without an appointment and they are both booked up today anyway.

**b** A visitor who has travelled some distance in bad weather asks you what the roads will be like that evening.

**c** A visitor has been waiting to see one of the solicitors for 20 minutes. You have rung through to his office twice – once to say the visitor had arrived and the second time to say that the visitor is still waiting. The visitor is now getting extremely impatient.

**d** At the moment the firm is recruiting for a junior legal clerk. A young man arrives and announces that he has come for an interview. According to your records he should have come tomorrow. When you tell him this he is devastated and tells you that he is going on holiday the following day.

**e** A visitor asks for a leaflet on buying and selling a house. Normally you have several in stock but there are none left in the display, the door to the stockroom is locked and you don't have a key.

**f** At 4 p.m. a man arrives. According to your records he was due at 1400 hours. He argues that he was definitely told to come at four and would never have agreed to a 2 p.m. appointment. When you tell him the solicitor he was going to see has now gone out he becomes very angry and says that you are all inefficient idiots.

### Core unit link

Your evidence relating to organisational procedures and how you interact with your visitors will link to unit 202, performance indicators 1–4. The way you follow security procedures should cross-reference to unit 202, PIs 13–15.

### Evidence collection

**1** List the organisational and security procedures you have to follow in relation to visitor entry and access to the buildings or offices. State where you would find these if you needed to refer to them at any time. Include your own explanation of:

## Core unit link

Many of your verbal communications in question two can be linked to unit 201, and this may include discussions you have to solve a visitor's problem. If you also provide written information or extract information for visitors, all these activities may link to performance indicators 3–6.

Again for question three check how your evidence relates to unit 202, PIs 1–4 as well as 13–15, in addition to unit 201, PIs 14, 21, 24 and 25.

The evidence from question four should relate to unit 201, PIs 1, 2, 10, 20, 24 and 25.

If you plan to work effectively, follow guidelines, take responsibility for your work and identify/report problems when they arise, check if your question five evidence links to unit 201, PIs 9, 10, 13 and 14.

### Evidence planning Continued

- the areas that are restricted, if any
- the type of visitor identification system you use
- the information you obtain from visitors on arrival – and why
- how you try to ensure visitors return identification on departure.

Write a personal account to say how you follow security procedures and ask your supervisor to countersign and date it to confirm that this is accurate.

2 Obtain a copy of your organisational chart showing the main departments or sections, or prepare your own summary to identify these for your assessor. Attach a copy of your staff list which includes internal extension numbers, or keep a copy available to show your assessor. Then describe three complex enquiries you have received (or might receive) from visitors and, for each one, identify the person you would contact in each case. In each case say how you would communicate with this person and what you would do if the person was not available.

3 Check that you know the location of your organisational procedures for dealing with awkward or aggressive visitors. If you need to deal with a difficult visitor during the period you are being assessed, write an account of what happened and ask your supervisor to add his or her own comments to confirm what you did.

4 Obtain witness testimony from one or two of your colleagues who regularly expect visitors, to confirm that you contact them promptly when visitors arrive and can cope effectively if there is a slight delay or minor problem.

5 Your assessor will want to observe you receiving and dealing with visitors in a professional way and see how you check that you have met visitors' needs. Prepare for this by thinking about the ways in which you ensure that a visitor's needs have been met. You should also note that, on this occasion, your assessor will also be a visitor with needs to be met!

### What if?

What should you do if you are not expected to inform your colleagues about visitors' arrivals? In this case your assessor will ask 'what if?' questions to check what you *would* do if the situation arose.

### Key skills reminder

If you are taking Key Skills awards, remember to discuss with your tutor or trainer how your evidence for this unit could also count towards those awards.

# Unit 209

# Store, retrieve and archive information

## Unit summary and overview

This option unit is divided into three sections:

- process information
- retrieve information
- archive information.

All organisations need to store information safely and accurately so that it can be retrieved quickly and easily whenever it is needed. Because many people do these tasks every day there are normally procedures in place to ensure that they do them in the same way. Otherwise important information could easily be lost or mislaid. Information that must be kept but is no longer required regularly is normally archived to free up storage space. Again there will be procedures to follow to ensure that this is done correctly.

In this unit you will learn about different types of information storage system as well as the legal requirements relating to the storage, retrieval and archiving of information.

Because you will apply your knowledge to all three activities – processing, retrieving and archiving information – this unit has *not* been split into separate sections. Instead the headings follow the knowledge requirements of the unit and specific information relating to each section is included where appropriate.

# The importance of storing, retrieving and archiving information effectively and efficiently

## Link to option units

As you gather your evidence for this unit you should also obtain evidence for your core units. Watch for the Core unit link logo which suggests how the evidence you may collect may count towards both this unit and your core units.

Remember that you might be able to identify other links yourself, because of your own job role and the evidence you have obtained.

Talk to your assessor if you need further guidance on how your evidence should be cross-referenced.

## Remember

It only needs one person to 'guess' where to store a few important documents for chaos to ensue when they are needed.

## Did you know?

An **information system** refers to the methods and equipment used to store documents, either manually or electronically. **Procedures** are the sequence of activities you must follow when you use

The ability to find what you put away, quickly and easily, has always been a bonus! It saves time, confusion and arguments. There is an added benefit if the item you want has been stored carefully so that it is in pristine condition. Turning the house upside down to find your GCSE certificate before an important interview will add to any stress you already feel. Finding that it has been reduced to a crumpled piece of card because it was jammed at the back of a drawer is not likely to make your day any easier!

At home, you may be a naturally tidy person who takes pride in looking after your possessions and someone who firmly believes in a place for everything and everything in its place. Or you have a far more casual approach to life and happily scatter your belongings around as the mood takes you. In this case it will be more good luck than good management if you ever actually find what you want.

Businesses, however, can't rely on good luck. They receive and produce a huge amount of information every day and need to ensure that this is stored safely and can be found quickly – time after time. This is because staff at all levels regularly need to refer to information to make important decisions, and it is essential that the information be complete and absolutely up to date. In other cases documents must be kept for a minimum period of time to comply with legal requirements, as you will see on page 310.

For these reasons there must be a proper system in place, so everyone knows where particular documents can be found. Even more important, everyone must then follow the procedures that have been devised. These ensure that each person uses the system in the same way.

It isn't enough just to make sure that the information is stored in the right place. It also has to be kept safely and maintained in good condition. This means that papers should be placed securely in folders and stored in good-quality, lockable cabinets. Electronic systems must be backed up daily, and back-up tapes or disks should ideally be kept off the premises for extra security and protection.

There must also be procedures to regulate which documents can be retrieved and by whom. Some may be confidential so that access to them must be restricted. In a manual system, users also need to be able to check which documents or folders have been borrowed from the system in case they also need that information urgently.

Finally, in a well-organised system, paper files must be routinely cleared. Information that is no longer of any use at all may be thrown away, but most documents will be archived. This means they are kept safely but usually away from the main working area. In many organisations the basement is a favourite place for keeping archives. This frees up space in the main files because historic documents required only infrequently have been removed from the system. If files were never archived, the organisation would be using more and more valuable space for storage and have to expand continually to store all the information it had retained. Archiving is rather different in an electronic system, as you will see on page 237.

A summary of the main benefits of an efficient and effective storage system is shown in the table below.

| Key benefits of an efficient and effective information system |
| --- |
| ✓ The system is easy to understand and use |
| ✓ Information is kept safely |
| ✓ Information is stored promptly so that users have access to the most recent information |
| ✓ Information is found quickly, which saves time and enables people to react promptly to situations |
| ✓ Paper documents are kept in good condition |
| ✓ There isn't unnecessary duplication of papers or folders |
| ✓ Any borrowed files are recorded and their location is known |
| ✓ All legal requirements relating to the storage and security of information are met |
| ✓ Space is saved because historic information is archived |
| ✓ The system is flexible and can be adapted to meet future needs |

**Did you know?**

The best filing cabinets are fire- and impact-resistant so that they won't split open if there is an explosion or if they are thrown out of the building in an emergency. Even the best cabinet can withstand high temperatures for only up to about 90 minutes, so to save valuable papers in a fierce blaze a cabinet may be thrown downstairs or even out of the nearest window to safety!

**Did you know?**

**Culling** or **disposing** of papers means throwing them away. **Archiving** means keeping papers safely but moving them out of the main system because the files are no longer 'active'. Never carry out either of these activities without your supervisor's agreement.

# Information systems and their main features

There are two main types of information system:
- **paper-based** or **manual** systems in which paper documents are kept
- **electronic systems** into which documents have been scanned or created.

Organisations may use either one or, in some cases, both systems – as you will see in the case study later in this unit. Despite talk of a 'paperless office', even in the most technically advanced organisation there will usually still be some paper notes kept relating to current events or activities.

Both types of system are described in the sections that follow.

# Manual information systems

The main features of a manual system relate to the equipment, the methods of storing the information and the way in which the information is classified (ordered) within the system.

## Standard equipment

### Find out

Filing cabinets are available in a range of colours today and may be chosen to match an office colour scheme. In some cases, lateral files can be used as wall partitions or to divide up space in an open-plan office area. Find out which systems are in operation in your organisation and why they are used.

There are three types of cabinet used to store files.

- **Vertical filing cabinets** are the most commonly found in offices. They have between two and five large drawers – although four is the most popular number. Cabinets may be made of metal or wood, are lockable and are fitted with a safety mechanism to prevent more than one drawer being opened at once, to prevent the cabinet tipping forward on to the user.

  Inside the drawers there are usually suspension pockets that hang from side to side, often in a continuous row. Each pocket has a tab at the front, giving the name of the file folder it contains.

- **Lateral filing cabinets** are wider and not as deep. They are like large open cupboards with a sliding door or blind that can be pulled down when the cabinet is not in use. Instead of shelves there are rows of suspended pockets, each with tabs on the side. File folders are inserted sideways, usually to the right of the tab.

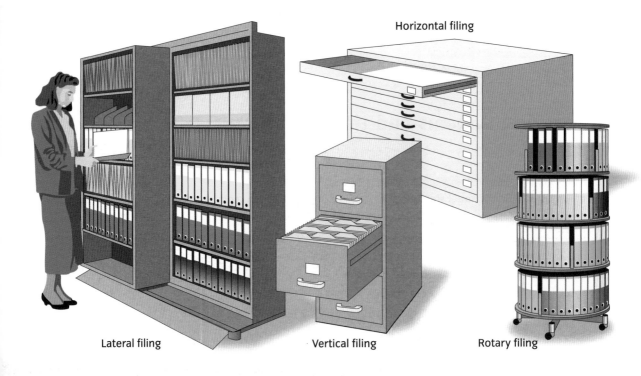

Horizontal filing

Lateral filing      Vertical filing      Rotary filing

A variation is a multi-purpose lateral cabinet that has rows of pockets and some shelves designed to hold lever arch or box files (see opposite).

- **Rotary filing systems** are similar to the rotating display stands you see in many shops. They hold A4 lever arch or box files, or special folders, and spin to give all-round access to the files.
- **Horizontal filing cabinets** are used for documents that are very large or must not be hole-punched, such as drawings, maps and photographs. You may find them in an architect's or surveyor's office.

## Storage materials

A variety of materials are available for holding documents within a filing system.

- **File folders** are used to store most papers. They are available in a variety of colours and with optional fastenings. Some organisations colour-code their files, which makes it easier to identify different categories. In most organisations the papers are fastened into the folders. In others it depends on the type of information being stored, and some don't fasten papers in at all.
- **Document wallets** (sometimes called envelope wallets) are used for carrying small quantities of documents or storing them on a temporary basis.
- **Ring binders** are used for storing small quantities of documents on a particular topic.
- **Lever arch files** are a larger version of ring binders, for greater quantities of documents on a certain topic.
- **Box files** are used to store documents that cannot or must not be hole-punched, such as important legal documents, presentation documents, catalogues and bound reports.
- **Index pages** or dividers are used to separate documents filed in ring binders or lever arch files.

**Find out**

How many examples of storage materials for holding files can you find in your workplace? Check whether you are expected to secure papers into all folders, some of them or none of them – and why.

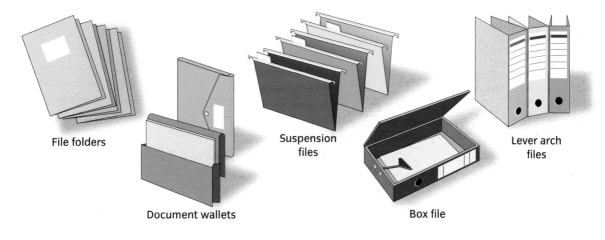

File folders

Document wallets

Suspension files

Box file

Lever arch files

## Classification systems and indexes

All files are kept in a particular order. They may be stored in one of three ways: alphabetically, numerically or chronologically. The difference between these methods is explained in the table below.

| Method | Variations | Main use | Examples |
|---|---|---|---|
| **Alphabetical** | By name | When *the name* of the person or organisation is the most important factor | Customer files Staff records |
| | By location | When *the place* is the most important factor | Branch office files Overseas contacts |
| | By subject | When *the topic* is the most important aspect | A manager's personal files Purchasing files (by product) |
| **Numerical** | By sequence | When the files *are linked* to unique reference number (often allocated by a database) | Customer files in a large organisation |
| | Alpha-numerical | When *letter codes* as well as numbers are allocated, e.g. S = Sales, then S1, S2 etc. | Departmental files in a large organisation |
| **Chronological** | | When *the date* is the most important factor | Exam results Travel files |

### Alphabetical filing systems

These are most suited to small organisations and to a manager's personal files. This is because they cannot be expanded very easily. You are likely to find that some letters are particularly popular ('B' is one example) and soon become congested. Then all the files have to be reorganised to make space for the new ones.

The advantage with this system is that it is *direct*. If you know the name or place or topic then you can go straight to the file you want. A disadvantage – particularly with subject filing – is that you may need to file papers in more than one place because they relate to more than one topic. How to cope with this is covered on page 317.

It is important that everyone who uses the system knows how to file correctly and there is rather more to this than knowing your alphabet! For example,

**Remember**

The danger with classifying by subject is that topics may be repeated by accident (e.g. 'staff', 'employees' and 'personnel'). This can be prevented by referring to a master index that lists all the topics. In any case, never start a new topic without the permission of your supervisor.

would you put MD Products under 'M' or 'P'? And should Flora McDonald come before or after Tom Mackintyre? And what about Four Gates Hotel? Should this come before or after The Five Alive Club? And do you put files relating to Manchester in England in the same place as those for Manchester in New Hampshire, USA?

If these types of questions give you a headache, you need to check the rules to use! These are summarised in the table below.

## Alphabetical filing

| Rule to follow | Example of filing order |
|---|---|
| **PEOPLE** | |
| Surname first | Adams, Kate |
| Short names before long | Adams, Kate |
| | Adamson, Joanne |
| For identical names, follow first name(s) or initial | Adamson, Joanne |
| | Adamson, Martin |
| Nothing always comes before something | Akhtar, P |
| | Akhtar, Parveen |
| Treat Mac and Mc as Mac and file before 'M' | MacDonald, T |
| | McGowan, M |
| | Marte, D |
| Ignore apostrophes | Oliver, T |
| | O'Sullivan, B |
| **ORGANISATIONS** | |
| Ignore the word 'The' | BBC, The |
| Treat numbers as words | Seven Sisters Garden Centre |
| | Six Steps Nursery |
| If names are identical use street or town to decide the order | Top Shop, Martin Way |
| | Top Shop, Westminster Parade |
| Initials come before full names (ignore 'and' and '&') | BBC, The |
| | BVM Supplies |
| | B & Z Consultants |
| | Bath Tourist Office |
| Treat Saint and St as Saint | Sainsbury's, J plc |
| | St Mary's College |
| | Salisbury College |
| File public bodies under name, or town/city if the names are identical | Maidstone Borough Council |
| | Medway Council |
| | Magistrates' Courts Service, Leeds |
| | Magistrates' Court Service, Leicester |
| | Ministry of Defence |

### Find out

If there are too few documents for a new file, papers may be put into a miscellaneous file. There may be one for the whole system, for each letter of the alphabet or none at all in your system. This is because some firms ban miscellaneous files on the basis they are just a dumping ground for 'hard to file' documents and the papers in them go unnoticed. Is this true in your workplace?

**Remember**

An excellent example of alphabetical filing by name is *The Phone Book*. *Yellow Pages* is an equally good example of subject filing. Check out both to see how this is done professionally.

*The Yellow Pages is an excellent example of subject filing.*

### Numerical filing systems

These are mainly used by organisations that deal with large numbers of files because they can be constantly expanded. There is no reshuffling needed when you are simply allocating the next number to a new file.

The problem with this system is that you can't go direct to a file because – in most cases – you don't know the number. It is therefore *indirect*. You need an index to help you find the file you need (see below). Alternatively you need to refer to a reference number. This is why many organisations routinely quote a reference number on every document they produce. This isn't just to help their customers but also the staff who must file the firm's copy of the document in the right place.

### Chronological filing systems

**Find out**

Find out what classification systems are used in your workplace. Remember there may easily be more than one. A manager's personal files may be alphabetical by subject, customer files could be numerical and linked to a database, and expense claims could be filed in date order.

These are used only for specific types of documents. Internal financial documents are one example, such as bank statements or petty cash vouchers. The key identifying feature of these is the *date*. In a computer system it is important that the date be entered in the same format each time (e.g. 23.1.06 or 23/1/06 or 23.01.2006).

## Index systems

An index system is essential to guide users to files stored in numerical or alpha-numerical order. Index systems may also be used to keep small amounts of important information on particular topics, such as individual customers, suppliers or stock.

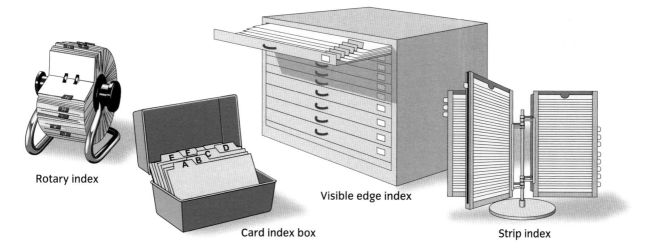

Rotary index

Card index box

Visible edge index

Strip index

Today many indexes are created and maintained on computer, because the information can be entered and edited easily and entries can be found quickly by searching on specific criteria. If the system is large or electronic filing is in operation, then special software is used to index the documents (see page 308). On a smaller system an index list can be created on a word-processing package or more detailed records held on a database.

These are the more traditional systems:

- **Index cards** are stored in a small cabinet with the key information written at the top. Guide cards help the user to quickly locate a card under a particular letter. The size of the cards means that additional reference information can be included on them.
- **Strip index cards** are small strips of card slotted into a special holder. Each strip contains the name and the file number.
- **Rotary cards** are slotted on to a small drum and rotate so that you can flip through the cards to find the one you need. The cards and the box are both small so can easily fit on a person's desk.
- **Visible edge cards** are larger. The key information is written at the bottom of each card and is always visible in the holder. The remainder of the card can be used to add other relevant information, such as customer details.

An example of a numeric index is shown below.

> **Remember**
>
> Index cards are always kept in alphabetical order. You use the system by looking for the name and reading off the file number alongside. Never remove the card from the system in case it gets lost. Write down the number instead.

| A numerical index | |
| --- | --- |
| **Reference number** | **Name** |
| 68209 | Simon Pearson |
| 68210 | Adele Storozuk |
| 68211 | Rachel Mitchell |
| 68212 | Muhammad Daud |
| 68213 | Rehana Iqbal |
| 68214 | Marina Parente |

# Electronic information systems

If you create documents on a computer, name them and save them in folders on your system, then you are already storing information electronically. An electronic filing system goes one step further. In addition to storing computer-created documents, all the documents that are received by the business every day are also added to the electronic files by scanning them into the system.

The following are the main features of an electronic information system:

- **A computer system**. If this is networked then it means that all users can find and read the saved documents on their own computer, if their access level allows them to do so (see page 318–319).
- **A scanner** that 'reads' the document and digitises the image. The scanner is connected to the operator's computer and uses special software that transfers each image into the computer.

- **Document management software**. This converts the paper files into electronic (digital) images and creates a file record. It also allows the operator to adjust, change or enhance the image if that is necessary. It then indexes the document so that it can be easily retrieved. There are many ways of indexing, such as using keywords, customer numbers, dates, postcodes and geographic areas.
- **Storage media**, typically CD-ROMs, that hold the electronic images. A major benefit is that copy disks can be stored off the premises so that, in the case of a disaster such as a fire, the back-up information is readily available.

Users of the system can search for a document using a variety of methods, including entering keywords or the appropriate date of inputting.

Incoming mail is scanned as images

Images processed by administator on a computer system and stored as index data

## Snapshot – Information management systems

If you thought that paper-based filing systems are normally limited to a few battered metal cabinets in a corner, then a visit to www.kardex.co.uk should help to change your mind. Kardex is one of the largest suppliers of document management systems in the UK, and offers sophisticated systems that not only save space but also reduce health and safety hazards relating to the movement and storage of vast amounts of paper. Their systems include mobile shelving, which moves from one side to the other to save space, double-sided rotating filing systems, called TimesTwo, which revolve within an outer shell, and large automated storage cabinets called Datastack where files can be retrieved simply by entering the number into the keypad.

### Find out

Find out more about different types of paper-based filing systems and equipment online at any of the following websites: www.cavetab.co.uk, www.kardex.co.uk, www.railex.co.uk, www.rackline.co.uk.

*A Kardex information management system.*

Kardex also provide software to enable files to be found quickly and easily and a wide range of other, more basic, filing equipment and supplies. On the website, the explanations and graphics will help you to understand more about some of the modern methods of handling information today. You can also read case studies about the systems that have been installed in organisations such as Manchester City Council, IBM and Eversheds (a leading law firm).

# Legal and organisational requirements covering the security and confidentiality of information

There are four main legal considerations relating to the storage of information:

- **The Data Protection Act 1998**. This is the main Act that regulates the activities of all organisations storing data on individuals. This was described in full in unit 202, on page 152.
- **Retention periods**. These relate to the length of time records may be held. There are specific legal requirements relating to some types of document. The main ones are shown in the table below.

**Find out**

Find out the retention policies in your organisation for keeping documents such as tax records, staff records and accident reports. Find out, too, if there is a retention schedule in your organisation which says when, and how, this type of information can be destroyed.

## Information storage and retention periods

| Record | Statutory retention period (i.e. required by law) |
|---|---|
| Accident reports | Three years after date of last entry on record |
| Attendance records | Three years |
| Income tax/NI records | Minimum of three years after the end of the tax year to which they relate |
| Statutory Maternity Pay and Statutory Sick Pay records | Three years |
| Payroll records | Seven years |
| Accounts documents | Between three and six years, depending on the size and type of organisation |
| Tax documents | Six years |
| **Record** | **Recommended retention period** |
| Application forms and interview notes | One year where these relate to unsuccessful candidates |
| Health and safety records relating to staff | Permanently |
| Disciplinary records | Six years from the end of employment |
| Redundancy records | Six years from the end of employment |
| Parental leave records | Five years from birth or adoption or, if the child is disabled, until the child is 18 |
| Working time and training records | Six years from end of employment |
| Trade union agreements | Ten years from the end of the agreement being in force |

With many types of records this is in case of any legal claims that may be made against the organisation, such as someone claiming that he or she was discriminated against at an interview. Organisations normally have specific retention policies to ensure these requirements are met.

- **Electronic documents as legal evidence**. There have been concerns that documents stored in an electronic system may not be allowed as evidence in a court case because they might have been altered or amended at some stage. To help prevent these problems, the British Standards Institute (BSI) has produced a code for organisations that explains the steps they must take to process electronic information so they are adopting 'best practice'.
- **Industry-specific legislation**. Some organisations may have to comply with additional legislation relating to their own particular type of industry and/or records held. You will see how this affects staff in the health service in the case study on page 323.

## Organisational policies and procedures

Organisations cannot assume that their staff will know the legal requirements affecting information they handle. They must therefore devise policies and procedures that control access to confidential information. There should also be strict procedures for the disposal of confidential information. There is no point in protecting sensitive information when it's active and then just throwing it in the wastepaper bin once it isn't! In addition to procedures to cover the shredding of paper files, guidance should also be given on how electronic media such as CD-ROMs that contain confidential documents are destroyed.

Certain information is particularly sensitive:

- personal information on individuals, such as their age, address, medical history and details of personal relationships or problems
- financial information about individuals, including how much they earn or how much money they owe
- financial information about your organisation or department
- future business plans of your organisation and decisions made at meetings
- information on customers, clients or contacts that would be highly valuable to a competitor.

### Confidentiality in a manual system

In a paper-based system, procedures will control the handling, movement and archiving of confidential documents or files. An example of a procedure to control this is shown on page 312.

**Did you know?**

The best type of shredders 'cross-cut' rather than shred paper in strips. The toughest have a heavy duty motor so that they can cope with floppy disks, CDs, DVDs, staples, paperclips and credit cards – and whole files in one go. An alternative to buying one of these machines is to use a shredding service instead.

### Remember

If you work for a doctor, solicitor, accountant or other business that handles sensitive information on individuals, your contact of employment may include an express clause to prevent you disclosing this to people outside your workplace. Even without this clause, you still have a duty to your employer not to divulge confidential information (see page 117).

## Example of a procedure for handling and storing confidential files

1 All confidential information must be stored in the red file folders provided. These are pre-marked with the word CONFIDENTIAL on the cover.

2 These files must be stored in the red cabinets in each department and the cabinet kept locked at all times. The departmental manager and the senior administrator are the authorised key holders.

3 Access to these files is only by agreement with the departmental manager or senior administrator.

4 The senior administrator is responsible for keeping confidential files up to date and for archiving the files. Archived confidential files are kept in a secure, locked cabinet in the basement.

5 No confidential files must be taken out of the office without the express agreement of the departmental manager.

6 Confidential papers must be destroyed by cross-shredding, under the supervision of the senior administrator.

### Find out

What confidential information is stored in your organisation? What procedures control how it is handed? How does this affect the type of information you can store or retrieve?

### Confidentiality in an electronic system

This will be controlled through levels of access to the system, as you will see on page 318.

### Over to you

Carry out the following tasks and then check your answers with those on the CD-ROM.

1 Check how accurately you can file alphabetically by rearranging the list below into the order the files should be placed in a filing cabinet.

| | |
|---|---|
| 9 Elms Hotel | Okunowo M |
| Oscar Bears Nursery | NBC Builders Ltd |
| Office of Fair Trading | McInnes T |
| Newson PK | Natural Foods Ltd |
| N & S Transport | Mercer M |
| O2 | O'Sullivan, T |
| O'Brien K | The Open University |
| MacIntyre J Ltd. | |

2 Your company deals with a number of agencies in European countries. These files are stored geographically, first by country and then by city. For example, in Germany the file for the agency in Stuttgart would come after that for Berlin. The following files have become muddled under their respective countries and the countries themselves are in the wrong order. Rearrange these correctly.

| Spain | France | Switzerland | Italy | Denmark |
|---|---|---|---|---|
| Madrid | Paris | Berne | Milan | Copenhagen |
| Alicante | Nice | Zurich | Rome | Arhus |
| Barcelona | Lyon | Geneva | Naples | Aarlborg |
| Malaga | Lille | Basle | Venice | Odense |

**3** A sales administrator keeps her files in subject order. She groups these under main headings but sometimes sub-divides them. From the list below, identify how they should be ordered in the filing cabinet.

Sales conference

Exhibitions – UK

Advertising – local

Travel – UK

Training – external

Expenses

Exhibitions – overseas

Agency agreements

Catalogue – current year

Training – in-house IT

Catalogues – past years

Travel – overseas

Press releases

Publicity campaigns

Training – in-house health and safety

Advertising – national

Training – in-house consumer law

Representatives' reports

**4** Rearrange the following alphabetical list of staff members twice.

**a** Put them into the correct order when they are filed by their pay reference number, which is based on part of their NI number.

**b** Put them into the correct order when they are listed by the date on which they started work, with the longest-serving employee first.

| Nazam Asghar | 2839041 | 14/03/96 |
|---|---|---|
| Ann Balshaw | 7130922 | 15/09/02 |
| Stuart Barton | 5602814 | 17/06/05 |
| Kamran Inayat | 3301281 | 12/05/92 |
| Paul Hipson | 8310282 | 14/02/03 |
| Tracey Isherwood | 6203192 | 25/01/01 |
| Giuseppe Ponti | 1273012 | 07/07/01 |
| Noreena Seedat | 2390172 | 31/10/04 |
| Ann Storozuk | 5273812 | 02/09/85 |
| Tanzeela Tabusam | 1325301 | 06/11/91 |
| Lesley Underwood | 6224391 | 17/04/98 |
| Alan Wright | 4020311 | 23/01/87 |

**5** Kardex promote their systems by saying that they systems are safer because users don't have to bend and stretch to reach files, climb up ladders or carry heavy files. They also say that automated systems make it easier for disabled employees to work productively.

**a** Suggest five safety precautions you can take when you are filing, regardless of which systems you use. Compare your ideas with other members of your group or your colleagues.

**b** Suggest how an automated system may help a business to comply with the terms of the Disability Discrimination Act. (If you have forgotten about this Act, look back at unit 202, page 141.)

## Core unit link

Helping to process information effectively helps your organisation to achieve its main purpose and therefore links to unit 202, performance indicator 1. Following procedures, guidelines and codes of practice (and querying these if you are unsure about anything) links to unit 202, PIs 2 and 5, as well as unit 201, PI 14.

Maintaining security and confidentiality links to unit 202, PIs 13–15.

Understanding the specific legislation that relates to your own organisation and your own role links to unit 202, PIs 7 and 8.

## Evidence collection

Your assessor will want to observe you storing, retrieving and archiving documents and have a professional discussion about the work that you do and the systems that you use. Start to prepare for this by noting down the following information.

1 What type of information system(s) do you use at work (i.e. whether you use only paper-based systems, an electronic system or both) and the main features?

2 What procedures must you follow in your workplace to comply with security and confidentiality requirements? You do not need to obtain a copy of these procedures. Note down the title of those that you must follow, where they are located and then say how these affect the way you work.

3 What classification systems do you use for any paper-based filing you do and/or the indexing systems you use in an electronic system?

4 What retention periods have been set for the records kept in your organisation?

## What if?

What should you do if you do not use both manual and electronic systems? In this case your assessor will ask you 'what if?' questions to check your competence.

# Confirming information to be collected, stored, retrieved and archived

## Information to be collected and stored

In most organisations there is a specific system everyone follows so that you know which documents are ready for storing and which are not. Few managers would be pleased to discover that several of the documents on which they are currently working have suddenly disappeared off their desks and into the filing system!

**In a manual system**, documents are filed only after they have been read or dealt with. There are two main ways in which the documents may be collected:

- You may visit certain members of staff or a manager to collect papers for filing. These will routinely be placed in a separate 'filing' basket in their office or workspace so that you know to empty this basket, and no other.
- Members of staff may place documents for filing in a large basket or tray near to the filing cabinets themselves.

**In an electronic system** you are more likely to be given a batch of original documents to scan into the system and there will be specific procedures in place stating what you must do with these afterwards. These may be stored in a temporary file for a short period, in case there are any queries or problems, before being systematically shredded.

## Information to be retrieved – and absence records

It is sensible to check that you understand exactly what information you have been asked to retrieve. Otherwise you can be hunting for hours simply because you don't really know what you are looking for!

There is normally a procedure to prevent individual papers being removed from a file, so instead the whole file has to be taken away and recorded in an 'absent' system. This tells other users where it is, in case they also need it urgently. The borrowed file may be listed in an 'absence book', kept near the filing system. Alternatively you can substitute an absent card for the file itself, stating who has taken it and when it is due to be returned.

## Information to be archived

Archiving means that the information is being put into long-term storage. This normally applies only to paper-based systems. The types of file that can be archived is normally controlled by specific procedures that must be followed by all users. You will find out more about these on page 326.

**Find out**

In some organisations staff put a 'release mark' (usually a small tick or cross) on documents to be filed, so that current paperwork isn't filed by mistake. Find out if this is the case in your workplace.

**Did you know?**

Bar codes can be allocated to file folders. These are then scanned into a computer to record files being taken from, and returned to, the system – rather like books in and out of a library.

# Methods used to collect, process and store information

On page 315 you saw that information to be stored is often collected from filing baskets. This section therefore concentrates on the correct way to process this information and store it.

**How to ...** Process information correctly to store in a paper-based system

- Check that the document has been released or marked for filing.
- Make sure that multi-page documents are complete and in the right order. Remove any paperclips and staple the document, to prevent other papers being 'hooked' behind it.
- Pre-sort paper documents into alphabetical or numerical order, depending on your system. Store pre-sorted documents in a concertina (expanding) file.
- Repair any torn papers with transparent sticky tape.
- Punch papers centrally, using either the ruler on the punch or the central notch as a guide.
- Locate the file you need and remove it carefully from the cabinet.
- Double-check you have the right folder.
- Put it on a stable surface and insert the new documents with the most recent on the top.
- Replace the folder in exactly the right place in the cabinet.

## Problems you may encounter

It can be extremely irritating to start to file documents and then find that, every two minutes, you seem to be encountering a problem. The temptation to dump all the problem papers back into the filing tray may be huge, but try to resist this, if only because they will still be there, staring at you, tomorrow!

There may be specific procedures to cover the following issues, otherwise the points below may help you.

- **There is no file for that person or topic**. This may be because it is a new customer or topic. You may need permission before you can start a new file. As a first step, check your miscellaneous files in case there are other papers on the same person or topic. Then check the procedures in your workplace for starting a new file. These will be devised to avoid 'tiny' files of one or two documents and to prevent the duplication of existing or similar files.

- **Your document could go in several files**. In some organisations you would photocopy the document and put it in all of them. In others you put it into the most obvious one and put a cross-reference note in the others, to say where it has been filed.

- **The file is missing**. Check the file records and the book that records borrowed files. If you don't have any such records then ask your colleagues if they have seen it and start looking on desks to see where it is. Then report the problem to your supervisor – perhaps with a suggestion that borrowed files should be recorded.

- **The folder is so full you can't fit anything else into it**. The normal procedure is to start a new file and label each folder with the date on which it was started and closed – but you need to check whether this is done in your workplace.

### Did you know?

*Yellow Pages* is a wonderful example of cross-referencing. If you look in the wrong place there is a note telling you where to look for the entry you want. Your cross-reference system should work in the same way!

### Remember

The tabs on file folders are for writing names on. They are not for tugging! If you do that they are likely to break off in your hand.

● **The folders are so tightly packed** in a drawer you can't remove the one you want. Try to slide your hand between them carefully and support the folder you need underneath as you lift it, particularly if it is heavy or bulky. Then check your organisation's procedures for archiving files or expanding the space available for storing active files before reporting the problem to your supervisor.

**Remember**

If all paper documents were retained after scanning into an electronic system, this would defeat one of the main reasons for having the system in the first place, which is to save space.

**How to ...** Process information correctly to store in an electronic stystem

● Check that the documents have been identified for scanning.

● Scan each one into the system. On some systems you can scan back-to-back images at the same time, which is quicker.

● Check that each image is readable. If not, enhance the image using the methods available in your system.

● Enter the correct key indexing words, so that each document can be easily found.

● Enter additional protection if required, to restrict access to confidential documents.

● Process the paper document according to the procedures for your system.

# Procedures to follow to access information systems

Access to paper-based systems and/or particular files is normally determined by the procedures relating to confidential files, as you saw on page 311. In electronic systems, access levels are set to control whether any documents can be amended or changed and how they are archived. An example of access levels is shown below.

| Level | Permitted actions | Effect |
|---|---|---|
| 1 | No access allowed/ documents invisible | This protects highly confidential or sensitive documents from being found or read<br>The document does not appear when searches are made |
| 2 | Read-only or visible access | Users can read the document only. |

| Level | Permitted actions | Effect |
|---|---|---|
| 3 | Read and edit | Users can access the document and make changes<br>These are recorded by the system |
| 4 | Enter and index documents | Users can scan new documents into the system, index them and save these in the appropriate folder |
| 5 | Authorisation access | Users can distribute documents to other people |
| 6 | Administrator access | Users can change the access level of other users, change how documents are indexed or stored, and amend the rules for archiving |

**Find out**

If you use an electronic information system, find out what access levels apply and what level you have been allocated as a user. It may also be interesting to find out who has certain access levels – and why.

If you work with an electronic system, your access level as a user will be pre-set, depending on the work you do. This will be controlled by the senior administrator in charge of the system.

# Ensuring information required is accurate

Apart from updating files, you will normally access files to retrieve information that is required for a particular purpose. Whether these are paper-based or electronic, the process is virtually the same.

**Did you know?**

If someone asks you for a 'hard copy', this means they want the information on paper rather than electronically.

**How to ...** Retrieve information in a paper-based system or an electronic system

- Obtain specific details on the information required, the format in which it is required and the timescale for obtaining it.

- Identify the criteria you need to find the information. In a paper-based system this is the file reference number or name. In an electronic system, it is the key words that you need to enter.

- If you find you are not allowed access to this information, promptly inform the person who gave you the task that you cannot obtain this.

- Locate the information. Check each document to see whether it matches the details you were given. Important details include the name or heading, the date and any specific reference numbers.

- In an electronic system, print out or email the document required to the person who requested it.

- In a paper-based system, your procedures are likely to state that you cannot remove a document from a file – although you can photocopy it. If the file is removed, the name of the borrower and the date may need to be recorded in an absence book or log.

- If you are unable to find the information use your own initiative to see whether you can solve the problem (see below). Otherwise report the matter to the person who asked you for the information and the person who is responsible for the system.

# Problems that can occur with information systems, and who to report them to

On page 317 you saw the type of problems that can occur when you are trying to store information into a system. Some of these can haunt you when you are trying to retrieve information, too, as you will see!

- You know which file you want, but it is missing from the system.
- The file is there, but the document you need is missing.
- In an electronic system, all your keywords and searches draw a blank.

First of all, don't panic! That never helped anyone and can easily mean you overlook the obvious – like the file is in front of you on your own desk! It helps if you think that there is a limited number of reasons for your problem no matter which type of system you use.

- **The document isn't visible**. This could be the case if it is confidential so it isn't in the main system or it is hidden in an electronic system.
- **You weren't given the correct information** (or didn't understand your instructions) so you are looking in the wrong place. Go back to the person who asked you to find the information and ask for more details to narrow down your search.
- **Someone has borrowed it**. Bear in mind this can happen only in a manual system. Check the borrowed-file log. Then check recent entries to see whether it says the file was borrowed but returned; then see whether the original borrower took it again or still has it. It's also worth checking the top of all cabinets and desks and all out-trays and trying to find out who was last working on it and when.
- **The document or file has been misfiled** so it is in the wrong place (or indexed wrongly in an electronic system). If a folder has gone missing, check similar names or numbers under which it could have been placed. Similarly, for a document think about other names it could have been filed under. If you have a numerical system, check file folders with a similar number (e.g. 8973 or 9873 if the file you want is 8937). In an electronic system, try other searches on similar keywords. Narrowing it down to a specific date range can also be useful.
- **The file or folder is completely lost**. Don't give up hope until you have sent out an email asking for help and information. Someone may have taken it home or suddenly find it in a desk drawer. In that case, don't be surprised if it mysteriously reappears one morning without a word said!

**Remember**

Folders can slip between suspension files in many systems. Check underneath them – on the base of a drawer – if a folder has gone missing.

**Did you know?**

In offices, items going missing is normally because of carelessness, not theft. Libraries, however, have bigger problems. In 2005 the British Library confirmed that 6995 items were now officially listed as 'not being at the correct position on the shelf'. This may be because they have been misplaced or mis-catalogued, but officials were also worried they may have been stolen.

### Reporting a problem

If folders or documents are regularly going missing then there is likely to be a problem with the system or the users. Perhaps there are no proper procedures? Or perhaps some people ignore the procedures or don't understand how the system works and so mess it up. Any system is only as good as the people who use it.

If you have tried your best to solve the problem on your own, without success, you should report it to the person who is responsible for your information system. This is likely to be your supervisor or line manager.

# Providing information in the required format and within agree timescales

There will always be a reason why you are asked to provide information. It is important to establish the urgency of the request. If the person who asked you needs it urgently – and is waiting for it impatiently right now – then it helps if you have assigned it the same priority. If you think it doesn't really matter when you find it, then within a day or so there are likely to be problems! Once you have been given a deadline you should work towards achieving this unless you have negotiated a different timescale because of your current workload or for some other legitimate reason.

If you encounter problems and your immediate efforts to solve these are unsuccessful, you must tell the person who asked you for the information promptly. This helps that person to consider revising any deadlines or even amending the task given the new situation. You may also find that you have an important ally in trying to find the missing information or in investigating what went wrong to cause the problem in the first place.

### Remember

When you are asked to provide information, the three important questions to ask are:

- *What* information is wanted?
- *When* is it wanted for?
- *How* is it wanted (as an original document, photocopy, sent electronically)?

### Snapshot – Information-handling services for business

A variety of organisations offer specialist services to businesses to help them process information securely and accurately.

- Scanning services will visit a business to scan documents or collect documents and scan them off-site. The original documents are then returned, destroyed or kept securely in a separate storage area. You can find out more at www.e-file-uk.com.

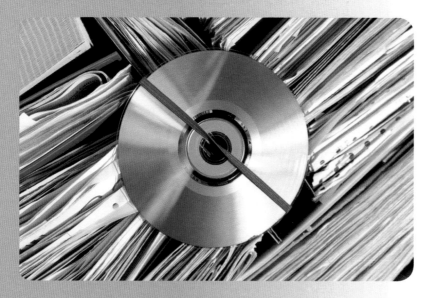

- There are document collection and archiving services for both paper-based records and for computer backups. Documents can be collected 365 days a year and taken to be stored in a secure environment. Backup tapes and other media are stored in fire-proof facilities and are available 24/7 in the event of a crisis. You can find out more details at www.atix.co.uk.

- Archive rental spaces are available together with storage boxes. Find out more at www.admiralstorage.co.uk and check out their archive/document storage facilities.

- Some specialist organisations also offer information 'health checks'. Consultants visit the firm and assess the current system and identify its strengths and weaknesses. How well would your system stand up to this type of close inspection? Find out how it works at www.audata.co.uk.

## Case study What's up Doc?

*Read the case study below and then answer the questions that follow. Then check your answers with those on the CD-ROM.*

Margaret Baines is Practice Manager at St George's Surgery, a group practice of GPs in East Lancashire, where she oversees the smooth running of all aspects of the practice. This means ensuring that all the administrative systems work effectively, including the storage and retrieval of medical records.

All general practices keep hundreds of patient records – in a group practice like St George's there are several thousand. If paper records are kept these are usually stored in a small paper folder known as a 'Lloyd George'. These no longer exist in practices that have chosen to have a 'paperless' system where everything is scanned into an electronic filing system.

St George's has opted to be a 'paper light' practice. Past information is still kept in paper form but incoming paper based information is scanned into EMIS – the computerised system used by the practice. To this is added patient information received electronically, such as lab reports from local hospitals. For consultations, doctors have the patient's Lloyd George folder on their desk and find current information on their computer. When information is scanned into the system it is 'tagged' with keywords so that the doctor can differentiate between the different electronic documents showing on screen to choose which they want to open. This is rather like the keywords you see for each entry in a search engine like Google. Consistency in allocating keywords is vital for doctors to be able to quickly spot the right document, so only trained administrators are allowed to do this task.

All medical practices must comply with relevant legislation and record retention periods, such as keeping a patient's record safely until he or she dies or transfers to another practice. In either of these cases the paperwork is sent to the medical agency for the area. For St George's this is LASCA (Lancashire and South Cumbria Agency) whose courier makes weekly visits to all practices to collect the 'green bag' containing medical records and other confidential information.

Medical practices, like other organisations that hold personal information, must comply with the Data Protection Act 1998. A different act – the Access to Medical Reports Act 1988 – states that patients must give their permission before a doctor can give information about their health to someone else. So if an insurance company or your employer want a medical report about you, they need your agreement and you can also opt to read the record before it is sent out. This costs £10 and you have 21 days in which to contact your GP and arrange to see it. This is always done in the presence of a medical professional who can explain any terms that have been used. Administrators at the practice know that they must not release medical reports until day 22 unless the patient has definitely stated that they do not wish to see the record. They also know a copy of the report must be kept for a minimum of six months in case of any queries or disputes at a later date.

Margaret is a firm believer in the benefits of electronic filing, such as the reduction in the amount of paper that needs to be stored. To keep this to a minimum, the records are culled to reduce the number of bulky medical notes and remove any duplicated information. This is done only by the doctors themselves to ensure that nothing of medical importance is thrown away by accident.

Margaret likes the safeguards that are built into the electronic system, such as the fact that if a name is misspelt, an address is incorrect or a date of birth isn't accurate then the system will query the entry. This means information doesn't go missing through misfiling. She also likes the fact that she can set security and confidentiality access levels to be appropriate for the level of expertise of the user and 'need to know'. For safety, the system is backed up every night and the back-up copy taken off-site. EMIS also guarantees an eight-hour maximum response time service if the system fails for any reason. You can find out more about the system at www.emis-online.com/index.asp.

**Questions**

1  *Three possible ways to keep medical records are mentioned. What are they?*

2  *Why do the doctors at St George's need both a computer and the paper record when they see a patient?*

3  *Identify two benefits of storing medical records electronically.*

4  *Why are only trained staff allowed to scan information into the electronic system?*

5 **a** Suggest one reason why an employer might want a medical report on an employee.

**b** Explain why an administrator cannot just post a copy of the report to the patient.

6 Why do you think LASCA send a courier to collect medical records from practices?

7 Why is the culling of paper records done only by the doctors?

8 Suggest two reasons why a back-up copy of the system is stored off-site each night.

# When information should be archived and the procedures to follow

## Archiving and paper-based systems

Many problems with paper-based systems start to occur over a period of time. These include:

- folders becoming full, so that no more documents can be added
- cabinet drawers becoming full, with no space for new files
- insufficient room for more cabinets in a limited amount of office space
- congestion in certain areas of a cabinet, particularly for files stored alphabetically
- unimportant or duplicated documents within files, together with more important documents.

For all these reasons, at regular intervals, the whole information system needs to be reviewed. This includes taking the following actions:

- Prune or cull folders by removing unimportant or duplicated documents.
- Destroy unimportant files that will never be needed again – such as those relating to an organisation that no longer exists.
- Destroy files that have been retained under the organisation's retention policies but are now beyond their final date.
- Archive files that must be kept but are now inactive and move them to another area.

There are normally specific procedures to control when archiving can take place and who must decide which files can be moved – and where to. An example is shown opposite.

## Example of a procedure for archiving paper-based files

1  A file should be considered for disposal or archiving when on the following applies.
   - No papers have been added for two years or more
   - The contents of the papers cover a period of more than five years
   - The file has reached the end of a natural cycle (e.g. a member of staff has left the company).

2  All requests for disposal or archiving must be referred to the senior administrator.

3  When a file is closed, the date of closure must be written on the front of the file and entered on to the master file list.

4  Once a file is closed, no documents must be added to it.

5  The documents held in files for disposal must be shredded. Where possible the file folder should be reused and any transparent pockets or other storage items removed for reuse.

6  Files for archiving must be clearly labelled with an 'archive' label and placed in a secure storage box. The name of the file must be entered on the box label.

7  The archive storage box must be placed in the basement, or some other place for long-term storage, in accordance with the archiving classification procedures.

## Archiving and electronic systems

Some organisations operate a manual system for storing current files but then arrange for archived files to be scanned into an electronic system. This can be done on the premises using a stand-alone electronic archiving machine that scans the documents directly on to CD-ROMs. Alternatively, this process can be carried out off the premises by a specialist firm (see page 322–323). This is an ideal alternative if there is no space for storing archived files in paper form.

If all files are retained electronically then there is usually no need to archive them. They can still be instantly retrieved in the system if required.

### How to ... Archive information

- Check that you know exactly which files can be archived.
- Check that you clearly understand the procedures for archiving information in your organisation.
- Remove the file folders from the main system.
- Transfer these to the archive storage boxes.
- Depending on your organisation's system, clearly label each box with the files it contains or number the box and make a separate record listing the files contained in the box.
- Close the box and place it in its correct sequence in the archive storage area.

## Changing places

*Your assessor will ask you how you will adapt your knowledge of storing, retrieving and archiving information if you change your job in the future. You will need to think about the way in which aspects of these tasks would change if you worked for a different organisation.*

Donna works as a school administrator. All the filing is paper-based. Donna keeps the general files in a vertical cabinet in her office in subject order under topics such as timetables, building maintenance, equipment and stationery. Staff files are kept in a similar cabinet in the head's office and are filed in alphabetical order. Donna doesn't keep student files – those are kept by the tutors and the year heads. Donna is responsible for ensuring both filing cabinets are locked each night and that no files are taken from either cabinet without the head's agreement.

Beth works as sales administrator for a company making and suppling specialist equipment to customers all over the world. Customer files are paper-based and stored alphabetically, in geographical regions, under countries of the world and then the name of the firm. Beth says the system has improved her geography immensely! The sales manager is insistent that filing be done daily in case there is a query regarding a customer so that he can be sure that the files will always include the most up-to-date paperwork.

Abida works in the HR department of a large organisation. All staff records are stored electronically. They include details of staff training, appraisals, salaries, sick leave and other personal details. There are six levels of access to the files – Abida has level four access which allows her to read and update documents and also index new documents that are added to the system. She is obviously aware she must never discuss the information she reads in the files. Under the Data Protection Act, for a fee of (currently) £10, a member of staff can ask for a copy of his or her own record. In the last six months Abida has twice printed out information for a member of staff to meet this request.

Simon works for a public relations company that also offers a reading and press cuttings analysis service for its clients. This means that the company needs to scan magazines and newspapers for stories relating to its clients and copy these. To do this without breaking copyright laws it has a licence from the Newspaper Licensing Agency. The company has an electronic filing system for all its client files and Simon scans all new cuttings into these. He can also forward a copy to a client electronically, as an email attachment.

Jamila works for an insurance broker. The customer files are paper-based and kept in alphabetical order by surname, but Jamila also records the dates on which policies are due for renewal. This enables the broker to remind each customer when the renewal premium needs to be paid.

1 For any *one* person listed above, identify the differences he or she would find if moving to your organisation and doing your job.

2 For any *one* person listed above, say how you would need to adapt your skills if you did their job rather than your own.

 **Over to you**

1 You have been asked to work with Alec this week, to file a backlog of papers. You soon start to suspect he hasn't much idea what to do. How would you solve each of the following problems he has encountered?

  **a** He has absolutely no idea how to punch papers so that they are aligned properly in a folder.

  **b** He was told to file a document relating to Mr J. Allan this morning. Your supervisor has just picked up the file and the document is missing – though Alec swears he put it in the file.

  **c** You spot him trying to punch holes in a bound report from your firm's accountants.

  **d** He has several papers waiting to go into four borrowed files that were supposed to be returned two days ago.

  **e** When he tugs a heavy folder by the tab, it breaks off in his hand.

  **f** He has no idea what to do with an email about recalled goods that relates to four customers.

  **g** He has a document to file in a confidential file to which neither of you has access.

2 Your friend Bushra works for a small firm of architects. She needs to store large drawings that are produced by the firm, together with reports and correspondence between the organisation and its clients. Her problem is that space is limited and her paper-based storage system is overflowing.

  **a** Suggest two benefits that the firm could gain by changing to an electronic storage system.

  **b** Suggest an alternative method of freeing up space in the organisation's active system.

  **c** If Bushra's boss didn't want to convert to electronic filing, and there was no basement or spare storage room available, what else could she suggest to solve the problem?

## Core unit link

Checking that you clearly understand the information you must obtain and checking documents to ensure they match these requirements may link to unit 201, performance indicators 1 and 4.

Agreeing a deadline for providing information, working to achieve these and reporting problems (and/or admitting your mistakes!) links to unit 201, PIs 7–13. Trying to improve your own performance and acting on feedback may link to unit 201, PIs 15 and 16.

Setting high standards for yourself and being supportive to others may link to unit 201, PIs 20, 24 and 25.

## Evidence collection

1 Keep an information log that you can discuss with your assessor. This doesn't need to include every document you handle! Instead it should be a summary of the type of information you store and retrieve on a routine basis. In particular it should include any problems you have encountered and how you have tried to solve these.

2 Write an account of the work you routinely undertake when you are storing or retrieving documents for your line manager or other people in your workplace. Include any deadlines you have been given or specific information regarding the format of documents you have to supply. Ask the person who gave you the work to countersign and date your account to confirm its accuracy.

3 Write a separate account listing the tasks you undertake when you are archiving files. Ask the person who supervised you doing the work to countersign and date your account to confirm it.

## What if?

What should you do if no problems arise during the time you are being assessed? In this case your assessor will ask you 'what if?' questions to confirm your competence.

## Key skills reminder

If you are taking Key Skills awards, remember to discuss with your tutor or trainer how your evidence for this unit could also count towards those awards.

# Use a telephone system

## Unit summary and overview

This option unit is divided into three sections:

- making calls
- receiving calls
- dealing with message systems.

Using a telephone system is one of the most fundamental tasks required of any administrator. Yet there is a huge difference between worst and best practice – as any customer who rings a firm will testify. This is despite the fact that there were over 60 million mobile phone users in the UK in 2004! It would appear that widespread mobile ownership hasn't helped inexperienced staff to use a business telephone system very effectively.

In this unit you will find out how to make calls professionally and effectively so that you achieve the aims of the call as well as projecting a positive image of yourself and your organisation. This is equally important when you receive calls and have to prove that you can deal with them promptly and transfer callers safely to other extensions without any difficulty. You will also learn how to deal with messages efficiently, no matter what type of messaging system is used in your organisation.

This unit starts with a brief overview of different types of telephone systems and their main features before covering the knowledge and skills required for the three sections listed above.

# Features of telephone systems and how to use them

**Link to option units**

As you gather your evidence for this unit you should also obtain evidence for your core units. Watch for the Core unit link logo which suggests how the evidence you may collect may count towards both this unit and your core units.

Remember that you might be able to identify other links yourself, because of your own job role and the evidence you have obtained.

Talk to your assessor if you need further guidance on how your evidence should be cross-referenced.

**Find out**

In most large firms a designated person operates a switchboard or screen-based console which is often the first point of contact for callers. In a small firm, incoming calls may be routed directly through to extensions so that they can be answered from any phone. Which is the case in your organisation?

There is a very wide range of telephone systems for business users. The specific system in your organisation will have been chosen based on the following main factors:

- the size of the business
- the number of employees who regularly use the telephone
- the amount and type of business done over the telephone
- whether the telephone system is to be linked to the computer network
- the features, extras and applications required on the central system (see the snapshot on page 339).

In addition, there are many manufacturers making competing systems. For that reason, if you change jobs, you may well find that the phone system in your new place of work is different from the one you are used to. It may also have some different features

The best way to learn about your particular telephone system is to understand the type of features commonly found, then check which ones you have. These will be given in the handbook for your system. You then have to learn how to use them. Ideally you will be shown how to use your phone system by a colleague who knows it well, but even then it can be difficult to remember all the features available unless you use them regularly. The best way is to concentrate first on those you need to understand to deal with calls efficiently yourself. These are in the Group A list in the table opposite.

Display phone

Cordless headset phone

Conference phone

## Main features of business telephone systems

**Group A – Common features you need to know and understand**

| | |
|---|---|
| Callback | Enables you to automatically recall an engaged extension when it is free; this saves you from having to keep trying |
| Divert or call forwarding | Enables you to redirect calls from your extension to another one; on some systems you can divert calls to another outside number or to a mobile<br>Use this if you will be away from your desk for some time, to save other people having to answer your calls or to prevent them remaining unanswered |
| Interrupt | This feature tells you when another call is waiting; you will normally hear a beep on the line<br>Ideally you will speed up your current call (or arrange to ring back) to deal with the incoming call |
| Last number redial | Automatically redials the last number you called |
| Message waiting | A light or beep shows that a voicemail message is waiting (see below)<br>If the phone is linked to your computer system, the message waiting will show on screen |
| On hold/reminder call holding | On hold enables incoming calls to be held while the correct person is found to deal with the call<br>Reminder call holding prompts you that the caller is still waiting to be connected |
| Transfer | Transfer enables you to put a call through to another internal extension; you need to know how to do this speedily and efficiently (see page 347)<br>On some systems you can transfer to external numbers too |
| Redirect | Enables you to reroute a transferred call if, for example, the first person is not available and you have to redirect the call to someone else |
| Speed dialling | Enables you to use abbreviated dialling for long numbers or set up your own abbreviated numbers for people you call regularly |
| Voicemail | An individual answering service for each person as callers can leave voice messages in individual mailboxes when people are away or engaged on another call<br>You can retrieve your messages from any extension or from an external phone |

**Group B – Additional features you may have available**

| | |
|---|---|
| Call barring | Prevents extension users making certain types of call (e.g. to international numbers)<br>Only 999 can never be barred |
| Caller display or Calling Line Identity | Shows the number of the caller<br>If the system is linked to an address book feature it may also show the person's name and company |

### Did you know?

**Automated attendant** is the official term for the recorded message that answers a phone and tells callers how to use the keypad to choose who they wish to speak to – e.g. 'Press 1 for Sales, 2 for Customer Service ...'. The problem with some systems is that callers find themselves in a seemingly endless loop, vainly trying to find the combination that will let them speak to a real human

**Main features of business telephone systems** Continued

**Group B – Additional features you may have available**

| | |
|---|---|
| Conference calls | Allows you to speak to more than one extension at a time or to one or more outside callers and extension holders at a time |
| Computer telephony integration | Links the computer network to the phone system<br>Enables, for example, pop-ups to appear on screen to announce callers<br>Outgoing calls can be made by clicking on a name on screen |
| Direct dial inwards | Enables callers to phone extensions and departments direct without going through the switchboard |
| Discriminating ringing | The ring tone between external calls and internal calls is different, so that you know which is which<br>A variation of this is when lights are programmed to flash differently depending on the type of call |
| Distinctive ringing | Different ring tones are programmed for different extensions, so that you can tell which one is ringing |
| Do not disturb | Blocks calls to your extension while it is set |
| Hands-free | Enables you to continue working because you listen and speak through a speaker, not the handset<br>Not suitable for confidential calls but useful if more than one person needs to listen in to a call |
| Listen on hold | Linked to the above, this enables you to replace the receiver if you have been asked to hold, so that you can carry on working<br>You can then pick up the receiver again when the person comes back on the line |
| Secrecy button | Pressing this means the caller cannot hear you<br>It is far more effective than trying to cover the mouthpiece with your hand while you talk to a colleague about the call! |
| VoIP (Voice over Internet Protocol) | This means free calls and voicemails can be sent over the Internet; see also snapshot on page 349 |

**Find out**

Some organisations have specific procedures that relate to making telephone calls. For example, you may not be allowed to make international calls or to call important customers unless you have had specific training. Find out what procedures exist in your firm that relate to making telephone calls. (See also page 342 for procedures relating to receiving telephone calls.)

# Making calls

Many people are more worried about making business telephone calls than they are about receiving them. Yet the advantage is that when you are making a call you can prepare for it. You also know what you are going to talk about. When you answer a call you have no idea what the caller might want or what type of questions you might be asked! For that reason, a good way to develop your telephone skills is to start by making simple calls yourself, both to your colleagues internally and to outside contacts. As you become more experienced you will find it easier to prepare to make more complex calls, even to people you have never met before.

# Identifying the purpose of a call before you make it

The purpose of a call – in other words, the reason for making it – should influence the way you communicate with the other person, both in terms of the words you use and your tone of voice. You should hardly ring to give someone bad news – such as your technician cannot now visit as promised – in the same bright and breezy tone of voice you would use to tell them their order had arrived! In addition, you should expect a rather different response, especially if you are telling someone there is a problem of some kind. You need to prepare for dealing with that, too.

Thinking about the purpose of the call can therefore help you to prepare in two ways.

- You can think about the aim of the call, what you have to achieve and how to do this.
- You can consider how the other person may react to what you are saying and how you should respond.

Remember that when you are communicating with someone by telephone the person cannot see your body language or facial expressions, and you cannot see his or hers. You therefore have fewer clues to guide you about the person's feelings and attitude and his or her response to what you are saying. You therefore need to listen carefully not just to the words people use, but to other sounds – such as sighs or 'tuts'! A stunned silence should also tell you quite a lot.

**Remember**

Regardless of why you are calling, your manner should always be more formal and professional when you are making a business call. It shouldn't be the same as the way you speak on your mobile or home phone.

**Did you know?**

Even though the other person cannot see you, if you smile during the conversation this shows in your voice and helps you to sound friendlier and nicer to deal with.

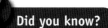

**How to ...** Prepare to make a call

*If you are calling to provide information*

- List the points you have to make, so you don't miss anything out.
- Make sure you understand the information yourself.
- Check that the order of the points is sensible, so that you introduce the topic properly.
- Think about questions you might be asked.
- Remember not to speak too quickly if any of the information is complicated or technical.

**Remember**

Don't try to rush your calls. You may know what you want to say but you have to allow the other person some thinking time to consider what you have said.

---

**How to ... Continued**

- Think about whether the recipient will be pleased to receive your call or not. This should influence your tone of voice and the way you present the information.

*If you are calling to make an enquiry or to ask for information*

- List the questions that you need to ask in a logical order.

- Leave space underneath each one to write down the answer.

- Be prepared to ask someone to slow down if he or she is answering too quickly.

- Be prepared to ask someone to explain a term you do not understand.

---

**Remember**

It is always better to use an online enquiry service because use is free. If you must telephone a directory enquiry service always have a pen in your hand to note down the number. Agreeing that the service connects your call is far more expensive!

# Methods of obtaining names and numbers of people

The method you use to obtain the name and number of someone you have to call will depend on the type of person you are calling and the resources available at your workplace. You may just have a shared BT phone book in a drawer, or there may be a series of directories and a comprehensive customer database. The main options are identified in the table below.

| Various methods of obtaining names and numbers | |
|---|---|
| **Type of contact** | **Alternative sources** |
| Frequent contact | Telephone memory number store<br>Computerised address book<br>Paper-based address book |
| Customer | Computer database (if linked to the telephone system, the call can be made with a click of your mouse!)<br>Customer contact list<br>Customer file |
| Local first-time contact | *The Phone Book*<br>*Yellow Pages* for your area |
| National first-time contact | Online at one of the free services (e.g. www.yell.co.uk or www.192.com or www118500.com and click 'online services')<br>Phone directory enquiries (e.g. 118 500: BT number) but this is chargeable<br>If a business, check the website |
| International first-time contact | If a business, check the website<br>If in the USA or Canada, try www.worldpages.com<br>An International directory enquiry service (e.g. 118104) |

# Using the telephone system to contact people

On virtually all telephone systems you use a slightly different method to make internal as opposed to external calls.

- To contact someone inside the organisation, lift the handset and key his or her extension number.
- To make an external call, you first need an outside line. You normally obtain this by keying 9 and then keying the area code (unless it is a local call) and the number.
- To make a call to a number or area that is normally barred on your extension, you will need to go through your switchboard operator.

# Projecting a positive image of yourself and your organisation

You will project a positive image of yourself and your organisation if you are polite, efficient and professional. This means opening and closing the call properly, having a pleasant but business-like manner and using appropriate words and phrases. If it's also obvious that you know what you are talking about, people will be doubly impressed! Key points to note are listed in the 'How to ...' box.

> **Remember**
>
> Words to avoid during a business phone call include: 'yeah', 'cool', 'ace', 'hang on', 'you what?' and – if you can manage it – 'OK'!

## How to ... Project a positive image when you make a telephone call

- Ask for the person and/or department you need to contact.
- If asked by the switchboard operator, identify yourself by saying your name and the name of your organisation. If you have an unusual name then be prepared to repeat it or spell it. Otherwise wait until you are connected to the person you want to speak to and introduce yourself then.
- Tell the person why you are ringing.
- Don't use slang, technical words, jargon or current expressions.
- Use your natural voice. There is no need to try to alter your accent. Just concentrate on speaking clearly and not too quickly.
- Try to use the person's name during the conversation. That helps you to remember who are speaking to and it makes the person you are calling feel more important. Remember, though, that unless you know someone well, it is usual to use their surname during a business conversation.

**How to ... Continued**

- If you have to give any figures (such as your own telephone number), say the figures in pairs rather than in threes, and use 'zero' rather than 'nought' as it's clearer.

- If you don't understand anything or the other person is speaking too quickly, ask for the information to be repeated. This is far better than concluding the conversation and finding you have to ring back!

- Remember, if you made the call then you should be the one to end it. When you have discussed everything on your list start to draw the call to a conclusion.

- Before you ring off, summarise the main points you have discussed (see below) to check you agree on everything.

- If the person has been helpful or done you a favour, conclude by thanking him/her.

# Summarising the outcomes of a telephone conversation before ending a call

When you are talking to someone for quite a time, especially if you are discussing various options, it is very easy to lose track of what was decided or agreed. Summarising the outcome of a telephone conversation before you ring off helps to overcome that.

Doing this is easy if you have been making clear notes as the conversation progressed. The simple way now is to read each note back to the other person. If he or she agrees with what you are saying, put a tick next to the note. If not, then put a cross – or cross out those notes – and write the correct version instead. Read this back and tick it when the person agrees.

When you have completed the call, you can quickly summarise the key points yourself by extracting and listing all the notes that you've ticked.

## Snapshot – Additional features on modern systems

The task of purchasing a business telephone system today is not for the faint-hearted. Not only are there many different systems available, the jargon used is almost undecipherable unless you are an expert. Decisions have to be made regarding the number of incoming lines and extensions that will be required, as well as what type of additional features are needed. You have already read about the automated attendant feature on page 333. Other extras features can include the following.

- **Call sequencing.** All callers are greeted with a pre-recorded message and then queued automatically. A further message is given every few minutes after that if the caller is still in the queue.

- **Automated caller distribution** (ACD). This automatically places calls to the next available extension. It is more sophisticated than call sequencing because different types of call can be identified and prioritised and the caller given an estimated time to be answered. Managers can also obtain reports showing how quickly calls are being dealt with.

**Snapshot** Continued

- **Music on hold.** This is a common feature but on some systems the operator can choose the music or even link the system to the local radio station.

- **Bulletin board**. This gives pre-recorded information to callers about the company's products or service. Many multiplex cinemas use one to give details of programmes and screening times.

- **Call logging**. This tracks and records calls from extensions showing the number called, the duration of the call and the cost.

- **Call management system**. This tracks and records calls made and received by extension holders, including speed of response and numbers of missed calls.

Operators who manage a system from a central console can view the state and identity of all calls in progress and those held in queues on their screen. During quiet times they can use the same PC to do other work – such as word-processing or sending emails. Some systems link to databases held in Microsoft Access and sophisticated searches can be carried out to find names and numbers.

### Over to you

1 Jamie Symmonds owns Sportsdays Exclusive, an agency specialising in offering experience and hospitality days linked to special sporting events. Customers can buy anything from a day out at the races or Wimbledon, to travel and tickets for football or cricket matches at home and abroad.

Jamie employs four staff who handle telephone enquiries. The current telephone system has been installed for quite some time and he is thinking of upgrading it. Suggest five features that would be invaluable on the new system and give a reason for each of your choices. Check your answers with the suggestions on the CD-ROM.

2 Sara Broughton has just started working for Jamie as an administrator. He has asked her to call a hotel chain they use regularly to query a bill they have received. Read the conversation below and then answer the following questions. Then check your answers with the suggestions on the CD-ROM.

 a Identify what Sara did right when she made the call.

 b Identify where she went wrong.

 c State your opinion of the manner of the person she spoke to.

 d What do you think Sara should do now – and why?

Sara's conversation:

**Sara:** 'Good morning, is that the Sherwood Hotel Group? This is Sara Broughton of Sportsdays Exclusive. I'd like to query an invoice we received from you yesterday.'

**Sherwood Hotels:** 'Just a moment, please, I'll put you through to Accounts.'

(*After a short pause*) 'Accounts. Can I help you?'

**Sara:** 'Oh, yes please. My name is Sara Broughton of Sportsdays Exclusive. I'd like to query an invoice we received from you yesterday.

**Sherwood Hotels:** 'Do you have the account reference number?'

**Sara:** 'Er ... yes (*rustle of paper*) It's ZK2039482/4. You see, the bill is for five rooms for two nights but we previously cancelled one of the rooms so the bill should be for only ...'

**Sherwood Hotels:** (*Interrupts*) 'Just a second. Can I check the details with you? We have charged you for five executive doubles at the Westbury Sherwood for two nights at the rate of £120 per room per night + VAT.'

**Sara:** 'Yes, that's the problem. We only used four rooms, you see. We cancelled the other one.'

**Sherwood Hotels:** 'What's your cancellation number?'

**Sara:** 'What? I mean, sorry – I don't understand what you mean.'

**Sherwood Hotels:** 'Well, when you cancelled, we would have given you a cancellation number.'

**Sara:** 'I don't know, sorry, I didn't work here then. Perhaps it was cancelled online at your website?'

**Sherwood Hotels:** (*Impatiently*) 'It doesn't make any difference, we would still give you a number. Perhaps you could check your records or talk to someone who might have done the cancellation and ring me back when you've found it?'

**Sara:** 'Er, well, yes. OK. Will do. Bye.'

**Sherwood Hotels:** 'Bye.' (*Puts phone down*)

## Evidence collection

1  Check out your own telephone system at work against the list of features on page 333–334. Identify all the features that relate to your particular system and the phone you use every day at work. Then score your own

**Core unit link**

When you are providing information to other people and focusing on their communications to you, this links with unit 201, performance indicators 1 and 2.

Using your telephone system professionally to achieve your organisation's objectives, following the procedures that relate to your role and promoting the image of yourself and your organisation may link to unit 202, PIs 1–5, and unit 202, PI 14.

---

**Evidence collection** Continued

ability to use each one effectively. Keep your notes as the basis of a professional discussion with your assessor about the system you regularly use at work.

2  Keep notes that you have made when you have prepared for three or four calls. Ideally these should include further notes you made during the conversation and show how you ticked off particular points when you summarised the call at the end.

3  If you regularly make internal calls to one or two colleagues in other departments or areas of your organisation, summarise the types of call you regularly make to them and ask them to write a brief statement underneath to confirm that you communicate clearly and project a positive image and to sign and date this statement. Don't ask external contacts for the same type of evidence unless you have the specific agreement of your supervisor.

---

**Remember**

No matter how busy you are, incoming calls should be answered promptly and pleasantly. Don't let any irritation about being interrupted show in your voice. If no one ever rang your organisation you'd probably not have a job!

# Receiving calls

One of the most nerve-wracking tasks when you have just started working for an organisation is having to answer the telephone when you don't know much about the organisation, the work it does or who does what. Yet it is still quite possible to deal with a caller in a pleasant, professional manner, without knowing the specific answers to a query, as you will see in this section. Provided you sound positive and helpful and can *either* transfer the call to someone who can help *or* take an accurate and complete message so that someone can call back promptly, then you have done a good job and still given a positive image of yourself and the organisation.

**Remember**

To *every* caller you are seen as a representative of your organisation whenever you answer the phone, whether you have worked there for one day or for ten years!

## Following procedures when receiving calls

Some organisations have specific procedures for dealing with calls received – from the speed at which calls must be dealt with, to the ways callers must be greeted. In a large organisation the procedures may be in writing and new staff may be allowed to make or answer calls only after a short period of training. In a small firm there may be no specific training, but your line manager or supervisor will be just as keen to maintain high standards. In this situation, the best strategy is to watch other people and copy what they do.

**Did you know?**

If you can tell the difference between the distinctive ring tones on your system for internal and external callers, then you can tailor your response to the type of caller who is contacting you.

The procedures you can expect are likely to include the following:

- *The greeting to be given to callers by anyone answering on behalf of the organisation.* This can range from the formal ('Good morning, Jackson and White. How may I help you?') to the informal ('Hi, Software Solutions, Arif speaking. What can I do for you?')

- *The way in which departmental or individual extensions should be answered.* This will depend on whether it is standard practice to give the name of the department, and/or just your name. Variations include 'Hello. Customer Service, Ruth speaking' and 'Carl Sims, Accounts. Can I help you?' It is normally not good practice just to say the extension number, as this is meaningless to external callers.

- *The action to take if one of your colleagues is unavailable to take the call.* For example, should you arrange for your colleague to contact the caller, or should you ask for the caller to call back later? Professional and business firms are likely to want potential customers to be phoned back promptly so that they don't lose possible new business. Organisations that receive lots of general enquiries from members of the public, such as an entertainment complex or leisure centre, are more likely to ask the caller to call back again later, to reduce their own telephone costs.

- *The firm's policy on personal calls.* Since the advent of mobile phones this has become less of an issue, as staff rarely receive private calls on a business line. Most firms have no objections to personal calls being received provided the privilege isn't abused and staff don't spend work time chatting to friends. Personal calls should be kept short and your friends and family should ring you at work only when it's absolutely necessary. Similarly, you should make a personal call on a work phone only if it's about an urgent and important matter.

**Remember**

If you take your mobile to work, keep it on message mode when you are at your desk – or on vibrate if you are expecting an urgent call. And, in case you forget once or twice, check that your ring tone wouldn't alarm or offend anyone.

# How to identify the caller and his or her needs

## Identifying the caller

If you are fortunate to answer a handset that has a display screen, then the caller's number – or even his or her name – will appear on the display so that you can give a personal greeting. Otherwise one of the first things to find out is the name of the caller. If the caller represents a business organisation, you need that name as well. This sounds very straightforward but there are a few pitfalls for the unwary.

- The caller has a very common name, such as Brown or Khan, so you need to ask for the first name too, otherwise your caller could be one of several different customers or contacts.
- The name is foreign or very unusual. You haven't a clue how to spell it and don't like to ask.
- You can't understand what the person is saying, perhaps because he or she has a foreign or strong regional accent. You ask for the name to be repeated but it's just as incomprehensible the second time, so you give up.
- The caller launches straight into the reason for ringing and doesn't give you a name and you forget to ask. This is more likely to happen with a call from a private individual rather than a business contact, especially if the caller is very old or very young.

Despite all these potential difficulties, it is important that you establish the caller's identity properly for several reasons:

- You may need to find the customer file, to obtain relevant information.
- You may need to pass on information to a colleague about the call.
- You may need to send out information to the caller by post.
- If your organisation deals with several people with the same name, you could end up calling the wrong person back.

### How to ... Make sure you know the caller's identity

- Never pick up the telephone without a pen and paper next to you.
- Automatically start to make a written note whenever you receive a call.
- If the caller gives you his or her name, write this down in capital letters at the top.
- Use the name during the conversation. It will help you to remember the name; it will also check you are pronouncing it correctly!

- Ask the caller to spell the name if it is unusual. Beware of letters that sound the same over the phone (T and D; P and B). Differentiate these using the phonetic alphabet – e.g. 'Is that T for Tango or D for Delta?' If you don't know the phonetic alphabet any simple words or names can be used – T for Tilly and D for David will have the same effect!

- If you realise you are starting to write down what the caller wants and there is no name on your note, wait for the next time the caller pauses. Then say: 'I'm sorry, but could you please give me your name first.'

**Remember**

Always make sure that you can use the caller's name when you conclude a call – e.g. 'Thank you for calling, Mrs Evans. Goodbye.' If that becomes your standard way of saying goodbye, then you can never conclude a phone call without knowing the caller's name!

## Identifying the caller's needs

Unless you have been told just to ask for a caller's name or just to transfer callers to another extension, you should always try to find out why the caller is ringing. There are several reasons for this:

- You need to know the reason for the call before you can decide whether you can deal with the matter yourself or need to pass it on to someone else.
- If you cannot help the caller yourself, knowing what the caller wants means you can connect up to the best person to provide help or information.
- If you are putting the call through to your supervisor or line manager, it helps that person to decide whether to deal with it or let someone else handle it. In either case you are providing invaluable thinking time to prepare for the call before connecting the caller.
- If you are going to take a message for someone, you will need to find out what the call is about.

**Remember**

It is far better and more tactful to say 'Could I tell Sue Kelly why you are calling, please?' than 'What do you want to speak to her about?'

Most callers will happily say why they are calling. In fact, in some cases, it might be the first thing they tell you! Otherwise you will have to ask. However, in other cases you must be prepared for some people to refuse to give you the reason, particularly if you work for a solicitor or accountant, when clients regularly discuss sensitive or confidential issues. Never take a refusal personally. If you have to pass on a message or transfer the call, simply give the name and say that the caller preferred not to discuss the reason for the call.

# Giving accurate and up-to-date information to callers

Many callers ring to obtain information. There are two aspects to this you must consider:

- The first is whether the information is accurate and up to date.
- The second is whether or not it is confidential.

How to deal with confidential information is covered below. First, you need to ensure that you are not misleading callers by giving them incorrect or outdated information, either accidentally or deliberately!

If you work in an organisation where you are frequently answering general enquiries, then you should have the information you need at your fingertips, either in printed format or on a screen. An obvious example is an up-to-date product catalogue and price list, or access to the product database.

If your job means that you answer far more wide-ranging calls and enquiries, then you are less likely to have everything you need close at hand, and the effort of checking fiddly details may be too much – particularly on a busy day with a fussy caller you want to get rid of. The temptation to say the first thing that comes into your head may be huge!

You are wise not to do this. Trying to convince your supervisor a few days later that there was a really good reason why you told a customer a load of rubbish may work the first time, but would certainly backfire if you tried it regularly!

Finally, if a caller is making a complaint, remember to stay non-committal. Take down all the facts and say you must pass them on. Above all, never agree that your organisation or your colleague must have been at fault. You can't possibly know this and if you admit liability at the outset this can cause serious problems for anyone who has to follow up the complaint.

# Why confidentiality and security are important when dealing with callers

People who telephone your organisation have a right to expect that personal, sensitive and confidential information they discuss over the phone will go no further. In some organisations, such as medical practices and legal firms, being discrete and keeping such information confidential may be an express term in your contract of employment. Even if it is not, don't forget that not disclosing confidential information is one of your implied responsibilities to your employer – as you saw on page 117 in unit 202.

If you are told confidential information over the telephone there are three things to remember:
- Don't repeat the information to anyone except the person who should receive it.
- Don't leave notes about the call lying around for anyone to read.
- If you write the information in a message, put this in a sealed envelope.

# Information that could affect confidentiality and security – and how to handle it

There are various types of information that you should never disclose to callers without specific authority. These include:

- personal information about your colleagues (e.g. someone's home address or telephone number)
- information about other customers or your dealings with them
- information about your company's future plans
- financial information about your company.

Depending on the type of organisation you work for – and how it operates – you may find there are many other types of information that you mustn't discuss with callers, both internal and external. Your boss may be keen that you keep certain departmental plans and discussions confidential, especially if you work in an organisation where the managers are very competitive.

**Did you know?**

The easiest way to keep sensitive information confidential is just to say you don't know the answer and refer the caller to your boss. This is easier and quicker than defending a decision not to tell!

# Identifying the appropriate person to whom you should transfer a call

Transferring calls on a telephone system is a very basic operation but one that sometimes goes horribly wrong. One of the most annoying experiences for any caller is waiting to be transferred, not knowing quite what will happen next, only to end up listening to the dialling tone again or even silence. If this has happened to you, then you will know how frustrating and infuriating it can be.

It is important to identify the appropriate person to take the call first time round because otherwise you end up shunting your poor caller from pillar to

post, in a vain attempt to find someone to help. This not only makes you look incompetent but it makes your organisation look careless and slipshod. You will identify the appropriate person only if you know:

- exactly why the caller is ringing
- who deals with what in your organisation.

You then need to look up that person's extension number and transfer the call. How to do this is revealed below.

# Information to give when transferring calls

**Remember**

Another way to 'transfer' a call is to hand the phone to your colleague to deal with the matter. It is still important to provide your colleague with a brief summary about the caller and the reason for ringing – in the same way that you would if you were transferring the call to another office or department.

The second most annoying experience for a caller, after having eventually been transferred successfully, is to find the person to whom they are now speaking has absolutely no idea who they are or why they are ringing! Equally, it is very annoying to find your colleagues transferring a call by saying 'This call is for you – it came through to us by mistake' then putting the phone down. So you have no choice but to start from scratch with an already impatient caller.

The golden rule is to keep both parties informed. This helps everyone, takes very little effort and no more time at all.

## How to ... Transfer a call properly

- Explain to the caller where (or to whom) you are transferring the call and why – e.g. 'I'm going to transfer you to Cath Singleton. She's our HR administrator and will be able to tell you if an alternative interview date is possible. Please hold the line a moment.'

- Press the button on your system that will put the call 'on hold'. On most systems this will mean the caller will be listening to music for a while.

- Key the extension number for the person you want.

- When the number is answered, ask for the person you need. Then give the name of the person holding on and the reason for the call and why you are transferring it – e.g. 'I've a Simon Mills on the line. He's got a letter inviting him for interview next Tuesday but he can't make it and wants to change the date. I said you'd be able to help him. Is that OK?'

- With most systems, when you replace your handset, the call is automatically transferred to that extension.

- If you discover that the person you want on that extension isn't available, you normally key a specific button on your handset to get the call back again and speak to the caller.

- Don't try to transfer your caller to yet another extension unless they are happy with this idea. Instead you may be safer taking a message and arranging for one of your colleagues to call back instead.

## Snapshot – Calls of the future – Internet telephony

It is very likely that, within the next ten years, virtually all the telephone calls we make will be free of charge. This is because we will be using the Internet to make our calls, rather than standard phone lines. The technical term used for this is VoIP or Voice over Internet Protocol.

If this seems baffling, think about it this way. Computers already communicate over the Internet. It only takes the addition of a little bit of software, plus a microphone and speakers, to be able to speak to another online computer user rather than send emails. So a business executive in a hotel on the other side of the world can speak to the office or phone home via a laptop, rather than a mobile or (very expensive) hotel phone. And the call would be free, regardless of distance. And you can use your computer to call your online friends, wherever they are. And your employer can use the computer network to send and receive calls and voicemails, rather than main phone lines. And so on.

The prospects for growth are so great that, in 2005, eBay spent $4 billion to buy Skype, a pioneering Internet phone company, which has 54 million customers around the world, 1.9 million of whom are in Britain. This means eBay buyers and sellers can talk to each other for nothing in future. Skype is becoming so popular that some people think it won't be long before people say 'skype me' rather than 'call me'! But that is ignoring the responses of the other main Internet service providers, such as Google, who already offer a competing service. To find out more, check out www.google.com/talk.

### Remember

You still need to summarise the conversation of calls you have received, as well as those you make, to check that you both agree on all the points that have been discussed.

## Over to you

1 Suggest the best way to deal with each of the following situations. Then check your ideas with the suggestions on the CD.

   a Mark, one of your colleagues, regularly says the first thing that comes into his head to get rid of a caller. Last week he told a customer that your offices would be open on Monday – a bank holiday – merely because he never bothered thinking about it. You have now found out that this same customer made a special journey to your offices and waited outside for over half an hour, thinking the office was closed for lunch, before giving up and going home.

   b You are being pestered by one of your business contacts to give the home address of one of your colleagues because he wants to send her a card on St Valentine's Day. You know she likes him – but you also know nothing about him.

   c An elderly customer likes to ring for a chat. He is on the phone for long periods of time and you struggle to get rid of him.

   d The newest addition to the staff, Sandra, just seems to guess how the telephone system works. To your knowledge she has cut off at least two people this week, and is now trying to avoid answering the phone when it rings by pretending to be busy with lots of urgent jobs.

2 Whenever you make telephone calls yourself at work, someone else is the recipient. Over the next two weeks, every time you make a call, score each person you speak to out of 10 for their overall manner and attitude, professional approach, helpfulness and ability to handle your call effectively. Make a special note of the factors that most impress you, and those that most annoy you. If possible, compare your list with the findings of other people from their experiences as a telephone user.

## Core unit link

Interacting with other people sensitively and supporting diversity links to unit 202, performance indicators 11 and 12. Treating other people with respect and consideration and helping and supporting other people links to unit 201, PIs 24 and 25.

Maintaining confidentiality of information and reporting any concerns about this links to unit 202, PIs 14 and 15.

## Evidence collection

Your assessor will want to observe you receiving and transferring calls and taking messages. You can prepare for this in the following way.

1 Identify the procedures in your organisation that relate to the way in which calls must be answered and transferred, and make of a note of where they are kept. Be prepared to discuss with your assessor these procedures and how they affect your work.

2 Think about the way in which you try to present a positive image of yourself and your organisation when you are receiving calls. Note down five or

six techniques you use to achieve this – such as answering promptly and giving the correct greeting – so that you can use these as a basis for a professional discussion with your assessor.

3   Keep a log to record the more difficult calls you receive. Examples would include occasions when you struggled to identify or understand the caller, times when you were asked to divulge confidential information or when you had to deal with argumentative or irritated callers. Make sure you say what you did to try to resolve the matter.

4   Write a brief statement about how you routinely deal with incoming calls and transfer these when necessary or relay messages as requested. Ask two people to whom you routinely transfer calls (or for whom you take messages) to sign and date your statement to confirm that its accuracy.

# Dealing with message systems

The ability to take messages is essential because you will often deal with people who telephone your organisation at a time when the person they want to contact is not available. On these occasions, precise and efficient message-taking can make all the difference between a call for information or action being dealt with correctly – or being ignored.

There is a skill to taking and passing on messages effectively. It includes obtaining the key information you need. This is listed in the table below.

**Did you know?**

Omitting a key item of information – such as the reason for ringing or even the caller's number – can mean that the message is almost meaningless to the recipient. This can be either because it isn't clear what is wanted or because the caller cannot be contacted with a response.

| Essential information when taking or leaving a message |
|---|
| **When taking a message** |
| ✓ Full name of caller |
| ✓ Company name or home address |
| ✓ Landline telephone number (direct line number or also get extension number) |
| ✓ Mobile number |
| ✓ Reason for phoning |
| ✓ Action required |
| ✓ Date and time |
| **When leaving a message** |
| ✓ Your name |
| ✓ Your organisation |
| ✓ Your telephone number (preferably direct line number) |
| ✓ Essential details |
| ✓ Action you want |
| ✓ Date and time message left |

# Types of message system and their main features

There are several message systems to choose from. The preferred method will depend on where you work, as you will see in the 'Changing places' feature on page 357.

- **Voicemail** enables an extension holder to leave a message for a caller who can listen to this and then, if need be, leave his or her own message. Ideally this will include the option to speak to someone who is instantly available – e.g. '... or you can press zero to speak to our switchboard'. Voicemail is becoming increasing popular but there are advantages and disadvantages, listed in the table below.

## Advantages and disadvantages of voicemail

**Advantages**
- Messages can be allowed to go to voicemail if the recipient is very busy
- Voicemail messages can be saved or deleted, depending on their importance
- There is no danger of the message being accidentally changed or altered by someone else if callers leave it themselves
- Callers accessing voicemail (should) have the option to press 0 to speak to the operator if they prefer
- Voicemail updated daily can provide business contacts with a summary of a person's movements and commitments that day
- Voicemail can be accessed from any phone, including a mobile, by ringing the number and entering a personal code – this enables anyone working away from the office to routinely check voicemail for new messages

**Disadvantages**
- People can choose not to respond – especially to 'difficult' callers, because they know the call will go to voicemail instead
- A form of 'telephone tennis' may ensue – you leave a message on my voicemail, I leave one on yours etc.
- A switchboard operator may put callers straight through to an extension linked to voicemail, without offering them the opportunity to speak to someone instead
- It may be more difficult to understand a complex message received verbally than in writing (e.g. by email)

- **Answering machines** were once a common feature in many offices but are now declining in popularity given the alternatives that are available. If you work in an organisation where there is an answering machine remember that someone must listen to this every morning, and after lunch if the offices have been closed.
- **1571** is an answering service which, for a small fee, can be customised with a personal message by the account holder. This can be useful

**Did you know?**

'Missed calls' are those where callers rang but didn't leave a message. Many systems record these and give the time of the call and the number of the caller. In some cases the number may be withheld – either deliberately by a caller or because the caller was ringing through a switchboard or from abroad.

for a small business which can quickly check messages that have been left, as well as the numbers of callers who rang but did not leave a message.

- **Answering services** are organisations that will receive calls, take messages and provide a daily summary which they will fax or email to their clients. They are mainly used by small businesses where the key person is frequently away and needs to be able to rely on a professional response to queries.
- **Paper messages** are the traditional method of recording information left by a caller when the recipient is away from his/her desk or away on that day. They may be written on a printed form that includes headings to cover the key facts that must be included (see page 360). If you work for an organisation that does not have printed message forms then you can soon prepare your own on a computer and save it. Then just enter the information on a blank form and print it out. This is far better than a scribbled note, which may be difficult to read and from which you may omit several items of important information.

### Find out

Find out more about professional answering services online by searching www.google.co.uk – pages from the UK – to see which service you might be tempted to use if you owned your own business.

## How to ... Take a telephone message

- Jot down notes on a piece of paper as you are listening and then write them out properly. This gives you the opportunity to extract the correct information and put it in the right order.

- Listen carefully. Be patient if someone is nervous. Ask someone who is speaking rapidly to repeat anything you do not hear properly.

- Check you have the key facts about the person – the full name, organisation or private address, telephone number and/or mobile number.

- Double-check any figures you are given or information relating to dates, places and products.

- Read the message back to the caller to check that you have understood everything correctly.

- Write it out promptly. Use simple, straightforward words that cannot be misunderstood and include all the key facts in a logical order.

- Be specific about days and dates and give both to be on the safe side. Never say 'today' or 'tomorrow' in case the message is read on a different day.

- Include your own name and the date and time of the call.

- If the message is urgent, pass it on immediately.

- If the recipient will be away from the office for some time, pass the message to your supervisor.

### Did you know?

Instead of writing out a paper message, an alternative is to send the message by email or to complete an electronic message form, such as those available at www.caliente.com.

# The importance of keeping your message system up to date

There is absolutely no point in having any type of message system unless the messages are checked regularly. If you have a mobile phone then you will know this. If you have had it set to voicemail then you will check these as soon as you possibly can, otherwise you might miss something urgent or important. Exactly the same criteria apply in business.

You also need to delete messages that you have dealt with and/or passed on, so that outdated ones are not left on the system.

## How to ... Deal with message systems

- Update the message that callers will hear, as required, to make sure that it includes current information.
- Check the system for callers' messages every morning and immediately after every other occasion when the system has been left in operation.
- Note down the calls received, the key information in each case, and the response requested.
- Pass on or transfer recorded messages to the required recipient.
- If required, respond within any requested deadlines, even if this is just to acknowledge receipt of the call.
- Delete messages once they have been dealt with or transferred.

## Case study Phones for all!

*Read the case study below and then answer the questions that follow. Then check your answers with those on the CD-ROM.*

When Lucy Watts was interviewed for the job of receptionist/administrator at Mirfield Solicitors she was worried that she might not get the job because she had used only a basic phone system before. But according to Ian Tyler, the senior partner who interviewed her, Lucy's knowledge of the system was far less important than her reference, which said she was excellent at talking to people on the telephone, discrete and especially good at handling difficult calls. In any case, Lucy was told that she would receive training on the system from Aisha, the other receptionist.

On her first day, Lucy was introduced to Helen and Oliver, two of the solicitors she would be working for. In Helen's office, Lucy was fascinated to see a pop-up screen appearing on her computer whenever the phone rang, showing the number of the person calling, sometimes with the person's name as well, ticking off the seconds until Helen answered. After five rings the call automatically went to voicemail and a little envelope icon appeared on the screen. Helen's screen also showed how many calls she had missed so far that morning and how many voicemails were waiting for her.

Helen was less impressed! She said that the pop-up screen often distracted her when she was typing something. On a busy day when she may be on the phone for long periods, her voicemail messages stacked up and then, while she was trying to answer them, more were arriving because her phone was engaged. And the call management system told the senior partners when any staff weren't responding to their calls or messages promptly!

Oliver had a different opinion. 'It's a brilliant system,' he argued, 'state-of-the-art, digital communications with CTI, CLI, DDI and voice over IP.' 'Ignore him,' said Helen, drily. 'He hasn't a clue what it means, he just thinks it makes him sounds good!' Oliver grinned. 'Take no notice of Helen, too,' he said 'she's a technophobe. Hates computers. She'd still be using a quill pen if we'd let her!'

Later that morning Lucy sat with Aisha watching her give the standard greeting of 'Good morning, Mirfield Solicitors' to all callers. 'Most callers phone the extensions direct,' Aisha said. 'This gives me more time to deal with callers who ring into the switchboard – usually first-time enquirers.'

'Putting calls through is much quicker now,' she added. 'I just key the extension, type the name of the caller and any key notes, such as 'property

purchase', and that shows in the pop-up box on the extension holder's computer I then move on to the next caller. It leaves fewer calls on the switchboard and saves me having to wait for extension holders to answer'.

On Aisha's screen she could check the status of calls and check extensions to see whether any calls were waiting and whether there were unanswered voicemail messages in a mailbox. 'This helps me to distribute calls better,' she said. 'It's no use putting a call through to someone who is frantically busy. Group hunting also helps me. All the solicitors who can deal with the same type of enquiry are placed in a small group. The phone system will find the first free extension in each group automatically.'

'What do you do if every phone in the group is engaged?' asked Lucy. 'Is there a message pad?' 'No,' said Aisha cheerfully, 'we got rid of paper messages when we installed the new system. Ian didn't like them because they got buried under paper on a desk or could even be left lying on an empty desk. Every message now is sent either by voicemail or email. It's up to you. You can put callers through to the extension where they can leave a message themselves or, if it's a new enquiry, you take a message and then ring through to the extension yourself and leave the message on voicemail. We prefer it because all the solicitors routinely check their voicemail when they are out of the office, such as during a day in court, just by phoning in to their own mailbox. They can also save or delete the message – it's up to them. So you see, Lucy, this new system has made it easier for us to be really efficient. It just takes a little getting used to – that's all!'

**Questions**

1   **a**   *What three skills contributed to Lucy getting the job at Mirfield Solicitors?*

    **b**   *Explain why the senior partner rated those skills so highly.*

2   **a**   *Explain how the information on Helen's pop-up screen was supposed to help her to work more efficiently.*

    **b**   *What did Helen not like about the system?*

    **c**   *Suggest why every call didn't display both the number and the name on her screen.*

3   *Identify the meaning of each of the following terms used by Oliver. You will find these by referring to the information on pages 333 and 334 of this unit.*

    **a**   *CTI*

    **b**   *CLI*

    **c**   *DDI*

    **d**   *Voice over IP.*

4   Explain four ways in which the new system helps Aisha to deal with calls effectively.

5   Give three reasons why the firm prefers to use voicemail for all its telephone messages.

6   Suggest two reasons why the firm prefers to have a receptionist to answer incoming calls personally rather than an automated attendant.

7   The system includes a call management facility for the senior partners. What does this mean and why it may be useful?

## Changing places

*Your assessor will ask you how you will adapt your knowledge of using a telephone system if you change your job in the future. You will need to think about the way in which aspects of these tasks would change if you worked for a different organisation.*

Roger works for a small engineering firm. There are three external lines and ten extensions on the telephone system. An incoming call rings on the phones of all members of staff in the office as well as in the workshop. If Roger is very busy he uses the 'Do not disturb' feature to silence his phone, but his colleagues get annoyed if he does this too often! There is no voicemail or direct dialling into an extension but there is music on hold for callers. When Roger transfers a call on his system he has to identify the line on which the call has been received – e.g. 'call on line 2 for you'. This is easy to identify because the relevant line flashes on his phone when he puts the call on hold before contacting one of his colleagues. If he has to take a message he relays this by email.

Jessica works as administrator at the head office of a firm of retailers with 40 branches throughout the UK. Each Monday the Sales Director holds a series of conference calls with his branch managers and finance director to review the previous week's sales figures. It is Jessica's job to set up the conference calls, and the telephone system they use was specially chosen with this in mind. If Jessica takes a message she types this out on her computer before putting a hard copy on the recipient's desk.

Yasmeen works as an administrator for a housing association. The phone system just has one incoming line and three extensions. Yasmeen receives all the incoming calls on her telephone and greets all callers with the standard greeting. If a call is received for her boss, she always announces the name of the caller and, if possible, the reason for the call before putting the call

**Changing places** Continued

through. If Yasmeen takes a message, she writes it out on a printed message form.

Vikki works as an administrator in a communications and website agency. All the staff have laptops which they use for communicating with the firm and each other – by email and VoIP – when they are working away. The phone system in the office has direct dial-in, voicemail, music on hold and was chosen with the emphasis on allowing each account manager to liaise with clients quickly and easily and to include colleagues in conference calls when campaigns are being planned.

Shamim works for a production company that sells its goods all over the world. She regularly makes and receives calls to and from abroad and knows which members of staff can help her if she needs a translator in Spanish, German, Russian and Japanese! The phone system and the computer system are linked, which means that Shamim can reach regular contacts in the company database just by clicking on their name. She doesn't need to look up lengthy dialling codes and key them into the system. She does, however, need to take account of time differences and is well aware of the best times to ring contacts in America and the Far East.

1  For any *one* person listed above, identify the differences he or she would find if moving to your organisation and doing your job.

2  For any *one* person listed above, say how you would need to adapt your skills if you did their job rather than your own.

## Over to you

You work for an insurance firm. Jason, a new recruit, is struggling with phone messages. This morning, when you were all very busy, he answered the telephone and took a message for Jacqui Spence, the motor insurance supervisor, which he has now written out on a telephone message form. He asks you to check it before he puts it on Jacqui's desk.

---

**MESSAGE FORM**   ☐ URGENT   ☐ NON-URGENT

To:   Jacqui Spence          Dept:  Motor Insurance

Date: Tuesday               Time:  10.15 am

---

Caller's name   Peter

Organisation    Marstons or Marsdens?

Tel no    893029          Ext No

☐ Telephoned               ☐ Please return call

☐ Returned your call       ☐ Please arrange appointment

☐ Called to see you        ☐ Left a message

**Message:**

He phoned 'cos he says he's fed up with us. A few weeks ago, when he tried to renew his insurance for his works van, someone told him the model number was wrong, and changed it, and told him it would cost £40 more to renew it. He checked his papers and the model number was right, he says. But we didn't agree with him. And it's still wrong,

he says. And he rang the garage last week where he bought it and they said that he is right and we are wrong. And he wants his £40 back and he wants us to change the records and if we don't sort it all out for him he's going somewhere else. He also said we do all his insurance for his business, and if we don't sort this out he's going somewhere else for absolutely everything.

He sounded very angry.

Taken by: Jason Edwards

---

Read the message and then answer the following questions. Check your answers for questions 1–4 with the suggestions on the CD-ROM and check your written message with your tutor or trainer.

**Over to you** Continued

1 Identify three key facts Jason has missed out and suggest the problems this could cause for Jacqui.

2 Suggest the questions Jason could have asked to obtain this information.

3 Identify two other omissions from the message.

4 Jacqui is away on holiday this week. Suggest what should be done with the message.

5 You check in the files and find out that the caller was Peter Bryant of Marston's Builders. Rewrite the message so it is a summary of the key points that were made rather than an account of everything that the caller said!

## Core unit link

Focusing on information people are communicating and providing written information to other people links to unit 201, performance indicators 1 and 6. Identifying and reporting any problems when they occur and taking responsibility for any mistakes you may make links to unit 201, PIs 10 and 13. Setting high standards for your work and showing commitment for achieving these links to unit 201, PI 20.

## Evidence collection

If you take telephone messages and send these to the recipient on a printed form, ask for at least ten of these to be returned to you afterwards with a brief comment added that the message was complete and accurate. Try to make sure that the messages chosen are from as many different people as possible and demonstrate your performance over a period of 4–6 weeks. Your recipients should sign and date their comments.

If you send messages by email, save these in a folder on your computer to show to your assessor and ask one or two recipients for written confirmation that they were correct.

You can also ask recipients of voicemail messages to save one or two of your messages so that your assessor can listen to these.

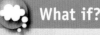

## What if?

What should you do if you don't transfer any calls to other offices or departments during your assessment period? In this case you can transfer a call to a colleague in the same office but you must still demonstrate that you can pass information obtained from the caller to the recipient.

# Operate office equipment

## Unit summary and overview

This option unit relates to the operation of a range of office equipment used to carry out administrative tasks.

If you use office equipment regularly to carry out your work then this unit would be suitable for you. Particular types of equipment are not specified in the unit, but those most frequently used by administrators are computer printers, photocopiers and, to a lesser degree, fax machines (which have declined in use since the advent of email). Other examples include scanners, mailroom equipment (such as letter openers, postage scales and franking machines) and miscellaneous items including shredders, laminators, binding machines, printout calculators and audio equipment.

There is emphasis in this unit on the most commonly used items, but whichever type of equipment you use the information here will help you to use it more knowledgeably and effectively.

# Types of office equipment, their features and use

Administrators use a wide range of equipment to undertake many tasks quickly and effectively. As a simple example, consider what would happen in your workplace if there was a power cut. How many jobs could still be done, and how many would just have to wait no matter how urgent they were?

The type of equipment used will vary depending on the work carried out and, more importantly, the volume of work undertaken. A small inkjet printer is fine for light to medium use but would not be suitable for high levels of production. In this case you would be more likely to find a laser printer installed and shared by several users. This may also save space as well as providing better quality printouts more quickly.

Similarly, if you work in a small firm where photocopying requirements are relatively light, you will be using a very different machine from that found in an office where thousands of copies are required every day.

The type of organisation you work for, and the documents you handle, will also determine whether you need to use additional equipment, such as a fax machine, scanner or ancillary items such as a binding machine. Your overall job role will determine whether you also need to be proficient with using other equipment, such as that found in a mailroom.

Office equipment can be divided into several broad areas of use. Bear in mind that you don't have to use every type described below to achieve this unit!

## Computer printers

These are used to produce hard (paper) copies of documents created or stored on a computer. There are two main types, inkjet and laser, and there are several differences between the two:

- **Inkjet printers** are smaller, cheaper and usually slower. They are often supplied one per workstation. They work by shooting very fine jets of ink on to the surface of the paper. Most take two ink cartridges, one containing

**Link to option units**

As you gather your evidence for this unit you should also obtain evidence for your core units. Watch for the Core unit link logo which suggests how the evidence you collect may count towards both this unit and your core units.

Remember that you might be able to identify other links yourself, because of your own job role and the evidence you have obtained.

Talk to your assessor if you need further guidance on how your evidence should be cross-referenced.

**Did you know?**

**Multifunction devices** are popular with smaller businesses because they combine several operations in one machine, such as printing, photocopying, scanning and faxing. They save space and it is a cheaper solution than buying separate, specialist devices. The disadvantage is that if they break down the business is disrupted to a far greater extent.

**Did you know?**

Inkjet printers print a line at a time, laser printers print a page at a time (like photocopiers). This is why they operate much more quickly.

a colour and one containing black. Normally both must be installed for the printer to work, whether or not you are printing in colour.

- **Laser printers** are generally larger and more expensive. They operate more quickly and the print quality is normally crisper. Each printer may be used by several workstations. The printer works by shining a laser beam on to a photo-sensitive drum and then uses toner to create an image on the paper. Laser printers use toner cartridges. Colour laser printers require three separate cartridges in magenta, yellow and cyan.

The range of features on a printer varies, depending on the type of printer and the price paid. The main ones are listed in the table below.

**Did you know?**

Manufacturers are now concentrating on features to reduce running costs – particularly that of replacement cartridges. Epsom has launched a laser printer that can be converted to a colour printer by adding the appropriate cartridges and then back again by replacing these with black ink cartridges.

### Potential main features of computer printers

| Feature | Meaning/variations |
| --- | --- |
| Duplex printouts | Can do back-to-back printing |
| Media capacity | Size of the paper tray (or how often it needs to be refilled!)<br>This can range from 100 to 850 pages |
| Media size | Maximum size of paper that can be used<br>Many printers accept only A4 paper but some will take up to A3 size |
| Media type | Relates to the type of paper that is used<br>Typically media types include plain paper, envelopes, transparencies, labels, photo paper, high-gloss film, matte paper, recycled paper |
| Memory | Number of pages that can be held in the printer memory |
| Mono or colour | Whether the printer produces only black ink copies or will also produce colour copies |
| Monthly usage | The number of printouts expected a month (e.g. 30000 or 60000)<br>Exceeding this figure on a regular basis means the printer is likely to break down more often or need replacing sooner |
| Networkable | Means it can be linked to several computers |
| Noise (dBA) | Rated in dBA (units of sound) in operation<br>Quieter printers are around 40, noisier ones 60 or more |
| Print resolution | Rated in dpi (dots per inch)<br>The higher the dpi the better the print quality |
| Print speed | Rated in ppm (pages per minute) and will be much slower for top-quality colour prints and photos than for draft mono printers<br>Inkjet can range from 3 to 9; laser from 6 to 24. |

**Remember**

A multifunction machine can operate as both a laser printer and a photocopier.

## Photocopiers

Photocopiers are standard items in all offices. They are used to make copies of many types of document, such as those items received in the mail or stored in the files. They are also useful for making multiple copies of computer printouts that would take too long to produce on a small inkjet printer.

Photocopiers vary tremendously in terms of their size, speed and features. Some are small desktop models while others are very large, sophisticated machines which link to the computer network. For this reason, the way in which they operate varies considerably.

The main features found on photocopiers are listed in the table below.

**Did you know?**

Digital photocopiers can be linked to other types of digital equipment. They can therefore receive documents sent electronically direct from computer users to be copied or faxed. All multifunction devices that also operate as scanners and faxes are digital.

| Potential main features of photocopiers | |
| --- | --- |
| **Feature** | **Meaning/variations** |
| Copying speed | Can range from as slow as 15 pages a minute to over 100 |
| Duplexing | Two-sided copying may not be available, may be a manual operation of may be automatic with different options |
| Finishing unit | This may collate multipage documents, hole punch or staple as required |
| Image density and other adjustments | Adjusts exposure for light/dark text or dirty backgrounds (e.g. newspapers) Adjustments may also be available for photographs, pale originals etc. to improve copy clarity |
| Image rotation | Enables image to be rotated to adjust crooked image or to print on differently orientated paper (e.g. portrait to landscape) |

| Potential main features of photocopiers Continued ||
| Feature | Meaning/variations |
| --- | --- |
| Interrupt facility | Enables a long job to be temporarily stopped while an urgent job is done |
| Memory | Pages are scanned into memory before printing<br>Routine jobs can be programmed into the machine and recalled as required |
| Mono or colour | Whether the copier produces only black and white copies or whether colour copies are an option<br>Digital colour copiers are expensive and printing in colour is slower than in mono |
| Networkable | Means it can be linked to several computers |
| Paper trays and capacity | Can range from one small A4 paper tray to two paper trays, one large capacity and the other adjustable for A3 paper<br>There may also be a bypass tray for labels or transparencies |
| Reduce/enlarge | Enables copies to be reduced or enlarged to fixed pre-set ratios. The best ratio is chosen automatically on some machines |
| Sample copy | Enables a test copy to be made automatically |
| Stack | This is the opposite of collate – multiple pages are inserted but each is copied and stacked separately |
| User ID/counter | Enables usage per user to be logged; users must enter PIN to gain access to machine |
| Zoom | Allow reproduction ratio to be set in 1% steps for more precise reduction/enlargement |

## Fax machines

Fax machines are used to transmit text, graphics and photographs to other fax machines but there are many differences between various types. There are small, cheap desktop machines that use special (thermal) paper. At the other extreme are large, plain-paper machines that operate virtually automatically 24 hours a day, 7 days a week and link to the computer network. This means that messages can be prepared and sent from individual users and received messages are automatically forwarded to their computers. All fax machines can be used as photocopiers, although this is obviously a slow process on small machines.

The types of features found on fax machines are given opposite.

## Potential main features of fax machines

| Feature | Meaning/variations |
|---------|--------------------|
| Automatic features | More expensive machines offer options such as automatic fax forwarding to PCs, delayed fax sending until a later time (when phone rates are cheaper), automatic collection from another machine (called 'polling') and sending the same fax to many numbers automatically (called 'broadcast') |
| Cover sheet | The option to produce a front page summarising the key details of the fax |
| Fax memory | Enables originals to be scanned before sending and incoming faxes to be held in memory if the machine is busy or is out of paper or ink |
| Flatbed or document feeder | Some large fax machines have a 'flatbed' like the document glass on a photocopier<br>Most, however, receive the original document by feeding it into the machine |
| Mono or colour | Colour fax machines are available but most are black and white |
| Plain or thermal paper | Plain paper fax machines are now common<br>These use the same type of paper as photocopiers and printers, which is cheaper<br>Thermal paper is supplied on a roll and copies fade over time if exposed to light |
| Speed dialling/ memory/auto-redial | Most faxes store frequently used numbers in memory and a limited number can be dialled in one touch<br>Most will also try to reconnect if a number is engaged |
| Verification or confirmation report | The option to receive a printed report after sending each fax to check transmission went smoothly |

## Document and image scanners

Scanners are used to convert documents and other images – such as photos – into file formats that can be stored on a computer. This means that application forms, illustrations, correspondence and drawings received through the post can be saved on the firm's computer system rather than in a filing cabinet.

Scanners look very much like a streamlined version of a desktop photocopier. You lift the lid to see a glass plate underneath. When you put the document or image on top and select Scan, instead of producing a paper copy you create a computer file that you can save, email to someone or print.

The main features of scanners are listed below:

| Potential main features of scanners | |
|---|---|
| **Feature** | **Meaning/variations** |
| Automatic document feeder (ADF) | Allows documents to be stacked and fed automatically into the scanner |
| Duplexing | Enables documents to be scanned back and front, without having to be reloaded separately |
| Networking | Can be connected to a networked computer system |
| Preview | This provides a quick scan of the document, or the size of image you have selected |
| Scan area | The larger the area, the larger the document size that can be scanned |
| Scan resolution | The number of dpi (dots per inch) or ppi (pixels per inch) The more you choose, the higher resolution the image but the more computer memory is required |
| Scan settings | Options here include colour, greyscale (like black and white photographs), line art (for printed text) or halftones (for images that will appear in newspapers and magazines) |
| Scan speed | Given as ppm (page per minute) or ipm (image per minute) The faster this is, the quicker the images are scanned |

## Mailroom equipment

Organisations that send and receive vast amounts of mail each day, such as credit card companies, have specialist mailrooms with extremely sophisticated equipment. The whole process is mechanised, from opening the envelopes and extracting the contents of incoming mail, to collating and inserting items in pre-printed envelopes, then sealing, weighing and franking outgoing mail items in one operation.

Administrators who assist with the mail are likely to work with far more basic items. The key items are usually a letter-opening machine, date stamp, electronic scales and a franking machine.

- **A letter-opening machine** makes a slit in the envelope, very close to the edge, so that the contents aren't damaged. The envelopes are stacked in a hopper and pass automatically through the machine, making the whole operation very quick and easy.
- **A date stamp** records the date (and sometimes the time) when the item was received in case there are any queries later. The stamp should never be placed so that it obscures part of the information.

*A franking machine.*

- **Electronic scales** are pre-programmed with current postal rates. You simply select the class of postage and any special fee services on the keypad and the amount of postage is displayed. These scales cannot be used for very large, heavy items – those must be weighed on larger scales or taken to a post office for weighing.
- **A franking machine** puts a printed postal impression on each envelope. This means no stamps are required. The machine will also print labels for parcels. Envelopes or labels can include an advertisement for the organisation; this operates also as a return address if the item is undeliverable.

Some machines incorporate electronic scales so that the item is weighed and franked in one operation.

The main features of franking machines are listed below.

**Find out**

From 4 September 2006, postage charges will be calculated based on size and thickness as well as weight. The Royal Mail Pricing in Proportion system means that franking machines have to be updated with new rates. You can find out more at www.pitneybowes.co.uk/comms/pip/pip.htm.

| Potential main features of franking machines | |
|---|---|
| **Feature** | **Meaning/variations** |
| Automatic date change | Date automatically updates and is programmed for leap years! |
| Disk drive | Included on computerised franking machines only<br>A disk which contains the software must be entered for the machine to work |
| Feeder | Some accept mail of different thicknesses with flaps open or closed, in others mail must be batched into similar items<br>The feeder can operate continuously or be set to feed one piece at a time |

| Potential main features of franking machines Continued | |
|---|---|
| **Feature** | **Meaning/variations** |
| Hopper | Holds mail prior to processing |
| Meter | This produces the postage impression and records the total amount spent |
| Meter display | Shows the options selected by the operator |
| Sealer | Automatically seals mail if required with a water spray |
| Stacker | Collects the franked mail; different sizes are available. |
| System display | On computerised franking machines these enable the operator to undertake various operations (e.g. changing the advert, overriding the high-value lock, to protect against high postage values being entered in error), pre-set certain jobs |
| Tape or label roll | Produces postage labels for parcels and envelopes that cannot be franked |
| Weighing device | If incorporated, weighs mail and calculates the postage required which is then sent to the meter for printing on the envelope |

**Did you know?**

Many photocopiers have finishing units attached so that they can be set to collate, staple or hole-punch automatically. Smaller machines may offset your copies for you to keep them separate, but you will then have to staple or punch the documents manually.

## Miscellaneous equipment

Other commonly used equipment is often associated with preparing multipage documents so that the presentation looks professional. At the very least you may be asked to staple or hole-punch these documents. For a

*A comb binding machine.*

professional finish you may also be expected to bind the document and put it into a printed cover.

- **Staplers** can be manual or electric. Heavy-duty staplers are needed for thick documents.
- **Hole punches** need to be heavy duty for thick documents.
- **Thermal binders** use heat to seal the pages to the spine.
- **Comb binding machines** incorporate a punch to make holes in the paper. They then open a plastic comb over which the pages are inserted. The comb is then closed. Combs can be cut to fit but the depth selected must be appropriate to the papers used.
- **Wire binders** operate in a similar way, but the binding is made of wire, not plastic.
- **Slide binders** literally slide over the left-hand edge of the pages. They are cheap but there is a disadvantage because the pages won't open flat.

In addition, you may use these items:

- **A laminator**. This puts a thin protective plastic film over documents that are to be pinned up or handled frequently.
- **A guillotine** or paper trimmer. These cut or trim documents to size.
- **A shredder**. This is a device to destroy sensitive or confidential documents so they cannot be read. Cross-cut shredders are more effective than strip-cut because they slice the document in two directions, not one.
- **Audio equipment**. This will be relevant if you transcribe audio media as part of your job.
- **Calculators**. Some include the facility to produce a printout of the calculation.

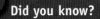

**Did you know?**

There's a right (and wrong) way to use even the most basic items. Stapling so that you obscure the print is unprofessional, so is punching holes that aren't aligned so your papers are all over the place! See page 376 for how to do this properly!

*A shredder.*

*When using a shredder, make sure you don't destroy a document you still need!*

## How to choose equipment and resources appropriate for a range of administrative tasks

'Equipment' refers here to the machinery you need to do a task. 'Resources' refers to the materials you need. You can't produce printouts or photocopies without paper, and you can't finish documents professionally if you don't have any folders or binders to put in the machine. For some tasks you may need special resources, such as transparencies, coloured card, printed folders or a different size of envelope.

*Choose equipment* for a task based on:
- the type of task you have been given
- the equipment you have available in your workplace
- the suitability of each type of equipment, in terms of its main use and features, for the task you have to do.

*Choose resources* for a task based on:
- the task you are doing, its purpose and the eventual recipient(s)
- the equipment you will be using
- the special requirements of the person who gave you the work.

For example, if you are producing a multipage document that will be given to an important external customer you would be expected to use quality paper

**Remember**

Organisations are restricted by copyright law in the amount and type of copies they can make and what they do with them. Turn back to page 153 in unit 202 to refresh your memory!

and special folders to create a good impression. If you are doing a similar task for an internal staff meeting then you would probably use standard paper and staple the documents instead.

There are, however, other factors to consider when you are planning to use certain resources or equipment:

- You need to check that the items you need are available, as special resources may have to be ordered in advance.
- Even with routine resources, you need to check that there are sufficient supplies in the stock cupboard. Grabbing the last armful of folders and squirreling them away so that no one else can get them is not the way to operate! If supplies are limited, talk to your supervisor if helping yourself could cause serious problems for everyone else.
- If certain types of equipment are shared items, then there may be a booking system in operation. Check this first and make your booking early. You can always change it later if necessary.

Finally, you need to check that the resources are available before you promise to do a task by a certain deadline – or allow time for them to be obtained. You should also take the equipment you have, and its limitations, into consideration. It might not take long to produce 50 copies of a 40-page document on a fast photocopier or laser printer; it would be a much longer and more tedious job if all you had available was a small inkjet printer or an antiquated desktop copier.

## Over to you

1 Check that you understand the description of all the equipment given in the previous section. If there is any type of equipment that you are unsure about, find out more at www.euroffice.co.uk/display_tab.asp?T5=Office-Machines.

2 Select *one* item of equipment that you use regularly from the 'Miscellaneous equipment' section on page 370–371. Then list its key features and explain why you use it. Check your answer with your tutor or trainer.

3 For *two* items of equipment you use regularly to do routine tasks, identify the resources that you need to do these tasks. Check your answer with your tutor or trainer.

4 Identify the most likely result in each of the following situations. Compare your ideas with other members of your group or your colleagues and check against the answers on the CD-ROM.

a You use your desktop stapler to fasten 30 pages together.

b You use your desktop punch to hole-punch 40 pages in one go.

c You staple the pages diagonally 4 cm in from the top left-hand corner.

    **d** You divide a large batch of pages you have to punch to put in a ring binder so that you can use your desktop punch, but forget to set the ruler or check the arrow mark.

    **e** You use your stapler while you are talking to someone and don't watch what you are doing.

    **f** You promise your boss you can produce 200 printouts of a document in five minutes on your inkjet printer.

**5** In Chris's office are the items of equipment listed in table A below. He also uses the resources in table B. For each of the following tasks he has to do, identify the equipment and the resources (where appropriate) that he should use. Check your answers against those on the CD-ROM.

### Chris's equipment

Desktop copier in own office (takes A4 paper and card only)
Large-volume copier in next office with all features listed on page 365–366
Inkjet printer
Thermal binder
Shredder
Scanner
Fax machine
Franking machine
Laminator
Rotary paper trimmer

### Chris's resources

A4 white paper
A4 white card
Coloured A4 card
Presentation folders
Staples
A3 white paper
Padded bags for dispatch

    **a** Take three copies of a confidential document he has just amended from his boss's draft and destroy the draft.

    **b** Take five copies of this month's staff duty rota to be placed on all notice boards.

    **c** Send an email containing a copy of a drawing he has just received.

    **d** Send another copy of the drawing to a foreign client with no email address.

    **e** Produce 40 A6 invitations to an informal staff event.

**f** Produce and despatch a copy of a 100-page stapled report for your office in Scotland.

**g** Take one copy of a full page in today's *Financial Times* newspaper. Note: this is a broadsheet newspaper that is A3 size.

**h** Produce 15 bound copies of a 20-page report for an important customer visit next week.

**i** Take three copies of a handwritten security report.

**j** Make 100 stapled copies of a five-page document he has just prepared on his computer.

## Evidence collection

1 You will need to prove to your assessor that you can locate and select the equipment and resources you need for a task. Start a log to record this information. Suggested headings are given below. You can then use this as a basis for a professional discussion with your assessor about how and why you made these choices.

| Date | Description of task | Equipment selected | Resources selected |
|------|---------------------|--------------------|--------------------|
|      |                     |                    |                    |
|      |                     |                    |                    |
|      |                     |                    |                    |
|      |                     |                    |                    |

2 Discuss with your assessor how many samples of work you produce using equipment should be included in your portfolio. These can form the basis of a professional discussion about the tasks that you do.

**a** In each case note the date you produced the work and whether you did it on your own or not. If you worked as a member of a team, identify your own role and ask your supervisor to countersign your statement.

**b** Attach any written instructions you were given relating to how the work should be done or what resources you had to use. If the instructions were verbal, make a note of these on your work sample and ask the person who gave you the work to countersign and date your note to confirm it is correct and that the work you produced met their requirements.

### Core unit link

When you communicate with people who give you work to check and discuss their exact requirements, this may link to unit 201, performance indicators 1–3.

Bear in mind that much of the work you carry out may also support your organisation's mission and objectives and link to unit 202, PI 1. If you need to follow or check legal restrictions on the amount and type of copying that can take place in your organisation, this links to unit 202, PIs 2, 3 and 5. If any work you produce is confidential, this may link to unit 202, PI 14.

# Following manufacturers' instructions when operating equipment

All office equipment, apart from the most basic items, is sold complete with instructions. This might be one folded page tucked in the box or a manual of 20 or 30 pages. It contains all the basic information the manufacturer thought users should know (other features could be included only on a CD-ROM). The problem is that many people can't be bothered to read it, or start off with good intentions and lose interest by the third page. Even worse, they don't understand what they are reading and try to guess what to do, stabbing at a few buttons here and there to see what happens next.

It doesn't help, of course, if you are unfortunate to have a manual that is over-facing or difficult to understand. If you see 15 pages of tiny print, very few drawings and oddly translated words and phrases than you are unlikely to be inspired to read very much. This is why most of us, for example, can do basic operations on a DVD player or on a mobile phone but never got around to mastering the finer points!

The dangers with ignoring manufacturers' instructions are several.
- It will probably take twice as long to do a basic operation.
- You can easily make a mess of a job.
- You may do something that is hazardous or even dangerous.
- You could even damage the equipment.

This is why it is important to know what manufacturers intend you to do. You will then use the equipment safely, in the most efficient way and you won't break it.

**Did you know?**

The best way to learn to use an item of equipment is to be trained properly by someone who knows how to use it. This is why many photocopier dealers offer a demonstration or training session as part of the package when they supply a new machine.

# Keeping waste to a minimum

Anyone who uses equipment carelessly, or without knowing what they are doing, is likely to waste a considerable amount of resources. This can be as minor as tapping the wrong figures into a calculator – and ripping off the resulting printout and throwing it in the bin – to producing 500 crooked photocopies that all need throwing away.

'Danger' items of equipment that have the most potential to create waste are computer printers and photocopiers, particularly in the hands of the untrained or unwary! You can also ruin a good job you produced using either of these items by careless paper trimming or incorrect stapling, punching or binding.

**Remember**

You can align punched holes on multiple batches of paper by setting and using the guide ruler on the punch correctly. Alternatively gently hold the papers horizontally and align the crease with the arrow on the punch.

## How to ... Keep waste to a minimum

- Check that you understand your instructions before you start work.
- Use the print preview function on your system to check your document before printing it.
- Take a printout in draft mode (File/Print/Properties/Draft in MS Word) to save ink or toner.
- Use the correct paper for your equipment, and make sure you insert it the right way up (look for an arrow on the packet).
- Keep your equipment clean (see page 378).
- Repair any torn originals before faxing, photocopying or scanning them and clean up any obvious dirty marks.
- If you are photocopying a multipage original, check that it is in the right order with all the pages the right way up.
- Double-check the settings on your equipment before starting any operation.
- Always take a test printout or photocopy and check it before starting a long job.
- Use duplex mode to make double-sided copies – if this is available.
- Learn which waste is re-useable. Wrongly franked envelopes and labels can still be used or a credit obtained. Some spoiled papers may be useful as scrap pads.
- Put any waste paper that cannot be used into a recycling container.

# Keeping equipment clean and hygienic – and the standards for this

There are two main reasons for keeping equipment clean.
- The quality of the output is better. Dirty photocopier or scanner glass will result in blotchy copies or stored documents that need cleaning up before they are much use. Dirty print heads on an inkjet printer or fax machine will result in poor-quality printouts.

**Find out**

There are certain key areas that must be kept clean for equipment to work properly. They include the document glass on photocopiers and scanners, print heads and rubber rollers on printers and fax machines, and sensors on computerised franking machines. Investigate the key areas on the equipment you use.

- It is more hygienic because cleaning removes bacteria that live on dirty equipment and workstations (see page 379 and unit 110, page 172–173). This is crucial when items of equipment are shared – such as earphones or telephone handsets – but is also important because some contagious conditions, such as dermatitis, can be spread by shared use of dirty equipment.

## How to ... Clean electrical equipment safely

- Turn off the power switch and disconnect the power cord before you start.

- Keep the area around the power outlet – including the plug – clean and free from dust (which might cause a short-circuit). Wipe dust away with a dry cloth.

- Check any air vents – these attract dirt. Keep them clean by brushing the dust away; never use water.

- Use the correct materials to clean the equipment. These will be listed in your handbook. Never use flammable substances of any type, and do not use liquid or aerosol cleaners if the instructions say you should avoid them.

- The outer casing can usually be cleaned with a damp (not wet) cloth, moistened with a mild detergent mixed with water.

- Never try to clean inside equipment such as a photocopier or in sealed areas in a fax, scanner or printer.

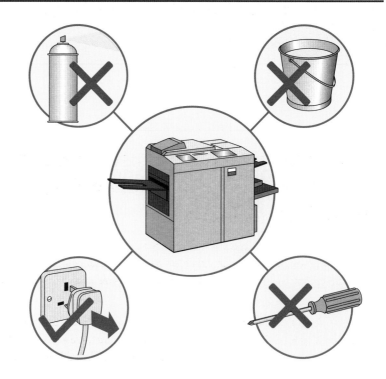

## Snapshot – Time to call in the experts!

If you are fortunate, you may work in an office where specialist cleaners are employed to clean your computers, printers, scanners, faxes and photocopiers as part of an equipment maintenance service. In this case you have little to worry about because, at regular intervals, a team of experts will descend to clean everything for you.

Demand for their services is increasing as more and more firms realise that it is rather silly spending vast amounts of money on equipment and then neglecting to maintain it properly. The workplace is more hygienic and staff are less likely to suffer from minor ailments. According to one specialist firm, Equipment Cleaning Services Ltd, the worst offender is the telephone, closely followed by the desktop and then the computer keyboard. They suggest a simple test. Place a piece of white paper on your desk, carefully lift your keyboard and turn it upside down, then give it a *gentle* tap over the paper. Another test is to run your hand over the top of a fixed item of equipment, like a fax machine or photocopier, and see how much dust you collect on the way.

Most specialist firms operate in London or the south of England but are generous enough to give potential customers tips online. You can read how to keep your computer, printer and photocopier clean on the HY-TEC East London website at www.hy-tec.co.uk/computers.asp.

In the United States, office equipment cleaning firms are one of the fastest growing business opportunities. If you become an expert at keeping your organisation's equipment clean, perhaps you might be tempted to start out in business for yourself!

# Following manufacturers' instructions and organisational procedures when dealing with equipment faults

Even the cleanest equipment sometimes goes wrong or breaks down, which is why every handbook and manual contains a 'troubleshooting' guide. This lists the most common faults that can occur and tells you what to do to put them right.

It also tells you the faults that need to be reported, particularly if your equipment is leased or rented under a service contract. Never be tempted to ignore these instructions. Even if the equipment is still usable you could be causing further damage unless the problem is put right. In some cases – such as an electrical fault – you could be putting yourself in danger unless you take immediate action.

It is quite probable that your organisation has procedures restricting the type of actions that can be taken by individuals to repair faults themselves, particularly if they have not received specific training. For example, there may be one nominated person who must be contacted to remedy paper jams in the photocopier, and only a mailroom supervisor may be authorised to investigate a franking machine fault before calling in the mechanic. You may also have to contact an IT helpdesk for assistance with a printer or scanner problem.

**Remember**

Before you ring your helpdesk with a problem, do carry out a basic check to make sure your machine is plugged in, the power switch is down and the equipment is switched on!

**Remember**

Reduce paper jams in your office by storing the paper flat in a dry place, removing it from paper trays at weekends especially if the weather is humid, fanning paper before you put it into the machine, setting the paper guides carefully, and never over-filling the paper tray or cassette.

# Equipment and resource faults you are likely to experience

**Paper jams** are top of the list of faults that can occur on printers, photocopiers and fax machines. The equivalent on a franking machine is a **mail jam**. Paper jams occur when too many sheets of paper are being taken at one time, or when the paper has been fed on a slant rather than straight.

There are many reasons why paper jams occur. Perhaps the wrong type of paper has been used, the paper is damp or creased, the paper guides haven't

been set correctly, or the paper hasn't been loaded properly. On most printers and fax machines you can access the jammed paper by removing a cover – but you need to know where this is, so check the handbook. To release jammed paper in a photocopier you need to be trained what to do because if you touch some of the surfaces by mistake you could easily burn yourself.

**Running out of ink or toner** is another problem you may experience, so learn how to replace the cartridges for your printer. Then dispose of the used ones carefully, as described on page 377. If you notice stocks are running low then warn the person responsible for ordering more, before there is a crisis!

Other types of faults will vary, depending on your equipment and the resources you use.

- **Communication problems** can occur with fax machines. There are many reasons – you may be trying a wrong number, the receiving fax may be faulty, or there may be a problem with the phone line. Your manual will tell you what to do if a communication error occurs.
- **Memory problems** can occur with any equipment that stores information. Examples are fax machines, photocopiers and some types of franking machine.
- **Connection problems** can occur if the power cord connecting the equipment to the mains is taut, if heavy items are placed on the cord, or if it is connected by an extension cord or through a multiplug adaptor.
- **Overheating** can occur in any equipment with an air vent if this is blocked or if the machine is placed too close to a wall. Some equipment will automatically shut down in this situation. Alternatively the fuse may blow because of the fault, in which case there will be no power to the machine. The problem must be remedied before the fuse is replaced.
- **Resource faults** can include faulty cartridges, damp or creased paper, and cheap paper that won't feed properly into the machine. Remember that faulty goods can be returned to the supplier for a refund, so if you open a cartridge and find immediately that it won't work you can insist that it be replaced. Do check first, though, that you have removed any protective tapes that would stop it operating!

**Did you know?**

If you can't find your manual and need to fix a problem quickly, check online before you panic. Many manufacturers provide instructions and guidance for users on their websites.

**Find out**

**Routine maintenance** is intended to prevent faults from occurring. This is why it is often provided as part of a service contract for expensive equipment like photocopiers. Find out if this applies to any of the equipment you use.

**Did you know?**

Many types of electrical equipment are fitted with circuit-breakers which cut the power off if there is a power surge. This can occur in a thunderstorm and can seriously damage a machine. You would need to contact a technician in your firm to reset the breaker.

## Case study In the driving seat!

*Read the case study below and then answer the questions that follow. Then check your answers with those on the CD-ROM.*

Sajida Mulla works as an administrator at CarChange UK, a small engineering company specialising in adapting cars for mobility-impaired drivers. This may mean installing hand controls, rotating car seats, a wheelchair hoist or making other changes to the vehicle at the driver's request.

Sajida's work involves assisting the two design engineers, Matt and Josh. Both create technical drawings on their computers using a CAD (computer aided design) package to show how modifications to the vehicles will be made. These are copied on to A3 paper for the production staff and copies are sent to suppliers who provide the parts that will be needed. Some small suppliers don't have email addresses, so Sajida reduces the drawings to A4 size on the photocopier so that they can be faxed instead.

The drawings may be discussed at a production planning meeting and notes for amendments made on them. Sajida scans these updated drawings into the computer system to make sure there is a record. She also scans any original printouts into the system if the original CAD drawing file has been deleted for any reason. The scanner, printer and photocopier were all purchased so that they could handle A3 documents as well as A4.

Sajida also does routine photocopying work, such as copying correspondence and meeting notes. It is company policy to photocopy back-to-back, whenever possible, to save paper. Any spoiled papers must be put into the recycling bin, not the waste bin.

CarChange UK also keeps car dealers informed of its work so that they can inform customers who would qualify for adaptations under the Motability grant scheme. Twice a year Sajida produces over 1000 presentation packs to send to dealers. She types the information on her computer and inserts photographs and drawings into the pages and then takes a test copy on her own small inkjet printer and checks it carefully. The final work is printed on the laser printer in the next office because it produces the sets quickly and in colour. The packs are then fastened using a thermal binder.

Sajida's boss is considering replacing some of the equipment with a multifunction device that can be used as a fax, photocopier and scanner. Matt and Josh have mixed views about this. They are worried that if a serious fault occurs this will hold up their work. Sajida likes the idea because she will then have only one piece of equipment to keep clean, rather than three!

**Questions**

1   List the items of equipment that Sajida uses as part of her job.

2   a   What two methods are used to send the drawings to the suppliers – and why?

    b   Why do you think the drawings must be reduced for one method of transmission?

3   What important feature was required when the scanner, the printer and photocopier were purchased – and why?

4   Give two reasons why it is vital that Sajida takes a test copy of her presentation packs.

5   If Sajida wants to insert a drawing into a document that isn't stored on her system, how will she do this?

6   Why are the presentation packs prepared on the laser printer and not the inkjet?

7   What is CarChange's attitude to waste and the environment? Give two examples to support your answer.

8   From the information given, suggest one advantage and one disadvantage of installing a multifunction device.

# The importance of meeting work standards and deadlines

**Work standards** refers to the quality of work you are expected to produce. **Deadlines** refers to the timescale in which you must produce it. You first read about these in on pages 35–52 in unit 201. Both of these are essential. It is no use producing high-quality work that is completed two weeks late, and equally useless producing work on time that is unusable because it is too much of a mess.

It may be tempting to think that quality and deadlines don't matter as much if you are producing work that will be used only internally, but this is a dangerous strategy for several reasons. The people who see your work will think you're sloppy, unreliable or both; the work will have to be redone if someone suddenly decides to send it outside the organisation, and you may find that you slip into bad habits all too easily especially if you have a boss who is too soft or very tolerant! If you change boss or workplace then you are likely to get rather a shock.

It is important to meet both work standards and deadlines because you will be given tasks to do for a reason – and someone will be relying on you to do a good job, on time. For that reason it is always sensible to check all the details about a job carefully before you start, including the deadline.

> **Remember**
>
> If a deadline is impossible, given the equipment you have to hand, you will need to try to negotiate a more realistic completion date. If you don't know how to do this, turn back to page 37–38 and find out!

**Remember**

If communal equipment you are using breaks down or develops a fault, put a notice on it to warn other people not to use it.

**Questions**

1   *List the items of equipment that Sajida uses as part of her job.*

2   **a**   *What two methods are used to send the drawings to the suppliers – and why?*

    **b**   *Why do you think the drawings must be reduced for one method of transmission?*

3   *What important feature was required when the scanner, the printer and photocopier were purchased – and why?*

4   *Give two reasons why it is vital that Sajida takes a test copy of her presentation packs.*

*Make sure you don't gain a reputation for leaving work areas untidy!*

**How to ...** Leave a work area ready for the next user

5   *If Sajida wants to insert a drawing into a document that isn't stored on her system, how will she do this?*

6   *Why are the presentation packs prepared on the laser printer and not the inkjet?*

7   *What is CarChange's attitude to waste and the environment? Give two examples to support your answer.*

8  *From the information given, suggest one advantage and one disadvantage of installing a multifunction device.*

# The importance of meeting work standards and deadlines

**Work standards** refers to the quality of work you are expected to produ‹
**Deadlines** refers to the timescale in which you must produce it. You first
read about these in on pages 35–52 in unit 201. Both of these are essenti
It is no use producing high-quality work that is completed two weeks lat
and equally useless producing work on time that is unusable because it i
too much of a mess.

## Changing places

It may be tempting to think that quality and deadlines don't matter as much if you are producing work that will be used only internally, but this is a dangerous strategy for several reasons. The people who see your work will think you're sloppy, unreliable or both; the work will have to be redone if someone suddenly decides to send it outside the organisation, and you may find that you slip into bad habits all too easily especially if you have a boss who is too soft or very tolerant! If you change boss or workplace then you are likely to get rather a shock.

It is important to meet both work standards and deadlines because you will be given tasks to do for a reason – and someone will be relying on you to do a good job, on time. For that reason it is always sensible to check all the details about a job carefully before you start, including the deadline.

# Leaving equipment, resources and the work area ready for the next user – and what the standards are

When you are working in a communal area and sharing equipment and resources, it is infuriating to find you are sharing with someone who leaves it looking like a bombsite. If you are the type of person whose bedroom floor normally represents some type of serious obstacle course then take note!

**Changing places** Continued

Quite simply, you should leave an area as you would want to find it. If you leave it in a tip, be prepared to be hauled back to tidy it up – or to be labelled as everyone's least favourite person to work with. Even if your organisation doesn't have official standards you must follow, your colleagues certainly will have!

- Don't spread your work and belongings out all over the place. Try to control the space you use from the start.

- Complete each part of a job before you start the next.

- Stack all your completed work neatly to one side.

- Never leave a large job on the copier and walk away, even for a short time.

- If you are interrupted, or have to leave the area and are in the middle of a task, put your work in one place with a note on it identifying yourself as the 'owner' and saying when you will return to remove it.

- When you have finished the task, clear up after yourself and put everything back in its proper place.

- Check that all working surfaces – and the floor – is clear of papers, rubbish or sundry items you have been using, like paperclips.

- Put any unused resources back in the store cupboard.

- Never take the last one of anything without notifying someone first!

 **Over to you**

- Never leave the copier when it has run out of toner or paper because you can't be bothered to refill it!

*Your assessor will ask you how you will adapt your skills if you change your job in the future. You will need to think about the way in which your role might change if you worked for a different organisation.*

Louise works as an administrator in the Business, Administration and Technology department in a large college. Each administrator in the office has an inkjet printer attached to a computer. There is also a networked digital photocopier which all staff can use for photocopying. Teaching staff are expected to make their own photocopies but Louise does photocopying for the Head of Department. There is a fax machine in the office which is mainly used to send off completed forms for staff training and development and to book places at conferences. In a crisis it has also been used to send an urgent official order to the stationery supplier!

Iqra works as an administrator for a communications agency that prepares sales kits, marketing brochures, user guides, technical documentation and even speeches for its clients. The creative staff work in teams, each with their own administrator, like Iqra. Iqra uses a colour digital multifunction machine that can do normal copying functions but also has special booklet features, will save images scanned or created on a PC, can send scanned images or document data to computers or by email or fax, and will print different types of output including detailed graphics and files containing colour graphics, photos and text.

Kirsty works as administrator for a local car dealership and repairer. She prints out documents on an inkjet printer and has a small desktop photocopier in one corner of her office. One of her jobs is processing the outgoing mail and

## Core unit link

Organisational procedures relate to unit 202, performance indicators 2 and 5. Following guidelines and procedures links to unit 201, PI 14.

From question two, agreeing realistic targets, using your time wisely and employing effective working methods and meeting deadlines link to unit 201, PIs 7–12. Taking responsibility for your work, setting high standards and taking account of feedback to make improvements can link to unit 201, PIs 13, 15, 16 and 20. Producing work that protects or improves the image of your organisation links to unit 202, PI 5.

Showing consideration for other people, as in question three, links to unit 201, PI 24.

In question four putting your organisation's values into practice links to unit 202, PI 3. Understanding your rights and responsibilities in relation to health and safety when you use and operate equipment may link to unit 202, PIs 6–9, and unit 201, PI 21.

Question five's confirming and reading written material to check the correct action you should take links to unit 201, PI 4.

## Evidence collection

she uses a small digital weighing machine and franking machine. She also produces invoices for car services and repairs and records payments received. She does this on a small calculator with a printout facility.

Amina works as an administrator in a large medical practice. She scans the results of patient tests into the electronic filing system using a small desktop scanner and uses audio equipment to transcribe tapes given to her by the doctors. These contain notes for the files and correspondence for specialists. Printouts are made on a networked laser printer which is used by all the administrators in the practice.

Andrew works as an administrator for a small firm of accountants. Each accountant has a computer for producing and processing clients' accounts. Once these have been checked and printed Andrew has to photocopy them and bind them using a wire binding machine. Two copies are sent to each client, one for signing/returning to be kept in the client's file. The firm also produces tax guides and financial information sheets for its customers. These are produced on a small colour laser copier in the marketing office. One copy of each guide is laminated and put up in reception.

1 For any *one* person listed above, identify the differences he or she would find if moving to your organisation and doing your job.

2 For any *one* person listed above, say how you would need to adapt your

## What if?

skills if you did his or her job rather than your own.

1  Decide the probable consequences of each of the following. Check your ideas with the suggestions on the CD-ROM.

## Key skills reminder

a  guessing the amount of postage for a large item of mail

b  photocopying a six-page document for a meeting with one page missing and two upside down

# How did you do in the quizzes?

## Your final score to quiz on page 17

25–30    You certainly have no need to worry about being under-confident!
         You might, though, want to think whether you are sometimes seen as
         overbearing and sometimes you don't take enough care over what you are
         doing or think about your effect on other people. It can be difficult for your
         friends and colleagues if they are shy or quiet, because you may sometimes
         overwhelm them.

17–24    You nearly always get the balance right. You are confident enough to do
         your job effectively and take care to check things when you are not certain
         what to do. You are also considerate of other people's feelings.

10–16    You really struggle on many occasions when you feel you are on show. You
         need to work at trying to conquer your nerves by concentrating on the
         event or the other person, rather than yourself. Start by trying to put other
         people at their ease whenever you are in an unfamiliar situation.

## Your final score to quiz on page 41

18–20    You sound too good to be true! Do you honestly never gossip by the water-
         cooler?

12–17    You try hard to manage your time well but are still human! Just remember
         to focus more on busy days.

6–11     Vow to be more self-disciplined. Start by making a determined effort not to
         indulge in time-wasting activities any more.

0–5      It's amazing you ever get around to going to work in the first place!

## Your final score to quiz on page 47

8–10     You are a natural planner and very well organised. If you are flexible as well
         then you are an asset in any workplace.

5–7      You try hard and in your private life that's fine. You could do better at work
         though.

2–4      Oh, dear. But at least you could say every day is a new experience!

0–1      What day is it? Any idea?

## Your final score to quiz on page 65

17–20    To your colleagues you are a headache. They try to keep as far away from
         you as possible. Have you noticed yet?

13–16    If you notice that people are starting to tolerate you rather than enjoy
         working with you, don't be surprised.

8–12     You are normally a great colleague but you are far more inclined to think
         about yourself first and other people later, if at all.

0–7      You are a super colleague who everyone trusts and admires.

## Your final score to quiz on page 95

20–24: You sound a bit too good to be true. Remember it's not ethical to tell white lies in quizzes either!

14–20: You normally have high standards and values and when you are in doubt you are prepared to think twice or check with someone else.

8–13: You are sometimes tempted to be less than ethical – which lets you down. 'Do to others as you would be done by' should be your new motto!

0–7: You are treading such a fine line it is only a matter of time before you are caught and lose your job! Unless, of course, the firm you work for is as unethical as you are, in which case they may treat you in the same way that you treat them!

# Index

Page numbers prefixed by a unit number indicate that the reference is to material on the CD-ROM.